Jeanne Ellis Ormrod
University of Northern Colorado

HUMAN LEARNING
Principles, Theories, and Educational Applications

Merrill, an imprint of
Macmillan Publishing Company
New York

Collier Macmillan Canada, Inc.
Toronto

Maxwell Macmillan International Publishing Group
New York   Oxford   Singapore   Sydney

To Richard, Christina, Alex, and Jeffrey

Cover Illustration: Marko Spalatin

This book was set in Bookman.

Administrative Editor: David Faherty
Production Editor: Ben Ko
Art Coordinator: Lorraine Woost
Cover Designer: Brian Deep

Library of Congress Catalog Card Number: 89–63045
International Standard Book Number: 0–675–21044–5
Printed in the United States of America
2   3   4   5   6   7   8   9—94   93   92   91

PREFACE

Human learning is a complex and fascinating process. I have been excited about how much psychologists have learned about learning since the turn of the century. Yet I have been discouraged about how little of their knowledge of the learning process has been used to help people learn more efficiently and effectively. For many years I searched for a textbook that explains principles and theories of human learning in a readable and down-to-earth fashion and that also applies those theories and principles to educational practice. I continued to hope that someone would write such a book, but finally realized that the "someone" would have to be me.

I have written this book with particular students in mind: students who would like to learn about learning, but often do not have much background in psychology. Such students may benefit from studying the historical roots of learning theories but prefer to focus their energies on studying contemporary perspectives and ideas. These students might find learning theories fascinating but lose patience when they cannot see the relevance of those theories to everyday practice. These students are capable of reading a dry, terse textbook but probably learn more effectively from a textbook that shows how different concepts relate to one another, presents numerous examples, and, especially, emphasizes meaningful learning—true *understanding*—of the material it presents.

Even though I am listed as the sole author of this book, I have not written it alone. Many people have helped me with the process:

- Frank DiVesta, my adviser and mentor at Penn State, who taught me a great deal about learning and who absolutely refused to let me graduate until I also learned a great deal about writing.

- Dave Faherty, my administrative editor at Merrill Publishing, who has provided me with the guidance I needed in my first book-writing endeavor, but who has also given me free rein to follow my instincts.

- Livingston Alexander, Western Kentucky University; Sarah Huyvaert, Eastern Michigan University; Janina Jolley, Clarion University of Pennsylvania; Joseph Kersting, Western Illinois University; Gerald Larson, Kent State University; John Newell, University of Florida—Gainesville; Mark Lewis, University of Texas at Tyler; and James O'Connor, California State University—Bakersfield, who read earlier drafts most thoroughly and conscientiously and whose suggestions have greatly improved the final product.

- My colleagues at the University of Northern Colorado—Kyle Carter, Kathy Cochran, John Cooney, Randy Lennon, Teresa McDevitt, Dale Shaw, Lee

Swanson, and especially Ellen Wagner—who have cheered me on over the past 18 months.

- My husband, Richard, and my children, Christina, Alex, and Jeffrey, who have been eternally supportive of this project, and who have provided me with numerous examples of human learning in action.

- My parents, James and Nancy Ellis, who long ago taught me the value of higher education.

- My students, who urged me to write this book in the first place.

Jeanne Ellis Ormrod

CONTENTS

INTRODUCTION TO HUMAN LEARNING

Definitions and Perspectives of Learning

WHEN my son Alex was in kindergarten, his teacher asked me please to do something about his shoes. Alex had been leaving the house every morning with his shoes carefully and lovingly tied by his mother, but by the time he arrived at school the laces were untied and flopping every which way, a state to which they returned within ten minutes of anyone else's retying them. I had repeatedly suggested to Alex that we double-knot his laces, but Alex had rejected that method as too babyish. As an alternative, I had purchased numerous pairs of shoes with Velcro straps instead of laces, but the stuff always seemed to separate from the straps within a month. I had of course also had a series of shoe-tying lessons with Alex, but they had never been successful. The teacher was justifiably irritated that she had to tie Alex's shoes so many times in one day and asked that Alex learn to tie those shoes himself. Her request reflected such exasperated desperation that I guiltily sat down with him one more time and demonstrated how to put two laces together into a presentable bow. This time, however, I accompanied my explanation with a magical statement: "Alex, when you learn how to tie your shoes, I will give you a quarter." Alex had shoe-tying perfected in five minutes, and we haven't had a complaint from school since—at least not about his shoes.

When my daughter Tina was in fourth grade, she experienced considerable difficulty with a series of homework assignments in subtraction. She had never learned basic subtraction facts, despite my continual nagging to do so, with the result being that she could not solve two- and three-digit subtraction problems successfully. One night, after her typical half-hour tantrum about "these stupid problems," my husband explained to Tina that subtraction was nothing more than reversed addition, and her knowledge of addition facts could help her with subtraction. Something must have clicked in Tina's head, because we haven't been subjected to any more tantrums about subtraction. Multiplication, yes, but not subtraction.

Human learning takes many different forms, some of which are easily seen and some of which are not. Some instances of learning are readily observable, such as when a child learns to tie shoes. But other instances of learning are more subtle, such as when a child gains a new understanding of mathematical principles. People learn for many different reasons. Some learn for the rewards their achievements bring: for example, good grades, recognition, or money (consider my capitalistic son). But others learn for less obvious reasons—perhaps for a sense of accomplishment, or perhaps simply to make their lives easier.

In this book, I will describe human learning from the various perspectives that have evolved in psychological theory throughout the twentieth century. As you will soon discover, learning is a complicated process, and psychologists disagree even about such basic issues as what learning is, how it occurs, and which factors are necessary for it to occur at all.

THE IMPORTANCE OF LEARNING

When it comes to learning, many species have things easy compared to humans, or so it seems. Birds, for example, are born with a wealth of knowledge that we humans have to learn. Birds instinctively know how to build their houses; we either have to be taught somehow about framing, drywalling, and roofing, or else we have to hire someone to do it for us. Birds know, without being told, exactly when to fly south and how to get there; we have to look at our calendars and road maps. Birds instinctively know how to care for their young; we have to go to prenatal classes, read child-care books, and learn how to change diapers.

On the other hand, it is the humans, not the birds, who are getting ahead in this world. Over the years, humans have learned to make increasingly stronger and more comfortable homes for themselves, while birds are still making the same flimsy, drafty nests they have been building for thousands of years. Humans have developed fast, dependable modes of transportation for themselves and their goods, while birds are still winging it. And humans are learning how better to feed and care for themselves and their young, so that each generation grows taller, stronger, and healthier than the one before. Birds, meanwhile, are still eating worms.

The learning process allows the human race a greater degree of flexibility and adaptability than any other species on the planet. Because so little of our behavior is controlled by instinct and so much is controlled by what we learn, we are able to benefit from our experiences. We know which behaviors are likely to lead to successful outcomes and which are not, and we modify our behaviors accordingly. And as adults pass on to children the wisdom gleaned from their ancestors and from their own experiences, each generation is just that much more capable of behaving intelligently. Let's face it: we can get from New York to Miami in 2 hours, but how long does it take the birds?

DEFINING LEARNING

My son Alex's learning to tie his shoes and my daughter Tina's learning how subtraction relates to addition are both examples of learning. Consider these instances of learning as well:

- The mother of a five-year-old boy insists that her son assume some household chores, for which he earns a small weekly allowance. The allowance, when saved for two or three weeks, enables the boy to purchase small toys of his own choosing. As a result, he develops an appreciation for the value of money.

- A college freshman from a small town is exposed, for the first time, to political viewpoints different from her own. After engaging in heated political debates with her classmates, she evaluates and modifies her own political philosophy.

- A toddler is overly affectionate with a neighborhood dog, and the dog responds by biting the boy's hand. After that, the child cries and runs quickly to his mother every time he sees a dog.

Learning is the means through which we acquire not only skills and knowledge, but values, attitudes, and emotions as well.

Just what do we mean by the term *learning*? Different psychologists conceptualize and define learning differently. Here are two definitions that reflect common, but very different, conceptions of what learning is:

1. Learning is a relatively permanent change in behavior due to experience.

2. Learning is a relatively permanent change in mental associations due to experience.

What things do these definitions have in common? Both speak of learning as involving a "relatively permanent" *change;* in other words, the change will last for some period of time, although not necessarily forever. Also, both definitions attribute that change to *experience;* in other words, learning takes place as a result of some event in the learner's life. Other changes, such as those due to maturational changes in the body, organic damage, and temporary body states (e.g., fatigue, drugs), are not attributable to experience, and so do not reflect learning.

How do the definitions differ? The first speaks of a change in *behavior,* an external change that can be observed. The second focuses on a change in *mental associations*—an internal change that cannot be observed. Herein lies the most fundamental difference in perspective in the theories of learning that we examine in this book.

The first definition reflects the perspective of a group of theories collectively known as *behaviorism.* These theories focus on the learning of tangible, observable *behaviors,* or *responses,* such as tying shoes, solving a subtraction problem, or complaining about a stomachache to avoid going to school.

The second definition reflects the perspective of a group of theories collectively known as *cognitivism.* These theories focus on the thought processes (sometimes called mental events) involved in human learning rather than on behavioral outcomes; examples of such processes include the way a child interrelates addition and subtraction facts, the memory gimmick a student uses to remember French vocabulary words, and the idiosyncratic meanings a student has attached to her understanding of basic physics principles.

In this book, I will describe both of these two major perspectives in considerable detail; I will also include perspectives that are somewhere between the two extremes. Most psychologists tend to align themselves with one perspective or the other, and I, whose graduate training and research program have been rooted firmly in cognitivist traditions, am no exception. However, I firmly believe that both the behaviorist and cognitive perspectives have something important to say about human learning and that both provide useful suggestions for education.

THE NATURE OF PRINCIPLES AND THEORIES

The systematic study of human behavior, including human and animal learning processes, has emerged only within the last hundred years, making psychology a relative newcomer to scientific inquiry. But in a century's time, thousands of experiments have been conducted to investigate how people and animals learn, and the occurrence of patterns in the results of these experiments have led psychologists to generalize about the learning process through the formulation of both principles and theories of learning.

Principles, or *laws*, of learning identify specific elements that consistently influence learning and describe the particular effects of these variables on learning. For example, consider this learning principle:

> *A behavior that is followed by a satisfying state of affairs (a reward) is more likely to be learned than a behavior not followed by a reward.*

In this principle, a particular factor (a reward consequent to a behavior) is identified as having a particular effect on learning (an increase in the frequency of behavior). The principle can be observed in many different situations, including these:

- A pigeon is given a small pellet of food every time it turns its body in a complete circle. It begins turning more and more frequently.
- Dolphins who are given fish for "speaking" in Dolphinese quickly become quite chatty.
- A boy who completes a perfect spelling paper and is praised for it by a favorite teacher works diligently for future success in spelling assignments.
- A high school girl who receives compliments on her new hairstyle continues to style her hair that way.

Principles are most useful when they can be applied to a wide variety of different situations. The "reward" principle is an example of such broad applicability; it can be applied to both animals and humans, and it holds true for different types of learning and rewards.

Theories of learning provide explanations about the underlying mechanisms involved in the learning process. Whereas principles tell us *what* factors are important for learning, theories tell us *why* these factors are important. For example, consider this theory:

> *People learn what they pay attention to. Reward increases learning because it makes people pay attention.*

Here we have an explanation of why a reward affects learning. Attention is identified as the underlying process responsible for the observed effect of reward on learning.

Advantages of Theories

Theories have several advantages over principles. First, theories allow us to summarize the results of many research studies and integrate numerous principles of learning. In that sense, theories are very concise, or parsimonious. Second, theories provide starting points for conducting new research; they suggest research questions worthy of study. For example, the theory that attention is more important than reward for learning leads to the following prediction:

> *When an individual's attention can be drawn to the information to be learned, learning can occur in the absence of reward.*

In fact, this prediction has been supported by research (e.g., Faust & Anderson, 1967).

Research conducted outside the context of a particular theoretical perspective will frequently yield results that are trivial and nongeneralizable. Interpreted from a theoretical perspective, however, those same results become significant. For example, consider an experiment by Seligman and Maier (1967). In this classic study, dogs were placed in individual cages and given a number of painful and unpredictable shocks. Some dogs were able to escape the shocks by pressing a panel in the cage, while others were unable to escape. The following day, the dogs were placed in different cages, and again shocks were administered. This time, however, each shock was preceded by a signal (a tone) that the shock was coming, and the dogs could escape the shocks by jumping over a barrier as soon as the tone was presented. The dogs who had been able to escape the shocks on the preceding day learned to escape in this new situation, but the dogs who had been unable to escape previously did *not* learn to escape the shocks now that they could do so. On the surface, this experiment, while interesting, might not seem especially relevant to human learning. However, Seligman and his colleagues have used this and other experiments to develop their theory of *learned helplessness:* individuals who learn that they have no control over unpleasant or painful events in one situation are unlikely, in later situations, to attempt to escape or avoid those aversive events even when it is possible for them to do so. As you will learn in Chapter 6, studies such as Seligman and Maier's research with dogs, because they have led to the development of learned helplessness theory, have implications for classroom practice.

A third advantage of theories over principles is that theories explain learning, whereas principles only describe it. An understanding of the mechanisms underlying learning processes will ultimately help psychologists and educators design learning environments that facilitate human learning to the greatest possible degree. For example, the teacher who is familiar with the theory that attention is a key factor in learning may decide to employ a variety of techniques, including rewards, that increase student attention to learning materials. On the other hand, the teacher familiar only with the principle that rewarded behaviors are learned may use rewards, such as small toys, that are counterproductive because they distract students' attention away from their academic tasks.

Disadvantages of Theories

Theories have at least two disadvantages as well. First, no theory explains all we know about learning. Current theories of learning tend to focus on specific aspects of learning. Behaviorist theories, for example, limit themselves to situations in which learning involves a behavior change. Cognitive theories tend to focus instead on how information is organized or remembered. Observed phenomena that do not fit comfortably within a particular theoretical perspective are excluded from that perspective.

Second, theories affect what new information is published, therefore biasing the knowledge that we have about learning. For example, a team of researchers may propose a particular theory of learning and conduct a research study to support their idea. However, the results of the research are exactly opposite to what they expected, therefore casting doubt on their theory. If these researchers are fully committed to demonstrating that their theory is correct, they are unlikely to publish results that will indicate otherwise! In this way, theories may sometimes impede progress toward a truly accurate understanding of the learning process.

A Perspective on Theories and Principles

The theories I describe in this book are dynamic, changing models of the learning process. Each theory is based on several decades of research results, and each has some validity. However, as research continues in the decades ahead, theories of learning will undoubtedly be revised to account for new evidence that emerges. In this sense, no single theory can be considered "fact."

At the same time, learning principles are relatively enduring conclusions about cause-effect relationships in the learning process. Principles generally maintain their validity longer than theories do. The "reward" principle was introduced by Edward Thorndike in 1898, and has remained with us in one form or another ever since (although I will describe some exceptions to the principle at the end of Chapter 5). Thorndike's theory of *why* reward affects learning, however, has been largely replaced by other explanations.

Both principles and theories provide a means to predict the conditions under which learning is likely to occur. To the extent that principles and theories are useful in this way, we are better off with them—imperfect and temporary as they may be—than without them.

APPLYING PRINCIPLES AND THEORIES TO CLASSROOM SITUATIONS

A great deal of learning takes place in schools. Most students learn such basic skills as reading and subtraction. Unfortunately, students may also learn things their teachers never intended for them to learn. For example, while they have learned to read, they may also have learned that studying means memorizing, word-for-word, what they read. And while they have learned their subtraction facts, they may also have learned that mathematics is frustrating or incomprehensible.

The learning that takes place in schools should not be left to chance. The better we understand the factors that influence learning and the processes that underlie it, the better we can train teachers and design instructional materials to maximize learning that will benefit students, and minimize learning that will interfere with their later achievements.

The theories that I have included in this book portray human learning from different perspectives, and at times even contradict one another. Yet I hope you will take an eclectic perspective, resisting the temptation to choose one theory over others as the "right" one. Different theories are applicable in different situations, depending on the content being taught, the teacher's objectives for an instructional unit, and the specific characteristics of the student population. At the same time, each theory provides unique insights into how and why humans learn (e.g., see Catania, 1985), and how schools might be designed to enhance student learning. It is probably more helpful to think of theories in terms of their usefulness rather than their correctness.

As theories of learning are revised over the years, educational practices will also change. In the meantime, educators can use current theories to help students learn more effectively and less painfully than they seem to learn now. The time has come to make schools places of success and pleasure rather than places of failure and pain.

OVERVIEW OF THE BOOK

In Part Two of the book, we will explore principles and theories of learning from the behaviorist perspective, beginning with an introduction and historical overview of behaviorism in Chapter 2. We will then examine in depth the two most commonly used models of learning within the behaviorist perspective: classical conditioning (Chapter 3) and operant conditioning (Chapters 4 and 5). We will also look at the role of unpleasant events, such as punishment, in the learning process (Chapter 6).

In Part Three, we will turn to cognitive perspectives of learning, beginning with an introduction and overview of cognitivism in Chapter 7. In Chapter 8, we will examine social learning theory, an approach to learning that has evolved over the years from its behaviorist roots into a cognitive model of how people learn through observation of their fellow human beings. We will then examine in depth the internal, mental processes involved in learning, including perception and attention processes (Chapter 9) and the various components of the human memory system (Chapters 10 through 12). Some specific educational applications of cognitivism are covered in Chapter 13.

Finally, in Part Four, we will turn to some of the more complex forms of human learning: concept learning (Chapter 14), and transfer and problem solving (Chapter 15).

As we proceed, we will consider numerous applications for teaching and instruction. I believe that psychology has much to say about how learning and instruction can be improved. I hope that, once you have finished Chapter 15, you will agree with me.

SUMMARY

Learning allows humans a greater degree of flexibility and adaptability than any other species. Currently, two major theoretical perspectives help us understand how people learn. The behaviorist perspective emphasizes relationships among observable stimuli and responses. The cognitive perspective emphasizes the role of internal mental processes involved in learning. Principles (descriptions of what variables affect learning) and theories (explanations of why those variables have the effects they do) from both behaviorism and cognitivism help educators optimize learning environments and facilitate student achievement.

PART TWO

BEHAVIORIST VIEWS
OF LEARNING

C H A P T E R 2

Overview of Behaviorism

Outline

Assumptions of Behaviorism

Early Theorists in the Behaviorist Tradition
Ivan Pavlov
Edward L. Thorndike
John B. Watson
Edwin R. Guthrie
Clark L. Hull
Burrhus Frederic Skinner

Contemporary Behaviorism

Educational Applications of Behaviorism
Emphasis on Behavior
Drill and Practice
Breaking Habits
Attention to the Consequences of Behavior

Summary

B EHAVIORISM, the first psychological perspective to have a significant impact on our understanding of how human beings learn, is the topic of Chapters 2 through 6. In this chapter, I will present an overview of the major assumptions of the behaviorist approach to learning, provide a historical perspective of some of the key theorists who have contributed to the behaviorist movement, and discuss some general applications of behaviorist theories to educational practice. In the chapters that follow, I will cover more specific aspects of behaviorism, including classical conditioning (Chapter 3), operant conditioning and its educational applications (Chapters 4 and 5), and aversive control of behavior (Chapter 6).

ASSUMPTIONS OF BEHAVIORISM

Before the advent of behaviorism around the turn of the century, the two dominant perspectives in psychology were *structuralism* (e.g., Wilhelm Wundt's work) and *functionalism* (e.g., John Dewey's writings). Although these two perspectives differed considerably in their underlying assumptions and topics of study, they shared a common characteristic: they lacked a precise and carefully defined research methodology. The primary means of investigating learning and other psychological phenomena, especially for the structuralists, was a method called *introspection:* people were simply asked to "look" inside their minds and describe what they were "thinking."

However, beginning with the works of the Russian physiologist Ivan Pavlov and the American psychologist Edward Thorndike, a more objective approach to the study of learning was introduced, an approach that focused on the measurement of observable phenomena rather than on internal mental events. With the advent of methodologies that emphasized stimuli and responses in learning, the behaviorist movement was born.

As will become clear later in the chapter, behaviorists have not always agreed on the specific processes that account for learning. However, most of them do share certain basic assumptions about learning:

1. Underlying most behaviorist theories is the assumption of *equipotentiality:* principles of learning apply equally to different behaviors and to different species of animals, including human beings. Behaviorists often use the term *organism* to refer to both humans and other animals.
2. Because of the equipotentiality of organisms across species, principles of learning developed from research with one species should apply to

other species as well. Behaviorist principles derived primarily from research with such animals as rats and pigeons are often applied to human learning situations.

3. Organisms enter the world as "blank slates" (the assumption of *tabula rasa*). Aside from certain species-specific instincts, people and animals are not born predisposed to particular behaviors.

4. The study of learning is a science similar to the physical sciences. As such, it must focus on events that can be observed and measured. Only two kinds of events fit the criteria of observation and measurement: *stimuli* (S) within the environment and *responses* (R) performed by an organism.

5. Many behaviorists believe that internal processes (thoughts, motives, emotions, etc.) cannot be directly observed or measured, and therefore should not be considered in the scientific study of learning. The organism is described as a "black box"; things that impinge on the box (stimuli) and emerge from it (responses) can be studied, but the processes that occur within it cannot.

6. Principles of learning are based on the relationship between stimuli and responses; hence, behaviorism is often called *S-R psychology*.

7. Rather than using the term *learning,* behaviorists often talk about *conditioning;* an organism is conditioned by environmental events. What is learned, being largely the result of one's past and present experiences, is often beyond an organism's control.

8. Learning can only be assumed to have occurred when a change in behavior is observed. Some behaviorists propose that if no behavior change occurs, learning has not taken place.

9. The learning of all behaviors, from the most simple to the most complex, should be explained by as few learning principles as possible, an assumption reflecting a preference for parsimony (conciseness) in explaining learning and behavior.

Not all behaviorists would agree with all nine of these assumptions. For instance, many theorists disagree with the "black box" assumption, believing that the role of internal factors—those within the organism (O)—is an important consideration in understanding learning. Such *neo-behaviorist* theorists are sometimes called S-O-R (stimulus-organism-response) theorists rather than S-R theorists.

EARLY THEORISTS IN THE BEHAVIORIST TRADITION

Numerous theorists contributed to the rise of behaviorism in the psychology of learning during the early decades of the twentieth century. The contributions of six of them—Pavlov, Thorndike, Watson, Guthrie, Hull, and Skinner—will be briefly described in this chapter. Two of these six, Ivan Pavlov and B. F. Skinner, have had such significant impact on psychological theory and educational practice that their theories will also be considered in more detail in Chapters 3 and 4.

Ivan Pavlov

The Russian physiologist Ivan Pavlov, while investigating salivation reflexes in dogs, discovered that a dog would learn to salivate not only to food, but also to other environmental events that it associated with food—for example, the laboratory assistant who often brought the dog its meals. Through a systematic study of how dogs salivate to different stimuli, Pavlov developed a theory of learning most commonly known as *classical conditioning* (Pavlov, 1927).

Pavlov's theory of learning begins with a stimulus-response connection, in which a particular stimulus (e.g., meat) leads to a particular response (e.g., salivation). When that stimulus is repeatedly presented in association with one or more other stimuli (e.g., the lab assistant or the sound of his footsteps in the hall), those other stimuli also begin to lead to a similar response. This process of classical conditioning, which will be described in greater detail in Chapter 3, was integrated into the work of other early psychologists, such as John Watson and B. F. Skinner, and is now perceived as a powerful force in learning, particularly in the development of emotional responses.

Edward L. Thorndike

In 1898, Edward Thorndike introduced a theory of learning that emphasized the role of experience in the strengthening and weakening of stimulus-response connections, a perspective now known as *connectionism* (Thorndike, 1898, 1911, 1913). In Thorndike's classic first experiment (his doctoral dissertation), a cat was placed in a "puzzle box" with a door that opened when some device (for example, a wire loop) was appropriately manipulated. Thorndike observed the cat initiate numerous, apparently random movements in its attempts to get out of the box; eventually, by chance, the cat triggered the mechanism that opened the door and allowed escape. When returned to the box a second time, the cat again engaged in trial-and-error movements but managed to escape in less time than it had previously. With successive trials in the box, the cat, although continuing to demonstrate trial-and-error behavior, managed to escape within shorter and shorter periods.

From his observations of the cat in the puzzle box, Thorndike concluded that the learning of a behavior is affected by the consequence of that behavior (e.g., escape from a confining situation). Thorndike's *law of effect* is paraphrased as follows:

Responses to a situation that are followed by satisfaction will be strengthened; responses that are followed by discomfort will be weakened.

According to Thorndike, learning consists of trial-and-error behavior and a gradual "stamping in" of some behaviors (those leading to satisfaction) and "stamping out" of other behaviors (those leading to discomfort). In other words, rewarded responses increase, and punished responses diminish and disappear.

In addition to his law of effect, Thorndike proposed that practice influences S-R connections as well. His *law of exercise* is paraphrased as follows:

Stimulus-response connections that are repeated are strengthened; stimulus-response connections that are not repeated are weakened.

In other words, practice facilitates the learning of responses. Responses that are not practiced eventually disappear.

Thorndike later revised both his law of effect and his law of exercise (Thorndike, 1935). The original law of effect implied that reward and punishment have opposite but equal effects on behavior: one strengthens and the other weakens. However, Thorndike's later research (1932a, 1932b) indicated that punishment may not be effective in weakening responses. For example, in one experiment (Thorndike, 1932a), human subjects were given a multiple-choice Spanish vocabulary test in which they were to choose the English translation for each of a long list of Spanish words. Every time subjects chose the correct English word (out of five alternatives), the experimenter said "Right!" (i.e., the response was rewarded); every time subjects chose an incorrect alternative, the experimenter said "Wrong!" (i.e., the response was punished). In responding to the same multiple-choice question over a series of trials, subjects increased the responses for which they had been rewarded, but did not necessarily decrease those for which they had been punished. In his *revised law of effect* (e.g., Thorndike, 1935), Thorndike continued to maintain that rewards strengthen the behaviors they follow, but deemphasized the role of punishment. Instead, he proposed that punishment has an *indirect* effect on learning—as a result of an annoying state of affairs, an organism may engage in certain other behaviors (for example, crying or running away) that interfere with performance of the punished response.

Thorndike also conducted research (described by Trowbridge & Cason, 1932) that cast doubt on the effect of practice alone on learning. For example, in one experiment, human subjects were blindfolded and asked to draw a series of four-inch lines. Subjects could not see the results of their efforts, and they received no information from the experimenter about the correctness of their drawings. Without feedback, subjects did not improve in accuracy despite their practice, a result that led Thorndike to repudiate his law of exercise.

Despite the weaknesses of Thorndike's early ideas, his work provided a significant contribution to the study of learning. The idea that the consequences of responses influence learning continues to be a major component of behaviorism today.

John B. Watson

Although Pavlov and Thorndike are considered among the earliest contributors to the behaviorist tradition, it was actually John Watson (1913) who introduced the term *behaviorism* and who served as the most vocal advocate for the behaviorist perspective in the early part of the century.

In his major writings (Watson, 1914, 1919, 1925), Watson adamantly called for the introduction of scientific objectivity and experimentation into the study of psychological phenomena. He emphasized the necessity for focusing scientific inquiry on observable behaviors rather than on such unobservable phenomena as "thinking." Not only was Watson opposed to the study of internal mental events, he denied any existence of the mind at all! Thought, he proposed, was nothing more than tiny movements of the tongue and larynx, and thus was a behavior just like any other.

Greatly influenced by the work of both Pavlov and another Russian, Vladimir Bechterev (1913), Watson adopted the classically conditioned S-R *habit* as the basic unit of learning and extended it to human learning (Watson, 1916; Watson & Rayner, 1920). Watson proposed two laws that described how such habits were developed. First, his *law of frequency* (similar to Thorndike's law of exercise) stressed the importance of repetition:

> *The more frequently a stimulus and response occur in association with each other, the stronger that S-R habit will become.*

Second, Watson's *law of recency* was as follows:

> *The response that has most recently occurred after a particular stimulus is the response most likely to be associated with that stimulus.*

In other words, the last response to a stimulus is the one that will occur the next time the stimulus is presented. Through his law of recency, Watson was able to reject Thorndike's law of effect. According to Watson, reward has only an indirect effect on learning in that the most *recent* response is the one that is rewarded. For example, when a cat is in a puzzle box, the last response is the one that leads to escape and so is most likely to be connected to that stimulus situation.

Watson asserted that past experience accounts for virtually all behavior. His extreme environmentalism, which denied that heredity had any effect on behavior whatsoever, was reflected in the following infamous quote:

> Give me a dozen healthy infants, well-formed, and my own specified world
> to bring them up in and I'll guarantee to take any one at random and train

him to become any type of specialist I might select—doctor, lawyer, artist, merchant-chief, and yes, even beggar-man and thief, regardless of his talents, penchants, tendencies, abilities, vocations and race of his ancestors (Watson, 1925, p. 82).

Watson's influence continued to be felt long after he retired from academia in 1920. His strong advocacy of psychology as an objective and precise science and his insistence that environment plays a key role in human behavior led to a behaviorist tradition that dominated the first half of the century.

Edwin R. Guthrie

Edwin Guthrie's *contiguity theory* (Guthrie, 1935, 1942) was similar to John Watson's ideas in that it emphasized S-R connections and rejected the role of reward in developing these connections. Guthrie's basic principle of learning was as follows:

A stimulus that is followed by a particular response will, upon its recurrence, tend to be followed by the same response again. This S-R connection gains its full strength on one trial.

In other words, if an individual responds to a particular stimulus in a particular way at one time, that individual will make the same response the next time the same stimulus is encountered, and a habit is formed. Guthrie contended that the critical factor in learning is the *contiguity* of stimulus and response.

Guthrie also shared John Watson's belief that *recency* is critical in learning: an organism will respond to a stimulus in the way it last responded to that stimulus. A reward facilitates learning only to the extent that it removes the organism from the stimulus, thus preventing different responses from being associated with that stimulus.

Guthrie's notion of *one-trial learning*—that an S-R connection is fully formed on one pairing—was quite different from Thorndike's idea that responses are gradually "stamped in." Guthrie explained the gradual learning of complex behavior by proposing that complex behavior is actually composed of many tiny S-R connections; with each practice trial, more and more appropriate S-R connections are formed, thus leading to the gradual changes observed in overall behavior.

The parsimony of Guthrie's notion of the contiguity of stimuli and responses as the basis for all learning is definitely appealing. However, Guthrie conducted little research to support his theory, and later research has cast doubt on the notion that learning is as simple as Guthrie described it (Bower & Hilgard, 1981). However, three techniques for breaking S-R habits, which Guthrie derived from his theory, continue to be used in educational and therapeutic practice. We will discuss each of them later in this chapter.

Clark L. Hull

It was primarily the work of Clark Hull (1943, 1951, 1952) that introduced "organismic" characteristics—characteristics unique to different organisms—into behaviorist learning theory. Like many of his predecessors, Hull maintained that learned S-R habits form the basis of behavior. Furthermore, he agreed with Thorndike about the importance of rewards in the learning process. However, he believed that the presence of a particular stimulus and one's past experiences with that stimulus are not the only determinants of whether a particular response will occur or how strongly it will be made. Hull proposed that a number of other factors—intervening variables—unique to each organism and each occasion must be considered to predict the likelihood and strength of a response's occurrence. Hull's theory was therefore the first major theory of the S-O-R genre.

According to Hull, one intervening variable that affects the occurrence of a response is *habit strength,* the degree to which a particular stimulus and a particular response are associated. The more often a response has previously been rewarded in the presence of the stimulus, the greater is the habit strength, and the more likely the response is to occur.

A second intervening variable critical for response is the organism's *drive,* an internal state of arousal that motivates its behavior. Hull suggested that some drives (e.g., hunger and thirst) are directly related to an organism's survival. Others (called *acquired drives*) serve no apparent biological purpose, but are instead the result of previous associations of neutral stimuli with drive-reducing stimuli such as food. To illustrate, one might become "driven" by a need for approval if approval had previously been associated with a candy bar. Rewards increase the strength of a S-R habit by reducing the organism's drive; for example, food reduces hunger.

Hull proposed that intervening variables such as habit strength, drive, stimulus intensity (an intense stimulus is more likely than a weak stimulus to bring about a strong response), and incentive (based on the amount and immediacy of reward) all work together to increase the likelihood and relative strength of a particular response. At the same time, *inhibitory factors* (e.g., fatigue) decrease the likelihood and strength of the response.

According to Hull, an organism might learn several different responses to the same stimulus, each with a different degree of habit strength. The combination of the various S-R habits for a given stimulus, with their respective habit strengths, is known as a *habit-family hierarchy.* When a stimulus is presented, an organism will, if possible, make the response for which the habit strength is the strongest. However, if that response is for some reason blocked, the organism will make the second response, or, if again foiled, the third response, and so on down the hierarchy.

As an illustration of this concept of habit-family hierarchy, consider Stan, who is confronted with a homework assignment involving the multiplication of fractions. Stan may first try to complete the assignment using the technique his teacher taught him for multiplying fractions. When he finds he cannot remember the technique, Stan may instead ask his friend Angela if he may copy her answers. If Angela refuses the request, Stan may resort to a third response in his hierarchy: telling his teacher that the family dog ate his homework.

Hull developed a series of mathematical formulas through which the occurrence and strength of responses could be predicted, once the various intervening variables were measured and their values entered. The precision of Hull's formulas permitted a careful testing of his theory through research, and many specifics of the theory were found to be incorrect (Bower & Hilgard, 1981; Klein, 1987). For example, learning apparently can take place in the absence of drive; you will see some examples of such learning later in the book (e.g., in Chapters 7 and 8). In addition, Hull proposed that a reward is a stimulus that reduces drive, yet some rewards actually appear to *increase* drive (e.g., Olds & Milner, 1954).

Hull's theory was probably the predominant force in learning research throughout the 1940s and 1950s. Although many details of the theory did not hold up under empirical scrutiny, Hull's emphasis on intervening variables made such notions as *motivation* and *incentive* prominent concepts in learning research. And his many productive students—among them, Kenneth Spence, Neil Miller, John Dollard, and O. H. Mowrer—have continued to advance and modify Hullian ideas.

Burrhus Frederic Skinner

B. F. Skinner is unquestionably the best known psychologist in the behaviorist tradition. Originally a fiction writer, Skinner was lured into psychology by the ideas of Pavlov and Watson (Skinner, 1967). His principles of *operant conditioning*, first proposed in 1938, have undergone little change in the past fifty years (e.g., Skinner, 1938, 1953, 1958, 1966b, 1971; Skinner & Epstein, 1982). Operant conditioning principles have served as the basis for thousands of research studies and have been applied extensively in both educational and therapeutic settings. I will present an overview of Skinner's ideas here, and then describe operant conditioning again in more detail in Chapter 4.

Skinner, like Thorndike and Hull, has proposed that behaviors are learned when they are followed by certain consequences. Unlike his predecessors, however, Skinner has spoken only about the strengthening of responses, not the strengthening of S-R habits. Skinner's use of the term *reinforcement* instead of "reward" reflects his concern that psychologists remain objective in their examination of behavior and not try to guess what subjects find pleasing (rewarding) or why the reinforcement has the effect on behavior that it does.

To study the effects of reinforcement using precise measurement of responses in a carefully controlled environment, Skinner developed a piece of equipment, now known as the Skinner box, that has gained widespread popularity in animal learning research. As shown in Figure 2–1, the Skinner box used in studying rat behavior includes a metal bar that, when pushed down, causes a food tray to swing into reach long enough for the rat to grab a food pellet. In the pigeon version of the box, instead of a metal bar, a lighted plastic disk ("key") is located on one wall; when the pigeon pecks the key, the food tray swings into reach for a short time. Through observation of rats and pigeons in their respective Skinner boxes under varying conditions of reinforcement, Skinner has developed a set of principles of learning that focuses on a description of behavior rather than an explanation of it (hence, some psychologists view Skinner's model as a "nontheory").

Skinner's most fundamental principle of operant conditioning, his *law of conditioning*, is paraphrased as follows:

> *A response that is followed by a reinforcing stimulus is strengthened and is therefore more likely to occur again.*

A corollary to this principle, Skinner's *law of extinction*, is:

> *A response that is not followed by a reinforcing stimulus is weakened and is therefore less likely to occur again.*

Unlike Watson, Skinner has acknowledged the existence of thought, particularly as it is reflected in verbal behavior (e.g., Skinner, 1963). However, he has contended that the *causes* of mental events (including thoughts)

Figure 2–1

A prototypic Skinner box: the food tray swings into reach for reinforcement.

lie in the environment; therefore, a stimulus-response approach to the study of learning, which emphasizes the impact of environment on behavior, is still the most appropriate approach.

Although his own research has focused almost exclusively on the simple responses of animals, Skinner has nonetheless extended his conditioning principles to complex human behavior in general (e.g., Skinner, 1948b, 1957, 1971) and to educational practice in particular (e.g., 1954, 1958, 1968, 1973). The numerous educational applications of operant conditioning (e.g., programmed instruction, behavioral objectives, and behavior modification) will be described in Chapter 5.

CONTEMPORARY BEHAVIORISM

Although much of the work in human learning has been shifting toward a cognitive perspective in recent years, the behaviorist movement is still very much alive and well. Pavlov's classical conditioning and Skinner's operant conditioning remain as major theoretical perspectives that are continually refined by ongoing research (still conducted primarily with animals) and are applied successfully in educational and clinical settings.

Recent trends in behaviorist research reflect several differences between contemporary behaviorism and the more classical theories presented in this chapter. One trend is an increased focus on motivation in relation to learning and performance (Herrnstein, 1977). A second change from early behaviorist theory is increased attention to the role of negative consequences (e.g., punishment) in learning. Early theorists such as Thorndike, Guthrie, and Skinner maintained that punishment had little or no effect on behavior; however, a growing body of research (some of which I will present in Chapter 6) indicates that negative consequences *do* impact behavior. Still a third trend is an increasing recognition that learning and performance must be considered as separate, albeit related, entities. A number of contemporary psychologists (e.g., Bandura, Grusec, & Menlove, 1966; Brown & Herrnstein, 1975; Estes, 1969a; Herrnstein, 1977) have proposed that many behaviorist laws are more appropriately applied to an understanding of what influences the *performance* of learned behaviors, rather than what influences learning itself.

EDUCATIONAL APPLICATIONS OF BEHAVIORISM

Behaviorist theories have numerous implications for teaching methodology. Some educational practices suggested by behaviorist ideas are emphasis on behavior, drill and practice, methods for breaking habits, and attention to the consequences of behavior.

Emphasis on Behavior

Behaviorists define learning as a change in behavior due to experience. This emphasis on behavior has two implications for education. First, students should be *active responders* throughout the learning process rather than just passive recipients of whatever information is being taught. For example, students should not just listen (a nonobservable response), but also should talk, write, and do (observable behaviors).

A second implication of a behavioral emphasis relates to the *assessment* of student learning. Regardless of how effective teachers think a certain lecture or a particular set of curriculum materials might be, they should never assume that learning is occurring; rather, they should observe whether student behaviors have changed as a result of that instruction. Only behavior changes—for example, improved test scores or better study habits—can actually confirm that learning has taken place. This emphasis on behavior as the only means by which learning can be assessed points to the importance of frequently observing and measuring student responses in some way.

Drill and Practice

Many behaviorists have stressed the principle that repetition of stimulus-response habits strengthens those habits. If responses to particular stimuli are to be learned thoroughly, then *practice* is essential. For example, basic addition and subtraction facts will be better learned and more quickly recalled if they are repeated numerous times (e.g., through the use of flashcards). In a similar way, many reading teachers advocate that the best way for students to improve their reading level is simply to read, read, read.

Breaking Habits

Guthrie's notion of recency—that an organism will respond to a stimulus in the same way it responded on the most recent previous encounter with that stimulus—implies that habits, once formed, are difficult to break. The trick in breaking a habit, from the point of view of the recency principle, is to lead an individual, somehow or other, to make a new response to the same old stimulus.

As an example, Guthrie (1935) described a girl who, upon entering the house after school each day, had the nasty habit of throwing her hat and coat on the floor rather than hanging up her garments. Despite repeated entreaties by the child's mother to change the sloppy behavior, the habit continued. One day, however, rather than admonishing the girl, the mother insisted that her daughter put her hat and coat back on, go outside, reenter the house, and hang up her clothes. The "hanging up" response, being the most recently exhibited, now became a new habit for the girl, and the "throwing on the floor" response disappeared.

Guthrie proposed three ingenious techniques specifically designed to break habits.

Exhaustion Method. One way to break a stimulus-response habit is to continue to present the stimulus until the individual is too tired to respond in the habitual way. At that point, a new response will be made, and a new S-R habit formed. For example, in breaking a bucking bronco, the persistent rider (the stimulus) stays on the horse's back until the horse is too exhausted to continue bucking; a new response (behavior reflecting acceptance of the rider, such as standing still) then becomes associated with the "rider" stimulus. Similarly, a teacher might eliminate a child's spitball-throwing behavior by keeping that child after school to make and throw spitballs until the child is too tired to continue.

Threshold Method. Another way of breaking a habit is to begin by presenting the stimulus so faintly that the individual does not respond to it in the habitual manner. The intensity of the stimulus is then increased so gradually that it continues *not* to be responded to. For example, when a student has test anxiety (i.e., a test stimulus leads to an anxiety response), a teacher might eliminate that anxiety by first presenting tasks that are enjoyable to the child and only remotely resemble a test; over time, the teacher can present a series of tasks that increasingly but gradually begin to take on testlike qualities.

Incompatible Stimulus Method. A third method for breaking an S-R connection is to present the stimulus when the habitual response cannot occur and when an opposite, or *incompatible*, response will occur. For example, Guthrie recommended tying a dead chicken around a dog's neck to teach the dog not to catch and eat chickens. The dog will struggle to get rid of the annoying chicken, a response that is incompatible with catching and eating the chicken. Similarly, imagine a classroom of highly achievement-motivated students who are overly competitive with one another. To reduce the competition among students, the teacher might divide the class into small groups and assign each group an academic task that requires cooperation rather than competition (e.g., developing an argument for one side of an issue in a class debate). Assigning grades on the basis of group performance rather than individual performance will enhance the likelihood that students will cooperate. Hence, cooperation will replace competition in that classroom environment.

Attention to the Consequences of Behavior

Many behaviorists, among them Thorndike and Skinner, emphasize the importance of reinforcement to learning. Students are most likely to learn and exhibit behaviors that lead to positive results. The kinds of reinforcers that are effective, and the many ways in which reinforcement principles can be incorporated into classroom practice, will be addressed in greater detail in Chapters 4 and 5.

SUMMARY

Behaviorism encompasses a group of theories that share several assumptions, including the applicability of common principles of learning across many species, the "blank slate" nature of organisms, and the need to focus on external, observable events. Early learning theorists—Pavlov, Thorndike, Watson, Guthrie, Hull, and Skinner—have all viewed learning somewhat differently, but each has made a unique contribution to our understanding of how humans learn. The impact of behaviorism in contemporary educational practice can be seen in an emphasis on observable behavior, the use of drill and practice, methods for breaking habits, and concern for the positive and negative consequences of student behaviors.

C H A P T E R   3

Classical Conditioning

Outline

I have a thing about bees. Whenever a bee flies near me, I scream, wave my arms frantically, and run around like a wild woman. Yes, yes, I know, I would be better off if I remained perfectly still, but somehow I just can't control myself. My overreaction to bees is probably due to the several painful bee stings I received as a small child.

The learning of an involuntary response to a particular stimulus, such as my fearful reaction to bees, can be explained by a theory of learning known as *classical conditioning*. This paradigm originated with the work of Ivan Pavlov, so we will begin this chapter by reviewing his classic research. We will then explore how Pavlov's learning paradigm can be applied to an understanding of human behavior. We will survey some of the phenomena associated with classical conditioning, such as extinction, spontaneous recovery, stimulus generalization and discrimination, higher-order conditioning, and sensory preconditioning. Finally, we will look at ways of eliminating undesirable responses using the classical conditioning model and at some specific implications of the model for educational settings.

PAVLOV'S EXPERIMENT

Pavlov, a Russian physiologist whose work on digestion earned him a Nobel Prize in 1904, was conducting a series of experiments related to salivation in dogs. To study a dog's salivation responses, he would make a surgical incision in the dog's mouth, thus allowing the dog's saliva to be collected and measured, and strap the dog into an immobile position. He would then give powdered meat to the dog and observe its resulting salivation. However, Pavlov noticed that the dog soon began to salivate before it even saw or smelled the meat—in fact, it salivated as soon as the lab assistant entered the room with the meat. Apparently, the dog had *learned* that the lab assistant meant food was on the way and responded accordingly. Pavlov devoted a good part of his later years to a systematic study of this learning process upon which he had so inadvertently stumbled, and summarized his research in his book *Conditioned Reflexes* (Pavlov, 1927).

Pavlov's original study of classical conditioning went something like this:

1. He first observed whether the dog salivated to the ringing of a bell. As you might imagine, the dog did not find a bell especially appetizing and so did not salivate.

2. Pavlov then rang the bell again, but this time the ringing was immediately followed by the presentation of some powdered meat. The dog of

course salivated. He rang the bell several more times, and each time meat was presented immediately afterward. The dog salivated on each occasion.

3. Pavlov then rang the bell again *without* presenting any meat. Nevertheless, the dog salivated. The bell, to which the dog had previously been unresponsive (step one), now led to a salivation response. There had been a *change in behavior due to experience;* in the behaviorist definition of the term, *learning* had taken place.

Let's analyze the three steps in Pavlov's experiment in much the same way that Pavlov did:

1. A *neutral stimulus* (NS) is a stimulus to which the subject does not respond. In the case of Pavlov's dog, the bell was originally a neutral stimulus that did not elicit a salivation response.

2. The neutral stimulus is presented just before another stimulus, one that *does* lead to a response. This second stimulus is called an *unconditioned stimulus* (UCS), and the response to it is called an *unconditioned response* (UCR), because the subject responds to the stimulus unconditionally, without having had to learn to do so. (Pavlov's original term was actually unconditional, but the mistranslation to unconditioned remains in most classical conditioning literature.) For Pavlov's dog, meat powder was an unconditioned stimulus to which it responded with the unconditioned response of salivation.

3. After being paired with an unconditioned stimulus, the previously neutral stimulus now elicits a response, so it is no longer neutral. The NS has become a *conditioned stimulus* (CS) to which the subject has learned a *conditioned response* (CR). In Pavlov's experiment, the bell, after being paired with the meat—an unconditioned stimulus—became a conditioned stimulus that led to the conditioned response of salivation. The diagram in Figure 3–1 shows graphically what happened from a classical conditioning perspective.

Figure 3–1
A classical conditioning analysis of Pavlov's dog

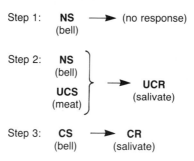

Pavlov's study of classical conditioning continued long after this initial experiment, and many of his findings have been replicated with other responses and in other species, including humans. Let's take a closer look at the process of classical conditioning and some examples of its occurrence in human learning.

THE CLASSICAL CONDITIONING MODEL

Classical conditioning has been demonstrated, not only in dogs and laboratory rats, but also in newborn human infants (Lipsitt & Kaye, 1964; Reese & Lipsett, 1970), unborn human fetuses (Macfarlane, 1978), and even organisms as simple as a flatworm (Thompson & McConnell, 1955). The applicability of classical conditioning clearly extends widely across the animal kingdom.

As illustrated by Pavlov's dog, classical conditioning occurs when two stimuli are presented at approximately the same time. One of these stimuli

The conditioned stimulus may serve as a signal that the unconditioned stimulus is coming.

is an unconditioned stimulus: it has previously been shown to elicit an unconditioned response. The second stimulus, through its association with the unconditioned stimulus, begins to elicit a response as well: it becomes a conditioned stimulus that brings about a conditioned response.

Classical conditioning is most likely to occur when the conditioned stimulus is presented just *before* the unconditioned stimulus. For this reason, some psychologists describe classical conditioning as a form of *signal learning*. By being presented first, the conditioned stimulus serves as a signal that the unconditioned stimulus is coming, much as Pavlov's dog might have learned that the sound of a bell indicated that yummy meat powder was on its way.

Classical conditioning usually involves the learning of *involuntary* responses, responses over which one has no control. When we say that a stimulus *elicits* a response, we mean that the stimulus brings about a response automatically, without the individual having much control over the occurrence of that response. In most cases, the conditioned response is similar to the unconditioned response (see Klein, 1987, or Hergenhahn, 1988, for exceptions), with the two responses differing primarily in terms of which stimulus elicits the response, and sometimes in terms of the strength of the response.

CLASSICAL CONDITIONING IN HUMAN LEARNING

Classical conditioning theory is frequently used to help us understand how people learn a variety of involuntary responses. For example, many people develop aversions to particular foods as a result of associating those foods with an upset stomach (Garb & Stunkard, 1974). To illustrate, after associating the taste of creamy cucumber salad dressing (CS) with the nausea (UCS) I experienced during pregnancy, I developed an aversion (CR) to cucumber dressing (CS) that lasted for more than a year.

For many people, darkness is a conditioned stimulus for going to sleep, perhaps because it has frequently been associated with fatigue. I once became uncomfortably aware of how conditioned I was when I attended my daughter's "astronomy night" at school. We parents were ushered into a classroom and asked to sit down. Then the lights were turned off, and we watched a half-hour filmstrip describing a NASA space museum. Although I am usually quite alert during early evening hours, I found myself growing increasingly drowsy, and probably only my upright position in an uncomfortable metal chair kept me from losing consciousness altogether. In that situation, the darkness elicited a go-to-sleep response, and there were no stimuli (certainly not the filmstrip) eliciting a stay-awake response.

Classical conditioning is also a useful model for explaining some of the fears and phobias that people develop. For example, my bee phobia can probably be explained by the fact that bees (CS) had previously been associated with a sting (UCS), such that I became increasingly fearful (CR) of the nasty insects. In a similar way, people who are bitten by a dog sometimes become afraid of a particular breed, or even of all dogs.

Probably the best known example of a classically conditioned fear of an animal is the case of "Little Albert," an infant who learned to fear white rats through procedures used by John Watson and Rosalie Rayner (1920). Albert was an even-tempered, eleven-month-old child who rarely cried or displayed fearful reactions. One day, Albert was shown a white rat. As he reached out and touched it, a large steel bar behind him was struck, producing a loud, unpleasant noise. Albert jumped, obviously very upset by the startling noise. Nevertheless, he reached forward to touch the rat with his other hand, but the steel bar was struck once again. After five more pairings of the rat (CS) and the loud noise (UCS), Albert was truly rat-phobic: whenever he saw the rat he cried hysterically and crawled away as quickly as his hands and knees would allow. Watson and Rayner reported that Albert responded in a similarly fearful manner to a rabbit, a dog, a sealskin coat, cotton wool, and a Santa Claus mask with a fuzzy beard, although none of these had ever been paired with the startling noise. (Watson and Rayner never "undid" their conditioning of poor Albert. Fortunately, the ethical standards of the American Psychological Association would now prohibit such negligence.)

When I was growing up, my mother had an effective means of keeping my behavior within reasonable limits. Whenever I began to step out of bounds, she simply gave me "The Look," a scowl accompanied by a wrinkled brow and sinister, piercing eyes. I suspect that this facial expression must have been paired with physical punishment sometime in my early childhood years, because The Look alone was eventually sufficient to send me to my bedroom in quick retreat. A threat of punishment such as The Look can be anxiety-arousing enough to control a child's behavior without one's actually having to resort to the punishment threatened. However, a threat can only become a conditioned stimulus if it has in fact been associated with punishment at one time or another, with that punishment following the threat in close proximity (Klein, 1987).

The use of punishment itself is a controversial procedure because stimuli frequently associated with it—the home or school environment, or a child's parent or teacher—can become a conditioned stimulus also leading to fear and anxiety responses. We will examine punishment in more detail in Chapter 6, and will look at guidelines for minimizing the chances that negative side effects from punishment will develop.

Fear of failure is still another example of a response that may be classically conditioned. In some cases, people who are unusually afraid of failing may have previously associated failure with unpleasant circumstances, perhaps painful punishment from an angry parent or the ridicule of insensitive classmates. Yet occasional failure is a natural consequence of attempting new endeavors, whether in school, at home, or elsewhere. Teachers and parents must be careful that failure does not become such a strong conditioned stimulus for children that they resist engaging in new activities and attempting challenging but possibly risky problems.

The examples of classical conditioning at work should help you understand this learning process and recognize a classically conditioned response when you see one. We will now turn to other aspects of classical conditioning.

BASIC CONCEPTS IN CLASSICAL CONDITIONING

Pavlov described a number of phenomena characteristic of classical conditioning. We will examine several of them: extinction, spontaneous recovery, stimulus generalization, stimulus discrimination, higher-order conditioning, and sensory preconditioning.

Extinction

Let's return for a moment to Pavlov's dog. Remember that the dog learned to salivate to the sound of a bell alone after that bell had on several occasions been presented in conjunction with meat powder. But what would happen if the bell continued to ring over and over without the meat powder's ever again being presented along with it? Pavlov discovered that repeated presentation of the conditioned stimulus alone led to successively weaker and weaker conditioned responses. Eventually, the dog no longer salivated to the bell; that is, the conditioned response disappeared.

The disappearance of a conditioned response when a conditioned stimulus is repeatedly presented without the unconditioned stimulus is a phenomenon Pavlov called *extinction*. For example, The Look from my mother no longer has the effect it used to: whatever punishment was once associated with it has long since disappeared (besides, now I'm bigger than she is).

Sometimes conditioned responses will extinguish, and sometimes they will not. The unpredictability of extinction is a source of frustration to anyone working with people who have acquired inappropriate, yet involuntary, conditioned responses. Later in the chapter, we will discuss an alternative procedure for situations in which inappropriate responses *don't* extinguish.

Spontaneous Recovery

Even though Pavlov quickly extinguished his dog's conditioned salivation response by repeatedly presenting the bell in the absence of meat powder, when he entered his laboratory the following day he discovered that the bell once again elicited salivation in the dog, almost as if extinction had never taken place. This reappearance of the salivation response after it had previously been extinguished is something Pavlov called *spontaneous recovery*.

In more general terms, spontaneous recovery is a recurrence of a conditioned response when a period of extinction is followed by a rest period. For example, if I am near lots of bees for a period of time, I eventually settle down and regain my composure. However, my first response on a later encounter with a bee is to fly off the handle once again.

Pavlov found that a conditioned response appearing in spontaneous recovery is typically weaker than the original conditioned response and extinguishes more quickly. In situations in which a CR spontaneously recovers several times, each time after a period of rest has elapsed, each response is weaker than the one before it and extinguishes more rapidly.

Stimulus Generalization

You may recall that Little Albert, after being conditioned to fear a white rat, also became afraid of a rabbit, a dog, a fur coat, cotton wool, and a fuzzy-bearded Santa Claus mask. When individuals respond to other stimuli in the same way that they respond to conditioned stimuli, *stimulus generalization* is occurring. The more similar a stimulus is to the conditioned stimulus, the greater the probability that stimulus generalization will occur. Albert exhibited fear of all objects that were white and fuzzy like the rat, but he was not afraid of his nonwhite, nonfuzzy toy blocks. In a similar way, a child who fears an abusive father may generalize that fear to other men, but not to women.

In some cases, generalization of conditioned fear responses may actually increase over time—that is, as time goes on, an individual becomes fearful of an increasing number of objects (McAllister & McAllister, 1965). Thus, conditioned responses that are not quickly extinguished may actually become more frequent because they are being elicited by a greater number of stimuli.

Stimulus Discrimination

Pavlov observed that when he conditioned a dog to salivate to a high-pitched tone, the dog would generalize that conditioned response to a low-pitched tone. To teach the dog the difference between the two tones, Pavlov repeatedly presented the high tone in conjunction with meat powder and presented the low tone without meat. After several such presentations of the two tones, the dog eventually learned to salivate only to the high tone. In Pavlov's terminology, differentiation between the two tones had taken place. Psychologists today more frequently use the term *stimulus discrimination* for this phenomenon.

Stimulus discrimination occurs when one stimulus (the CS +) is presented in conjunction with an unconditioned stimulus, and another stimulus (the CS −) is presented without that UCS. The individual learns a conditioned response to the CS + but does not generalize the response to the CS −. For example, if a child who is abused by her father simultaneously has positive interactions with other adult men, she is not as likely to generalize her fear of her father to those other individuals.

Higher-order Conditioning

Pavlov also discovered a phenomenon known as *second-order conditioning*, or more generally as *higher-order conditioning*. When a dog had been conditioned to salivate to the sound of a bell, and the bell was later presented in conjunction with a neutral stimulus such as a flash of light, that neutral stimulus would also elicit a salivation response, even though it had never been directly associated with meat. In other words, the light flash became a conditioned stimulus through its pairing not with the unconditioned stimulus, but with another conditioned stimulus.

Higher-order conditioning works like this: first, a neutral stimulus (NS$_1$) becomes a conditioned stimulus (CS$_1$) by being paired with an unconditioned stimulus (UCS) and therefore elicits a conditioned response (CR). Next, a second neutral stimulus (NS$_2$) is paired with CS$_1$, and then independently elicits a similar conditioned response—that second stimulus has also become a conditioned stimulus (CS$_2$).

A diagram of higher-order conditioning appears in Figure 3–2.

Steps one and two depict the original conditioning; steps three and four depict higher-order conditioning, in which a second neutral stimulus becomes a CS$_2$ by virtue of its being paired with the CS$_1$.

Figure 3–2
An example of higher-order conditioning

Step 1: **NS**$_1$
         (bell)
                    ⟶   **UCR**
         UCS   (salivate)
         (meat)

Step 2: **CS**$_1$ ⟶   **CR**
         (bell)   (salivate)

Step 3: **NS**$_2$
         (light)
                    ⟶   **CR**
         CS$_1$ (salivate)
         (bell)

Step 4: **CS**$_2$ ⟶   **CR**
         (light)   (salivate)

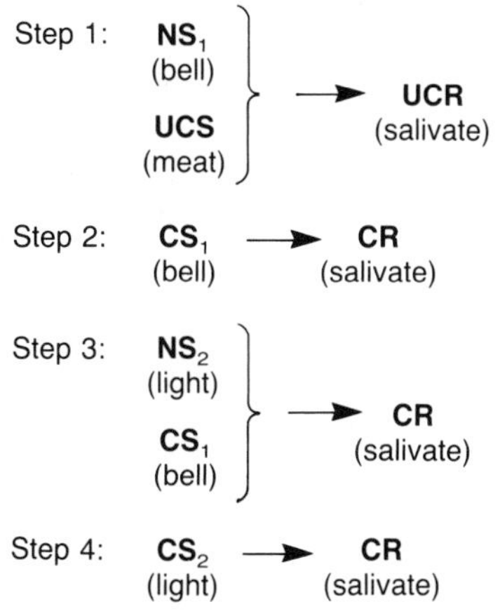

Higher-order conditioning is a possible explanation for some of the fears that students exhibit in the classroom (e.g., Klein, 1987). Let's say, first of all, that failure has previously been associated with painful physical punishment. Then another situation—perhaps a test, an oral presentation in front of classmates, or even school itself—becomes associated with failure. The painful punishment is the UCS. Failure, originally a NS_1, becomes a CS_1 after its association with the UCS. Some other aspect of school (e.g., a test), while first a NS_2, becomes an additional conditioned stimulus (CS_2) through its association with CS_1. In this way, a student may develop test anxiety, fear of public speaking, or even school phobia—fear of school itself.

Sensory Preconditioning

Higher-order conditioning is one way an individual can develop a conditioned response to a stimulus that has never been directly paired with an unconditioned stimulus. *Sensory preconditioning* is very similar to higher-order conditioning, except that the steps occur in a different order. Let me first illustrate the process by once again conditioning Pavlov's poor, overworked dog. Suppose that we first present the sound of a bell and a flash of light simultaneously. Then we pair the bell with meat powder. Not only does the dog salivate to the sound of a bell, we discover that it also salivates to the flash of light!

In more general terms, sensory preconditioning occurs like this. First, two neutral stimuli (NS_1 and NS_2) are presented simultaneously. Then one of these neutral stimuli (NS_1) is associated with an unconditioned stimulus (UCS), thus becoming a conditioned stimulus (CS_1) and eliciting a conditioned response (CR). In cases of sensory preconditioning, the second neutral stimulus (NS_2) *also* elicits the conditioned response (i.e., NS_2 has become CS_2) by virtue of its prior association with CS_1.

Klein (1987) has suggested that sensory preconditioning may be an alternative explanation for some cases of test anxiety. School (NS_1) is first associated with tests (NS_2). If school is later associated with some traumatic event (UCS), then not only will school become a conditioned stimulus (CS_1) eliciting anxiety (CR), but tests may become a conditioned stimulus (CS_2) as well. A diagram of how test anxiety might develop through sensory preconditioning is presented in Figure 3–3.

CHANGING INAPPROPRIATE CONDITIONED RESPONSES

Conditioned responses are often not easily eliminated because they are involuntary: people have little or no control over them. Yet some classically conditioned responses (e.g., some irrational fears) may be detrimental to an individual's functioning. How can we get rid of counterproductive conditioned responses? Extinction and counterconditioning are two possible methods.

Figure 3–3
An example of sensory preconditioning

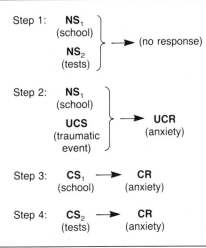

Extinction

One obvious way in which a conditioned response might be eliminated is through the process of extinction. If the conditioned stimulus is presented in the absence of the unconditioned stimulus frequently enough, the conditioned response should disappear. Often this is exactly what will happen.

Unfortunately, though, extinction is notoriously unpredictable as a means of eliminating conditioned responses: it simply doesn't always work. There are at least three reasons why:

1. The speed at which extinction occurs is unpredictable. If, during the conditioning process, the conditioned stimulus was sometimes presented in conjunction with the unconditioned stimulus but sometimes alone (i.e., the stimulus pairings were inconsistent), extinction is likely to be particularly slow (Humphreys, 1939).

2. People tend to avoid a stimulus they have learned to fear, thus reducing the chances of encountering the conditioned stimulus in the absence of the unconditioned stimulus. For example, a student who has learned to fear mathematics after a history of failing the subject typically avoids math as much as possible, thus minimizing any chance of associating math with success.

3. Even when a response has been extinguished, it may reappear through spontaneous recovery. You can never be totally sure when a response will spontaneously recover and when it will not.

Counterconditioning

In an alternative procedure to extinction, called *counterconditioning*, one conditioned response is replaced with a new, more appropriate conditioned response. Counterconditioning tends to be more effective than extinction in eliminating undesirable conditioned responses; it also minimizes the chances that those responses will recur through spontaneous recovery.

Mary Cover Jones's classic work with "Little Peter" (Jones, 1924) provides an excellent example of counterconditioning. Peter was a two-year-old boy who had somehow learned to be afraid of rabbits. To rid him of his fear, Jones placed Peter in a high chair and gave him some candy. As he ate, she brought the rabbit into the far side of the same room. Under different circumstances the rabbit might have elicited anxiety; however, the pleasure Peter felt as he ate the candy was a stronger response and essentially overpowered any anxiety Peter might have felt about the rabbit's presence. Jones repeated the same procedure every day over a two-month period, each time sitting Peter in a high chair with candy and bringing the rabbit slightly closer than she had the time before, and Peter's anxiety about rabbits eventually disappeared.

In general, counterconditioning involves these components:

1. A new response is chosen that is *incompatible* with the existing conditioned response. Two responses are incompatible with each other when they cannot be performed at the same time. Because classically conditioned responses are often emotional in nature, an incompatible response is often some sort of opposite emotional reaction. For example, in the case of Little Peter, happiness was used as an incompatible response for fear. Since fear and anxiety create bodily tension, any response involving relaxation would be incompatible.

2. A stimulus that elicits the incompatible response must be identified; for example, candy elicited a "happy" response for Little Peter. If we are seeking to develop a happy response in a student for a stimulus that has previously elicited displeasure, we need to find a stimulus that already elicits pleasure—perhaps a friend, a party, or a favorite food. If we want someone to learn a relaxation response, we might ask that person to imagine lying in a cool, fragrant meadow or on a lawn chair by a pool.

3. The stimulus that elicits the new response is presented to the individual, and the conditioned stimulus eliciting the undesirable conditioned response is *gradually* introduced into the situation. In treating Little Peter's fear of rabbits, Jones initially presented the rabbit at some distance from Peter, only gradually bringing it closer and closer in successive sessions. The trick in counterconditioning is to ensure that the stimulus eliciting the desirable response is always *stronger* than the stimulus eliciting the undesirable response; otherwise, the undesirable response might prevail.

Counterconditioning provides a means through which many conditioned anxiety responses can be decreased or eliminated. For example, *systematic desensitization* (e.g., Wolpe, 1958, 1969), a therapeutic technique designed to replace anxiety with a relaxation response, is now widely used as a means of treating such difficulties as fear of public speaking and test anxiety. I should point out, however, that treating test anxiety alone, without remediating possible academic sources of a student's poor test performance as well, may reduce test anxiety without any concurrent improvement in test scores (Tryon, 1980).

A technique I recommend to many graduate students who dread their required statistics course because of mathematics anxiety is that they find a math textbook that begins well below their own skill level—at the level of basic number facts, if necessary—so that the problems are not anxiety-arousing. As they work through the text, the students begin to associate mathematics with success rather than failure. Programmed instruction (described in detail in Chapter 5) is another technique that can be useful in reducing anxiety about a given subject matter, because it allows a student to progress through the material in small, easy steps.

GENERAL EDUCATIONAL IMPLICATIONS
OF CLASSICAL CONDITIONING

The durability and generalizability of some classically conditioned responses point to the need for a positive classroom climate for our students. When schoolwork, a teacher, or even the school environment itself is associated with punishment, humiliation, failure, or frustration, school and its curriculum can become sources of excessive anxiety.

Some classroom activities—tests, oral presentations, and difficult subject matter—are particularly likely to be associated with unpleasant circumstances such as failure or embarrassment, and many students may soon become anxious when involved in them. Teachers should therefore take special precautions when asking students to engage in any "risky" activities. For example, I suspect that many students have early unpleasant experiences in public speaking because they receive little if any instruction about how to prepare and deliver an effective oral presentation. If students are asked to speak in front of a group, they should be given specific suggestions regarding what material to present and how to present it in such a way that classmates will react positively rather than derisively.

Mathematics is a difficult and anxiety-arousing subject for many students. I firmly believe that mathematics anxiety is so prevalent because most schools teach too much, too fast, and too soon, so that students quickly begin to associate mathematics with frustration and failure. Part of the problem may lie in the tendency to teach mathematical concepts before children are cognitively ready to deal with them. According to Jean Piaget (whose ideas I will present in Chapter 7), children do not acquire certain capabilities for mathematical reasoning until age eleven or twelve at the earliest. One of these late acquisitions is the ability to understand the idea of proportion, the concept underlying fractions and decimals. Yet schools typically introduce fractions and decimals sometime around fourth grade, when students are only nine or ten years of age.

Educators have often argued that school should be a place where a student encounters more success than failure, and classical conditioning provides a justification for their argument. This is not to say that students should never encounter failure; people need feedback about what they are doing wrong as well as what they are doing right. However, when students experience failure too frequently, either in their schoolwork or in their social relationships, school may quickly become a conditioned stimulus that leads to counterproductive conditioned responses such as fear and anxiety. These responses, once conditioned, may be very resistant to extinction and may interfere with a student's learning effectively for years to come.

SUMMARY

Through a systematic study of the salivation response in dogs, Ivan Pavlov developed his theory of classical conditioning, an explanation of how certain involuntary responses develop. Classical conditioning occurs when two stimuli are presented at approximately the same time. One is an unconditioned stimulus that has been previously shown to elicit an unconditioned response. The second stimulus, through its association with the unconditioned stimulus, begins to elicit a response as well: it becomes a conditioned stimulus that brings about a conditioned response. The classical conditioning paradigm is frequently used as an explanation of human fears such as test anxiety, fear of failure, and school phobia. Undesirable conditioned responses can sometimes be eliminated by either extinction or counterconditioning.

C H A P T E R   4

Operant Conditioning

Outline

The Operant Conditioning Model
Reinforcement Defined
Three Important Conditions for Operant Conditioning
What Behaviors Can Be Reinforced?

Operant Conditioning and Classical Conditioning Contrasted

Basic Concepts in Operant Conditioning
Free Operant Level   Terminal Behavior   Extinction
Superstitious Behavior   Shaping

The Nature of Reinforcers
Primary and Secondary Reinforcers
Positive Reinforcement, Negative Reinforcement, and Punishment
Different Kinds of Reinforcing Stimuli

Factors Affecting the Effectiveness of Reinforcement
Timing   Magnitude and Appeal   Consistency

Schedules of Reinforcement
Ratio Schedules: Reinforcing a Certain Number of Responses
Interval Schedules: Reinforcing the First Response After a Time Period
Differential Schedules: Reinforcing Rates of Responding

Stimulus Control
Stimulus Generalization   Stimulus Discrimination
Stimulus Control in the Classroom

Eliminating Undesirable Behaviors
Extinction
Differential Reinforcement of Other Behaviors
Reinforcement of Incompatible Behaviors

When Reinforcement Doesn't Work
Reinforcer Doesn't Reinforce   Reinforcement Is Inconsistent
Change Isn't Worthwhile   Shaping Proceeds Too Rapidly

Skinner on Education

Summary

DIFFERENT individuals work for different rewards. When my son Alex needs money to buy something he wants desperately, he will engage in behaviors he never does otherwise—for example, scrubbing the bathtub or sweeping up rotten crabapples that have fallen on the driveway. My daughter Tina can rarely be enticed into doing household chores with financial incentives, but will make her bed and put away her clothes willingly if doing so enables her to have a friend spend the night.

The idea of reward (learning theorists more frequently use the term *reinforcement*) provides the foundation for B. F. Skinner's principles of *operant conditioning*. In this chapter, we will look at the operant conditioning in depth, contrasting it with classical conditioning and then examining such concepts as free operant level, terminal behavior, extinction, spontaneous recovery, superstitious behavior, and shaping. We will distinguish between primary and secondary reinforcers, and among positive reinforcement, negative reinforcement, and punishment. We will also look at the effects of different schedules of reinforcement, i.e., at the various patterns of responding that result when responses are reinforced intermittently. We will explore ways in which the environment can be structured, through means of stimulus control, so that appropriate responses are more likely, and we will also look at ways of reducing the occurrence of undesirable behaviors. Finally, we will look at what B. F. Skinner has to say about operant conditioning in the classroom.

THE OPERANT CONDITIONING MODEL

Skinner's principle of operant conditioning (Skinner, 1938) can be paraphrased as follows:

> *A response that is followed by a reinforcer is strengthened, and is therefore more likely to occur again.*

In other words, responses that are reinforced tend to increase in frequency. Because a response increase is a change in behavior, then, from a behaviorist viewpoint, reinforcement brings about learning. Skinner has found that rats will learn to press metal bars, and pigeons will peck at round plastic disks, to get pellets of food. Likewise, my daughter Tina will increase her housekeeping behavior if it allows her to see a friend, and my son Alex will do just about anything if the price is right.

Reinforcement Defined

Skinner has intentionally used the term *reinforcement* instead of *reward* to describe the kind of consequence that increases the frequency of a behavior. The word *reward* implies that the stimulus following a behavior is somehow both pleasant and desirable, an implication that Skinner has tried to avoid for two reasons. First of all, some individuals will work for what others would see as unpleasant consequences; for example, my daughter occasionally does something she knows will irritate me because she enjoys watching me blow my stack. Secondly, "pleasantness" and "desirability" are subjective judgments, and behaviorists such as Skinner prefer that psychological principles be restricted to the domain of objectively observable events. A reinforcer can be defined without any allusion to either pleasantness or desirability, in this way:

> *A reinforcer is a stimulus that increases the frequency of a response it follows.*

Notice how I have just defined a reinforcer totally in terms of observable phenomena, without reliance on any subjective judgment.

Now that I have given you definitions of both operant conditioning and reinforcers, I need to point out a major problem with my definitions: taken together, they constitute circular reasoning. I have said that operant conditioning is an increase in a behavior when it is followed by a reinforcer, but I cannot seem to define a reinforcer in any other way except to say that it increases behavior. I am therefore using reinforcement to explain a behavior increase, and a behavior increase to explain reinforcement! Fortunately, a paper by Meehl (1950) has enabled learning theorists to get out of this circular mess by pointing out the *transituational generality* of a reinforcer: the same reinforcer will increase many different behaviors in many different situations.

Three Important Conditions for Operant Conditioning

Three important conditions are necessary for operant conditioning to take place:

The reinforcer must follow the response. Reinforcers that precede a response rarely have an effect on that response. For example, about ten years ago, a couple of instructors at my university were concerned that grades, because they were "threatening," interfered with student learning; therefore they announced on the first day of class that everyone would receive an A for the course. Many students never attended class after that first day, so there was little learning for any grade to interfere with. Reinforcers must always, always *follow* the desired behavior.

The reinforcer must follow immediately after the response. A reinforcer tends to reinforce the response that has occurred just before it. Thus, reinforcement is less effective when its presentation is delayed: in the meantime, an organism may have made one or more responses that are reinforced instead. Once, when I was teaching a pigeon named Ethel to peck a lighted plastic disk, I made a serious mistake: I waited too long after she had pecked the disk before reinforcing her, and in the meantime she had begun to turn around. After eating her food pellet, Ethel began to spin frantically in counterclockwise circles, and it was several minutes before I was able to get her back to the pecking response I had in mind for her.

Our schools are notorious for delayed reinforcement. How many times have you completed an exam or turned in a written assignment, only to receive your grade days or even weeks later? Immediate reinforcers are typically more effective than delayed reinforcers in classroom situations (Kulik & Kulik, 1988). Furthermore, immediate reinforcers are probably the *only* effective reinforcers for animals and young children.

The reinforcer must be contingent upon the response. A reinforcer should never be presented unless the desired response has been exhibited. For example, teachers often specify certain conditions that must be met before children can go on a field trip: they must bring their permission slips, they must complete their assignments, and so on. When these teachers feel badly for children who have not met the stated conditions and allow them to go on the field trip anyway, the reinforcement is not contingent on the response, and the children are not learning acceptable behavior. If anything, they are learning that rules can be broken!

What Behaviors Can Be Reinforced?

Virtually any behavior—academic, social, psychomotor—can be learned or modified by means of operant conditioning. As a teacher, I keep reminding myself of what student behaviors I want to increase and try to follow those behaviors with positive consequences. For example, when a typically quiet student raises his hand to answer a question or make a comment, I call on him and give him whatever positive feedback I can. I also try to make my classes lively, interesting, and humorous, as well as informative, so that students are reinforced for coming to class in the first place.

Unfortunately, undesirable behaviors can be reinforced just as easily as desirable ones. Aggression and criminal activity often lead to successful outcomes: crime usually *does* pay. Disruptive behavior in class may get the teacher's attention in a way that no other behavior can. Getting "sick" will allow the school-phobic child to stay home from school. Students sometimes appear at my office at the end of the semester pleading for a higher grade than their class performance has warranted or for the chance to complete an extra-credit project. I almost invariably turn them down, for a simple reason: I want good grades to be contingent on good study habits throughout the semester, not on begging behavior at my office door. Teachers must be extremely careful about what they reinforce and what they do not.

OPERANT CONDITIONING AND CLASSICAL CONDITIONING CONTRASTED

Skinner has suggested that there are really two different kinds of learning: classical conditioning (he uses the term *respondent conditioning*) and operant conditioning. The two forms of conditioning are different in several major respects.

Classical conditioning results from the pairing of two stimuli, the UCS and the CS. The learned response is a direct and immediate reaction to the stimulus that precedes it; that is, the conditioned stimulus brings about, or elicits, the conditioned response. The conditioned response is automatic and involuntary, such that the organism has virtually no control over what it is doing. Skinner's term *respondent* reflects the fact that the organism's behavior is an involuntary *response* to a stimulus.

Operant conditioning, on the other hand, results when a response is followed by a reinforcing stimulus. The response is a voluntary one emitted by the organism, with the organism having complete control over whether the response occurs. Skinner's term *operant* reflects the fact that the organism voluntarily *operates* on the environment.

Figure 4–1 highlights the major differences between classical and operant conditioning.

In fact, because operant conditioning reflects a $R \to S_{Rf}$ model, where S_{Rf} is the symbol for a reinforcing stimulus, Skinner is not really an S-R psychologist at all—he is actually an R-S psychologist.

Figure 4–1
Differences between classical and operant conditioning

	Classical Conditioning (respondent)	**Operant Conditioning**
Occurs when:	Two stimuli (UCS and CS) are paired.	Response (R) is followed by a reinforcing stimulus (S_{Rf})
Nature of response:	Involuntary: elicited by stimulus.	Voluntary: emitted by organism.
Model:	$CS \to CR$	$R \to S_{Rf}$

Some theorists have questioned whether classical and operant conditioning really reflect different learning processes at all (e.g., see Bower & Hilgard, 1981). However, in most situations the traditional classical and operant conditioning models will help us understand many instances of learning, so I will continue to treat them as two distinct forms of learning.

BASIC CONCEPTS IN OPERANT CONDITIONING

A number of concepts are related to operant conditioning, including free operant level, terminal behavior, extinction, superstitious behavior, and shaping. Let's look at each of these.

Free Operant Level

An *operant* is a voluntary response emitted by the organism. The *free operant level* is the frequency of an operant in the absence of reinforcement—in other words, the prereinforcement, or *baseline*, frequency of the response. Students will vary in their free operant levels for different responses. For some students, getting-out-of-seat behavior will be quite frequent, while for others it will be rare. Similarly, some students will read frequently without being asked to do so while others will seldom read on their own initiative.

Terminal Behavior

The *terminal behavior* is the form and frequency of the desired response at the end of a reinforcement program. Let's say, for example, that a second-grade boy rarely stays in his seat for more than five minutes at a time, and when he does sit down, he slouches so low in the chair that his head is barely level with the desk. A teacher who plans to alter this child's classroom behavior through reinforcement may specify the terminal behavior as sitting up straight for a ten-minute period.

When using reinforcement to change behavior, it is essential that we describe the terminal behavior ahead of time in concrete terms. Specifying the exact form of the desired behavior (e.g., sitting up straight) and the frequency or duration of the behavior (e.g., ten minutes at a stretch) enables us to determine objectively whether our reinforcement program has been effective.

Extinction

In classical conditioning, when the CS is repeatedly presented in the absence of the UCS, the CR decreases and eventually disappears—that is, the response extinguishes. In operant conditioning, *extinction* occurs when a response is no longer followed by a reinforcer. A nonreinforced response will decrease—although sometimes a brief increase in the behavior will first be observed—and eventually return to its baseline rate. For example, a class clown who finds that no one laughs at her jokes anymore is likely to decrease her joke telling. A student who is never called on when he raises his hand may stop trying to participate in class discussions. A student who continues to fail exams despite hours of studying for them may eventually stop studying.

Although we want to extinguish undesirable behaviors such as disruptive joke telling, we need to take precautions that *desirable* behaviors are reinforced frequently enough that they *don't* extinguish. For example, a student whose studying produces no reinforcement at exam time needs assistance of some kind. If many other students also find the same exams too difficult to pass, something may be wrong with those exams or with classroom instruction. If only one student is failing, perhaps that student needs help in developing more appropriate study techniques, or more individualized instruction, or placement in a class better matched to his or her ability.

Superstitious Behavior

What happens when reinforcement is random and not contingent on any particular behavior? Skinner once left eight pigeons in their cages overnight with the food tray mechanism adjusted so that reinforcement was presented at regular intervals, regardless of what responses were occurring at the time. By morning, six of the pigeons were acting bizarrely: for example, one repeatedly thrust its head into an upper corner of the cage, and two others were swinging their heads and bodies in rhythmic pendulum movements (Skinner, 1948a).

Reinforcement administered randomly will often reinforce whatever response occurred immediately beforehand, and an organism will increase that response, thus displaying what Skinner has called *superstitious behavior*. A nonbehaviorist way of describing the learning of a superstitious behavior is that the organism thinks that the response and reinforcement are related when in fact they are not. For example, a student may have a "lucky sweater" to wear on exam days, or a football player may, before every game, perform a ritual totally unrelated to successful football.

Superstitious behavior in the classroom can occur either when reinforcements are not contingent on behavior or when students do not accurately see which of their many responses is responsible for bringing about reinforcement. It behooves the teacher to ensure that classroom reinforcers such as praise, attention, and grades *are* contingent on desired behaviors and that response-reinforcement contingencies are clearly specified.

Shaping

For the frequency of a response to be increased, that response must be reinforced. And for it to be reinforced, it must be emitted. But sometimes the free operant level of a response is so low that it rarely, if ever, occurs. What do we do then?

To handle such a situation, Skinner introduced a method called *shaping*, a technique also known as *successive approximations*. Shaping is a means of teaching a behavior when the free operant level for that behavior is very low, or when the desired terminal behavior is different in form from any responses the organism exhibits.

To shape a particular behavior, you begin by reinforcing the first response that in any way approximates the desired behavior and continue reinforcing that response until the organism emits it fairly frequently. At that point you reinforce only those responses that more closely resemble the desired behavior, then those that resemble it more closely still, until eventually only the desired behavior itself is being reinforced. In other words, shaping is a process of reinforcing successively closer and closer approximations to the terminal behavior until the terminal behavior is exhibited.

To illustrate, when I taught my pigeon Ethel to peck a lighted disk in her Skinner box, I began by reinforcing her every time she faced the wall on which the disk was located. Once this response was occurring frequently, I began to reinforce her only when her beak was near the wall, then only when her beak touched the wall, then only when she pecked within a two-inch radius of the disk, and so on. Within an hour, I had Ethel happily pecking the lighted disk and eating the food pellets that followed each correct peck.

Legend has it that a group of students once shaped a professor of mine a few days after he had given a lecture on shaping. Every time the professor stood on the side of the classroom near the door, they all appeared interested in what he was saying, sitting forward in their seats and taking notes feverishly. Every time he walked away from the door, they acted bored, slouching back in their seats and looking anxiously at their watches. As the class went on, they reinforced him only as he moved closer and closer to the door until, by the end of class, he was lecturing from the hallway!

In much the same way, we gradually shape such behaviors as handwriting, sedentary behavior, and mathematical problem solving. For example, kindergarten children are taught to write their letters on wide-lined paper, with the bottoms of the letters resting on one line and the tops touching the line above. As children progress through the primary grades, the spaces between the lines become smaller, and teachers are more particular about how well the letters are written. Gradually, children begin to write consistently sized and carefully shaped letters with the benefit of only a lower line, and eventually with no line at all. Teachers also shape the sedentary behavior of their students: as students grow older, they are expected to sit quietly in their seats for longer and longer periods. We can also think of mathematics as a shaped behavior: complex problem solving is introduced only after the more basic skills such as counting and number recognition have been mastered.

Teachers may also inadvertently shape undesirable behaviors, thereby intensifying them. For example, let's say that Molly frequently exhibits such disruptive behaviors as talking out of turn and physically annoying other students. Molly's teacher decides to eliminate these disruptive behaviors by ignoring (i.e., extinguishing) them. Although the teacher is able to ignore minor infractions, he finds himself unable to ignore Molly's more extreme disruptions and reprimands her for them. If Molly finds the teacher's negative attention reinforcing, as many students do, she may engage in more and more extreme disruptive behavior to get that attention. In other words, the teacher's strategy is counterproductive: because he ignores minor disruptions and reinforces major ones, he is unintentionally shaping Molly into an increasingly more disruptive student.

THE NATURE OF REINFORCERS

I have talked at length about how reinforcers can be used to change behavior. What about reinforcers themselves? I will first make two distinctions: the difference between primary and secondary reinforcers and the difference between positive and negative reinforcement—which I will also contrast with punishment. I will then describe a number of different kinds of reinforcers that can be effectively used to change student behaviors.

Primary and Secondary Reinforcers

A *primary reinforcer* is a reinforcer that satisfies a biological need. Food, water, oxygen, and warmth are examples of possible primary reinforcers. Physical affection and cuddling may also address biological needs (Harlow & Zimmerman, 1959), thus serving as primary reinforcers. There may be individual differences in what constitute primary reinforcers: for example, sex will be reinforcing to some individuals but not to others, and a certain drug will be a primary reinforcer for a drug addict but not for a nonaddicted individual.

A *secondary reinforcer*, also known as a *conditioned reinforcer*, is a previously neutral stimulus that has become reinforcing to an organism through repeated association with another reinforcer. Examples of secondary reinforcers, which do not satisfy any obvious biological necessities, are praise, grades, money, and feelings of success.

Some psychologists believe that secondary reinforcers are learned through the process of classical conditioning. A neutral stimulus is paired with an existing reinforcer (UCS) that elicits some form of biological satisfaction (UCR). That neutral stimulus becomes a CS (i.e., it becomes a secondary reinforcer) that elicits the same satisfaction (CR). For example, my daughter learned very early that she could use money (CS) to buy candy (UCS) to satisfy her sweet tooth. The more often a secondary reinforcer has

Primary vs. secondary reinforcers

been associated with another reinforcer and the stronger that other reinforcer is, the more powerful the secondary reinforcer will be (Bersh, 1951; D'Amato, 1955).

The relative influences of primary and secondary reinforcers on our lives probably depend a great deal on economic circumstances. When such biological necessities as food and warmth are scarce, these primary reinforcers, and the secondary reinforcers closely associated with them (e.g., money), may be major factors in reinforcing behavior. On the other hand, in times of economic well-being, when cupboards are full and houses are warm, such secondary reinforcers as praise, grades, and feelings of success are more likely to play a major role in the learning process.

Positive Reinforcement, Negative Reinforcement, and Punishment

In addition to the distinction between primary and secondary reinforcers, a distinction can also be made between positive and negative reinforcement. Let's examine these two forms of reinforcement and look at how they are different from punishment.

Positive Reinforcement. Up to this point, the reinforcers I have mentioned have all been positive reinforcers. *Positive reinforcement* involves the *presentation* of a stimulus after the response. Food, praise, a smile, and success are all positive reinforcers.

Negative Reinforcement. Negative reinforcement increases the response through the *removal* of a stimulus, usually an aversive or unpleasant one. For example, rats will learn to press a bar in order to terminate an electric shock: *removal* of the aversive shock is a negative reinforcer. As another example, many newer cars sound a loud buzzer if the keys are still in the ignition when the driver's door is opened; removal of the keys from the ignition is negatively reinforced because the buzzer stops.

The removal of anxiety or guilt can be an extremely powerful negative reinforcer. A child may confess to an offense committed days or even weeks earlier because she has been feeling guilty about the transgression all that time and needs to get it off her chest. Anxiety may drive one student to complete a term paper early, thereby removing an item from his "things to do" list. At the same time, another student confronted with the same term paper might procrastinate until the last minute, thereby removing anxiety—although only temporarily—about the more difficult aspects of researching and writing that paper.

Teachers may develop methods of classroom discipline that are effective over the short run but not over the long run because those teachers are negatively reinforced for using such discipline methods. For example, if Ms. Jones yells at Henry for talking too much, Henry may temporarily stop talking, and so Ms. Jones's yelling behavior is negatively reinforced. However, if Henry likes getting Ms. Jones's attention (a positive reinforcer), he will be chattering again before very long.

Punishment. Both positive reinforcement and negative reinforcement increase the responses they follow. Punishment, on the other hand, is likely to *decrease* those responses. I will describe the effects of punishment in more detail in Chapter 6, but will define punishment here so you can see how it differs from negative reinforcement. There are actually two different forms of punishment, frequently referred to as Punishment I and Punishment II. *Punishment I* involves the *presentation* of a stimulus, usually an aversive one. Scolding and spanking are examples of this form of punishment. *Punishment II* involves the *removal* of a stimulus, usually a pleasant one; examples include fines for misbehaviors (because money is being taken away) and loss of privileges. Figure 4–2 illustrates the differences among positive reinforcement, negative reinforcement, Punishment I, and Punishment II.

A particular source of confusion for many people is the difference between negative reinforcement and Punishment I. Although both involve an aversive stimulus, they differ in their time line. With negative reinforcement, the aversive stimulus *stops* when the response is emitted. With Punishment I, on the other hand, the aversive stimulus *begins* when the response is emitted. Figure 4–3 illustrates this difference graphically. The termination of an aversive stimulus negatively reinforces a response; the initiation of an aversive stimulus punishes a response.

Figure 4—2
Positive reinforcement, negative reinforcement, and punishment

Stimulus is:	Nature of Stimulus	
	"Pleasant"	Aversive
Presented after the response	Positive Reinforcement (response increased)	Punishment I (response decreased)
Removed after the response	Punishment II (response decreased)	Negative Reinforcement (response increased)

Figure 4—3
The difference between negative reinforcement and punishment is primarily one of time.

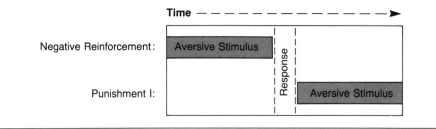

Different Kinds of Reinforcing Stimuli

Teachers often unnecessarily limit themselves to just a handful of reinforcers when using reinforcement in the classroom. In fact, a wide variety of events can be reinforcing to students. Let's look at various possibilities.

Material Reinforcers. A *material reinforcer*, or tangible reinforcer, is an actual object; food and toys are examples. For many people, the word *reinforcer* brings to mind such tangible consequences for good behavior. However, most psychologists recommend that a material reinforcer be used only as a last resort, when absolutely no other reinforcer works.

Social Reinforcers. A *social reinforcer* is a gesture or sign from one person to another that communicates positive regard. Praise, a smile, a pat on the back, and a hug are all social reinforcers. Social reinforcement is a common occurrence in the classroom and can be very effective. Teacher attention, approval, and praise are powerful classroom reinforcers (Becker, Madsen, Arnold, & Thomas, 1967; Drabman, 1976; Madsen, Becker, & Thomas,

1968; Schepis, Reid, & Fitzgerald, 1987; Ward & Baker, 1968). The approval of peers can be effective as well (Evans & Oswalt, 1968; Lovitt, Guppy, & Blattner, 1969).

Activity Reinforcers. Speaking nonbehavioristically, an *activity reinforcer* is an opportunity to engage in a favorite activity. (A quick quiz: Which word is the nonbehaviorist part of my definition, and why?) David Premack (1959, 1963) discovered that people will often perform one activity if doing so enables them to perform another. His *Premack principle* for activity reinforcers is as follows:

> *A normally high-frequency response, when it follows a normally low-frequency response, will increase the frequency of the low-frequency response.*

A high-frequency response is, in essence, a response that an organism enjoys doing, while a low-frequency response is one that the organism does not enjoy doing. Another way of stating the Premack principle, then, is that organisms will perform less preferred tasks so they can engage in more preferred tasks.

To illustrate, my own free operant level for housework is extremely low. I have found that I am more likely to do household chores if I make a higher-frequency behavior, such as reading a mystery novel or having a party, contingent on doing the housework. In a similar way, appropriate classroom behavior can be improved through the Premack principle. Young children can quickly be taught to sit quietly and pay attention if they are allowed to engage in higher-frequency "active" behaviors (e.g., talking and running around the room) only after they have been quiet and attentive for a certain period of time (Homme, deBaca, Devine, Steinhorst, & Rickert, 1963).

Although psychologists agree that the Premack principle works, they disagree as to *why* it works. If you are interested in exploring the theoretical underpinnings of the Premack principle, see the discussions by Bower and Hilgard (1981) and Timberlake and Allison (1974).

Intrinsic Reinforcers. In many situations, individuals will engage in certain responses not because of any external reinforcers but because of the internal good feelings—the *intrinsic reinforcement*—that such responses bring. Feeling successful after solving a difficult puzzle, proud after returning a valuable item to its rightful owner, and relieved after completing a difficult assignment are all examples of intrinsic reinforcers. People who continue to engage in responses for a long time without external reinforcers are probably working for intrinsic sources of satisfaction.

Positive Feedback. Material and social reinforcers may improve classroom behavior and lead to better learning of academic skills because they provide *feedback* to students about which responses are desirable and which are not (Gagné & Driscoll, 1988). For many students, the true reinforcers for learning are probably the internal reinforcers—feelings of success, competence, mastery, and pride—that scholastic accomplishments bring. For such students, external reinforcers, both material and social, are more helpful if they provide feedback that academic tasks have been performed well. Grades are probably also reinforcing for the same reason: good grades reflect high achievement, a reason to feel proud.

I once spent a half hour each day for several weeks working with Michael, a nine-year-old learning disabled boy who was having difficulty learning his cursive letters. Over the first three weeks, neither of us could see any improvement, and we were becoming increasingly frustrated. To give ourselves more concrete feedback on the results of our sessions together, I decided to start graphing Michael's daily performance. I explained to Michael how we would chart his progress on a piece of graph paper by marking off the number of cursive letters he could remember each day. I also told him that as soon as he had reached a certain dotted line (indicating twenty-six correct letters) three days in a row, he could have a special treat: his choice was a purple felt-tip pen.

At the beginning of each session, I tested Michael on his cursive letters, and together we counted the number he had right. We entered his performance on the chart in the form of a bar of the appropriate height, and then Michael practiced the letters he had missed. Michael's daily performance began to improve dramatically. Not only was he making noticeable progress, but he also looked forward to charting his performance and seeing a higher bar each day. Within two weeks, Michael had successfully met the criterion for his felt-tip pen: he had written all twenty-six cursive letters three days in succession. As it turns out, the pen was probably not the key ingredient for our success; Michael lost it within twenty-four hours of receiving it. Instead I suspect that the concrete positive feedback about his own improvement reinforced Michael's learning.

Positive feedback and the intrinsic reinforcement that such feedback brings are, from a teacher's perspective, probably the most desirable forms of classroom reinforcement. Keep in mind, however, that consistent positive feedback and resulting feelings of success and mastery can occur only when instruction has been carefully tailored to individual skill levels and abilities, and only when students have learned to value academic achievement. When, for whatever reasons, children are not motivated to achieve academic success, then other reinforcers, such as social and activity reinforcers, can be used.

Always remember that what is reinforcing for one individual may not be reinforcing for another. Reinforcement, like beauty, is in the eyes of the beholder. Even for the same individual, a reinforcer on one occasion may not be a reinforcer on another. Several other considerations influence the effectiveness of reinforcers; we will examine those now.

FACTORS AFFECTING THE EFFECTIVENESS OF REINFORCEMENT

At least three things influence the effectiveness of reinforcement in operant conditioning: timing, magnitude and appeal, and consistency.

Timing

Earlier in this chapter, I stressed the importance of *immediate* reinforcement for operant conditioning. In most cases, greater delays in reinforcement lead to slower acquisition of responses (e.g., Hockman & Lipsitt, 1961; Lett, 1973, 1975; Terrell & Ware, 1961). Fortunately, in situations when immediate reinforcement is impossible, the presence of other environmental cues indicating that reinforcement will come eventually may help to minimize the negative effect of a delay (Perin, 1943). For example, a teacher who wants to reinforce her students' persistence through a difficult lesson might say, "Because we have all worked so hard today, we will spend tomorrow practicing the class play."

Magnitude and Appeal

The larger and more appealing the reinforcer, the faster a response is learned and the more frequently it will be exhibited (e.g., Atkinson, 1958; Siegel & Andrews, 1962). For example, in a study by Siegel and Andrews (1962), three- to five-year-old boys learned more quickly when they were reinforced with such treats as candy, coins, balloons, and small toys than when they were reinforced with unexciting buttons.

Interestingly enough, however, it is not always the absolute magnitude of reinforcement that affects behavior as much as it is the *relative* magnitude compared with prior experience. For example, in a classic study by Crespi (1942), rats ran a runway to reach a food reinforcer at the far end. When rats accustomed to a small quantity of food were suddenly reinforced with a greater amount, they ran faster than rats who had always received that same large amount. Similarly, rats used to a large amount of reinforcement who then began receiving less food ran more slowly than rats who had always had that smaller amount. Crespi's results have been replicated in other rat studies (e.g., McHale, Brooks, & Wolach, 1982), although the results of analogous studies with infants have been inconsistent (e.g., Fagen & Rovee, 1976; Lipsett & Kaye, 1965).

The changes in behavior observed when quantities of reinforcement are increased or decreased are commonly known as *contrast effects*. One contrast effect—the *elation effect*—occurs when the amount of reinforcement is increased: the response rate becomes *faster* than it would be if the reinforcement had always been at that higher level. The opposite contrast effect—*the depression effect*—occurs when the amount of reinforcement is decreased: the result is that the response rate becomes *slower* than what it would be if reinforcement had always been that low. The depression effect may be at least partly due to negative emotions associated with a reduction in reinforcement (Flaherty, 1985).

Consistency

One of the most critical elements affecting the rate at which responses are learned and the rate at which they can be extinguished is the consistency of the reinforcement. To illustrate how consistency plays a role, consider this fantasy I have for the handful of students in my classes each semester who don't read their textbook:

> The student is locked in a small room. The assigned textbook lies on a nearby table. Every time the student opens the book to one of the assigned pages and looks toward the page, a small piece of delicious junk food falls from a hole in the ceiling.

Essentially, I would like to put unmotivated students into my own version of a Skinner box—the Ormrod box!

Now imagine twenty students in twenty Ormrod boxes. Ten of these students, randomly selected, are in Group A: they receive a piece of junk food every time they open the textbook and look at it. The other ten are in Group B: they get junk food for some of their book-reading responses (perhaps one response out of every four), but receive nothing for their efforts the rest of the time. Group A is receiving *continuous reinforcement:* every response is reinforced. Group B is receiving *intermittent reinforcement:* some of the responses are reinforced and some are not. Which group is going to increase its textbook-reading behavior faster? The answer, of course, is Group A, the group with continuous reinforcement. Continuously reinforced responses are acquired faster than intermittently reinforced responses.

Now suppose that, after a few hours in their respective Ormrod boxes, all twenty students have begun to show a high frequency of textbook-reading responses, so I turn off the junk-food-dropping mechanisms. Which students are first going to notice that they are no longer being reinforced? The answer is again Group A. Those students who have been reinforced for every single response will notice rather quickly that reinforcement has stopped, and their textbook-reading should extinguish rapidly. Group B students, on the other hand, have been receiving reinforcement for only twenty-five percent of their responses, so they are accustomed to nonreinforcement; these students will probably continue to read their textbooks for some time before they realize that reinforcement has ceased. Intermittently reinforced responses are extinguished more slowly than continuously reinforced responses.

Psychologists usually recommend that a response be reinforced continuously until the terminal behavior is reached and then be maintained through intermittent reinforcement so that it does not extinguish. Intermittent reinforcement can be administered using a variety of *reinforcement schedules*, each of which has a different effect, both on resistance to extinction and on the frequency and pattern of the response being reinforced. Let's take a look at these different schedules and the behavior patterns that result from each one.

SCHEDULES OF REINFORCEMENT

In this section I will describe three different groups of intermittent reinforcement schedules: ratio schedules, those in which reinforcement occurs after a certain number of responses; interval schedules, those in which reinforcement occurs for the first response after a certain time interval has elapsed; and differential schedules, those in which reinforcement is contingent on a certain rate of responding.

Ratio Schedules: Reinforcing a Certain Number of Responses

A *ratio schedule* is one in which reinforcement occurs after a certain number of responses have been emitted. That certain number can be either constant (a fixed ratio schedule) or variable from one reinforcement to the next (a variable ratio schedule).

Fixed Ratio (FR). In a *fixed ratio* reinforcement schedule, reinforcement is presented after a certain constant number of responses have been emitted. For example, reinforcement might be given after every third response (a 1:3 ratio schedule) or after every fiftieth response (a 1:50 schedule). Such a reinforcement schedule can lead to a high and consistent response rate over an indefinite period of time; for example, pigeons whose pecking is maintained on a high ratio schedule will peck as often as ten times per second (Ferster & Skinner, 1957).

Whitlock (1966) has described the use of a series of ratio schedules with a six-year-old boy who had been unable to acquire basic reading skills. At first, the boy was asked to read words presented to him on flash cards. Every time he read a word correctly, he received a plastic poker chip as a reinforcer, reflecting a continuous reinforcement schedule. Filled jars of thirty-six poker chips could be traded for a variety of activities; for example, with two jars he could play a game and with seven jars he could watch a cartoon. Once the boy was able to read from beginning reader storybooks, he was reinforced on a 1:2 fixed ratio schedule; that is, he received one chip for every two words read correctly. Eventually he was reinforced for every four words (a 1:4 schedule), then every page (one reinforcer for every 10–25 words), then every story (one reinforcer for every 50–70 words), and finally every four stories. After fifteen sessions of such individualized instruction, reinforcement was phased out altogether, and the boy was placed in his class's regular reading program; three months later he was still reading at grade level. (One thing has always struck me about this study: because so many poker chips were required to make a purchase, the boy must have actually bought very few activities. I suspect that his increasing success in reading was the true reinforcer in this case.)

Ratio schedules even as high as 1:1,000, when introduced through a series of successively higher ratios (as was done in the Whitlock study), have been found to maintain a response (Ferster & Skinner, 1957). In fact, high ratios typically lead to higher rates of responding than low ratios (Collier, Hirsh, & Hamlin, 1972; Stephens, Pear, Wray, & Jackson, 1975), although there is a tendency for organisms under high ratio schedules to exhibit a brief *post-reinforcement pause* after each reinforced response (Ferster & Skinner, 1957).

Variable Ratio (VR). A *variable ratio* reinforcement schedule is one in which reinforcement is presented after a certain variable number of responses have been emitted and is described by the average number of responses needed to obtain reinforcement. For example, a 1:5 VR schedule might be one in which reinforcement takes place after four responses, then after seven

Telephone solicitation reinforced on a variable ratio schedule.

more, then after three, and so on. As you can see, the occurrence of reinforcement in a VR schedule is somewhat unpredictable.

Playing a Las Vegas slot machine is an example of a response that is reinforced on a variable ratio schedule. The more times you put a quarter into the machine, the more times you will be reinforced by having quarters come back out again, but those quarters do not come out after any predictable number of quarters have gone in. In a similar way, telephone solicitation is also reinforced on a VR schedule. The greater the number of calls made, the greater the number of sales, but the soliciting caller never knows just which call will lead to reinforcement.

Margaret, one of my daughter's friends, has always been very persistent when she wants something; she seldom takes no for an answer. The source of her persistence became clear to me one evening when my daughter and I had dinner at a restaurant with Margaret and her mother. The girls gobbled their food quickly and went off to explore the restaurant while we ladies nursed our coffee. Margaret quickly returned to the table to make a request of her mother:

"Mom, can I have a quarter for a video game?"

"No."

"Please, Mom?"

"I said no, Margaret."

"But Tina has one." (I look absentmindedly into space.)

"No."

"I'll pay you back as soon as we get home."

"*No*, Margaret."

"*Pretty please?!*" (Margaret puts on a desperate face.)

"Oh, all right, here's a quarter."

Margaret's asking behaviors were clearly on a variable ratio reinforcement schedule, and she had learned that persistence paid off eventually.

Variable ratio schedules lead to higher response rates than fixed ratio schedules. Furthermore, responses reinforced on a VR schedule are highly resistant to extinction. In fact, pigeons working on very high VR schedules may expend more energy responding than they gain in food reinforcement, thus eventually working themselves to death (Swenson, 1980).

Interval Schedules: Reinforcing the First Response After a Time Period

An *interval schedule* is one in which reinforcement is contingent on the first response emitted after a certain time interval has elapsed. The time interval can be either constant (a fixed interval schedule) or variable from one reinforcement to the next (a variable interval schedule).

Fixed interval (FI). With a *fixed interval* reinforcement schedule, reinforcement is contingent on the first response emitted after a certain fixed time interval has elapsed. For example, the organism may be reinforced for the first response emitted after five minutes, regardless of how many responses may or may not have been made during those five minutes. Following reinforcement, another five-minute interval must elapse before a response is again reinforced.

A fixed interval schedule produces a unique response pattern: following reinforcement, the response rate tapers way off in a post-reinforcement pause until the end of the time interval approaches, at which point responding picks up again (e.g., Ferster & Skinner, 1957; Shimoff, Catania, & Matthews, 1981). To illustrate, my daughter has a spelling test every Friday. She gets the week's list of spelling words each Monday, so she has four evenings in which to study the list. Occasionally she begins on Wednesday, but she usually waits until Thursday night to study her spelling. If we were to graph Tina's studying behavior, it might look something like the graph in Figure 4–4. This "scallop" pattern is typical of behaviors reinforced on a fixed interval schedule. We do not see the high rate of responding with a FI schedule that is observed for fixed and variable ratio schedules, nor do we see as much resistance to extinction.

Variable interval (VI). A *variable interval* reinforcement schedule is one in which reinforcement is contingent upon the first correct response emitted after a certain variable time interval has elapsed. For example, the organism may be reinforced for the first correct response after five minutes, then the first response after eight minutes, then the first correct response after two minutes, and so on, with the VI schedule being identified by the average time interval.

Figure 4–4

Responses reinforced on a fixed interval schedule show a "scallop" pattern.

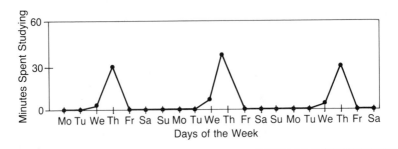

You may have a friend who really enjoys talking on the telephone, so that when you try to call him, you often hear a busy signal. If you have an urgent need to get in touch with your friend, you may continue to dial the phone number once every few minutes until eventually your call is completed. In a similar way, students who have been told that there is always the possibility of a pop quiz in class are likely to study a little bit every night. They never know on just what day that studying will pay off. Your pattern of dialing your gabby friend and students' pattern of studying for pop quizzes are typical of the response pattern observed for variable interval schedules: a slow, steady rate of responding. The longer the average time interval until reinforcement, the slower the response rate will be (e.g., Catania & Reynolds, 1968).

For both ratio and interval schedules, then, variable schedules lead to steadier response rates than fixed schedules, probably because of the unpredictability of the occurrence of reinforcement after a correct response. With a variable schedule, there is always the possibility that the next correct response will pay off. Variable schedules also appear to lead to greater resistance to extinction, again possibly because of their unpredictable nature.

When using ratio or interval schedules of reinforcement to prevent the extinction of a previously acquired response, the best schedule to use depends on the rate of response desired. In most cases, a variable ratio is recommended for a high rate of responding, with a variable interval schedule being better for a slow but steady rate. Ideally, when continuous reinforcement is first replaced by intermittent reinforcement, the ratio should be small (e.g., 1:2 or 1:3) or the time interval short. The ratio or interval can then gradually be extended until the response is being maintained on very little reinforcement at all.

Differential Schedules: Reinforcing Rates of Responding

When a particular rate of responding is required, a differential schedule of reinforcement is appropriate: a specific number of responses occurring within a specific length of time leads to reinforcement. There are at least three such schedules: reinforcement of a differential rate of high responding, reinforcement of a differential rate of low responding, and reinforcement of the *non*occurrence of the response (differential reinforcement of other behaviors).

Differential Rate of High Responding (DRH). A *DRH schedule* provides reinforcement only when a particular minimum number of responses has occurred within a particular period of time. For example, consider Margaret, the girl who persistently asked her mother for money to play a video game. Margaret may actually have been on a DRH schedule rather than a variable ratio schedule, in that she had to ask for a quarter several times *all at once* to get reinforced. With a ratio schedule, the length of time it takes to emit the necessary number of responses is irrelevant, but with a DRH schedule it is critical. Because a DRH schedule requires many responses to be made in a short period of time, a high response rate is typical.

Theoretically, studying for regularly scheduled exams is really on a DRH schedule: the more studying that occurs, the greater the probability of reinforcement at exam time. However, as Klein (1987) has pointed out, too many students instead treat exams as fixed interval schedules, thus showing the "goof off now, cram later" study pattern.

Differential Rate of Low Responding (DRL). A *DRL schedule* reinforces the first response after a certain time interval has elapsed in which the organism has not made the response at all. Although this might sound like a fixed interval schedule, remember that in a FI schedule, responses during the time interval, while not reinforced, are otherwise acceptable. One example of response on a DRL schedule is trying to start a car with a flooded engine. Repeated attempts at starting it will fail; you must wait for a few minutes, then try again, before you are likely to be successful.

Students' requests for their teacher's assistance are an example of responses that might be most appropriately reinforced on a DRL schedule. To reinforce students continuously when they ask for the teacher's help might lead to a high rate of such requests and a resulting overdependence on the teacher. On the other hand, reinforcing students who ask for help only after they have been working independently for a period of time will teach them that occasional questions are perfectly acceptable.

Learning the appropriate response pattern for a DRL schedule often takes time, because it requires one *not* to perform a behavior that has previously been reinforced (Reynolds, 1975).

Differential Reinforcement of Other Behaviors (DRO). A *DRO schedule* provides reinforcement when a particular response does not occur during a certain time interval. In other words, the organism is reinforced for doing anything else *except* that response for a certain length of time. For example, consider the teacher who says, "I am going to write on the chalkboard the name of every student who speaks out of turn today. If your name is not on the board by three o'clock, you may have a half hour of free time." That teacher is using a DRO schedule, because she is reinforcing children for *not* talking without permission.

Continuous reinforcement is clearly the most effective way of teaching a response. However, once the terminal behavior has been reached, the various intermittent reinforcement schedules—ratio, interval, and differential—can be beneficial both in preventing extinction (the DRO schedule excepted) and in controlling the frequency and pattern of that response.

STIMULUS CONTROL

Earlier in the chapter, I described Skinner's operant conditioning as an $R \rightarrow S_{Rf}$ model (where S_{Rf} is reinforcement) rather than the $S \rightarrow R$ model more typical of other early behaviorists. Actually, a stimulus that precedes a response *can* influence the likelihood that the response will occur again, although the role of this *antecedent stimulus* in operant conditioning is different from the role it plays in other behaviorist models such as classical conditioning.

To illustrate, here is a typical scenario in a high school class. The teacher begins to describe the evening's homework assignment to a class of quiet and attentive students but is interrupted by a bell marking the end of the class period. Immediately, the students, no longer interested in hearing their assignment, slam their notebooks shut and begin to push and shove their way toward the classroom door. These students are under *stimulus control:* they have learned that a particular response (leaving class) is acceptable under certain stimulus conditions (when the bell rings). A wise teacher would stand in front of the door while giving the homework assignment and not let the students leave their seats, bell or no bell. In that way, students would learn that leaving class is permissible only after a different stimulus—the teacher's movement away from the door—has occurred.

In operant conditioning, the antecedent stimulus does not directly elicit the response, as it does in classical conditioning. Instead, the stimulus *sets the occasion* for a response to be reinforced. When an antecedent stimulus influences the likelihood that a response will occur, we call that stimulus a discriminative stimulus, often symbolized as S + (Skinner uses the symbol S^D), and say that the response is under stimulus control. Responses to stimuli in operant conditioning reflect the phenomena of stimulus generalization and stimulus discrimination similar to the generalization and discrimination observed in classical conditioning.

Stimulus Generalization

When an organism has learned to respond in a certain way in the presence of one stimulus (the S +), it is likely to respond in the same way in the presence of similar stimuli; this operant conditioning phenomenon is known as *stimulus generalization.* Just as is true in classical conditioning, stimulus generalization is more likely to occur to stimuli similar to the discriminative stimulus. For example, kindergarten students may learn such appropriate classroom behaviors as raising their hands and waiting to be called on before speaking. Such behaviors are more likely to generalize to a similar situation (such as first grade) than to a dissimilar situation (such as the family dinner table). This tendency of organisms to generalize more as stimuli become more similar to the discriminative stimulus is known as a *generalization gradient.*

Stimulus Discrimination

In classical conditioning, stimulus discrimination occurs when one stimulus (the CS +) is presented in conjunction with an unconditioned stimulus, and another stimulus (the CS −) is presented in the absence of the UCS. Similarly, in operant conditioning organisms can learn that a certain response may be reinforced in the presence of one stimulus (S +) but not in the presence of another stimulus, one symbolized as S − (Skinner uses the symbol S$^\Delta$). Learning under what circumstances a response will and will not be reinforced is operant conditioning's form of *stimulus discrimination*.

$$(S+) R \to S$$
$$(S-) R \to (nothing)$$

Stimulus discrimination is essentially a process of learning that a conditioned response in the presence of S + should not be generalized to S −.

Consider the preschooler who has learned to say "bee" whenever she sees this symbol:

b

She then sees a similar stimulus:

d

and responds "bee" once again—that is, she generalizes. (Anyone who has worked with young children who are learning their alphabet letters has probably observed that, consistent with the generalization gradient, children are much more likely to generalize the "bee" response to the letter *d* than to less similar letters such as *j* or *s*.) If the teacher does not reinforce her for the "bee" response to the symbol *d*, the child will eventually learn to discriminate between the letters *b* and *d*.

Stimulus Control in the Classroom

Reinforcement plays a crucial role in helping children to learn in what situations particular responses are desirable and to generalize and discriminate among situations appropriately. Initially, teachers themselves can provide discriminative stimuli to serve as cues for letting students know how to behave. These stimuli may be either very explicit *direct cues* or more subtle *indirect cues* (Krumboltz & Krumboltz, 1972). For example, an elementary teacher whose students are preparing to walk to the lunchroom might provide a direct cue for appropriate behavior by reminding them to "go quietly and in single file." The teacher then reinforces the desired behavior by allowing students to proceed only when they behave as they have been instructed. A teacher who wishes to be more subtle in reminding students about the necessity for accomplishing a task quickly might use an indirect cue such as this one: "After you have all finished pages fourteen and fifteen in your workbooks, I will hand out next week's lunch menus." With a gradual shift from direct to indirect cues, teachers can help students become increasingly independent of reminders for good behavior. Eventually students should learn to identify for themselves the discriminative stimuli that signal the appropriateness of various behaviors.

ELIMINATING UNDESIRABLE BEHAVIORS

I have talked at length about how new responses are learned, modified, and maintained through operant conditioning. Sometimes, however, we may want instead to get rid of a behavior that has been acquired through reinforcement. At least four methods of reducing and eliminating misbehavior are possible: extinction, differential reinforcement of other behaviors, reinforcement of incompatible behaviors, and punishment. I will discuss the first three of these in the pages that follow; the fourth—punishment—falls outside the boundaries of reinforcement-based operant conditioning but will be covered in Chapter 6.

Extinction

A psychologist was once consulted about Jimmy, a child who had been hospitalized for an extended period. Nurses in the children's ward were very concerned because Jimmy kept banging his head on the side of his crib; whenever they heard him doing so, they would rush to his room and stop the behavior, thereby inadvertently reinforcing and maintaining the head-banging response. The psychologist successfully eliminated Jimmy's head-banging through a process of extinction: a protective helmet was strapped on Jimmy's head to prevent injury, and the nurses were instructed to ignore Jimmy during his head-banging episodes. At the same time, because Jimmy clearly craved attention, the nurses *did* attend to him on occasions when he was behaving appropriately.

Extinction—the withdrawal of reinforcement—can often be an effective method of eliminating inappropriate responses. Students who engage in disruptive behavior may stop if such behavior no longer gains them the teacher attention they seek (i.e., if the teacher ignores them). Similarly, cheating on classroom tests may soon extinguish if students are not given credit for those exams.

Unfortunately, however, extinction is typically not the most reliable method of eliminating unwanted behavior, for several reasons. First, it is not always possible to remove *all* reinforcers of a behavior; for example, although a teacher may be able to ignore the comments of a class clown, other students in the class may continue to reinforce those comments. Second, extinguished behaviors will sometimes show spontaneous recovery: a response that has been extinguished one day may pop up again at a later date. And third, some responses, because of the way they were originally reinforced, may be particularly resistant to extinction. As I stated earlier in the chapter, a response that has previously been reinforced on an intermittent schedule will be more resistant to extinction than one that has been continuously reinforced. When responses cannot be extinguished for any of these reasons, other methods will be more effective in reducing them.

Differential Reinforcement of Other Behaviors

As noted earlier, the differential reinforcement of other behaviors—a DRO reinforcement schedule—is a procedure whereby an organism is reinforced for *not* exhibiting a particular behavior during a specified time interval. For example, a teacher who praises a student who manages to get through an entire recess without fighting with any classmates is using a DRO schedule. The differential reinforcement of other behaviors tends to be a more effective and long-lasting technique than extinction (Uhl, 1973; Uhl & Garcia, 1969; Zeiler, 1971) and has been shown to be effective in reducing inappropriate classroom behavior (Parrish, Cataldo, Kolko, Neef, & Egel, 1986; Repp & Deitz, 1974).

Reinforcement of Incompatible Behaviors

In Chapter 2, I described Guthrie's methods of breaking habits. One of these—the incompatible stimulus, or counterconditioning, method—involves presenting a stimulus when the habitual response cannot occur, but when an opposite response is likely to occur instead. A similar method—reinforcement of incompatible behavior—can be used within the context of the operant conditioning model. The first step is to identify a response that is *incompatible* with the undesirable response, that is, a response that cannot be performed at the same time as the undesirable response. That incompatible behavior is then reinforced. For example, a child's inappropriate out-of-seat behavior may be reduced by reinforcing the child whenever she is sitting down. Similarly, an aggressive student can be reinforced whenever he is interacting in a prosocial manner with his classmates. Krumboltz and Krumboltz (1972) have described how the reinforcement of an incompatible behavior was effective in handling a chronic litterbug at a junior high school: the student was put in charge of the school's anti-litter campaign and given considerable recognition and praise for his efforts.

The reinforcement of incompatible behaviors sounds similar to the DRO schedule, but a subtle difference exists between the two methods. The DRO schedule involves the reinforcement of *nonoccurrence* of a particular response. The reinforcement of incompatible behaviors involves the reinforcement of a *specific, opposite* response.

When none of these techniques—extinction, differential reinforcement of other behaviors, or reinforcement of incompatible behaviors—proves effective, punishment may be a viable alternative for eliminating an inappropriate behavior, as you will learn in Chapter 6.

WHEN REINFORCEMENT DOESN'T WORK

The basic principle of operant conditioning—that a reinforced response will increase in frequency—has been used successfully in many different situations to change a wide variety of behaviors. When reinforcement doesn't work, the source of difficulty can often be traced to one of four circumstances: (1) the "reinforcer" is not reinforcing; (2) reinforcement is not consistent; (3) the individual loses too much, or gains too little, by changing a behavior; or (4) too much is expected too soon.

"Reinforcer" Doesn't Reinforce

A first-grade teacher once consulted me about one of her students, a boy so disruptive that he was only able to spend a half day in the classroom. In an effort to modify the disruptive behavior, the teacher had attached to the boy's desk a large sheet of heavy cardboard cut and painted to look like a clown, with a small red light bulb for a nose. When the boy exhibited appropriate classroom behaviors, such as sitting quietly or attending to his workbook, the teacher would light up the red nose. "I don't understand why his behavior isn't changing," she told me. "Maybe this clown isn't reinforcing to the boy," I suggested. "Nonsense!" exclaimed the teacher. "The clown has always worked with *other* children!"

One of the most common mistakes teachers make in using operant conditioning techniques is to assume that certain consequences will be reinforcing to students. Not all students will work for the same reinforcers; a consequence that increases the behavior of one child may not increase the behavior of another. For example, although most students find their teacher's praise reinforcing, some students do not (e.g., Pfiffner, Rosen, & O'Leary, 1985). A bright girl may view too much teacher praise as an indication to her classmates that she is teacher's pet; a teenage boy may value the friendship of peers who shun high achievers.

How can you determine what events will be reinforcing for different students? One way is to watch the students to see what kinds of consequences seem to affect their behavior. Another approach is to ask the students' parents, or even the students themselves. The one thing *not* to do is guess.

Reinforcement Is Inconsistent

Sometimes it is inconvenient to reinforce a behavior every time it occurs. But remember, continuous reinforcement brings about more rapid behavior

The "Reinforcer" must be reinforcing.

change than intermittent reinforcement. If a student's behavior has been particularly disruptive and time-consuming, a little extra time devoted *now* to the continuous reinforcement of appropriate behaviors, inconvenient as that may occasionally be, will probably save time over the long run.

Change Isn't Worthwhile

The individual may lose too much, or gain too little, by changing a behavior. Consider the college student who estimates that she will have to study at least twenty hours a week to get an A in her physics class. Although the A may be an effective reinforcer, it may not be worth the amount of time the student will have to spend to earn it. And consider the teenage boy who shies away from teacher praise because his peer group does not approve of academic achievement. It may be that teacher praise *is* a reinforcer to this boy, but he risks losing his status in the group if he is praised too frequently or profusely. Praise given privately, out of the earshot of peers, will probably be much more reinforcing than public praise.

I suspect that many people, consciously or otherwise, engage in a cost-benefit analysis when looking at the consequences of different behaviors. Although they may have learned that a certain response will be reinforced, they will nevertheless not respond in that way if they have too much to lose, or too little to gain, by doing so. For people to respond positively to reinforcement, it must be worth their while.

Shaping Proceeds Too Rapidly

Reinforcement is ineffective when too much is expected too soon. In many situations, establishing a desirable behavior requires a process of *shaping* that behavior. Remember that shaping involves the reinforcement of a series of responses that more and more closely approximate the terminal behavior. Each response should be well learned before reinforcement proceeds to a closer approximation. If an attempt at shaping moves too quickly, such that each response is not well established before a more complicated one is expected, the reinforcement program will be ineffective in bringing about behavior change.

To illustrate, let's say that a teacher wants to reinforce a hyperactive boy for sitting quietly in his seat; her goal (the terminal behavior) is for him to sit quietly for twenty minutes. On the first morning of the intervention program, the boy sits quietly for one minute, and so the teacher reinforces him. She probably does *not* want to move on to a two-minute criterion just because he has met the one-minute criterion once. Instead, she should continue reinforcing the boy for one-minute "sits" until it is clear, from the frequency of his sitting behavior, that she can begin to expect that behavior for a longer period of time.

SKINNER ON EDUCATION

B. F. Skinner has written prolifically on the weaknesses of our schools from an operant conditioning perspective (e.g., Skinner, 1953, 1954, 1958, 1968, 1973). He has contended that reinforcement in the classroom usually occurs inconsistently and too long after a desired response has occurred. Although "natural" reinforcers (e.g., the control of nature, or the intrinsically rewarding value of the subject matter) can and should be used to increase appropriate academic behaviors, in fact most classroom reinforcers are artificially imposed. A problem inherent in our educational system is that teachers must teach behaviors that will be useful to students in the *future* rather than in the present, so these behaviors are not likely to lead to the naturally positive consequences now that they might later. For example, although a student might find algebra useful several years from now as a practicing engineer, she does not find it particularly useful in her current life. As a result, teachers resort to artificial reinforcers such as teacher approval, grades, stickers, or free time to foster academic achievement. These reinforcers are often ineffective, however, partly because the relationship between them and specific responses is not well specified.

In desperation, teachers often find themselves punishing *mis*behaviors, through such aversive consequences as displeasure, ridicule, and failing grades, rather than reinforcing appropriate responses; as Skinner puts it, teachers "induce students to learn by threatening them for not learning" (Skinner, 1968, p. 57). Not only is such aversive control of behavior ineffective, but students will engage in behaviors that enable them to escape or avoid school tasks altogether.

Skinner has urged that education must begin to refocus itself on the reinforcement of student successes rather than on the punishment of student failures. He has proposed a "technology of teaching" whereby instruction is individualized, complex verbal behaviors are gradually shaped, reinforcement for appropriate responses is consistent and immediate, and learned behaviors are maintained through intermittent reinforcement schedules. Skinner's suggestions for how operant conditioning might be successfully applied to classroom situations, and the suggestions of other psychologists and educators as well, are the subject of the next chapter.

SUMMARY

The basic principle of operant conditioning is that responses that are followed by reinforcement increase in frequency. Many different kinds of behaviors can be modified using a variety of different reinforcers. Timing, magnitude, and consistency of reinforcement influence the rate at which new behaviors are learned; furthermore, different schedules of reinforcement influence the rate of acquisition and extinction, as well as the actual frequency of responding. Antecedent stimuli can also affect the occurrence of a response if the response has been reinforced in the presence of those stimuli. Undesirable responses can be eliminated through a variety of techniques, including extinction, the differential reinforcement of other behaviors, and the reinforcement of incompatible behaviors. B. F. Skinner believes that, in classroom situations, appropriate behaviors are usually reinforced inconsistently and undesirable behaviors are often unintentionally reinforced.

CHAPTER 5

Applications of Operant Conditioning

O PERANT conditioning has probably had a greater impact on educational practice within the past thirty years than any other single model of human learning. At least six educational innovations can be attributed directly to operant conditioning principles: (1) behavioral objectives, (2) programmed instruction and its offspring, computer-assisted instruction, (3) Fred Keller's personalized system of instruction, (4) contingency contracting, (5) behavior modification, and (6) self-control. In this chapter, I will describe the basic components of these innovations, present empirical evidence concerning their effectiveness, and then address common concerns regarding the use of behavioral techniques in classroom situations.

BEHAVIORAL OBJECTIVES

In its 1947 report, the President's Commission on Higher Education described the primary goal of the United States educational system as "the full, rounded, and continuing development of the person" (cited in Dyer, 1967, p. 14). At first glance, this might seem to be a worthwhile and appropriate goal for education, but at second glance, the statement provides very little *specific* information regarding what an educated person should be like. Dyer (1967) has presented the President's Commission report as an example of "word magic": it sounds nice, but on closer examination we realize we don't have a clue as to what the words really mean. When we don't know exactly what our educational objectives are, we don't know what or how to teach, nor do we know whether our instruction is accomplishing its goals.

A standard practice in using operant conditioning is to specify the terminal behavior in precise, observable terms before conditioning begins, thereby allowing us to develop appropriate methods of shaping the desired behavior and of determining when that behavior has been acquired. This principle of *a priori* specification of the terminal behavior in observable and measurable terms has been applied to classroom instruction in the form of *behavioral objectives*.

Ideally, a behavioral objective has three components (Mager, 1962). First, the outcome should be stated in terms of an observable and measurable behavior. Consider this objective:

The student will be aware of current events.

A student's "awareness" is not easily observable. The same objective can be stated in terms of one or more specific behaviors that a student should exhibit; consider this one as an example:

The student will recite the major cause of political unrest in South Africa.

Some verbs do not specify observable behaviors—for example, *understand, appreciate, know, be aware of,* and *remember*—whereas other verbs do communicate observable responses—for example, *write, compute, list, recite,* and *select* (Sax, 1980). Almost any objective can probably be conceptualized in behavioral terms when you consider what specific things people would have to do to convince someone that they had met the objective (Mager, 1972).

Second, a behavioral objective should specify the conditions under which the behavior should be exhibited. Sometimes we expect desired behaviors to occur in specific situations (stimulus conditions). For example, one of my objectives for my graduate course in educational testing is:

The student will correctly compute test-retest reliability.

However, I do not expect students to memorize the formula with which test-retest reliability is calculated. Hence, there is a condition under which I expect the behavior to occur, as follows:

Given the formula for a correlation coefficient, the student will correctly compute test-retest reliability.

Finally, the objective should include a criterion for judging the acceptable performance of the behavior. Many behaviors are not strictly "right" or "wrong," but vary on a continuum of relative "rightness" and "wrongness." In cases where right and wrong behaviors are not obvious, a behavioral objective should specify the criterion for acceptable performance, perhaps in terms of a certain percentage of correct answers, a certain time limit, or the degree of acceptable deviation from the correct response (Mager, 1962). Here are several examples to illustrate this point:

On weekly written spelling tests, the student will correctly spell at least eighty-five percent of the year's 500 spelling words.

Given a sheet of 100 addition problems involving the addition of two single-digit numbers, including all possible combinations of the numbers 0 through 9, the student will correctly write the answers to these problems within a five-minute period.

Given the formula for a correlation coefficient, the student will correctly compute test-retest reliability, with differences from a computer-calculated coefficient being attributable to rounding-off errors.

Formulating Different Levels of Objectives

Behavioral objectives have frequently been criticized for focusing on concrete, picayune details rather than on more central, but probably more abstract, educational goals. For example, many lists of behavioral objectives emphasize behaviors that depend on the rote memorization of facts rather than on behaviors that reflect more complex and sophisticated learning (Trachtenberg, 1974). Such "low-level" objectives may be prevalent simply because they are the easiest ones to conceptualize and write.

When objectives reflecting more sophisticated levels of learning are desired, which is more likely to be true as students get older, Benjamin Bloom's Taxonomy of Educational Objectives (Bloom, Englehart, Furst, Hill, & Krathwohl, 1956) can serve as a helpful aid in writing them. Bloom and his colleagues have identified six different levels of using and understanding information within the *cognitive domain* that are particularly useful in developing objectives:

1. Knowledge. Rote memorizing of information in a basically word-for-word fashion; for example, reciting definitions of terms or remembering lists of items.

2. Comprehension. Translating information into one's own words; for example, rewording a definition or paraphrasing a rule.

3. Application. Using information in a new situation; for example, applying mathematical principles to the solution of word problems, or applying psychological theories of learning to educational practice.

4. Analysis. Breaking information down into its constituent parts; for example, discovering the assumptions underlying a philosophical essay, or identifying fallacies in a logical argument.

5. Synthesis. Constructing something new by integrating several pieces of information; for example, developing a theory or presenting a logical defense of a particular viewpoint within a debate.

6. Evaluation. Placing a value judgment on data; for example, critiquing a theory or examining the internal and external validity of an experiment.

Bloom and his colleagues originally presented these six levels as a hierarchy, with each objective depending on the objectives preceding it in the list. Although the hierarchical nature of Bloom's cognitive domain is in doubt (Furst, 1981; Seddon, 1978), the taxonomy nevertheless provides a useful reminder that behavioral objectives should be written to encompass higher-level cognitive skills as well as the knowledge of simple, discrete facts (Hastings, 1977; Popham, 1988).

Advantages of Behavioral Objectives

From a teacher's perspective, behavioral objectives serve three useful functions (Mager, 1962). First, specification of the objectives of a unit in behavioral terms helps a teacher choose the most effective method of teaching that unit. For example, when teaching a unit on basic addition, you might use flashcards if the objective is *knowledge* of number facts, but should probably use word problems if the objective is the *application* of those number facts. A second advantage is that behavioral objectives are easily communicated from one teacher to another. For example, although teachers may differ in their conception of what "application of addition principles" means, they will be likely to interpret "correct solution of addition word problems" similarly. Finally, behavioral objectives facilitate the evaluation of both the student and the instructional program: when an objective is described in behavioral terms, both student accomplishment and program effectiveness can be evaluated on the basis of whether those specific behaviors are observed. From a student's perspective, behavioral objectives have an additional advantage: students who are told what behaviors they should be able to demonstrate at the conclusion of an instructional unit have tangible goals toward which to strive and are in a better position to judge correctly their own completion of those behaviors (McAshan, 1979).

The Effectiveness of Objectives

Because behavioral objectives specify the outcomes of instruction so explicitly, students typically view them favorably. However, research studies investigating the effectiveness of objectives for improving academic performance have yielded mixed results (Melton, 1978). Objectives tend to focus student attention toward certain information (that which is included in the objectives) and away from other information (that which has been omitted from the objectives). If the stated objectives encompass *all* important information, the use of objectives in the classroom will enhance learning. However, if the objectives include only a portion of the information the teacher deems important while excluding other, equally important, information, some critical information—that which is omitted from the objectives—is not as likely to be learned as it might otherwise be.

Unfortunately, schools typically have many goals in mind for each classroom in any given year. Writing behavioral objectives that cover each and every one of those goals can become a burdensome, if not impossible, task. As a result, many educators have more recently proposed that a smaller number of general, nonbehavioral objectives can be an acceptable alternative (Dressel, 1977; Gage & Berliner, 1984; Popham, 1988; Posner & Rudnitsky, 1986; Sax, 1980; Zahorik, 1976). Such vaguely stated objectives will not be as useful in student and program evaluation as behavioral objectives might be, nor will they allow the precise communication among teachers that behavioral objectives allow, but they can at least set the direction that instruction should take and thus keep teachers and students alike on track toward particular goals.

PROGRAMMED INSTRUCTION AND COMPUTER-ASSISTED INSTRUCTION

According to the operant conditioning model of learning, reinforcement must occur immediately after a response to have a significant impact on that behavior. However, many reinforcers of classroom learning are delayed by hours, days, or, in the case of a high school diploma or college degree, even years. To provide a means by which responses can be reinforced immediately, Skinner (1954) developed a technique most frequently known as *programmed instruction*, or *PI*.

In its earliest form, programmed instruction involved an adaptation of Pressey's (1926, 1927) teaching machine. This "machine" was a box enclosing a long roll of printed material that a student could advance past a display window, thereby viewing small portions of information successively and systematically. Since the teaching machine, programmed instruction has evolved into programmed textbooks and, more recently, computer-assisted instruction.

Regardless of the form it takes, programmed instruction consists of several standard features. First, the material to be learned is presented through a series of discrete segments, or *frames*. The first frame presents a small piece of information and poses a question about it. The student responds to the question, then turns to the next frame; there, the correct answer to the question of the previous frame is given, more information is presented, and another question is posed. The student continues through the frames, encountering new information, responding to questions, and checking answers against those provided by the program.

To illustrate the PI process, I have developed some possible frames for a unit on writing behavioral objectives, as follows:

Frame 1

An *objective* is a goal for an instructional unit. **(information)**

>Another name for the goal of an instructional
>unit is an _____. **(question)**

Frame 2

objective **(answer to previous question)**

A *behavioral objective* is an objective that specifies the goals of an instructional unit in terms of the *behaviors* that the student should be able to demonstrate at the completion of that unit.

>An objective that specifies instructional goals in
>terms of behaviors that the student can demonstrate is
>called a _____ objective.

Frame 3
---

behavioral

A behavioral objective should describe the desired behavior in such a way that the behavior is both *observable* and *measurable.*

> A behavioral objective is an instructional goal in which an observable and _____ behavior is described.

Frame 4
---

measurable

The student will write the correct answer to the problem "2 + 2 = ?" In this objective, the word *write* describes an observable behavior.

> Which of the following verbs is an example of an observable behavior: *think, appreciate, write,* or *learn?* _____

Intrinsic to programmed instruction are a number of concepts and principles based on operant conditioning, including the following:

1. Terminal behavior. The goal of instruction is specified before the instructional program is developed, in terms of the terminal behavior (behavioral objective) to be demonstrated upon completion of instruction.

2. Active responding. The student is required to make a response in each frame.

3. Shaping. Instruction begins with information that the student already knows. The new information to be learned is broken into tiny pieces, and instruction proceeds through a gradual presentation of increasingly more difficult pieces. As the successive pieces are presented and questions of increasing difficulty are answered, the terminal behavior is gradually shaped.

4. Immediate reinforcement. Because instruction involves a gradual shaping process, the probability is quite high that a student will provide correct answers to the questions asked. Each correct answer is reinforced immediately, in the form of feedback that it is correct.

5. Individual differences in learning rate. Programmed instruction is *self-paced,* allowing students to progress at their own rates of speed through an instructional unit.

The earliest form of programmed instruction was the *linear program*: all students proceeded through exactly the same sequence of frames in exactly the same order. A more recent trend is to use a *branching program*, a technique introduced by Norman Crowder (e.g., Crowder & Martin, 1961). Branching programs typically progress in larger steps than linear programs (i.e., more information is presented in each frame), so that error rates in responding are somewhat higher. A student who responds incorrectly is directed to one or more "remedial" frames for further practice on that part of the lesson before being allowed to continue with new information. To illustrate, let's resume our lesson on behavioral objectives (beginning where we left off, with Frame 4), but now using a branching format:

Frame 4

The student will write the correct answer to the problem "2 + 2 = ?" In this objective, the word *write* describes an observable behavior.

> Which of the following verbs is an example of an observable behavior: *think, appreciate, write,* or *learn?* _____

Frame 5

If you answered *think,* go to Frame 6.
If you answered *appreciate,* go to Frame 6.
If you answered *write,* go to Frame 7.
If you answered *learn,* go to Frame 6.

Frame 6

The verbs *think, appreciate,* and *learn* all describe internal mental events; they are not observable behaviors. Only the verb *write* describes an observable behavior.

Return to Frame 4 and try again.

Frame 7

Yes, the verb *write* is the only one of the four that describes an observable behavior. The other verbs—*think, appreciate,* and *learn*—cannot be directly observed.

The student will learn the alphabet. This is not a behavioral objective because the verb *learn* does not describe an observable behavior.

> The above objective could be changed into a behavioral objective by replacing the verb *learn* with which one of the following: *remember, memorize,* or *recite?* _____

Frame 8

If you answered *remember,* go to Frame 9.
If you answered *memorize,* go to Frame 9.
If you answered *recite,* go to Frame 13.

Frame 9

The verbs *remember* and *memorize* do not reflect observable behaviors. Only *recite* is a directly observable response.

The student will _____ *the Pledge of Allegiance.* One of these verbs would make this objective a behavioral objective: *know, say, memorize,* or *learn.*

Which verb can be used to make a behavioral
objective? _____

Frame 10

If you answered *know,* go to Frame 11.
If you answered *say,* go to Frame 12.
If you answered *memorize,* go to Frame 11.
If you answered *learn,* go to Frame 11.

Frame 11

No. *Knowing, memorizing,* and *learning* cannot be directly observed. Only *saying* is an observable behavior. Return to Frame 7 and review this section again.

Frame 12

Yes. Only the verb *say* describes an observable behavior.

Frame 13

[The lesson continues with new information.]

The major advantage of a branching program is that remedial instructional frames are provided only for students who have difficulty with a particular concept; other students can move on to new information without having to spend time on practice they do not need. Unfortunately, however, a branching program can be cumbersome, at least in its textbook form.

Students are referred to different frames, and often to different pages, for each response they make, so progression through the program is rarely smooth. Fortunately, this drawback of the branching program has been virtually eliminated by the advent of computer-assisted instruction.

Computer-assisted instruction, or *CAI*, is programmed instruction presented by means of a computer. It has a number of advantages not characteristic of other forms of programmed instruction. First, branching programs can be used without having to instruct students to proceed to one frame or another; the computer automatically presents the appropriate frame for any response the student has given. Second, because of the graphics capabilities of computers (e.g., they can present complex moving visual displays), CAI can present information in a way that traditional programmed instruction cannot. A good example is the use of simulation programs, programs that give students practice in performing skilled operations, such as flying an airplane, without the risk or expense that would be associated with performing those operations in real-life situations. Third, the computer can record and maintain ongoing data on each student, including such information as how far a student has progressed in the program, how often the student is right and wrong, how quickly the student responds, and so on. With such data, a teacher can monitor each student's progress through the program and can identify students who are having particular difficulty with the material. And, finally, a computer can be used to provide instruction when flesh-and-blood teachers are not available; for example, CAI is increasingly being used to deliver college instruction in rural areas far removed from university settings.

The Effectiveness of PI and CAI

Most research indicates that traditional (i.e., noncomputer-based) programmed instruction is no more effective than traditional instructional methods (Feldhusen, 1963; Lange, 1972; Reese & Parnes, 1970; Schramm, 1964). CAI, on the other hand, is frequently shown to be superior to traditional instruction, in terms of both increased academic achievement and improved student attitudes toward schoolwork (Kulik, Kulik, & Cohen, 1980). A cautionary note regarding the use of PI and CAI is in order, however. Some of the programmed instruction packages presently available have been criticized as being poorly conceived (Bell-Gredler, 1986; O'Leary & O'Leary, 1972). Programs do not always adequately incorporate such principles as active responding, immediate reinforcement of responses, or gradual shaping of the terminal behavior and are less likely to be effective when such principles of operant conditioning are violated.

KELLER'S PERSONALIZED SYSTEM OF INSTRUCTION

As Michael (1974) has pointed out, traditional college instruction suffers from a number of weaknesses, at least when viewed from the perspective of operant conditioning principles. For example, students' grades are often delayed by days or weeks, so achievement is not immediately reinforced. Furthermore, students are frequently asked to proceed to advanced material before they have mastered the more basic information necessary to understand it.

To remedy such weaknesses of college instruction, Fred Keller (1968, 1974) has developed the *personalized system of instruction* (also known as PSI or the Keller Plan) as an alternative approach to teaching college students. This approach, which is based on the assumption that all students can master the same material when given adequate study time and assistance, is currently being used in thousands of college courses across the country (Kulik, Kulik, & Cohen, 1979).

PSI encompasses the following features:

1. Discrete modules. Course content is divided into a number of units, or modules (typically between ten and twenty), each of which is treated as a separate, discrete portion of the course.

2. Emphasis on individual study. Most learning occurs through students' independent study of such written materials as textbooks and study guides. Additional assistance is provided by one-on-one tutoring when necessary.

3. Supplementary instructional techniques. Traditional group instructional methods (e.g., lectures, demonstrations, and discussions) are occasionally provided as supplementary presentations of the same information that also appears in the textbook or other assigned readings. These group classes are optional but serve to motivate and stimulate students.

4. Unit exams. Students' mastery of material is assessed by an examination on each module. Students receive immediate feedback about their exam performance.

5. Use of proctors. Proctors, usually more advanced students, administer and score exams and tutor students on topics with which they are having difficulty.

6. Self-pacing. Students report to class to take exams when they are ready to do so; in this sense, learning is self-paced. Some students proceed through the course very quickly, others more slowly.

7. Mastery. Students must demonstrate mastery of one module before proceeding to the next. Mastery is typically defined as passing a module exam at a certain criterion, such as eighty percent to ninety percent correct responses. When a student's exam performance does not meet the criterion, the "failure" is not recorded; however, the student must return again to take another exam on the same material before proceeding further in the course.

The teacher of a PSI course plays a different role from that of someone using a more conventional approach to instruction. The PSI teacher is less of a lecturer and more of a curriculum developer, exam writer, proctor coordinator, and record keeper. Rather than leading students through course content, the PSI teacher instead provides an elaborate system whereby students, with the assistance of study guides and tutors, find their own way through.

The Effectiveness of PSI

A meta-analysis of many research results concerning the relative effectiveness of PSI and more traditional teaching methods (Kulik, Kulik, & Cohen, 1979) has indicated the following: (1) students rate PSI courses more highly than courses using a traditional format, (2) course grades are higher in PSI than in traditional courses, and (3) achievement, as reflected by exam performance, is higher for students instructed by PSI than by more traditional approaches. This difference in achievement is evident both at final exam time and on follow-up tests several weeks later. The benefits of PSI over traditional methods are most apparent for low-ability students, who show better retention of course material for as long as two years after course completion (DuNann & Weber, 1976). Despite the higher achievement gained by PSI students, total study time for PSI and traditional courses appears to be about the same (Born & Davis, 1974; Kulik et al., 1979); PSI students spend more time in individual study but less time attending scheduled lectures. PSI also facilitates better study habits: PSI students tend to study regularly rather than procrastinating and cramming the way students in traditional courses often do (Born & Davis, 1974).

PSI is not without its problems, however. One difficulty lies in the required mastery of material; some students are unable to meet the criterion for passing exams, despite repeated testings (Sussman, 1981). A second weakness is the lack of interaction among students, interaction that many students see as beneficial to their learning (Gasper, 1980). A third problem is related to the self-paced nature of a PSI course, which is sometimes compromised if university policy requires that students complete a course within one quarter or semester (Sussman, 1981). Poorly motivated students are likely to procrastinate until finally they must withdraw from the course (Sussman, 1981; Swenson, 1980), although withdrawal rates from PSI courses do not appear to be appreciably higher than withdrawals from traditional courses (Kulik et al., 1979). Several techniques have been shown to reduce procrastination and withdrawal from PSI, among them setting target dates for the completion of different modules (Reiser & Sullivan, 1977), giving bonus points for early completion of modules (Bufford, 1976), and eliminating the necessity for completing the course within one college term (Sussman, 1981).

Keller's personalized system of instruction is probably most appropriately used when the main objective of a course is for students to learn a specified body of information. In that situation, the immediate feedback and emphasis on mastery of course material may well be reasons that PSI increases student achievement, particularly for low-ability students. However, when the course objective is something other than acquiring a body of information—for example, examination of controversial and unresolved issues, or the practicing of specific skills—PSI may not be the method of choice.

CONTINGENCY CONTRACTS

Programmed instruction and Keller's personalized system of instruction are instances of operant conditioning principles applied to the education of a large number of students. The amount of time needed to prepare materials for both of these techniques makes their use for only one or two students virtually impossible. When the behavior or learning of a single student is of concern, a *contingency contract* is often more practical.

A contingency contract is an agreement between a student and a teacher regarding certain expectations for the student (the terminal behavior) and the consequences of the student's meeting those expectations (the reinforcer). For example, a student and teacher may agree that the student should turn in all homework assignments, on time and with at least ninety percent accuracy, every day for a week. If the student accomplishes this task, the contract might specify that the student will have some time to engage in a favorite activity or that the teacher and student will spend time after school studying a topic of particular interest to the student. Although a contingency contract can be as simple as a verbal agreement, it more frequently takes the form of an actual written contract. As such, the conditions of the contract are negotiated in one or more meetings between student and teacher, and the contract is then dated and signed by both individuals.

A contingency contract can be used to reward academic accomplishment; it can also be used to modify classroom behavior. For example, a teacher might help a student to spend more class time attending to assigned work, or to engage in more prosocial behaviors on the playground, by contracting with the student that certain desired behaviors will lead to positive consequences. Contingency contracting has been shown to be an effective method of addressing such diverse problems as poor study habits (Brooke & Ruthren, 1984), juvenile delinquency (Rueger & Liberman, 1984; Welch, 1985), and drug addiction (Anker & Crowley, 1982; Crowley, 1984; Rueger & Liberman, 1984). It can also be a useful supplement to Keller's personalized system of instruction (Brooke & Ruthren, 1984).

Guidelines for Writing Contingency Contracts

Several guidelines should be kept in mind when developing contingency contracts.

The contract should specify the desired behavior of the student and the consequence (reinforcement) that will be contingent on that behavior. Both the desired behavior and the reinforcement should be specified in clear, precise terminology (Homme, Csanyi, Gonzales, & Rechs, 1970).

Early contracts should require small tasks that can be accomplished within a short period of time (Walker & Shea, 1984). Remember the problem with delayed reinforcement: contracts that provide reinforcement only after the desired behavior has been exhibited for a lengthy period of time simply may not work.

Reinforcement should be contingent on accomplishment of the desired behavior (Homme et al., 1970). Students occasionally tell their teacher that they *tried* to do a task, but for one reason or another could not. Teachers who reinforce students only for successful completion of the task specified in the contract, *not* for their self-described unsuccessful efforts, will give students a clear message that task completion is essential for school success.

A criterion for judging the quality of the desired behavior should be specified. When the task to be accomplished can differ considerably in quality, as is true for an exam or a written composition, a criterion of successful completion of that task should be included in the contract. In the case of an exam, the criterion might be a percentage of correct items. For written work, it is almost inevitable that some subjective judgment will be involved in assessing the work; however, criteria that will be considered in the evaluation—specific content to be included, organization, clarity, grammar, and so on—should be clearly stated as a part of the contract.

A former colleague of mine once overlooked this critical principle when he used contingency contracts to assign grades in his college classes. For example, some contracts stated that students would take exams on assigned readings without specifying acceptable scores for those exams. Other contracts read something like this: "For an A, the student will write a ten-page paper on the topic of behavior modification," without describing how well the paper was to be written or what should be included. My colleague found himself obligated to award A's for multiple choice exams with scores of twenty-five percent and for papers along the lines of "How I Behavior-Modified My Kid Brother at the Beach Last Summer."

When different contingency contracts are used with different students as a way of individualizing requirements for students, all contracts should nevertheless be equivalent in scope. Unless there are compelling reasons to do otherwise, contracts should require tasks that are equal in difficulty and that reflect equal levels of competence for all students. The need for equivalence across contracts is particularly critical when the reinforcers used are course grades: assigning grades based on student behaviors differing radically in difficulty level and quality typically renders those grades uninterpretable.

Contingency contracts are often considered a specific form of behavior modification. We turn next to more general behavior modification techniques.

BEHAVIOR MODIFICATION

Behavior modification, sometimes known as *behavior therapy* or *contingency management*, is probably the most straightforward application of operant conditioning principles. Based on the assumption that behavior problems are the result of past and present environments, behavior modification encompasses a number of procedures to modify an individual's environment to promote the reinforcement of acceptable behaviors and the nonreinforcement of inappropriate ones. Central to behavior modification techniques are such operant conditioning concepts as reinforcement, extinction, shaping, stimulus control, and the reinforcement of incompatible behaviors. The concepts of punishment and modeling, while not components of Skinner's model of operant conditioning, are also frequently used in behavior modification programs; these two aspects of behavior modification will be dealt with in Chapters 6 and 8 respectively.

Components of Behavior Modification

Although behavior modification encompasses a number of different techniques, some components are common to all of them.

For an A, ___Mary Lamb___ will read one book somehow related to education.

Signed:

___Mary L.___

___Dr. Schmoe___

For an A, ___John Goat___ will write a 500-page treatise on the use of computer-assisted instruction for teaching Chinese calligraphy to dysgraphic children.

Signed:

___John D___

___Dr. Schmoe___

When used to address individual student needs, contingency contracts should be equivalent in scope.

Both the present and the desired behaviors are specified in observable and measurable terms. Consistent with behaviorist tradition, behavior modifiers focus their attention on specific, concrete responses. The actual behaviors to be increased or decreased are called *target behaviors.* For example, in a program designed to decrease a child's aggressiveness, such target behaviors as screaming, hitting other people, and throwing objects might be identified (Morris, 1985).

An effective reinforcer is identified. You should never assume what consequences will be reinforcing to a student. Instead, you can identify one or more reinforcers that are likely to change an individual's behavior by observing what a student will work for or even by asking the student outright. When a behavior modification program is instituted in a school setting, social reinforcers, such as praise, or activity reinforcers, such as special privileges, are often effective. If material reinforcers are called for (only because other reinforcers don't work), having parents provide those reinforcers at home for behaviors exhibited at school often works very well (Barth, 1979; Wielkiewicz, 1986).

A specific intervention or treatment plan is developed. Developing a treatment plan involves determining the method by which the target behavior is to be modified. Sometimes a behavior's frequency can be increased simply by reinforcing that behavior every time it occurs. However, when the free operant level of a desired response (known in behavior modification terminology as the *baseline*) is very low, that response may have to be shaped through the reinforcement of successively closer and closer approximations. An undesirable behavior can be eliminated through such methods as extinction, the differential reinforcement of other behaviors (a DRO schedule), the reinforcement of incompatible behaviors, or stimulus control (i.e., limiting the situations in which the behavior is allowed).

Behavior is measured both before and during treatment. Only through the objective measurement of the target behavior during both baseline and treatment can we determine whether the behavior modification program is effectively changing the target behavior. One way of measuring the target behavior is simply to count each response that occurs; for example, if we have designed a program to modify Johnny's "hitting others" behavior, we would count each instance of hitting. A second method of behavior measurement is to examine the rate of responding by counting the number of responses occurring within a specified time interval; for example, we might count the number of times Johnny hits in each hour of the day. Still a third method, called *time-sampling*, involves dividing the time period during which the individual is being observed into equal intervals and then checking whether the target behavior occurred in each interval. For example, we might measure Johnny's hitting behavior by dividing his school day into five-minute intervals and then identifying those intervals during which hitting was observed.

Behaviors frequently persist because they are either intentionally or unintentionally reinforced, so it is often helpful to record the consequences of the behavior as well as the behavior itself. In addition, many behaviorists (e.g., Rimm & Masters, 1974; Sulzer-Azaroff, 1981) believe that antecedent events should also be noted to determine whether a behavior is under stimulus control. Figure 5–1 illustrates a time sample of Johnny's hitting responses, with events antecedent and consequent to those responses also recorded.

Behaviorists urge that target behaviors should be observed and recorded as objectively as possible. Ideally, they recommend that one person (e.g., the teacher) administer the program and at least two other individuals trained in observation techniques observe and record occurrences of the target behavior. If the method of behavior measurement is such that the behavior is being objectively and accurately recorded, the agreement between the recordings of the two observers (the *inter-rater reliability*) should be very high.

The treatment is monitored for effectiveness as it progresses and modified if necessary. When a desired behavior increases in frequency or an unwanted behavior decreases during the treatment program (compared to the baseline rate), the logical conclusion is that the behavior modification program is effective. When little change is observed from baseline to treatment, however, a change in the program is warranted. Perhaps the teacher is trying to shape behavior too quickly. Perhaps the reinforcer is not really reinforcing, and a different reinforcer should be substituted. Perhaps an undesired behavior that the teacher is attempting to eliminate through extinction is being maintained by reinforcers outside the teacher's control.

Figure 5–1

A time sample of target behaviors in conjunction with antecedent and consequent events

		student teased him	none observed		student hit him
Antecedent					
Target Behavior (hitting)	no	yes	yes	no	yes
Consequence		scolded	scolded		none

9:00   9:05   9:10   9:15   9:20
(Times indicate start of each 5-minute interval)

An unsuccessful treatment program should be carefully examined for these and other possible explanations for its ineffectiveness and then modified accordingly.

Treatment is phased out after the desired behavior is acquired. Once the terminal behavior has been reached, the behavior modification program should be gradually phased out. In many instances, the newly learned behaviors begin to have their own rewards: for example, the aggressive student who learns more acceptable social behaviors begins to acquire new friends, and the student who has finally learned to read begins to feel successful and to enjoy reading. In other situations, the target behavior may have to be maintained through intermittent reinforcement, as might be accomplished by a series of successively higher variable ratio reinforcement schedules.

Using Behavior Modification with Groups of Students

The emphasis until now has been on the use of behavior modification with individual students. But behavior modification can also be used to change the behavior of a group of students, even an entire classroom. Two methods have been shown to be particularly effective in working with groups: the group contingency and the token economy.

The Group Contingency. In a group contingency, the entire group must perform a desired behavior for reinforcement to occur. For example, in one study (Lovitt, Guppy, & Blattner, 1969), the performance of a class of 32 fourth-graders on their weekly spelling tests was effectively modified applying a group contingency. In phase one of the study, baseline data indicated that about 12 students (thirty-eight percent) had perfect spelling tests in any given week. In phase two, spelling tests were administered each of four days during the week; any student who obtained a perfect test score one day had free time on any successive days that the same test was repeated. During this individually-based contingency period, the average number of perfect spelling tests a week more than doubled to 25.5 (eighty percent). In phase three, the individual contingencies of phase two continued to apply; in addition, when the entire class achieved perfect spelling tests by Friday, the class could listen to the radio for 15 minutes. The group contingency of phase three led to 30 perfect spelling tests (ninety-four percent) a week!

The "good behavior game" is an example of how a group contingency can be used to reduce classroom misbehaviors. In research conducted by Barrish and her colleagues (Barrish, Saunders, & Wolf, 1969), a class of particularly unruly fourth-graders (seven of the students had repeatedly been referred to the principal for problem behaviors) was divided into two teams whose behaviors were carefully observed during reading and mathematics lessons. Every time an out-of-seat or talking-out behavior was observed for a member of a team, that team received a mark on its designated part of the chalkboard. The team that had fewer marks during the lesson would receive special privileges (e.g., first in the lunch line, free time at the end of the day); if both teams had five marks or fewer, both would win privileges.

Figure 5–2 shows the results of Barrish's study. Notice how baseline data was first collected for both math and reading periods. The good behavior game was instituted in the mathematics period on day 23: out-of-seat and talking-out behaviors decreased sharply during mathematics instruction while continuing at a high frequency during reading. On day 45, the game was initiated during reading instruction and stopped during math instruction; notice how the frequencies of misbehaviors changed accordingly. On day 51, the game was reinstituted in the math period, and again the misbehavior decreased to a low level in that class. By the way, these techniques of collecting *multiple baseline* data (data from two different situations) and of switching from reinforcement to nonreinforcement and then back again (a technique called *reversal*) are commonly used in behavior modification research as a way of ruling out coincidence as the reason for observed behavior changes.

Peer pressure and social reinforcement are clearly among the reasons that group contingencies are effective (O'Leary & O'Leary, 1972; Swenson, 1980). Misbehaving students are encouraged by other students to change their behaviors and are frequently praised when those changes occur. In addition, when increased academic achievement is the desired behavior, high-achieving students will assist their lower-achieving classmates by tutoring and providing extra practice in their academic work (Bronfenbrenner, 1970; Pigott, Fantuzzo, & Clement, 1986).

The Token Economy. The token economy, undoubtedly the most prevalent behavior modification technique in group settings, is a situation in which individuals who behave appropriately are reinforced with tokens, items that can later be traded in for *back-up reinforcers*—objects or privileges of each individual's choice. For example, a teacher using a token economy in the classroom might tell students that each completed assignment will be rewarded with one poker chip. Just before lunch, students can use their poker chips to buy small treats, free time in the reading center, or a prime position in the lunch line.

A token economy typically includes the following components:

1. A set of rules describing the responses that will be reinforced. The rules should be relatively few in number, so that they can be remembered easily.

2. Token reinforcers that can be awarded immediately when appropriate behaviors are exhibited. Such items as poker chips, check marks on a grid sheet, play money, and points can be used. Even class grades have been successfully used as tokens (McKenzie, Clark, Wolf, Kothera, & Benson, 1968).

Figure 5–2

Percent of one-minute intervals scored as containing talking-out and out-of-seat behaviors occurring during math and reading periods

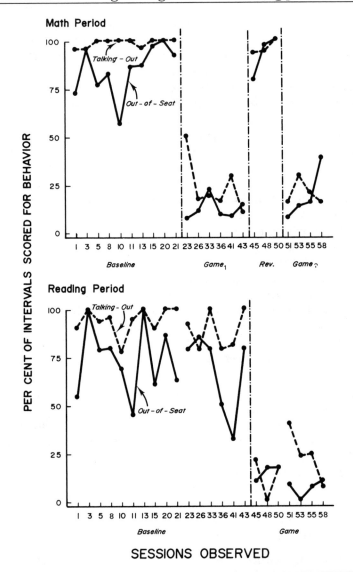

From "Good Behavior Game: Effects of Individual Contingencies for Group Consequences on Disruptive Behavior in a Classroom" by H. H. Barrish, M. Saunders, & M. M. Wolf, in K. D. O'Leary & S. O'Leary (Eds.), *Classroom Management: The Successful Use of Behavior Modification*, p. 375. Copyright 1972 by Pergamon Press, Ltd.

3. A variety of back-up reinforcers (objects, activities, and privileges) for which tokens can be exchanged. Examples of back-up reinforcers that have been shown to be effective in classroom token economies are free time (Osborne, 1969), participation in special events (Bushell, Wrobel, & Michaelis, 1968), and parent-awarded allowance (McKenzie et al., 1968).

4. A time and place (i.e., a "store") at which the back-up reinforcers can be "purchased." Young children should be allowed at least one purchase opportunity a day; for older children, one or two opportunities a week may be sufficient.

Token reinforcers are advantageous because they can be used to reward individual behaviors immediately and conveniently within a group setting. The fact that tokens can be traded for many different back-up reinforcers is another advantage; every individual can probably find at least one desirable item. The tokens themselves often become effective reinforcers (Hundert, 1976); perhaps they become secondary reinforcers through repeated association with other reinforcing objects and events or perhaps they are effective simply because they provide positive feedback that students are doing something right.

The Effectiveness of Behavior Modification

Behavior modification has been clearly shown to bring about behavior change and is often found to be effective when other techniques are not (O'Leary & O'Leary, 1972). Numerous studies point to its effectiveness in improving academic performance and study habits (e.g., Braukmann, Kirigin, & Wolf, 1981; Glover & Gary, 1976; Harris & Sherman, 1973; Iwata, 1987; Lovitt et al., 1969; McLaughlin & Malaby, 1972; Piersel, 1987; Rapport & Bostow, 1976). It is also useful in improving such behaviors as attention (Packard, 1970), social skills (Braukman et al., 1981; Iwata, 1987), and cleanliness (Taylor & Kratochwill, 1978). Furthermore, it can effectively reduce such undesirable behaviors as hyperactivity, impulsivity, aggression, and violence (Ayllon, Layman, & Kandel, 1975; Braukman et al., 1981; Mayer & Butterworth, 1979; Plummer, Baer, & LeBlanc, 1977; Shafto & Sulzbacher, 1977; Wulbert & Dries, 1977).

Behavior modification is particularly beneficial in classrooms of students who must be continually motivated to engage in appropriate academic and social behaviors. It is therefore used frequently in the education and therapy of special populations of students, including mentally retarded children (e.g., Haring, Roger, Lee, Breen, & Gaylord-Ross, 1986; Plummer et al., 1977), emotionally disturbed children (e.g., O'Leary & Becker, 1967; Rimm & Masters, 1974), and juvenile delinquents (e.g., Braukmann et al., 1981; Hobbs & Holt, 1976; Wolf, Braukmann, & Ramp, 1987).

Although it is clear that behavior modification works, it is not always clear just *why* it works. One likely factor underlying the effectiveness of behavior modification is the use of clearly specified response-reinforcement contingencies. Because desired behaviors are described in specific, concrete terms, students know exactly what is expected of them. And the immediate feedback they receive through reinforcement provides them with clear guidance as to when their behaviors are on target and when they are not.

SELF-CONTROL

Writing a textbook is a major undertaking. As I sit here in my basement pounding on the keys of my word processor day after day, I sometimes wonder why in the world I ever committed myself to such a project when I could instead be upstairs in my warm, comfortable living room reading mystery novels or watching television quiz shows. Yet each day I drag myself down to the basement to produce a few more pages. How do I do it? I do it by reinforcing myself every time I finish a small section of the book. For example, as soon as I finished the section on behavior modification that you just read, I gave myself permission to go upstairs to watch my favorite quiz show. Before I can watch another one, though, I need to finish this section on self-control.

Self-control, also known as *self-management*, includes a number of techniques through which people control their own behaviors by using

The author practices self-control.

operant conditioning techniques. Oftentimes students can change their own behavior simply by reinforcing themselves when they behave appropriately and withholding reinforcement when they do not (Mahoney & Thoresen, 1974; O'Leary & O'Leary, 1972; Rimm & Masters, 1974). I am able to maintain my book-writing behavior through use of the Premack principle: I let myself engage in enjoyable activities only after I have completed less enjoyable ones. Self-reinforcement has been shown to be an effective method for improving students' study habits and increasing their academic achievement (Beneke & Harris, 1972; Greiner & Karoly, 1976; Hayes, Rosenfarb, Wulfert, Munt, Korn, & Zettle, 1985; Stevenson & Fantuzzo, 1986).

Self-reinforcement can be as effective in modifying behavior as teacher-administered reinforcement. For example, in a study by Bandura and Perloff (1967), elementary school children were required to crank a wheel (described to them as "game equipment") numerous times to receive a token reinforcer. Some children were reinforced by the experimenter whenever they had cranked the wheel a predetermined number of times; other children were told to reinforce themselves each time they reached that predetermined level of performance. There were no significant differences in the number of wheel-cranking responses between the experimenter-reinforced and the self-reinforced children. Curiously, however, when the self-reinforced children were allowed to impose their own performance standards on themselves (i.e., they were able to choose the number of cranks needed for reinforcement), they were not easy on themselves: half of the children chose the most stringent performance standard possible (thirty-two cranks for each reinforcement), and *none* of them chose the least stringent standard (eight cranks per reinforcement). The results of Bandura and Perloff, and similar results reported by Lovitt and Curtiss (1969), suggest that, contrary to what we might expect, students do not necessarily take the easy road to reinforcement when that reinforcement is self-imposed. Instead, they are as demanding of themselves as teachers, sometimes even more so.

Another method by which behavior can sometimes be self-modified is simply to have an individual observe and measure his or her own responses, just as someone else might measure those responses in traditional behavior modification (Mahoney & Thoresen, 1974). The mere recording of responses is often enough to alter their frequency. For example, my family was once part of a research project in which randomly selected households recorded their own television-watching habits over a period of several weeks. We were instructed to mark down every instance of television viewing—including the date, time of day, length of time, and programs watched—on a specially designed record sheet. Every time I thought about turning on the television set, I remembered all the work I would have to go through to record my viewing, and, as often as not, I found something else to do instead. Thus, my television-watching behavior was modified simply through the process of my having to record it.

Self-recording of a target behavior has been found to increase study time and completion of classwork (Broden, Hall, & Mitts, 1971; Hallahan,

Marshall, & Lloyd, 1981; Harris, 1986). It can also be effective in reducing disruptive classroom behaviors such as talking out of turn, leaving one's seat without permission, and hitting other students (Bolstad & Johnson, 1972; Broden et al., 1971; Moletzsky, 1974).

Yet another method of self-control is a form of self-imposed stimulus control (Mahoney & Thoresen, 1974). To increase a particular desired behavior, the individual might be instructed to seek out an environment where that behavior is most likely to occur. For example, a student who wishes to increase the time actually spent studying each day should sit down at a table in the library rather than on the bed at home. Conversely, to decrease an undesired behavior, an individual should engage in that behavior only in certain situations. For example, I once knew a professor who, in an effort to stop smoking, gradually reduced the number of situations in which he permitted himself to smoke. Eventually, he was able to smoke in only one situation, facing a back corner of his office; it was at that point that he successfuly stopped smoking.

Self-control works only when individuals are themselves motivated to bring about a behavior change, and in such circumstances it works very well. Two precautions must be taken, however. First, self-control will only work when the capability for exhibiting a particular behavior is present; for example, students who wish to modify their study habits will only achieve higher grades if they possess adequate academic skills to ensure success. Second, individuals must be cautioned not to expect too much of themselves too quickly. Many individuals would prefer overnight success, but shaping, either of oneself or of another, is a slow and gradual process. Just as the dieter will not lose forty pounds in a week, it is equally unlikely that a habitually poor student will achieve honor roll status immediately. For self-control to be effective, your expectations for yourself must be practical and realistic.

CRITICISMS OF USING REINFORCEMENT IN THE CLASSROOM

Although instructional techniques based on operant conditioning principles are clearly effective, such techniques are not without their critics. Some criticisms are probably ill-founded, while others should be considered more seriously. We will first examine some of the common "bogus" complaints, and then turn to more genuine concerns.

Bogus Complaints

Many criticisms directed toward the use of reinforcement in the classroom reflect either a misunderstanding of operant conditioning principles or an ignorance of empirical findings. We will consider some typical examples of such criticisms.

Reinforcement as bribery

Reinforcement is bribery. The bribery argument is probably the most frequent complaint against the use of reinforcement in the classroom. However, the word *bribery* implies that the behavior being reinforced is somehow illegal or unethical. On the contrary, the appropriate use of reinforcement in the classroom can facilitate the attainment of educational objectives, all of which involve academically and socially desirable behaviors.

Reinforcement develops dependence on concrete, external rewards for appropriate behavior. It is often argued that students should learn because of its intrinsic rewards; they should learn for learning's sake. This argument can be countered in two ways. First of all, behavior modification does not necessarily involve material reinforcers. Social reinforcers, activities, feedback, and intrinsic reinforcers (e.g., feelings of success or accomplishment) are also effective in changing behavior, and the sensible behavior modifier will use them instead of material reinforcers whenever possible.

Second, even when material reinforcers must be relied on as the only means by which behavior can be changed, they are used to bring about positive changes in a student, changes that apparently *will not occur any other way*. Reinforcement is often used when more traditional methods of behavior change have failed, to increase desired academic and social skills and decrease counterproductive behaviors. If the choice comes down to either teaching Johnny to read by reinforcing him for reading or not teaching him to read at all, obviously Johnny must learn to read through whatever means possible. And we must remember, too, that, when material reinforcers are used, social events (e.g., praise) that are paired with them should eventually become reinforcing as well.

Reinforcing one student for being good teaches other students to be bad. "Hmmm," thinks Leslie. "Linda has been such a loudmouth the past few weeks that the teacher is now giving her candy so she'll keep quiet. Maybe if I start shooting my mouth off, I'll start getting some candy too." If students are thinking along these lines, then something is clearly wrong with the way reinforcement is being handled in the classroom. All students should be reinforced for their positive behaviors. Praise and positive feedback should not be limited to a handful of chronic misbehavers but should be awarded consistently to all students. If the behavior of a particular student can be modified *only* with material reinforcers, such reinforcement should be administered discreetly and privately.

Changing a problem behavior does not change the underlying cause of that behavior; other behavioral manifestations of that underlying cause will appear. Reflected in this criticism is Sigmund Freud's notion of *symptom substitution*: problem behaviors are a function of deep-rooted psychological conflicts, so that when a behavior is eliminated without treatment of its underlying cause, another problem behavior will emerge in its place. The best rebuttal to the symptom substitution criticism is an empirical one: when problem behaviors are treated through behavior modification, symptom substitution rarely occurs (Rimm & Masters, 1974).

One likely reason for this is that changing an individual's behavior may indirectly address its underlying causes as well. For example, consider the boy who is inappropriately aggressive on the playground. This boy might very well truly want to interact with his classmates, but aggression is the only way he knows of initiating this interaction. Reinforcing the boy for more appropriate methods of social interaction also helps him develop friendships, and the underlying cause for his aggression—his desire for companionship—is therefore dealt with at the same time.

Reinforced behaviors do not generalize to other situations. The argument here is that children may learn to engage in appropriate behaviors in the classroom where they are reinforced for doing so, but will not exhibit those behaviors in a setting where no reinforcement occurs. The fact is that reinforced behaviors often *do* generalize to other situations (Rimm & Masters, 1974). When they do not, their generalization can be taught by their reinforcement in different situations and by the reinforcement of similar behaviors (Morris, 1985).

Genuine Concerns

The bogus complaints listed can be easily rebutted. However, two major criticisms of operant conditioning techniques should be taken more seriously.

Attempts at changing behaviors ignore cognitive factors that may be interfering with learning. When students are capable of learning a new skill but are not motivated to do so, the use of reinforcement may be all that is needed to bring about the desired behavior change. However, when cognitive deficiencies (e.g., specific learning disabilities) exist that interfere with the acquisition of a new skill, reinforcement alone may be insufficient. In the latter situation, we may need to employ teaching techniques based more on cognitive learning theories, theories which will be explored in later chapters.

The extrinsic reinforcement of a behavior already motivated by intrinsic reinforcement may undermine the intrinsically reinforcing value of that behavior. Individuals often engage in activities because of the internal rewards—for example, pleasure or feelings of success—that those activities bring. A number of research studies (reviewed in Lepper & Greene, 1978) indicate that enjoyable activities can be increased by extrinsic reinforcers, but will then *decrease* to a below-baseline frequency once the extrinsic reinforcers are removed. For example, in one study, preschool children who had previously been reinforced for certain drawing activities were actually *less* likely to engage in drawing in a free-play situation than children who had not been reinforced (Lepper, Greene, & Nisbett, 1973). Similar results were obtained in a study with college students: students who were paid a dollar for each correct solution of a series of block puzzles were less likely to continue to work at such puzzles in the absence of reinforcement than students who had not been paid for their correct solutions (Deci, 1971). It appears, then, that externally reinforcing a behavior that is already occurring because of intrinsic motivation may actually undermine that intrinsic motivation (deCharms, 1968; Deci & Porac, 1978; Lepper & Greene, 1978; Mayer, 1987).

WHEN OPERANT CONDITIONING TECHNIQUES ARE MOST APPROPRIATE

Instructional methods based on principles of operant conditioning are probably more appropriate for certain groups of students than for others. Among the students who appear to benefit the most from the structure and clearly specified response-reinforcement contingencies of operant conditioning techniques are students with a history of academic failure, poorly motivated students, anxious students, and students for whom nothing else works.

Frequent success experiences and reinforcements, such as those provided by programmed instruction, are particularly beneficial to students who have had little success in their academic careers. Children officially identified as "mentally retarded" or "learning disabled" fall into this category, as do many juvenile delinquents and slow learners (children with below-normal intelligence whose test scores are not sufficiently low to qualify them for special class placement). Academic success is exactly what such students need to bolster the poor self-concepts that have resulted from a long string of academic failures.

Students with poor motivation for academic tasks can often benefit from operant conditioning techniques. Although some students thrive on the feelings that academic success can bring, others do not value academic achievement. The introduction of extrinsic reinforcers (material, social, or activity reinforcers) contingent on academic accomplishments may be helpful in improving the achievement of such students.

Highly anxious students appear to need structure in their curriculum to perform well on academic tasks (Dowaliby & Schumer, 1973; Grimes & Allinsmith, 1961). Such students need a classroom environment in which expectations for their behavior are specified and where response-reinforcement contingencies are clearly laid out. They also seem to require frequent success experiences and positive feedback. Many of the methods derived from operant conditioning principles address the needs of anxious children particularly well: behavioral objectives spell out desired behaviors in concrete terms, programmed instruction provides success and positive feedback, and behavior modification communicates quite clearly which behaviors will yield the reinforcers they seek.

Finally, there are some students for whom nothing else works. Techniques based on operant conditioning principles have been shown to be effective methods of changing even the most resilient of problem behaviors (Greer, 1983; Rimm & Masters, 1974). Such stubborn problems as childhood autism and juvenile delinquency have been dealt with more successfully by behavior modification than by any other method currently available.

On the other hand, methods based on operant conditioning are probably not well suited for everyone. Bright students may find the gradual, inch-by-inch approach of programmed instruction slow and tedious. A token economy in a classroom of highly motivated college-bound students may undermine the intrinsic desire of these students to achieve at a high level. Other learning theories, notably cognitive theories, can probably be applied with more success for these students.

SUMMARY

Principles of operant learning are manifested in a variety of educational practices. Behavioral objectives, which express educational goals in terms of precise, observable responses, are a direct outgrowth of the concept of terminal behavior. Programmed instruction, computer-assisted instruction, and Keller's personalized system of instruction incorporate such operant conditioning principles as active responding, shaping, and immediate reinforcement. Behavior modification encompasses a variety of techniques that have been shown to improve both academic achievement and social behavior. Through methods of self-control, such as self-reinforcement, individuals can effectively change their own behaviors. A number of criticisms have been directed toward the use of reinforcement in the classroom; some are legitimate while others probably reflect a misunderstanding of behavior modification techniques. Operant conditioning techniques are probably best used with special populations rather than as a matter of course with all students.

Aversive Control

Outline

I N the previous two chapters, we have focused on the influence of positive consequences (reinforcers) on learning. In this chapter, we will focus on the impact of *aversive* events on learning and performance, with particular attention to three different situations. We will first examine how people and animals learn to escape and avoid painful events. We will then look at the effects of punishment on learning and behavior. Finally, we will examine a phenomenon that occurs when people and animals are exposed to aversive stimuli that they can neither avoid nor escape, a phenomenon known as learned helplessness.

ESCAPE AND AVOIDANCE LEARNING

My university, like most others, abounds in faculty committees. When I first joined the faculty, I eagerly joined committees whenever I could, perceiving them as a means of meeting other faculty members and of having input into university decision making. Before long, however, I discovered that most faculty committees spend years chewing on the same old issues without ever arriving at consensus or otherwise accomplishing very much. Frustrated by the amount of time I was wasting, I soon found myself inventing excuses to leave committee meetings early ("I'm *so* sorry, but I have to take my son to the dentist"). Eventually, I stopped volunteering to join committees in the first place, thus avoiding them altogether. Committee meetings had become an aversive event for me. My learning to make excuses so I could leave meetings early and then learning not to volunteer in the first place is typical of what happens when an aversive stimulus is presented: organisms learn to *escape* and eventually to *avoid* that stimulus if they possibly can.

Escape Learning

Escape learning is the process of learning a response that terminates an aversive stimulus. For example, in Neal Miller's classic study of escape learning (Miller, 1948), rats were placed in one compartment of a two-compartment cage and then given a series of electric shocks. The rats quickly learned to turn a wheel that enabled them to run to the other compartment, thereby escaping the aversive shocks. In an analogous study with humans (Hiroto, 1974), people readily learned to move a knob to turn off an unpleasantly loud noise.

Just as is true in the laboratory, students learn various ways of escaping unpleasant tasks or situations in the classroom. Making excuses ("My dog ate my math problems!") can be a means of escaping homework assignments. Lying about one's own behaviors ("I didn't do it—*he* did!") is a way of escaping the playground supervisor's evil eye. Chronic truancy and hypochondriasis are ways of escaping the school environment altogether.

Because escape from an aversive stimulus terminates that stimulus, the escape response is *negatively reinforced*. When rats make a response that stops an electric shock, and children make a response that terminates the evil eye, and I make an excuse to leave a committee meeting, we are all reinforced by virtue of the fact that an unpleasant event is removed.

The more aversive a stimulus is, the more likely people are to learn to escape that stimulus (e.g., Piliavin, Dovidio, Gaertner, & Clark, 1981; Piliavin, Piliavin, & Rodin, 1975). For example, children who have particular difficulty with assignments are more likely to have dogs who eat their homework. And truancy is most likely to occur when school is an unpleasant environment for a student; chronic truants are often those students who have encountered repeated failures both with their academic work and in their relationships with teachers and peers.

Avoidance Learning

Avoidance learning is the process of learning to stay away from an aversive stimulus altogether. For avoidance learning to occur, an organism must have some sort of *pre-aversive stimulus*, a cue signaling the advent of the aversive stimulus. For example, rats who hear a buzzer (the pre-aversive stimulus) and are then given an electric shock easily learn to jump a hurdle as soon as the buzzer sounds, thereby avoiding the painful shock (Mowrer, 1938, 1939). Similarly, children quickly learn to pull a brass handle as soon

Common escape and avoidance responses

as a light flashes so that they can avoid an unpleasantly loud noise (Robinson & Robinson, 1961).

Avoidance learning appears in two forms: active avoidance learning and passive avoidance learning. In *active avoidance learning*, the organism must actively make a particular response to avoid the aversive event. Active avoidance learning provides an explanation of why many students study as diligently as they do. Unfortunately, most people do not find studying to be as enjoyable an activity as certain other activities (e.g., reading mystery novels or watching television quiz shows). Nevertheless, because studying behavior enables students to avoid an aversive stimulus (a failing grade), it is exhibited fairly frequently. But notice how rarely studying occurs when there is no signal of possible impending doom, such as an assigned research report or an upcoming exam.

In other situations, organisms learn that *not* making a particular response allows them to avoid an aversive event (e.g., Lewis & Maher, 1965; Seligman & Campbell, 1965); this form of learning is called *passive avoidance learning*. For example, people who feel awkward and uncomfortable in social situations tend not to go to parties or other social events. Likewise, students who have difficulty with mathematics rarely sign up for advanced math classes if they can help it.

What learning processes underlie avoidance learning? Probably the most widely cited theory of avoidance learning is Mowrer's two-factor theory (e.g., Mowrer, 1956; Mowrer & Lamoreaux, 1942). According to Mowrer's theory, avoidance learning is a two-step process that involves both classical conditioning and operant conditioning. In the first step, because the pre-aversive stimulus and the aversive stimulus are presented close together in time, the organism learns to fear the pre-aversive stimulus through a process of classical conditioning, as illustrated in Figure 6–1.

Figure 6–1
Learning to fear a pre-aversive stimulus through classical conditioning

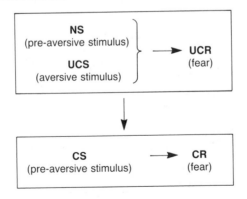

In the second step, an avoidance response is reinforced because the response leads to escape from the fear-inducing pre-aversive stimulus, thereby being negatively reinforced.

Other theories have been advanced as well (e.g., Bolles, 1975; D'Amato, 1970; Herrnstein, 1969; Seligman & Johnston, 1973). For example, rats can learn to avoid an aversive stimulus even when the allegedly fear-inducing pre-aversive stimulus is not escaped (Kamin, 1956), refuting Mowrer's notion that escape from this stimulus negatively reinforces the avoidance response. Such evidence has led some theorists to postulate that the actual reinforcer of an avoidance response is a feeling of relief (D'Amato, 1970; Denny & Weisman, 1964). Other research (e.g., Kamin, Brimer, & Black, 1963) indicates that fear is not necessarily involved in avoidance responses at all. Hence, such theorists as Bolles (1975) and Seligman and Johnston (1973) have abandoned behaviorism for a more cognitive explanation of avoidance learning: organisms simply form *expectations* about what situations are aversive and what behaviors enable them to avoid those situations.

Although there is disagreement about the best theoretical explanation of avoidance learning, there is general agreement on one thing: avoidance responses are very difficult to extinguish. When a previously aversive situation loses all sources of aversiveness, organisms nevertheless continue to avoid that situation. For example, dogs keep on escaping from a box that has been previously associated with shock long after the shock has been terminated (Solomon & Wynne, 1954).

One likely reason for the high resistance of avoidance responses to extinction is that when you avoid a formerly aversive situation, there is no opportunity to learn that the situation is no longer aversive. Let's examine students' avoidance of mathematics as an example. As I suggested in Chapter 3, mathematics anxiety may be a conditioned response acquired at a time when children are not cognitively ready to learn abstract mathematical concepts. Students with math anxiety may avoid math classes indefinitely, even though they may eventually develop the cognitive maturity necessary for comprehending previously troublesome concepts. If students never again enroll in another math class, they will never learn that they have nothing to fear!

Many psychologists believe that the best way to extinguish an avoidance response is to extinguish the fear that elicits the avoidance in the first place. One way of doing this is through *systematic desensitization*, a technique I described in Chapter 3: by relaxing while imagining a series of increasingly anxiety-arousing scenarios, fear of a situation can be reduced. Another approach is to prevent the avoidance response, thereby enabling the individual to experience the conditioned stimulus in the absence of a fear-elicited unconditioned stimulus. For example, if we have a math-anxious student that we know possesses adequate cognitive skills to succeed in mathematics, we might require that student to enroll in a math class.

In some cases it is probably true that students don't always know what is best for them!

But, undoubtedly, the best way to deal with both escape and avoidance behaviors in the classroom is to prevent their being learned in the first place, something we can accomplish only by minimizing aversive classroom stimuli. For example, educational objectives should be established with the cognitive maturity and acquired skills of each group of students clearly in mind so that students can realistically accomplish those objectives. And when students are then given adequate instruction, resources, and incentives to achieve success (a positive reinforcer) in their class work, they are more likely to seek out that work than to avoid it.

Escape and avoidance learning result when aversive stimuli can be terminated or avoided through one's responses; in these situations, the stimuli precede the responses. However, when aversive stimuli *follow* responses, we instead have a case of punishment.

PUNISHMENT

Punishment actually takes two forms. *Punishment I* (also called positive punishment) is the more commonly recognized form; it decreases the strength of a response when it is presented after that response. Typically, Punishment I involves the presentation of an aversive stimulus, for example, a spanking or an F. *Punishment II* (sometimes called negative punishment) decreases the strength of a response by virtue of the removal of a stimulus, usually a pleasant one. Losing a privilege and being fined (in which case money is lost) are examples of Punishment II. Punishment is a common occurrence in our daily lives; some psychologists believe that even the absence of reinforcement can be punishing.

Views on the effectiveness of punishment have changed considerably over the last fifty years. Early research indicated that punishment was a very ineffective means of changing behavior. For example, Thorndike (1932b) found that, although positive feedback facilitated students' learning of correct responses, negative feedback did not reduce incorrect responses. Similarly, Skinner (1938) found that when rats were punished for a response that had previously been reinforced, the response was temporarily suppressed but soon returned to its pre-punishment frequency. As a result, early behaviorists such as Thorndike, Skinner, and Guthrie discouraged the use of punishment.

Probably because of the negative views on punishment held by prominent learning theorists during the first half of the century, punishment as a means of behavior control was largely ignored until the 1960s. Until that time, concern centered more on disadvantages than on any possible advantages of punishment. More recently, however, research evidence has emerged to indicate that punishment *can* be effective in many situations.

In the following pages we will explore the many-faceted topic of punishment. We will begin by examining punishment's numerous disadvantages. We will then look at some evidence supporting the use of punishment as an effective means of behavior control and will also explore various theoretical explanations for its effect on behavior. Finally, we will discuss some guidelines for using punishment in the classroom.

Disadvantages of Punishment

Psychologists have cited a number of disadvantages associated with the use of punishment.

A punished behavior is not eliminated; it is only suppressed. Punishment suppresses a response; that is, it makes the response less likely to occur. However, this suppression effect is often only temporary: the punished behavior may reappear when the punishment stops or when the punisher is absent (Appel & Peterson, 1965; Azrin, 1960; Holz & Azrin, 1962; Skinner, 1938).

Punishment sometimes leads to an increase in the punished behavior. In some cases, this effect may be due to the fact that the "punishment" is actually reinforcing. For example, a teacher's reprimands may be reinforcing to the girl who craves her teacher's attention or to the boy who wants to look "cool" in front of his classmates. However, even in situations in which the punishment is truly punishing, it may nevertheless lead to an increase in the punished response. More specifically, when a behavior is punished in one situation, it may decrease in that situation but *increase* in a situation in which it has *not* been punished—an effect known as *behavioral contrast* (e.g., Reynolds, 1975; Swenson, 1980). For example, some children who behave badly at school may be described by their parents as being angelic at home. A child who is held to strict behavioral rules on the home front and is punished by a parent for breaking those rules may engage in the forbidden behaviors at school.

The response-punishment contingency may not be recognized. Punishment, particularly physical punishment, can distract an individual's attention away from the behavior that was punished. Children are often less aware of the response that was punished than of the punishment itself (Maurer, 1974). Punishment will clearly be ineffective if children do not know what they are being punished for.

Punishment often conditions negative emotional responses and may lead to escape and avoidance behaviors. When punishment involves a particularly aversive stimulus, the association of that stimulus with other stimuli (e.g., the punisher or the situation in which punishment occurred) can, through classical conditioning, lead to undesirable emotional responses to those other stimuli (Skinner, 1938). For example, when a teacher punishes a student at school, that punishment (the UCS) may be associated with the teacher and the classroom, both of which may then become conditioned stimuli (CSs) that elicit conditioned responses such as fear and anxiety.

Furthermore, a fear-eliciting stimulus often leads to escape and avoidance learning (e.g., Redd, Morris, & Martin, 1975). Escape and avoidance behaviors in school take many forms: running away, truancy, avoidance of school tasks, inattention or withdrawal in class, cheating, and lying (e.g., Becker, 1971; Skinner, 1938). Because such undesirable behaviors terminate an aversive stimulus (in this case, the aversive stimulus is the punishment), they are negatively reinforced and so are likely to increase.

Punishment may lead to aggression. When punishment produces pain, it evokes emotional arousal in an individual, arousal that may result in anger and aggression, especially in characteristically aggressive individuals (Azrin, 1967; Berkowitz & LePage, 1967; Walters & Grusec, 1977). Aggressive behavior in turn appears to reduce the emotional arousal (e.g., Hokanson & Burgess, 1962) and to feel good (Bramel, Taub, & Blum, 1968), the result being that aggression is reinforced.

Furthermore, punishment provides a model of aggression, thus communicating the message that aggression is acceptable. I am reminded of the many hypocritical interactions I have witnessed in the grocery store. A

Physical punishment models aggression.

mother yells, "How many times have I told you not to hit your sister?" and gives her child a solid whack. Children who observe others being aggressive are more likely to be aggressive themselves (Bandura, Ross, & Ross, 1961, 1963; Mischel & Grusec, 1966; Steuer, Applefield, & Smith, 1971). Particularly aggressive children (i.e., juvenile delinquents) are likely to come from homes where severe punishment has been frequent (Welsh, 1976).

Punishment does not illustrate the correct behavior. As Skinner (1938) has pointed out, punishment tells an individual what not to do, but not what should be done instead. Consider the boy who is consistently aggressive on the playground; it may be that aggression is the only way he knows of interacting with other children. Punishing this child for aggressive behavior without teaching him more appropriate social skills does not help him develop friendly relationships with his classmates.

Severe punishment may cause physical or psychological harm. Obviously, severe physical punishment can lead to bodily injury. In a similar way, severe psychological punishment, such as extreme embarrassment or deflation of self-esteem, can be equally harmful. The mother of a college friend of mine constantly degraded him with such remarks as "How can you be so stupid!" and "Can't you ever do anything right?" Throughout our four years in college, my friend fought numerous bouts with depression, and was in and out of mental institutions. The line between punishment and abuse is often a very fuzzy one.

Despite the many disadvantages I have listed, punishment can often serve as an effective method of behavior control. Let's now examine some instances when punishment *does* work. A bit later in the chapter I'll give you some guidelines in using punishment that will help avert the disadvantages just cited.

The Effectiveness of Punishment

Although early research cast doubt on the idea that punishment decreased behavior, more recently researchers have reported evidence that punishment can successfully reduce or eliminate undesirable behaviors (e.g., Azrin & Holz, 1966; Dinsmoor, 1954, 1955; Tanner & Zeiler, 1975; Walters & Grusec, 1977). Punishment is often used when methods such as extinction, the differential reinforcement of other behaviors (DRO schedule), or the reinforcement of an incompatible response are ineffective or impractical; furthermore, it appears that punishment may often be more effective than any of these other techniques (Boe & Church, 1967; Corte, Wolf, & Locke, 1971; Pfiffner & O'Leary, 1987; Walters & Grusec, 1977). Punishment is especially advised when a behavior is harmful either to oneself or another; in such cases, the use of punishment to eliminate such behavior rapidly may actually be the most humane course of action.

In a series of studies, Vance Hall and his colleagues (Hall, Axelrod, Foundopoulos, Shellman, Campbell, & Cranston, 1971) have demonstrated the speed with which punishment can bring about behavior change. For example, in one study, the aggressive behavior of a seven-year-old deaf girl named Andrea was virtually eliminated through the consistent use of punishment. Initially, this girl pinched and bit both herself and anybody else with whom she came into contact; the frequency of such responses (an average of seventy-two per school day) was so high that normal academic instruction was impossible. Following a baseline period, punishment for each aggressive act was initiated: whenever the girl pinched or bit, her teacher pointed at her sternly and shouted "No!" Figure 6–2 shows the changes in Andrea's behavior (the brief reversal to nonreinforcement for a few days was used to rule out coincidence as an explanation for the behavior changes). Even though Andrea was deaf, the shouting and pointing virtually eliminated her aggressiveness.

In a second study, Hall and his colleagues modified the whining and complaining behaviors of a boy named Billy. Billy frequently cried, whined, and complained of stomachaches whenever he was given a reading or arithmetic assignment, while apparently being quite healthy the rest of the day.

Figure 6–2
Number of bites and pinches by Andrea during the school day

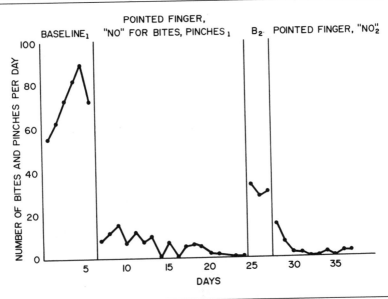

The treatment program consisted of giving Billy five slips of colored paper bearing his name at the beginning of reading and arithmetic periods every day, and then removing one slip of paper (Punishment II) each time Billy cried, whined, or complained. Treatment was instituted on day 6 for Billy's reading period and on day 11 for his math period (this multiple baseline approach is an alternative way of ruling out the "coincidence" factor). The effectiveness of the unusual punishment is clearly demonstrated in Figure 6–3 (note the temporary reversal to nonpunished baseline similar to that shown in Figure 6–2).

In yet another study by Hall and his colleagues, the grades of three tenth-grade students enrolled in a French class were modified using after-school tutoring as the punishment. These students—Dave, Roy, and Debbie—had been consistently earning D's and F's on daily quizzes. The teacher

Figure 6–3

Frequency of Billy's cries (C), whines (W), and complaints (C_1) during reading and arithmetic periods

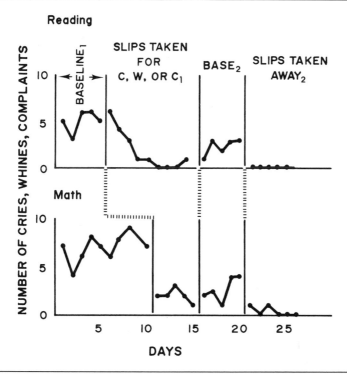

informed them that because they were obviously having difficulty with their French, they would have to come in for a half hour of tutoring after school whenever they received a grade lower than C. Quiz grades during baseline and during the time when poor quiz performance would be punished are shown in Figure 6–4 (note the multiple baseline approach once again). As you can see, none of the students ever needed to report for after-school tutoring! Apparently, the threat of punishment alone was sufficient to bring about desired study behaviors.

What is unique about the studies by Hall and his colleagues is that none of the punishments could be construed as being either physically or psychologically harmful or painful. Yet all of them—pointing and yelling "No!," withdrawing colored slips of paper, and requiring after-school tutoring—were clearly effective in bringing about dramatic behavior changes in different students. But just why does punishment work? Let's explore some possible explanations.

Figure 6–4
Quiz grades for three high school French class students

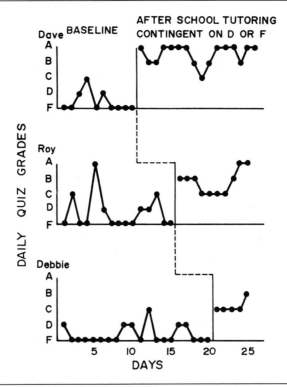

Reprinted with permission from "The Effective Use of Punishment to Modify Behavior in the Classroom" by R. V. Hall, S. Axelrod, M. Foundopoulos, J. Shellman, R. A. Campbell, & S. S. Cranston, 1972, in K. D. O'Leary & S. O'Leary (Eds.), *Classroom Management: The Successful Use of Behavior Modification*, p. 180. Copyright 1972 by Pergamon Press, Ltd.

Theoretical Perspectives on Punishment

A number of theories have been advanced to explain why punishment decreases the behavior that precedes it. Guthrie (1935) and Skinner (1953) offered two early theories based on the notion of incompatibility: punishment reduces a response only when it leads to a behavior (such as escape from the situation) that is incompatible with the punished response. Thus, Guthrie and Skinner argued that punishment affects the punished behavior indirectly (by bringing about a new response) rather than directly. An alternative theory (e.g., Estes, 1969b; Walters & Grusec, 1977) is also based on the notion of incompatibility, albeit the incompatibility of motives rather than behaviors. According to this explanation, punishment leads to motives (e.g., fear) that are incompatible with the motives that originally led to the behavior being punished. For example, when a rat who has learned to press a bar to obtain food is then punished for pressing that bar, the fear induced by the punishment may lower the rat's appetite.

Mowrer (1960) has proposed a two-stage theory of punishment similar to his theory of avoidance learning. First, when an organism is punished for a particular behavior, fear of the environment in which punishment occurred is established through a process of classical conditioning. Second, escape from that environment is reinforced because such escape reduces that fear (negative reinforcement). Punishment is effective to the extent that the escape response is incompatible with the punished response.

Still other theorists (e.g., Azrin & Holz, 1966; Fantino, 1973; Rachlin & Herrnstein, 1969) have reverted to Thorndike's original law of effect and suggest that punishment should be viewed in the same way as reinforcement—as a consequence that alters the frequency of future behaviors. These researchers advocate an atheoretical approach to punishment and focus more on what influences the effectiveness of punishment than on the reasons underlying its effectiveness (Walters & Grusec, 1977).

Using Punishment in Classroom Settings

The use of punishment as a means of behavior control is widespread in both child rearing and educational practice (Sears, Maccoby, & Levin, 1957; Wielkiewicz, 1986). One likely reason for the prevalence of punishment as a disciplinary measure is that because it tends to decrease or eliminate an undesirable behavior fairly quickly, the punisher is actually negatively reinforced for using punishment (i.e., by the termination of the unwanted behavior).

Two particular forms of punishment, time-out and response cost, are frequently used in classroom situations. Both are examples of Punishment II—the withdrawal of a reinforcer. A third type of punishment, the verbal reprimand (an example of Punishment I), is also useful in some instances. Let's examine the empirical evidence for all three.

Time-out. Time-out (e.g., Ullmann & Krasner, 1969; Walters & Grusec, 1977) involves placing the misbehaving individual in an environment without any reinforcers present—in other words, in a dull and boring situation. Often, this time-out environment is a separate room, furnished sparsely or not at all, from which the individual cannot interact with others. Other times, it may be a corner of the classroom screened from the rest of the room by partitions or tall furniture. In any event, the time-out environment should be neither reinforcing, as the hall or the principal's office is likely to be, nor frightening, as a dark closet might be (Walker & Shea, 1984; Wielkiewicz, 1986). Foxx and Shapiro (1978) have developed a procedure whereby time-out can be easily incorporated into a classroom context without requiring the availability of any special facilities. Students wear ribbons that make them eligible to participate in rewarding classroom activities. Students who misbehave remain in the classroom, but their ribbons are removed, making them ineligible to receive the reinforcers available to their classmates.

Time-out has been shown to be effective in reducing a variety of disruptive, aggressive, and dangerous behaviors (Drabman & Spitalnik, 1973; Mace, Page, Ivancic, & O'Brien, 1986; MacPherson, Candee, & Hohman, 1974; Mathews, Friman, Barone, Ross, & Christophersen, 1987; Rolider & Van Houten, 1985; Williams, 1959). It does not need to be lengthy to be effective, and in fact many psychologists advocate that durations of ten minutes (even as few as two minutes for preschool children) are sufficient. A key to using time-out effectively is that the inappropriate behavior must *stop* before the child is released from the time-out situation; release from time-out (a negative reinforcer) is therefore contingent on appropriate behavior.

Response Cost. Response cost involves the withdrawal of a previously received reinforcer; a ticket for speeding (resulting in the payment of a fine) and the loss of previously earned privileges are examples. Response cost has been shown to reduce such misbehaviors as aggression, inappropriate speech, disruptiveness, hyperactivity, and tardiness (Iwata & Bailey, 1974; Kazdin, 1972; McLaughlin & Malaby, 1972; Rapport, Murphy, & Bailey, 1982), and appears to be particularly effective when combined with reinforcement of appropriate behavior (Phillips, Phillips, Fixsen, & Wolf, 1971).

Verbal Reprimand. Although some students find teacher attention of any kind reinforcing, most students probably regard verbal reprimands as punishment. For example, in a study by O'Leary and his colleagues (O'Leary, Kaufman, Kass, & Drabman, 1970), reprimands were effective in decreasing the disruptive behavior of seven out of nine children. Softly spoken reprimands were noticeably more effective than loud ones, possibly because soft reprimands were less likely to be noticed by other children and thus less likely to draw the (potentially reinforcing) attention of other children to the child being punished. In addition to suppressing undesirable behavior, occasional reprimands also appear to enhance the positive reinforcement value of praise (Pfiffner & O'Leary, 1987).

Punishments such as time-out, response cost, and verbal reprimands appear to have fewer negative side effects than either physical punishment (e.g., spanking) or psychological punishment (e.g., withdrawal of love) (Walters & Grusec, 1977). However, teachers who use the more recommended forms of punishment to reduce inappropriate behavior must nevertheless monitor their effects on the behaviors being punished. For example, some individuals find time-out to be reinforcing rather than punishing (Solnick, Rincover, & Peterson, 1977), and their "punished" behaviors will increase rather than diminish.

In Chapter 4, I discussed the importance of reinforcement as a means of providing feedback about what is appropriate behavior. In much the same way, punishment is probably effective to the extent that it gives feedback about inappropriate behavior. Sometimes students are truly unaware of how frequently they are misbehaving (e.g., Krumboltz & Krumboltz, 1972), and the occasional punishment of inappropriate responses can provide reminders to keep these students on task. But how do we avoid such negative side effects as aggression, escape responses, and negative emotional reactions? Let's turn to some guidelines for using punishment in the classroom.

Guidelines for Using Punishment Effectively

Psychologists and educators have offered numerous suggestions on how to use punishment effectively, many of which decrease the chances of negative side effects. These guidelines are among the most commonly cited.

The "punishment" must be punishing. Punishment, like reinforcement, is defined by its effect on behavior. True punishment decreases the response it follows. If a given consequence does not decrease the response it is meant to punish, that consequence may not be aversive to the individual being "punished"; in fact, it may even be reinforcing.

Teachers and parents too often make assumptions about what consequences will be punishing for children. For example, a common "punishment" around our house is to be sent to one's room. For my two sons, such a consequence is truly aversive, as they would much rather socialize with the family in the kitchen or living room than be isolated in their rooms for any length of time. On the other hand, when my daughter Tina is banished to her bedroom, she is probably being reinforced: she rearranges her furniture, listens to her radio, or settles under the covers with a good book. And the behaviors for which she has been most often punished in this way— behaviors related in one way or another to annoying and teasing her brothers—seem to be increasing rather than decreasing.

The punishment must be strong enough to be effective, but not overly severe. Punishment that is too short or mild will not be effective (e.g.,

Tina is "punished"

Parke & Walters, 1967). For example, fines for such behaviors as speeding and drunken driving are obviously insufficient deterrents for some individuals. Similarly, grades in many college classrooms may be too lenient to discourage a student from academically unproductive behaviors. A college teacher may believe that by giving some students a C, she is punishing those students for their lack of class attendance and poor exam performance. Yet a C average is quite acceptable at most institutions, so the students may not be sufficiently "punished" to reduce their frequency of partygoing and Frisbee-throwing at times when they should be attending classes or reading their textbooks.

At the same time, punishment must not be overly severe, as it can then lead to such undesirable side effects as resentment, hostility, aggression, or escape behavior. Furthermore, although severe punishment may quickly suppress a response, that response may reappear at its original level once the punisher has left the scene (Appel & Peterson, 1965; Azrin, 1960).

Whenever possible, punishment should follow immediately after the inappropriate behavior. As is true for reinforcement, the effectiveness of punishment decreases dramatically when it is delayed (Trenholme & Baron, 1975; Walters, 1964; Walters & Grusec, 1977). The more closely punishment follows a misbehavior, the more effective that punishment will be.

Punishment should be consistent. Just as is true for reinforcement, punishment is much more effective when it is a consistent consequence of a particular response (Leff, 1969; Parke & Deur, 1972). When a response is punished only occasionally, with other occurrences of that response being either reinforced or ignored, the response disappears slowly, if at all. Supporting this idea is the fact that many juvenile delinquents come from home environments in which parental discipline has been administered inconsistently (Glueck & Glueck, 1950; McCord, McCord, & Zola, 1959).

Unfortunately, people can only be punished when they have been caught in the act. Thieves are rarely apprehended, and speeders are ticketed only when the highways on which they drive are patrolled. Many undesirable classroom behaviors, such as talking out, getting out of one's seat, being aggressive, and cheating, may be reinforced as frequently as they are punished. To deal with the difficulty of detecting some undesirable student behaviors, the next two guidelines—changing the situation so the misbehavior is less likely to occur and providing a positively reinforceable alternative behavior—are especially critical.

Whenever possible, the environment should be modified so that the misbehavior is less likely to occur. In other words, the temptation to engage in a misbehavior should be reduced or, if possible, eliminated. People on diets should not stock their kitchens with junk food. Troublemaking friends should be placed on opposite sides of the classroom or in separate classrooms. Cheating on an exam can be reduced by having students sit apart from one another or by administering two different forms of the exam (perhaps the same test items in different orders).

Desirable alternative behaviors should be taught and reinforced. Punishment of misbehavior is typically more effective when it is combined with reinforcement of appropriate behavior (Rimm & Masters, 1974; Walters & Grusec, 1977). A misbehavior is more likely to be suppressed permanently when alternative behaviors are reinforced, and particularly when those behaviors are incompatible with the punished behavior. For example, when punishing aggression on the playground, we should remember also to reinforce appropriate social behavior. We can punish a student for cheating, but we should also reinforce that student for demonstrating good study habits and for working well independently.

Punishment should be threatened once before it is administered. In other words, people should know ahead of time that a particular behavior will be punished, and they should know what the punishment will be. I remember an incident when I was about four years old, in which I was punished without warning. Sitting at lunch one day, apparently considering the old adage "Waste not, want not," I proceeded to lick a large quantity of peanut butter off my butter knife. An adult scolded me sternly for my behavior, and I was devastated. Being the Miss Goody-Two-Shoes that I was at that age, I would never have engaged in knife-licking behavior if I had known that it was an unacceptable response.

One common mistake made by many teachers and parents is to continue to threaten punishment without ever following through. One threat is advisable, but repeated threats are not. The father who constantly says to his son, "If you hit your brother again, Tommy, I'll send you to your room for the rest of the week," but never does send Tommy to his room, is giving his son the message that no response-punishment contingency really exists.

One of the reasons that teachers and parents often fail to follow through with threatened punishment is that they too often bluff, proposing punishment that is impractical or unrealistically extreme. Tommy's father does not punish his son because having Tommy spend the rest of the week in his room would be a major inconvenience for both of them. A teacher who threatens that certain behaviors will result in students not going on a promised field trip should make sure that leaving some students at school that day is logistically possible.

The behavior to be punished should be specified in clear, concrete terms. Students should understand exactly what behaviors are unacceptable. A student who is told, "If you disrupt the class again this morning, you will have to stay in during recess," may not understand exactly what the teacher means by "disrupt" and so may continue to engage in inappropriate classroom behavior. The teacher should instead take the student aside and say something like this: "Sharon, there are two behaviors that are unacceptable in this classroom. When you talk without permission and when you get out of your seat during seatwork time, you keep other children from getting their work done. This morning I expect you to talk and get out of your seat only when I give you permission to do so. Otherwise, you will have to stay in during recess today and sit quietly at your desk."

An explanation of why the behavior is unacceptable should be provided. Although behaviorists tend to focus their attention on responses and their consequences, a growing body of research indicates that punishment is more effective when *reasons* that certain behaviors cannot be tolerated are given (e.g., Baumrind, 1983; Hess & McDevitt, 1984; Perry & Perry, 1983). For example, notice how Sharon's teacher incorporated reasoning into her description of Sharon's inappropriate behaviors: "When you talk without permission and when you get out of your seat during seatwork time, *you keep other children from getting their work done.*"

There appear to be at least four advantages of providing reasons that behaviors are unacceptable:

1. When punishment is accompanied by reasoning, it appears to make the immediacy of punishment a less critical factor in its effectiveness (Walters & Grusec, 1977);

2. Reasoning increases the likelihood that when one behavior is punished, similar misbehaviors are also suppressed; that is, the effect of the punishment generalizes to other misbehaviors (Walters & Grusec, 1977);

3. When reasons are given, misbehaviors are likely to be suppressed even when the punisher is absent (Walters & Grusec, 1977); and

4. Older children apparently expect to be told why they cannot engage in certain behaviors and are likely to be defiant when reasons are not provided (Cheyne & Walters, 1970).

Some punishments are particularly ineffective and should be avoided. Among the punishments that are generally *not* recommended are physical punishment, psychological punishment, extra classwork, and suspension from school.

Physical punishment may be the only means of keeping very young children from engaging in potentially harmful behaviors. For example, the toddler who takes delight in sticking metal objects into electrical outlets should be quickly discouraged from such behavior, and a slap on the hand may be the only way of doing so. However, the use of physical punishment with older children is likely to provide a model of aggression for those children: consider evidence from descriptive studies that the great majority of abusive parents have been themselves abused as children (Steele & Pollack, 1968; Steinmetz, 1977; Straus, Gelles, & Steinmetz, 1980).

Psychological punishment, such as embarrassing or insulting a child, also is not recommended (e.g., Walker & Shea, 1984). Children who are consistently made to feel inferior or inadequate are likely to develop poor self-concepts that will interfere with their engaging in appropriate and constructive behaviors on future occasions.

Extra classwork is appropriate when it is a logical consequence of the misbehavior (for example, when students are failing exams), but in other situations it transmits the message that schoolwork is not fun. When Jimmy is punished for his disruptive classroom behaviors by being assigned an additional one hundred mathematics problems, Jimmy is unlikely to continue to regard mathematics in a very positive light.

Finally, suspension from school is typically an ineffective remedy for misbehavior. Most chronically misbehaving students are having difficulty with their academic work; many high school troublemakers, for example, are students with poor reading skills. To suspend such students from school puts these students at an even greater disadvantage and decreases still further the likelihood of academic success. Additionally, when students find school to be an aversive situation, removal from that environment is negatively reinforcing rather than punishing. (It is also negatively reinforcing to the administrators who have gotten rid of their troublemakers!)

An alternative, more effective punishment for chronic misbehavers is in-house suspension. In-house suspension is similar to a time-out in that punished students are placed in a quiet, boring room within the school building. However, in-house suspension typically lasts one or more days rather than just a few minutes, and students suspended in this manner are continually monitored by a member of the school staff. Students bring their schoolwork with them and therefore must keep up with their class-

Suspension is not an effective punishment

room assignments. In-house suspension tends to be effective because it does not allow students to escape the school environment, yet it prevents the social interactions with peers that most students find reinforcing.

Punishment should be used sparingly. The studies by Hall and his colleagues (Hall et al., 1971) that I described earlier provide several illustrations of how quickly punishment can reduce inappropriate behavior. An effective punishment is one that does not need to be administered often to be effective. Only when punishment is a frequent occurrence (in which case it is obviously not effective anyway) are the numerous disadvantages of punishment likely to appear.

When used properly, punishment is the fastest way of reducing or eliminating unacceptable behaviors. Remember, behaviorists define punishment as a consequence that decreases the response it follows. A "punishment" that clearly is not suppressing an undesirable behavior quickly should be replaced by a different consequence.

LEARNED HELPLESSNESS

Imagine that you are a student who is continually failing assignments and exams. You try all kinds of strategies to improve your grade—studying longer hours, memorizing your textbook word for word, having a friend drill you on key points, and even sleeping with your textbook open over your head (hoping that the information will sink in)—and still you get F after F after F. Eventually, you would probably just stop trying to achieve academic success and accept the "fact" that you have no control over the grades you receive.

When aversive stimuli are repeatedly presented—stimuli that cannot be avoided, escaped, or terminated—an organism will eventually give up and passively accept those aversive stimuli. This passive acceptance of uncontrollable events is a phenomenon known as *learned helplessness*.

Let me illustrate the phenomenon by describing research conducted by Seligman and Maier (1967). In the first phase of this classic experiment, dogs were given numerous painful and unpredictable shocks. Some dogs were able to escape the shocks by pushing a panel in the cage, whereas other dogs could not escape the shocks regardless of what they did. The following day, each dog was placed in a box that was divided into two compartments by a barrier. While in this box, the dog was presented with a series of tone-shock combinations, such that a tone was always followed by a shock; the dog could avoid the shock by jumping over the barrier into the other compartment as soon as it heard the tone. Those dogs who had been able to escape the shocks on the previous day quickly learned to escape the shocks on the second day. On the other hand, those dogs who had been previously unable to escape displayed learned helplessness: they made few attempts to escape, instead simply sitting still and whining as the shocks were presented.

People, too, begin to exhibit symptoms of learned helplessness when they cannot control the occurrence of aversive events (e.g., Hiroto, 1974; Hiroto & Seligman, 1975). According to Maier and Seligman (1976), learned helplessness is manifested in three ways. First, there is a motivational effect: the individual is slow to exhibit responses that will produce reinforcement or avoid punishment. Second, there is a cognitive effect: the individual has difficulty learning in future situations in which control of consequences *is* possible. Even when the individual's responses do lead to reinforcement or escape from an aversive stimulus, the individual tends not to learn from those experiences. And, third, there is an emotional effect: the individual tends to be passive, withdrawn, fearful, and depressed.

Learned helplessness has been offered as an explanation of clinical depression (e.g., Seligman, 1975): depressed people typically perceive that they have less control over their lives than nondepressed people. It may also be an explanation of why battered wives continue to remain with their husbands: they have learned that their husbands' abusive treatment is unpredictable and uncontrollable and that they themselves can do nothing to change the situation.

Learned helplessness may very well be a characteristic of some school children. Consider the learning disabled child as an example. Often unidentified as a student with special learning problems, the learning disabled child may encounter repeated failure in academic work despite efforts to achieve, and so may eventually just stop trying. I have also seen the learned helplessness phenomenon in presumably nondisabled students when I talk with them about certain subject areas. Many students, for example, attribute their mathematics anxiety to the fact that, as elementary school students, they could not comprehend how to solve certain problems no matter what they did or how hard they tried. Others show learned helplessness in the area of spelling: even when they know they have spelled a word incorrectly, they do not try to correct the spelling, excusing their behavior by such statements as "I'm just a bad speller" or "I never could spell very well" (Ormrod & Wagner, 1987).

In the last three chapters, we have explored how response-reinforcement contingencies increase certain responses and how response-punishment contingencies decrease others. To be successful in the school environment, students must be aware of those contingencies and be able to exhibit the responses that lead to positive outcomes. When students are unable to learn despite clearly specified contingencies and a slow, carefully designed curricular sequence, cognitive problems may exist that cannot be dealt with from a strictly behaviorist perspective. In such situations, cognitive learning theories, which I will describe in the next few chapters, may provide a more useful framework.

SUMMARY

Escape learning is the process of learning to terminate an aversive stimulus. Avoidance learning is the process of learning how to avoid an aversive stimulus altogether; avoidance responses, once learned, are very difficult to extinguish. Views on punishment have changed considerably in the past fifty years: early researchers found that punishment did little to reduce behaviors and cited numerous disadvantages of its use. More recently, however, some forms of punishment has been found to be effective in decreasing a variety of inappropriate behaviors, provided that certain guidelines are followed. When aversive stimuli are repeatedly presented without any opportunity to control their occurrence, the phenomenon of learned helplessness often results.

PART THREE

COGNITIVE VIEWS OF LEARNING

C H A P T E R 7

Antecedents and Assumptions of Cognitivism

D URING the past two decades, cognitive psychology has provided the predominant perspective within which learning research has been conducted and theories of learning have evolved. As we begin to explore this perspective, you will probably notice a change in our focus. In contrast to behaviorists, who emphasize the roles of environmental conditions (stimuli) and overt behaviors (responses) in learning, cognitive psychologists look more at how individuals *process* the stimuli they encounter—that is, how individuals perceive, interpret, and mentally store the information they receive from the environment. This focus on *information processing* underlies much of cognitive theory.

Early behaviorists chose not to incorporate mental events into their learning theories, arguing that such events were impossible to observe and measure and so could not be studied objectively. During the 1950s and 1960s, however, many psychologists became increasingly dissatisfied with such a "thoughtless" approach to human learning. Major works with a distinctly cognitive flavor began to emerge; publications by Noam Chomsky (1957) in psycholinguistics and by Bruner, Goodnow, and Austin (1956) in concept learning are examples. Ulric Neisser's *Cognitive Psychology*, published in 1967, was a landmark book that helped to legitimize cognitive theory as a major alternative to behaviorism (Calfee, 1981). Increasingly, cognitivism began appearing in educational psychology literature as well, with Jerome Bruner (e.g., 1961a, 1961b, 1966) and David Ausubel (e.g., Ausubel, 1963, 1968; Ausubel & Robinson, 1969) being two well-known early proponents. By the 1970s, the great majority of learning theorists had joined the cognitive bandwagon.

The roots of cognitive psychology, however, preceded the massive discontentment with strict S-R psychology by several decades. Some cognitive learning theories appeared in the 1920s and 1930s, notably those of the Gestalt psychologists of Germany, the American psychologist Edward Tolman, and the Swiss developmentalist Jean Piaget. These early theories have had considerable influence on contemporary cognitivism, and Piaget's theory in particular continues to provide a dominant perspective for developmental research.

Equally important to the cognitive movement was research conducted during the 1930s to 1960s in an area known as *verbal learning*. Verbal learning theorists originally attempted to apply a stimulus-response analysis to human language and verbal behavior, but soon discovered that the complexities of human language-based learning were sometimes difficult to explain from the behaviorist perspective. Increasingly, verbal learning theorists began to incorporate mental processes into their explanations of research results.

In this chapter, I will describe some of the contributions of the Gestaltists, Tolman, Piaget, and the verbal learning theorists. I will then introduce you to some of the unique assumptions, terminology, and methods of contemporary information processing theory. Finally, I will list some of the more general educational implications of the cognitive perspective.

EARLY COGNITIVE THEORIES

Many of the ideas and assumptions of cognitivism can be traced back to the early decades of the twentieth century, more specifically to the Gestalt psychologists of Germany, Edward Tolman of the United States, and Jean Piaget of Switzerland. Let's therefore look at some of the basic premises of these theorists.

Gestalt Psychology

During the early decades of the twentieth century, a perspective emerged in German psychology that was largely independent of behaviorism-dominated American psychology. This perspective, known as *Gestalt psychology,* was advanced by such theorists as Max Wertheimer (1912, 1945, 1959), Wolfgang Köhler (1925, 1929, 1938, 1940, 1947, 1959, 1969), and Kurt Koffka (1935). Gestalt psychologists emphasized the importance of organizational processes in perception, learning, and problem solving and believed that individuals were predisposed to organize information in particular ways. What follow are some of the most basic ideas of Gestalt psychology.

Perception may be different from reality. The origin of Gestalt psychology is usually attributed to Max Wertheimer's (1912) description and analysis of an optical illusion known as the *phi* phenomenon. Wertheimer observed that when two lights blink on and off sequentially at a particular rate, they often appear to be only one light moving quickly back and forth. (A similar effect can be observed in the blinking lights of many roadside signs.) The fact that an individual "sees" motion when observing stationary objects led Wertheimer to conclude that perception of an experience is sometimes different from the experience itself.

The whole is more than the sum of its parts. Gestaltists believed that human experience cannot be successfully understood when different aspects of experience are studied in isolation from one another. For example, the illusion of movement in the *phi* phenomenon is perceived only when two or more lights are present; no motion is perceived in a single light. A combination of elements may show a pattern not evident in any of the elements alone; to use a Gestaltist expression, the whole is more than the sum of its parts.

The importance of the interrelationships among elements in a situation can be seen in Köhler's (1929) *transposition* experiments with chickens. Hens were shown two sheets of gray paper, with one sheet being a darker shade of gray than the other. Grain was placed on both sheets, but the hens were only allowed to feed from the darker one. At a later time, the hens were shown a sheet of paper the same shade as that on which they had previously been fed, along with a sheet of an even darker shade. In this second situation, the hens tended to go not to the shade on which they had been reinforced earlier, but to the darker of the two sheets. The hens had apparently learned something about the relationship between the two sheets of paper; in a sense, they learned that darker is better.

The organism structures and organizes experience. The German word *gestalt* can be roughly translated to mean "structured whole." Structure is not necessarily inherent in a situation; instead, the organism imposes structure and organization on that situation. For example, the *phi* phenomenon represents a person's synthesis of two flashing lights into the perception of a single moving light.

Figure 7–1 provides another example of how experiences are organized. You probably perceive this figure as four pairs of lines with individual lines at each end. Now, however, look at Figure 7–2, in which the same lines appear within a particular context. You probably now see the same lines differently: as five pairs of lines forming the sides of five rectangles. The lines themselves are identical in both cases, but the way in which you organize them (i.e., which lines you group together) is different. The "structure" of the lines is something that you yourself impose upon the figure.

The organism is predisposed to organize experience in particular ways. Gestaltists believed that organisms are predisposed to structure their experiences in similar, and therefore predictable, ways. For example,

Figure 7–1

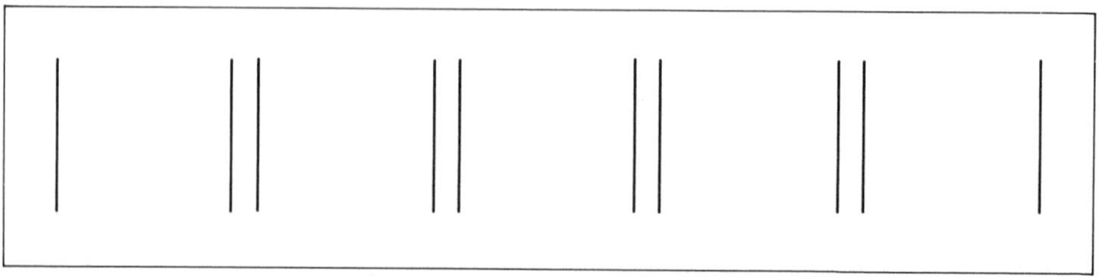

when you look at Figure 7–1, the *law of proximity* dictates that you see lines near each other as pairs. However, in Figure 7–2, the *law of closure* takes over: you complete the incomplete rectangles. Gestalt psychologists proposed a number of principles to describe how people organize their experiences, some of which we will explore in Chapter 9.

Gestaltists further proposed that individuals always organize their experience as simply, concisely, symmetrically, and completely as possible, a principle known as the *law of Prägnanz* ("preciseness"; e.g., Koffka, 1935). For example, you are likely to see rectangles in Figure 7–2 because rectangles are simple, symmetric figures. It is unlikely that you would fill in the missing pieces of that figure in a wild and crazy fashion such as that shown in Figure 7–3. People are very simple folks after all!

Learning follows the law of Prägnanz. According to Gestalt psychologists, learning involves the formation of memory traces. These memory traces are subject to the law of Prägnanz, so that over time they tend to be simpler, more concise, and more complete than the actual input. For example, upon

Figure 7–2

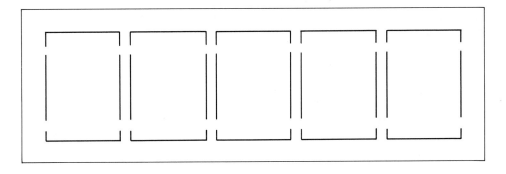

Figure 7–3

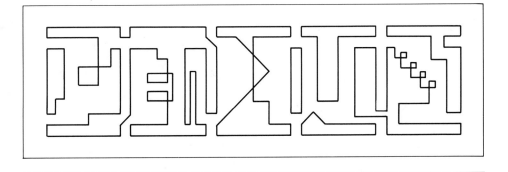

seeing the somewhat irregular objects in Figure 7–4, people are likely later to remember them as being a "circle" and a "square." As another example, consider a study by Tversky (1981), in which people studied maps and then drew them from memory. Distortions in the subjects' reproductions often followed the law of Prägnanz: curvy, irregular lines were straightened, slanted lines were represented as north-south or east-west lines, and map features were placed in better alignment with one another than they had been in the original maps.

Problem solving involves restructuring and insight. The American psychologist Edward Thorndike had previously described problem solving (such as that exhibited by cats in puzzle boxes) as a process of trial and error (Thorndike, 1898). Gestaltists proposed a very different view of how organisms solve problems. Köhler (1925), for instance, suggested that problem solving involves mentally combining and recombining the various elements of a problem until a structure that solves the problem is achieved. He described numerous observations of chimpanzees solving problems through what he perceived to be the mental manipulation of the problem situation. In one situation, a chimpanzee named Sultan was faced with a dilemma: some fruit was placed far enough outside his cage that he could not reach it. Sultan had had earlier experiences in which he had successfully used sticks to rake in fruit; however, the only stick inside the cage was too short. A longer stick was outside the cage, but, like the fruit, it was beyond Sultan's reach. The following scenario ensued:

> Sultan tries to reach the fruit with the smaller of the two sticks. Not succeeding, he tears at a piece of wire that projects from the netting of his cage, but that, too, in vain. Then he gazes about him (there are always in the course of these tests some long pauses during which the animals scrutinize the whole visible area). He suddenly picks up the little stick, once

Figure 7–4

Irregularly shaped objects may later be remembered as "circles" or "squares."

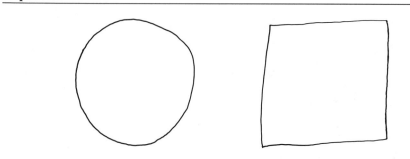

more goes up to the bars, directly opposite to the long stick, scratches it towards him with the [short stick], seizes it, and goes with it to the point opposite the [fruit], which he secures. From the moment that his eyes fall upon the long stick, his procedure forms one consecutive whole, without hiatus . . . (Köhler, 1925, p. 180).

In another situation, Sultan, again confronted with fruit placed outside the cage beyond his reach, had two hollow bamboo rods, one somewhat thinner than the other, and both too short to reach the fruit. After numerous "fruitless" attempts, he seemingly gave up and resorted to playing indifferently with the sticks. At one serendipitous point, Sultan found himself holding the two sticks end to end such that they formed a long, straight line. Immediately, he pushed the end of the thinner stick into the end of the thicker one, thus making a single long stick, ran over to the edge of the cage, and successfully obtained the elusive bananas.

In neither of the situations I have just presented did Sultan engage in the random trial-and-error learning that Thorndike had observed for cats. Instead, it appeared to Köhler as if Sultan thought about possible solutions to the problem, arranging the problem elements in various ways, until he arrived at a sudden insight as to a problem solution.

Gestalt psychology continues to have an impact on how cognitive psychologists conceptualize learning and cognition (e.g., Henle, 1985). In Chapter 9, we will examine several Gestaltist laws of perception that have been incorporated into contemporary views of perception and attention. In Chapters 11 and 12, we will look at the very critical role that organization plays in learning and memory and at some of the processes that determine just how individuals organize their experiences. Now, however, let's turn to an early American psychologist who was also influenced by the Gestalt theorists: Edward Tolman.

Edward Tolman's Purposive Behaviorism

Edward Chace Tolman (e.g., 1932, 1938, 1942, 1959) was a prominent learning theorist during the heyday of behaviorism, yet his work had a distinctly cognitive flair. Like his behaviorist contemporaries, Tolman valued the importance of objectivity in conducting research and used non-human species, especially rats, as the subjects of his research. Unlike his contemporaries, however, Tolman included internal mental phenomena in his perspective of how learning occurs and adopted a more holistic view of learning than was true of S-R theorists.

Among Tolman's contributions to contemporary cognitive theories of learning were the following ideas.

Behavior should be studied at a molar level. Whereas early theorists in the behaviorist tradition, such as Pavlov, Thorndike, and Watson, attempted to reduce behavior to simple stimulus-response connections, Tolman was adamant in his position that more global (molar) behaviors are the appropriate objects of study. Tolman argued that by breaking behavior down into isolated S-R reflexes rather than looking at it in its totality, the meaning and purpose of that behavior are lost. In this respect Tolman's view was similar to the "structured whole" view of the Gestaltists.

Learning can occur without reinforcement.   Tolman opposed the behaviorist idea that reinforcement is a necessary element in learning and conducted several experiments to support his contention. As an example, let's look at a study by Tolman and Honzik (1930) in which three groups of rats ran a difficult maze under different reinforcement conditions. Group 1 was reinforced with food for successful completion of the maze. Group 2 received no reinforcement for successful performance. Group 3 was not reinforced during the first ten days in the maze, but began receiving reinforcement on the eleventh day.

Before we examine the results of this experiment, let's make some predictions as to what should have happened in this situation if reinforcement were a necessary component of the learning process. Because Group 1 rats were continuously reinforced, we would expect their performance to increase. Because Group 2 rats were *not* reinforced, we would expect their performance to stay at a constant low level. And we would expect the rats in Group 3 to show no improvement in performance until after day 11, at which point they should show a pattern of behavior similar to Group 1 rats' first few days of performance.

The actual results of the Tolman and Honzik experiment are shown in Figure 7–5. Notice that the performance of Groups 2 and 3 improved somewhat even when they were not receiving reinforcement. Notice also that once the rats in Group 3 began receiving reinforcement, their performance in the maze equaled (in fact, it surpassed!) Group 1's performance. Apparently, Group 3 rats had learned as much as Group 1 rats despite their lack of reinforcement during the first ten days. Results such as these cast doubt on Thorndike's law of effect: perhaps reinforcement is not as critical a factor in learning as behaviorists have suggested.

Learning can occur without a change in performance.   Although behaviorists equated learning with behavior changes, Tolman argued that learning can occur without being evidenced in a change in performance, using the term *latent learning* for such unobservable learning. The Tolman and Honzik study just described provides an example of latent learning: Group 3 rats must have been learning just as much as Group 1 rats during the first ten days, even though their behavior did not reflect such learning. (Presumably, Group 2 rats were also learning more than they let on.) Tolman proposed that reinforcement influences *performance* rather than learning, in that it increases the likelihood that a learned behavior will be exhibited.

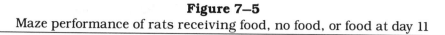

Figure 7–5

Maze performance of rats receiving food, no food, or food at day 11

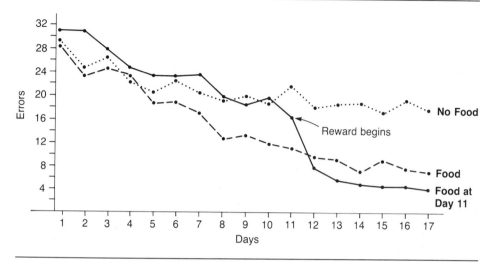

(Adapted from "Introduction and Removal of Reward, and Maze Performance in Rats" by E. C. Tolman and C. H. Honzik, 1930, *University of California Publications in Psychology, 4,* p. 267. Copyright 1930 by University of California Press. Adapted with permission.)

Intervening variables must be considered. As you may recall from Chapter 2, Clark Hull incorporated *intervening variables* into his theory of learning, arguing that variables such as drive, habit strength, and incentive play a critical role. The concept of intervening variables did not originate with Hull, however; as early as 1932, Tolman proposed that variables within the organism (e.g., cognitions and physiological states) have an effect on the behaviors observed. Thus, with Tolman's work, we have an early concern for *individual differences* in the learning process, a concern that continues in contemporary cognitivism.

Behavior is purposive. Tolman believed that learning should be viewed not as the formation of S-R connections but as a process of learning that certain events lead to other events (for example, that running a maze in a particular way leads to reinforcement). He proposed that once an organism has learned that a behavior produces a certain goal, the organism behaves to achieve that goal. In other words, behavior has a *purpose,* that of goal attainment. Because of this notion of goal-directed behavior, Tolman's view of learning is often referred to as *purposive behaviorism.*

Expectations affect behavior. According to Tolman, once an organism learns that particular behaviors produce particular results, it begins to form expectations about the outcomes of its behaviors. Rather than reinforcement affecting the response it follows, the organism's *expectation* of reinforcement affects the response it *precedes*.

When an organism's expectations are not met, its behavior may be adversely affected. For example, in an experiment by Elliott (cited in Tolman, 1932), rats received one of two different reinforcers for running a maze: an experimental group received a favorite rat delicacy—bran mash—while a control group received relatively unenticing sunflower seeds. The experimental group ran the maze faster than the control group, apparently because they were expecting a yummier treat at the end of the maze. On the tenth day, these rats were switched to the sunflower seed reinforcement that the control group rats had been getting all along. After discovering the change in reinforcement, these experimental group rats began to move through the maze more slowly than they had previously, and even more slowly than the control rats. Because both groups were being reinforced identically at this point (i.e., with boring sunflower seeds), the inferior performance of the rats in the experimental group was apparently due to the change in reinforcement, resulting in a depression effect similar to what I described in Chapter 4. As Tolman might put it, the rats' expectation of reinforcement was no longer being confirmed. As you or I might say, the rats were very disappointed with the treat awaiting them.

Learning results in an organized body of information. Through a series of studies, Tolman showed that rats who run a maze learn more than just a set of independent responses. It appears that they also learn how the maze is arranged—the lay of the land, so to speak. For example, in a classic study by Tolman, Ritchie, and Kalish (1946), rats ran numerous times through a maze that looked like Maze 1 of Figure 7–6. They were then put in a situation similar to Maze 2 of Figure 7–6. Since the alley that had previously led to food was now blocked, the rats had to choose among eighteen other alleys. Using S-R theory's notion of stimulus generalization, we would expect the rats to make their running response to a stimulus very similar to the blocked alley. We would therefore predict that the rats would choose alleys near the blocked one—particularly Alley 9 or Alley 10. However, few of the rats chose either of these routes. By far the most common choice was Alley 6, the one that presumably would provide a shortcut to the location in which the rats had come to expect food.

Based on such research, Tolman postulated that rats, and other organisms as well, develop *cognitive maps* of their environments: they learn where different parts of the environment are situated in relation to one another. Knowing how things are organized in space enables an organism to get from one place to another, often by the shortest possible route. The concept of cognitive map (sometimes called a mental map) continues to be a focus of research for contemporary researchers, psychologists and geographers alike (e.g., Downs & Stea, 1977).

Figure 7–6
Mazes used by Tolman, Ritchie, and Kalish (1946)

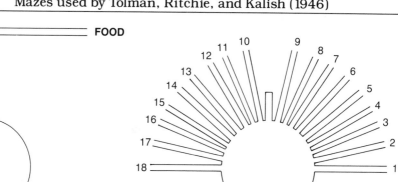

Tolman's notion of a cognitive map reflects his idea that learning is *organized:* rats integrate their experiences into an organized body of information from which they can then draw inferences (e.g., about shortest routes). We encountered this concept of organization in Gestalt psychology and will see it again in our discussions of Piaget's theory and verbal learning research.

Tolman developed his mentalistic view of learning through some rather ingenious adaptations of traditional behaviorist research methods. At about the same time, a Swiss developmentalist was using research methods radically different from those of American psychologists. It is to this theorist, Jean Piaget, that we turn now.

Jean Piaget's Developmental Theory

Independent of the Gestalt movement in Germany and of Tolman's work in the United States, the Swiss biologist Jean Piaget began a research program during the 1920s that has probably had greater impact on contemporary theories of cognitive development than that of any other single researcher. Piaget had interests in philosophy as well as biology and was particularly curious about the origins of knowledge, a branch of philosophy known as epistemology. To discover where knowledge comes from and the forms it takes as it develops, Piaget and his colleagues undertook at their Geneva laboratory a series of studies that have provided some unique insights into how children think and learn about the world around them (e.g., Inhelder & Piaget, 1958; Piaget, 1928, 1952, 1959, 1970, 1971, 1972, 1980; Piaget & Inhelder, 1969).

Although Piaget's theory dates from the 1920s, its impact on mainstream psychological thought was not widely felt until the 1960s, probably for several reasons. One likely reason is that Piaget, being Swiss, wrote in French, making his early work less accessible to English-speaking psychologists. Although his writings were eventually translated into English, Piaget's ideas gained widespread prominence and visibility largely through a summary of his early work written by the American psychologist John Flavell (1963).

A second reason that the Geneva research program was largely overlooked for more than three decades was Piaget's unconventional research methodology. Piaget employed what he called the *clinical method:* human subjects, usually children, were presented with a variety of stimulus situations and asked questions about them. Interviews were tailored to the particular responses that children gave, with follow-up questions varying from one child to the next. Such a procedure was radically different from the standardized and tightly controlled conditions typical of behaviorist animal research and was therefore unacceptable to many of Piaget's contemporaries.

But perhaps the most critical reason that Piaget's theory was so long in being introduced into the mainstream of psychological thought was that it was incompatible with the behaviorist perspective that dominated the field until the 1960s. Piaget focused on mental events—for example, on logical reasoning processes and the structure of knowledge—at a time when such mentalism was still being rejected by most other learning theorists. The cognitivism that began to emerge in the 1960s was more receptive to Piagetian ideas.

The recent popularity of Piaget's work may well be due to its currently being the single most global theory of intellectual development; it incorporates such diverse topics as language, logical reasoning, moral judgments, and conceptions of time, space, and number. In addition, Piaget's unique studies with children, often involving some clever problem situations, can be very revealing about the nature of children's thought. We will now look at some of Piaget's ideas most relevant to our understanding of human learning and cognition.

People are active processors of information. Whereas behaviorists portrayed organisms, including humans, as passive respondents to environmental conditions, Piaget portrayed human beings as being *actively involved* in the learning and interpretation of events around them. Rather than just responding to stimuli, people act on those stimuli and observe the effects of their actions. For example, consider Piaget's observation of his son Laurent at sixteen months of age:

> Laurent is seated before a table and I place a bread crust in front of him, out of reach. Also, to the right of the child I place a stick about 25 cm. long. At first Laurent tries to grasp the bread without paying attention to the instrument, and then he gives up. I then put the stick between him and the bread. . . . Laurent again looks at the bread, without moving, looks very briefly at the stick, then suddenly grasps it and directs it toward the bread. But he grasped it toward the middle and not at one of its ends so that it is too short to attain the objective. Laurent then puts it down and resumes stretching out his hand toward the bread. Then, without spending much time on this movement, he takes up the stick again, this time at one of its ends . . . and draws the bread to him.
>
> An hour later I place a toy in front of Laurent (out of his reach) and a new stick next to him. He does not even try to catch the objective with his hand; he immediately grasps the stick and draws the toy to him (Piaget, 1952, p. 335).

In this situation, Laurent is acting on his environment; he is obviously experimenting with the elements of the situation to see what outcomes he can achieve. (You may have noticed a similarity between Laurent's behavior and that of the chimpanzee Sultan that I described earlier in the chapter. Sultan, too, was an active problem solver rather than a passive respondent to environmental events.)

Knowledge can be described in terms of structures that change with development. Piaget proposed the concept of *schema* (the plural form is *schemata*) as the basic structure through which an individual's knowledge is mentally represented. Although Piaget's notion of schema is somewhat abstract, it can be roughly defined as a mental unit that represents a class of similar actions or thoughts. For example, an infant might have a schema for grasping and use it for grabbing everything from bottles to rubber ducks. A teenager is likely to have certain schemata of logic that may be applied to mathematical problems or to opinions about what is wrong with a certain system of government. As children develop, new schemata emerge, and existing schemata are modified and sometimes integrated with one another into *cognitive structures*. A good deal of Piaget's theory focuses on the development of the cognitive structures that govern logical reasoning, structures that Piaget calls *operations*.

Cognitive development results from the interactions of individuals with their physical and social environments. By interacting with the environment, individuals develop and shape schemata. In Piaget's example cited earlier, Laurent actively manipulated his physical environment—the stick and bread—and presumably learned that some objects can be used as tools to obtain other objects. Equally essential to children's development is their interaction with other people. For example, Piaget described young children as being *egocentric*—as having difficulty understanding that others don't share their perspective of the world. Through social interactions, both positive (e.g., conversations) and negative (e.g., conflicts over such issues as sharing and fair play), children begin to realize that they hold a perspective of the world uniquely their own.

The ways in which people interact with the environment remain constant. According to Piaget, people interact with their environment through two unchanging processes (functions) known as assimilation and accommodation. *Assimilation* is a process whereby an individual interacts with an object or event in a way that is consistent with an existing schema. For example, the infant who sees Mama's flashy, dangling earrings may assimilate those earrings to his grasping schema, clutching and pulling at them in much the same way that he grasps bottles. A second grader who has developed a schema for adding two apples and three apples to make five apples may apply this schema to the addition of two dollars and three more dollars. *Accommodation* is a process whereby an individual modifies an existing schema to account for a new event. For example, an infant who has learned to crawl must adjust her style of crawling somewhat when she meets a flight of stairs. A girl who calls a spider an insect must revise her thinking when she learns that insects have six legs but spiders have eight.

Assimilation and accommodation are complementary processes: assimilation involves modifying one's perception of the environment to fit a schema; accommodation involves modifying a schema to fit the environment. According to Piaget, these two processes typically go hand in hand, with individuals interpreting new events within the context of their existing knowledge (assimilation) but also modifying their knowledge as a result of those events (accommodation).

Learning results from the conjoint processes of assimilation and accommodation. Strictly speaking, learning itself is reflected in the process of accommodation, because it is through accommodation that cognitive changes occur. However, an environmental event cannot lead to accommodation of schemata unless that event can be related (assimilated) to those schemata in the first place. For example, consider this sentence:

> D. O. Hebb has proposed that learning is a process of developing cell assemblies and phase sequences.

Unless you know who D. O. Hebb is, and unless you are familiar with the concepts of cell assembly and phase sequence, you can learn very little from the sentence. Assimilation is almost always a necessary condition for accommodation to occur: you must be able to relate a new experience to what you already know before you can learn from it. This necessity for overlap between what you already know and the material to be learned is an important principle not only in Piagetian theory but in contemporary cognitive theory as well.

Cognitive development occurs in distinct stages, with the thought proc-esses at each stage being qualitatively different from those at other stages. A major feature of Piagetian theory is the identification of four distinct stages of cognitive development, each with its own unique patterns of thought. The schemata of each stage are modified and incorporated into the schemata of the following stage, thereby providing a foundation for that next stage. Accordingly, children progress through the four stages in the same, invariant sequence. The characteristics of Piaget's four stages are more completely described in other secondary sources (e.g., Flavell, 1963; Sund, 1976; Wadsworth, 1984), but I will discuss them briefly here.

The first stage, the *sensorimotor* stage, is evident from birth until about two years of age (the exact ages of each stage vary from child to child). This stage is characterized by behavior-based and perception-based schemata rather than by "thought" schemata. According to Piaget, sensorimotor chil-dren do not yet possess schemata that enable them to think about objects other than those directly in front of them. For the sensorimotor child, then, "out of sight, out of mind" definitely applies.

The second stage, *preoperations,* emerges when children are about two years old and continues until they are about six or seven. The appearance of language at this stage and of the ability to think about objects and events in their absence involves the development of internal, mental schemata representative of external events. According to Piaget, true "thought" first occurs at the preoperational stage. However, preoperational thought is char-acterized by a variety of illogical idiosyncrasies. For example, the child tends to confuse psychological phenomena with physical reality, a confusion man-ifested by such actions as attributing feelings to inanimate objects and believing that monsters and bogeymen are lurking under the bed.

A commonly used example of the illogical thinking of preoperational children is their reaction to a *conservation of liquid* problem. Imagine three glasses: Glasses A and B are tall, thin, and filled to equal heights with water, while Glass C is short, fat, and empty, as is shown in Figure 7–7.

Clearly, Glasses A and B contain the same amount of water. Now the contents of Glass B are poured into Glass C, thereby creating the situation shown in Figure 7–8.

Do Glass A and Glass C contain the same amount of water, or does one contain more?

Being logical, you would probably conclude that the two glasses hold identical amounts of water (excluding a drop or two that might have been lost in the process of pouring). The preoperational child, however, is likely to say that the glasses hold different amounts of water: most will say that Glass A has more because it is taller, although a few will say that Glass C

Figure 7—7

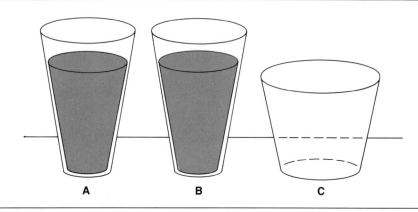

Figure 7—8

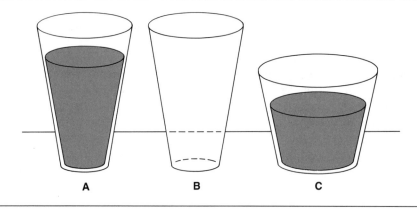

has more because it is fatter. The child's thinking tends to be ruled more by perception than logic during the preoperational stage and is therefore susceptible to outward appearances: the glasses *look* different so must *be* different.

Piaget's third stage of cognitive development, *concrete operations,* appears when children are about six or seven years old and continues until they are at least eleven or twelve. Children at this stage begin to think logically about conservation problems and other situations as well. However, concrete operational children are limited in one important respect: they can apply their logical operations only to concrete, observable objects and events. They have difficulty dealing with abstract information and with hypothetical ideas contrary to their own reality. For example, the concrete operational child should readily agree with the logic that

If all first graders are children,

And if all children are people,

Then all first graders are people

yet has trouble recognizing the logical validity of a similar problem that includes a contrary-to-fact premise:

If all first graders are children,

And if all children are hippopotamuses,

Then all first graders are hippopotamuses.

Concrete operational children, although generally very logical, cannot readily distinguish between logic and reality, and, after all, first graders are *not* hippopotamuses!

The fourth and final stage, *formal operations*, rarely appears before children are eleven or twelve and continues to evolve for at least several years after that. During formal operations, a child develops the ability to reason with abstract, hypothetical, and contrary-to-fact information. Other abilities essential to mathematical and scientific reasoning emerge as well. For example, proportional thinking develops, through which the child truly begins to understand the concept of *proportion*, as reflected in such mathematical entities as fractions and decimals. The child also begins to separate and control variables: in testing a hypothesis about which factor among many may bring about a particular result, the child tests one variable at a time while holding all others constant. In addition, with the onset of formal operations children are able to think about their own thought processes and to evaluate the quality and logic of those thoughts; for example, a child may notice a logical fallacy in something he or she has said.

I should point out here that recent research, while frequently confirming Piaget's assertions regarding characteristics of the different stages, does not support Piaget's proposed stage characteristics in their entirety (e.g., see Bee, 1985; Levin, 1983). For example, infants and young children apparently are cognitively more sophisticated than Piaget's descriptions of the sensorimotor and preoperational stages would indicate (Siegler, 1986). At the same time, Piaget may have overestimated the capabilities of adolescents and even adults (Siegler, 1986). For instance, many adults (including many college students) show behavior more characteristic of concrete operations than of formal operational thought (Sund, 1976).

The rate of cognitive development is controlled to some extent by maturation. One unique aspect of Piaget's theory is his assertion that children's progression through the four stages is limited by maturation, i.e., by genetically controlled physiological changes. Piaget contended that a necessary prerequisite for the transition to each successive stage is the occurrence of certain neurological changes that allow more sophisticated cognitive structures to develop. Because of physiological limitations, it would be virtually impossible for a two-year-old child to think logically like a concrete operations child, or for a seven-year-old to deal successfully with abstract ideas. In support of Piaget's proposal, research by Epstein (1978) and Hudspeth (1985) indicates that significant neurological changes do occur at the typical transition ages for progression from one of Piaget's cognitive stages to the next.

Many of Piaget's ideas are evident in contemporary cognitivism. The current notion that knowledge is structured and organized can be seen in Piaget's work as well as in that of Tolman and the Gestaltists. Also an important component of contemporary theories is Piaget's proposal that for learning to occur, an individual must be able to assimilate new information into existing cognitive structures—that is, there must be overlap between a new experience and prior knowledge. Finally, Piaget's notion of four qualitatively different stages of cognitive development, each influenced by physiological maturation and interaction with the environment and characterized by qualitatively different forms of thought, has provided the impetus for many studies of the development of cognition. Although not all of Piaget's ideas have been validated by research, his theory continues to be a dominant force in both the thinking and methodology of cognitive psychology.

Piaget's research program had a cognitivist flavor from its inception. Research by certain other theorists of his time, however, emerged from a behaviorist perspective and only gradually began to incorporate cognitivist ideas. Let's turn now to the work of these verbal learning theorists, psychologists who helped pave the way for a wider acceptance of cognitive views of learning.

Verbal Learning Research: A Transition from Behaviorism to Cognitivism

A logical outgrowth of the behaviorist movement was an extension of behaviorist principles to a uniquely human behavior: language. Verbal learning researchers, whose work peaked during the middle of the century (1930s through 1960s), began to study verbal behavior and the learning of verbal materials by applying an S-R approach to these phenomena.

Central to verbal learning research were two learning tasks, serial learning and paired associate learning, that were easily explained from an S-R perspective. *Serial learning* involves learning a sequence of items in their correct order; the alphabet, the days of the week, and the Pledge of Allegiance are all examples. Verbal learning theorists explained serial learning in this way: the first item in the list is a stimulus to which the second item is learned as a response, the second item then serves as a stimulus to which the third item is the learned response, and so on.

Paired associate learning involves learning pairs of items. Learning foreign language vocabulary words and their English equivalents (e.g., *le papier* is French for "paper") and learning state capitals (e.g., Denver is the capital of Colorado) are two examples. Verbal learning theorists described paired associates as being distinct stimulus-response associations: the first item in each pair is the stimulus and the second item is the response.

Increasingly, verbal learning studies yielded results that could not be easily explained in terms of S-R connections, and theorists began to introduce a variety of mental phenomena into their discussions of learning processes. In this section, I will describe some of the general learning principles that emerged from verbal learning research. Some of the findings are relatively easy to explain from a behaviorist perspective; others are not so easily explained.

Serial learning is characterized by a particular pattern. In a serial learning task, a *serial learning curve* is usually observed: people learn the first few items and last few items more quickly and easily than they learn the middle items (Hall, 1971; McCrary & Hunter, 1953; Roediger & Crowder, 1976). If we were to graph the speed with which the various items in a serial list are learned, we might obtain results similar to what you see in Figure 7–9. An example of the serial learning curve is the way in which most children learn the alphabet: they learn the first letters (A, B, C, D) and the last letters (X, Y, Z) before they learn the middle letters (e.g., H, I, J, K).

The fact that the first items in a serial learning curve are usually learned quickly is called the *primacy effect.* The fact that the last items are also learned quickly is called the *recency effect.* Verbal learning theorists explained both effects by proposing that the end points of the list (i.e., the first and last items) served as *anchors* to which the other items would then be attached in a stimulus-response fashion.

Overlearned material is more easily recalled at a later time. What happens when you learn information perfectly and then continue to study it?

Figure 7–9
A typical serial learning curve

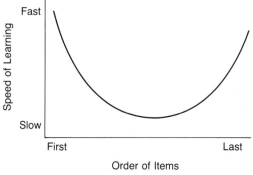

Speed of Learning

Fast

Slow

First   Last

Order of Items

This process of *overlearning*, in which you learn material perfectly and then practice the material for additional study trials, enables you to remember the information much more accurately at a later time (e.g., Krueger, 1929; Underwood, 1954). For example, Krueger (1929) found that overlearning of a list of words enhanced recall for up to a month after the learning session. As you may recall from Chapter 2, early behaviorists also emphasized the importance of practice.

Distributed practice is usually more effective than massed practice. Imagine that you have to study for a test. You estimate that you need six hours to master the test material. Would you do better on the test if you studied for six hours all at once or if you broke your study time into smaller chunks of time—say, six one-hour sessions? Research (e.g., Glenberg, 1976; Underwood, 1961; Underwood, Kapelak, & Malmi, 1976) has indicated that *distributed practice,* in which study time is spread out over several occasions, usually leads to better learning than *massed practice,* in which study time occurs all at one time. Thus, studying for a test over several short study sessions is more likely to be effective than one long cram session.

Learning in one situation often affects learning and recall in another situation. Imagine yourself having to learn two sets of paired-associates. The first one looks like this:

Set 1

house—dragon
plant—sled
lamp—music
onion—pillow

The second set looks like this:

Set 2

house—paper
plant—clock
lamp—turkey
onion—chair

After you have first learned Set 1 and then learned Set 2, you are asked to remember the responses to each of the stimulus words in Set 1. Will you have difficulty? You probably will, because you learned different responses to those same words when you learned Set 2. You would have an easier time remembering the correct responses you learned in Set 1 if you had not had to learn the Set 2 responses as well.

Verbal learning theorists observed that when individuals learn two sets of paired associates in succession, their learning of the second set often diminishes their ability to recall the first set (Hall, 1971), a phenomenon known as *retroactive inhibition*. They further observed that individuals in this situation often have difficulty remembering the second set as well as the first (Hall, 1971), a phenomenon known as *proactive inhibition*. This tendency for a set of paired associates learned at one time to interfere with the recall of a set learned either earlier or later is particularly likely to occur when the two sets have the same or similar stimulus words but different response words (Osgood, 1949).

Under different circumstances, learning one set of information may actually improve the recall of information learned at another time, a phenomenon referred to by verbal learning theorists as *retroactive facilitation* or *proactive facilitation*, depending on the order in which the two sets of information are learned (Hall, 1971). Facilitation is most likely to occur when two situations have similar or identical stimuli and similar responses as well (Osgood, 1949).

Verbal learning theorists (e.g., McGeoch, 1942; Melton & Irwin, 1940; Underwood, 1948) proposed that retroactive and proactive inhibition were major factors in forgetting verbal information; verbal learning theorists were therefore among the first to propose theories of memory. Although their explanations were based primarily on stimulus-response analyses, inhibition is still considered by many cognitive psychologists to play a role in memory and forgetting.

Characteristics of the material affect the speed with which the material can be learned. Verbal learning researchers discovered a number of characteristics that affect the ease of learning verbal material. Let's look at some of them.

Items are more easily learned when they are *meaningful*, that is, when they can be easily associated with other ideas (e.g., Cofer, 1971; Paivio, 1971). This principle was discovered very early by the German psychologist Hermann Ebbinghaus (1913). Ebbinghaus, who served as his own subject for a number of experiments in serial learning, observed that the associations he could make with words helped him to learn those words. He attempted to eliminate the influence of associations by using presumably meaningless nonsense syllables ("words" like JAD, MON, and ZIV). However, even many nonsense syllables have meaningfulness and evoke associations, thus making them relatively easy to learn (Hall, 1971). For example, the nonsense syllable JAD might make one think of "jade," and the syllable MON might remind one of "money."

Items are easier to learn when they are *pronounceable* (e.g., DiVesta & Ingersoll, 1969; Underwood & Schulz, 1960). For example, the nonsense syllable DNK should be learned faster than BPX because most people can pronounce it more easily.

Concrete items are easier to learn than abstract items (Gorman, 1961; Paivio, 1963); for example, items such as these:

turtle, hammer, sandwich

Some items are more meaningful than others.

are learned faster than items such as these:

truth, joy, experience

One probable reason that the concreteness of items makes them easier to learn is that concrete items can be more easily visualized. The extent to which visual images of items can be formed appears to influence the ease with which those items can be learned (Paivio, 1971). For example, it is easier to form a mental image of a turtle than it is to form an image of truth. Notice how, in discussing visual imagery, verbal learning theorists were beginning to talk about mental events. This phenomenon of visual imagery is particularly difficult to explain from an S-R perspective.

People often impose meaning when learning new information. The effect of meaningfulness on learning can be explained from an S-R perspective: when a stimulus word has many other words associated with it, one of those associations may in turn be associated with the response to be learned. What is more troublesome for an S-R approach is the fact that people will go out of their way to *make* information meaningful when they are trying to learn it. For example, when Bugelski (1962) asked subjects to learn paired associates involving nonsense syllables, subjects invariably reported that they imposed meanings to help them learn the pairs. To illustrate, when given this pair:

DUP—TEZ

one subject used the word *deputize* to help form the connection. Cognitive theories have emerged that probably explain this tendency for human beings to search for meaning better than a behaviorist approach can.

People organize what they learn. When people are allowed to recall items of a serial learning task in any order (a task known as *free recall*), they typically do *not* recall those items in their original presentation order. Instead, the order in which they recall items often reflects an organizational scheme of some kind (e.g., Bousfield, 1953; Jenkins & Russell, 1952). In a classic experiment by Bousfield (1953), college students were given a list of sixty words, fifteen from each of four categories: animals, names, vegetables, and professions. Although the words were presented in a random order, subjects tended to recall them in category clusters. For example, a typical recall order might have been something like this:

camel, giraffe, zebra, donkey, Jason, Adam, Howard, pumpkin, cabbage, carrot, lettuce, radish, milkman, baker, dentist

People even try to organize seemingly unorganized material (Tulving, 1962). This tendency people have to insist on organizing the information they learn is difficult to explain from behaviorist principles. However, as you will see in later chapters, it lends itself quite easily to an explanation based on cognitive learning theories.

People often use coding strategies to help them learn. People often change, or *code*, information in some way so that it is easier for them to learn (e.g., Bugelski, 1962; Dallett, 1964; Underwood & Erlebacher, 1965). Furthermore, when experimenters specifically tell subjects to use a certain coding strategy to help them learn information, learning is typically facilitated (Bugelski, Kidd, & Segmen, 1968; Hall, 1971). For example, when subjects are instructed in techniques for using visual imagery, they are able to remember a list of words more accurately than subjects not given such instructions (Bugelski et al., 1968).

People are more likely to learn general ideas than to learn words verbatim. In fact, when people focus on learning ideas rather than on learning information word for word, their learning is faster and their recall more accurate (Briggs & Reed, 1943; English, Welborn, & Killian, 1934; Jones & English, 1926). Verbal learning research focused on the learning of verbatim information. In doing so, it may very well have ignored the way in which human beings actually learn most verbal materials.

Clearly, verbal learning research provided us with a number of useful learning principles. It also provided us with two learning tasks, serial and paired associate learning, that continue to be used in learning research. At the same time, in trying to stretch S-R models of learning to explain human verbal behavior, it began to demonstrate some weaknesses of the behaviorist perspective. In more recent years, the focus of verbal learning research has been on how people learn meaningful verbal materials (e.g., prose passages) rather than artificially constructed serial lists or paired associates. In fact, the term *verbal learning* has been largely abandoned (for example, the *Journal of Verbal Learning and Verbal Behavior* became the *Journal of Memory and Language* in 1985) as verbal learning researchers have begun to embrace cognitivist ideas.

INTRODUCTION TO HUMAN INFORMATION PROCESSING THEORY

We have just seen how, even during the heyday of behaviorism, the work of the Gestalt psychologists, Edward Tolman, Jean Piaget, and verbal learning researchers was laying a foundation for cognitive learning theories. During the 1960s, discontent with the inadequacies of behaviorism became more widespread. The behaviorist perspective could not easily explain why people attempt to organize and make sense of the information they learn or why people often alter the form of information they learn—for example, remembering general meanings rather than verbatim input. Among learning psychologists there emerged a growing realization that mental events—cognition—could no longer be ignored (e.g., see Kendler, 1985).

The predominant approach to the study of human learning at present, as reflected in ongoing research and journal space, is a group of theories known collectively as *human information processing* (HIP). This approach encompasses a dynamic, rapidly changing view of how people acquire, process, and remember information; theories are revised so quickly that describing HIP has often been likened to taking a snapshot of a speeding locomotive. Different aspects of information processing theory will be described in more detail in later chapters, but let me introduce some of its assumptions, terminology, and unique research methods here.

Assumptions of Human Information Processing

The assumptions underlying contemporary information processing theories are radically different from those underlying behaviorism. What follow are some of the central assumptions of HIP.

Some learning processes may be unique to human beings. Because people possess some abilities unique to the species (complex language is an example), the processes involved in learning may be different in human beings from in other animals. Accordingly, almost all information processing research is conducted with human subjects, and theories formulated from this research are typically not generalized to other species.

Mental events are the focus of study. Mental events are centrally involved in human learning and must therefore be incorporated into theories of learning processes. To the extent that individuals think about the same situation differently, they will learn different information from that situation.

The study of human learning must be objective and scientific. Like behaviorists, HIP theorists underscore the importance of objective research. Unlike behaviorists, however, HIP theorists believe that mental events can be inferred from carefully designed experiments. Later in the chapter, I will describe some examples of how research involving observable behaviors can lead to inferences about nonobservable mental events.

Individuals are actively involved in the learning process. Rather than being merely passive victims of environmental conditions, people are active participants in the learning process, and in fact *control* their own learning. Individuals themselves determine how they mentally process the information they receive, and these cognitive processes in turn determine what, if anything, is learned in a given situation.

Learning involves the formation of mental associations that are not necessarily reflected in overt behavior changes. This assumption is essentially the same as Tolman's belief in latent learning. According to contemporary cognitive psychologists, learning involves an internal, mental change, but not necessarily the external behavior change that many behaviorists propose. Learning can therefore occur without being reflected in an individual's observed performance. (Of course, there is no way for others to know that learning has taken place until there *is* a behavior change of some sort.)

Knowledge is organized. An individual's knowledge, beliefs, attitudes, and emotions are not isolated from one another but are in fact all associated and interconnected. This emphasis on organization is one that we saw in all the early cognitivists—the Gestaltists, Tolman, and Piaget—as well.

Learning is a process of relating new information to previously learned information. Similar to Piaget's assertion that accommodation almost always involves assimilation, information processing theorists believe that learning is most likely to occur when individuals can relate a new experience to the information they have acquired from earlier experiences.

The Terminology of Human Information Processing

Information processing theory is characterized by its own unique terminology. Let's look briefly at some of the terms we will encounter frequently in the chapters that follow:

Cognitive Process. The term *cognitive process* refers to any internal mental event and includes such phenomena as perceiving, paying attention, interpreting, understanding, and remembering. True to its name, the information processing perspective emphasizes the importance of cognitive processes in human learning.

Learning vs. Memory. Up to this point, we have not really separated learning and memory, but information processing theorists do draw a distinction between these two terms. *Learning* is viewed, quite simply, as the acquisition of new information. *Memory,* on the other hand, is related to the ability to recall information that has been previously learned. In some instances, the word *memory* is used to refer to the process of retaining information. In other instances, it is used to refer to the "location" where learned information is placed; for example, we will be talking about short-term memory and long-term memory. The distinction between learning and memory is an important one; for a number of reasons that you will discover in later chapters, not everything that is learned is necessarily remembered.

Storage. Storage is the process by which new information is placed in memory. For example, if you can put this fact in your head:

Jeanne Ormrod's birthday is August 22nd.

then you are storing the information. We will be talking at great length about the processes that people use to store information in memory.

Retrieval. Retrieval is the process by which people "find" the information they have previously stored so that they can use it again. For example, I am hoping that, come mid-August, you will retrieve the date of my birthday and send me a tasteful card. Due to the fact that I will get cards from some of my readers and not from others, we can assume that retrieval is very easy in some cases and very difficult in others. (In still other cases, of course, we may assume that information retrieval is simply not resulting in a behavior change.)

Encoding. Encoding, the process by which information is modified before it is stored, often helps people store information more easily. Encoding sometimes involves changing information from one form into another. For example, I once had a combination lock for which the first two numbers of the combination were 22 and 8. I quickly learned these two numbers by encoding them as "the day and month of my birthday." In this case, I encoded numerical information into a verbal form. Encoding may also involve adding new information to the information presented, a process known as *elaboration*. For example, consider this information:

Jeanne Ormrod was born in Providence, Rhode Island.

Upon reading this, you might add some additional information to it, perhaps that I am a native New Englander or that I am a United States citizen, inferences that you might store along with the original information. Yet another encoding process is one of simplifying input, for example, by remembering the overall meaning, or gist, of a situation rather than the specific details of what happened (you might remember only that a certain textbook author talked about her birth).

Inference-drawing in HIP Research

Cognitive psychologists share with behaviorists the beliefs that the study of learning must be objective and that learning theories should be developed from the results of empirical research. However, cognitivists differ from behaviorists in one critical respect: by observing the responses that individuals make to different stimulus conditions, they believe that they can draw inferences about the nature of the internal cognitive processes that produce those responses. In fact, researchers have become increasingly ingenious in designing research that enables them to draw conclusions about specific cognitive processes. We will be seeing many instances of such inference-drawing in upcoming chapters, but let me describe a couple of examples here.

A simple example is provided in a classic experiment conducted by Peterson and Peterson (1959). In this experiment, adults were given three consonants (e.g., DXP), then immediately asked to count backward by threes from a certain three-digit number. Under these circumstances, subjects had great difficulty remembering the three consonants for more than a few seconds. Apparently, they needed to *process* those consonants to remember them, and their processing was prevented by the counting-backward task.

Another example of inference-drawing in cognitive research can be seen in a study by Bransford and Franks (1971). In this experiment, undergraduate students listened to a set of twenty-four sentences and answered simple questions about each one. The sentences were variations on four general ideas: a rock rolling down a hill, a man reading a newspaper, a breeze blowing, and ants eating jelly. To illustrate, the six sentences about the ants eating jelly were as follows:

The ants ate the sweet jelly which was on the table.

The ants in the kitchen ate the jelly which was on the table.

The ants in the kitchen ate the jelly.

The ants ate the sweet jelly.

The ants were in the kitchen.

The jelly was on the table.

Subjects then listened to a second set of twenty-eight sentences (variations on the same themes as before) and asked to indicate whether each had been in the first set. Most of the sentences (twenty-four out of twenty-eight) were *new* sentences; here are some examples:

The ants in the kitchen ate the sweet jelly which was on the table.

The ants in the kitchen ate the sweet jelly.

The ants ate the jelly which was on the table.

The jelly was sweet.

Subjects erroneously "recognized" most of these new sentences as being "old" ones. Sentences that contained a lot of information were particularly likely to be recognized as having been heard before; for instance, "The ants in the kitchen ate the sweet jelly which was on the table" was more likely to be recognized than "The jelly was sweet." From such results, Bransford and Franks concluded that people abstract ideas from the verbal information they receive (rather than learning it verbatim) and organize similar ideas together in their memories. Sentences in the experiment that included most or all of the information related to a single theme may have more closely resembled subjects' organized memories and therefore have seemed familiar to them.

Obviously, we cannot directly see the mental processing described by Peterson and Peterson, nor can we observe the organizational processes described by Bransford and Franks. Yet inferences about such mental events seem justified in light of subjects' behavior that we *can* see.

EDUCATIONAL APPLICATIONS OF COGNITIVE PSYCHOLOGY

The study of human information processing has numerous specific applications for educational practice, applications that we will consider in more detail in later chapters. However, let's take a brief look at some general educational implications of the cognitive perspective, including those of early cognitive theories.

Focus on Cognitive Processes

If learning is a function of how information is mentally processed, then students' cognitive processes should be a major concern to educators. Students' learning difficulties can often be attributed to ineffective or inappropriate cognitive processes; for example, learning disabled children tend to process information less effectively than nondisabled children (e.g., Swanson, 1987). Teachers must become aware not only of *what* students learn, but also of *how* they attempt to learn it.

Consideration of Students' Cognitive Levels (Piagetian Stages)

Educators must consider students' levels of cognitive development when planning topics and methods of instruction. For example, explanations based on concrete operational logic are unlikely to be effective ways of presenting ideas to preoperational kindergartners. Concrete operational elementary school children have difficulty understanding abstract ideas that do not tie in with their own experiences and will learn more effectively if the same information is presented through concrete, hands-on examples. Even high school and college students, if not completely formal operational, will need concrete experiences before being presented with abstract material.

Focus on Organization of Information

People organize the information they learn. Teachers can facilitate students' learning by presenting information in an organized fashion and by helping students see how one thing relates to another.

The Relationship of New Information to Previously Learned Information

New information is most easily acquired when people can associate it with things they have already learned. Teachers can therefore help students' learning by showing them how new ideas relate to old ones. When students are unable to relate new information to anything with which they are familiar, learning is likely to be slow and ineffective.

Emphasis on Student Control of Learning

B. F. Skinner (e.g., 1954, 1968) has argued from an operant conditioning perspective that students must actively respond if they are to learn. Cognitivists share that view with Skinner; however, they emphasize *mental* activity rather than physical activity. If students control their own cognitive processes, it is ultimately the students themselves who determine what information will be learned, and how.

AN OVERVIEW OF UPCOMING CHAPTERS

In the next chapter, we will look at social learning theory, a theory that originated from the behaviorist perspective (especially operant conditioning), but that has more recently begun to use cognitive ideas in its explanation of human behavior. In the succeeding five chapters, we will explore some of the ideas of cognitive psychology and human information processing in greater detail. In Chapter 9, we will look at the processes of perception and attention, processes that influence what information we receive in the first place. In Chapters 10 through 12, we will examine the human memory system, with a particular focus on the ways in which we store and retrieve information. Throughout these three chapters, we will consider many implications of memory theory for educational practice; however, we will look at some additional applications of cognitive psychology and human information processing in Chapter 13.

SUMMARY

Cognitivism is currently the predominant perspective within which human learning is examined and explained. The roots of cognitive theory can be found in research and theory dating back to the 1920s and 1930s—notably in Gestalt psychology, Edward Tolman's purposive behaviorism, and Jean Piaget's developmental theory. Mid-century verbal learning theorists, who initially attempted to apply an S-R analysis to the study of human language-based learning, increasingly began to incorporate mental events into their explanations of research results. Contemporary cognitivism, which most frequently takes the form of human information processing theory, is characterized by an emphasis on thought processes and the belief that many aspects of learning may be unique to the human species.

Social Learning Theory

THIS past summer, my sons Alex and Jeff spent quite a bit of time with their Uncle Pete, a large man who can pick them both up at the same time and carry them around on his shoulders. Uncle Pete's feats of strength were quite a contrast to Mom's and Dad's difficulties in lifting either boy alone, or even in opening pickle jars. Ever since the summer, Alex and Jeff have spoken often of wanting to be like Uncle Pete, and I have found that I can talk them into eating many foods they have previously shunned simply by saying, "This is what helps Uncle Pete get big and strong." The ploy still doesn't work for broccoli, however.

Some of my daughter's classmates have gotten in the habit of calling Tina every morning to find out what she will be wearing to school that day. Tina is apparently somewhat of a fashion trendsetter in school, and several other girls have been mimicking her attire. Given the apparel in which Tina leaves for school most mornings, I shudder at the thought of what her cronies must look like.

Almost daily, we see instances of people watching others and learning from them. Little boys often emulate hero figures like Superman, Batman, and Uncle Pete. Through watching and copying one another, preadolescent girls often begin to behave in similar ways, such as dressing alike, wearing their hair in faddish styles, and poking fun at the same boys. Children imitate their parents by developing similar hobbies and interests, by expressing similar political and religious beliefs, and by eventually raising their own children using the same disciplinary techniques used on them. Many skills acquired at school, including reading, writing, adding, and subtracting, are learned at least partly through watching and imitating what one's teachers and peers do.

This learning by observation and modeling is the focus of *social learning theory*, a theory that can best be described as a blend of behaviorist and cognitivist ideas (Bandura, 1977; Rosenthal & Zimmerman, 1978). In this chapter, we will look at the impact of both environmental and cognitive factors on human learning, particularly as they interact within an individual's social context. We will also look at how environmental and cognitive factors interact with one another and with behavior through the process of reciprocal determinism. We will then explore the phenomenon of modeling, looking at the mental processes involved, the characteristics of effective models, and the effects of modeling on behavior. Finally, we will examine a number of implications that social learning theory has for educational practice.

My daughter the trendsetter

THE SOCIAL LEARNING MODEL

Social learning theory is concerned with the learning that occurs within a social context. It focuses on how people learn from one another and encompasses such concepts as observational learning, imitation, and modeling. Although nonhuman animals probably can learn by imitation as well (e.g., Hayes & Hayes, 1952; Herbert & Harsh, 1944), social learning theory deals primarily with human learning, and so we will be leaving rat and pigeon studies behind.

The study of learning through imitation was launched by two of Clark Hull's students, Neal Miller and John Dollard (Miller & Dollard, 1941). However, not until the early 1960s did a theory of imitation and modeling, separate from its behaviorist roots, begin to take shape. The development of this theory, originally called observational learning, was due primarily to the research and writings of Albert Bandura of Stanford University (e.g., Bandura, 1969, 1973, 1977, 1986; Bandura & Walters, 1963). Bandura's perspective has evolved considerably over the past twenty-five years and continues to be the driving force in studies of imitation and modeling. Let's take a look at some of the major characteristics of contemporary social learning theory.

Principles of Social Learning Theory

A number of general principles underlie social learning theory. We will consider some of the key ideas that have shaped the evolution of the social learning perspective.

People can learn by observing the behaviors of others and the outcomes of those behaviors. Many behaviorists view learning largely as a matter of trial and error: people learn by engaging in different responses and then modifying them based on their consequences (i.e., reinforcement and punishment). In contrast, social learning theorists (e.g., Bandura, 1977) propose that most learning takes place not through trial and error but merely through watching the behavior of other individuals (*models*).

Learning and performance are distinct from each other. Behaviorists define learning as a relatively permanent change in behavior due to experience; thus, no learning can occur without a behavior change. In contrast, social learning theorists argue that because people can learn through observation alone, their learning will not necessarily be reflected in their performance. In other words, learning may or may not result in a behavior change. Something learned at one time may be reflected in behavior exhibited at the same time, at a later time, or never (a notion similar to Edward Tolman's concept of latent learning).

Reinforcement plays a role in learning. The role of reinforcement in social learning theory has evolved as the theory itself has evolved. In Miller and Dollard's (1941) early theoretical analysis of learning through imitation, reinforcement was a critical factor in learning. Operant conditioning continued to be a major component of Bandura's early work (e.g., Bandura & Walters, 1963) as well. More recently, however, the role of reinforcement has been reconceptualized (e.g., Bandura, 1977; Rosenthal & Zimmerman, 1978). Contemporary social learning theorists propose that reinforcement has less critical, *indirect*, effects on learning, effects that we shall examine shortly.

Cognitive processes play a role in learning. Within the past twenty years, social learning theory has become increasingly "cognitive" in its analysis of human learning. For example, contemporary social learning theorists such as Bandura maintain that an individual's awareness of response-reinforcement contingencies is an essential component of the learning process. They also assert that expectations of future rewards—incentives—can have a major impact on the behaviors that people exhibit. Finally, as you will see, social learning theorists incorporate such cognitive processes as attention and retention (memory) into their explanations of how learning occurs.

Let's turn now to the ways in which environmental factors—reinforcement and punishment in particular—play a role in modeling. We will then look at the ways in which cognition is also involved.

ENVIRONMENTAL FACTORS IN SOCIAL LEARNING: REINFORCEMENT AND PUNISHMENT

If we were to explain imitation from an operant conditioning perspective, we might propose that people imitate others because they are reinforced for doing so. In fact, this explanation is exactly what Miller and Dollard proposed back in 1941. According to these theorists, an individual uses another person's behavior as a discriminative stimulus for an imitative response. The observer is then reinforced in some way when imitation is exhibited. For example, let's say that a French teacher carefully enunciates:

Comment allez vous? (Discriminative stimulus)

Students repeat the phrase in more or less the same way:

Comma tally voo? (Response)

The teacher then praises them for their efforts:

Very good! (Reinforcement)

From an operant conditioning perspective, modeling of other people is maintained by an intermittent reinforcement schedule: people are reinforced for imitating the behaviors of others often enough that they continue to do so. Eventually imitation itself becomes a habit, a phenomenon Miller and Dollard called *generalized imitation.*

How the Environment Reinforces Modeling

Clearly, people are often reinforced for modeling the behavior of others. Bandura has suggested that the environment reinforces modeling in several different ways.

The observer is reinforced by the model. People often reinforce others who copy what they themselves do. For example, a group of teenage girls is more likely to welcome another girl into the group if she dresses as they do. A gang of delinquent boys will probably accept a new member only if he acts "tough."

In the French lesson I just described, the model—the teacher—reinforced students for imitative behavior. Teachers and parents often reinforce children for copying appropriate behaviors. For example, occasionally I hear one of my children use polite, "adult" language on the telephone, perhaps along this line: "I'm sorry, but my mother is busy right now. If you will give me your name and number, I'll have her call you back in a few minutes." Such a statement is similar to what I myself tell callers, and I am likely to praise my child profusely. On the other hand, a statement like this one: "Ma! Telephone! Hurry up and get off the potty!" has *not* been learned through observation of the adults in my house, and I certainly do not reinforce it.

The observer is reinforced by a third person. On some occasions, an individual is reinforced by a third person rather than by the model. For example, children are often reinforced by parents and teachers when they imitate other children. Something I frequently tell my youngest child Jeff is this: "Oh, you're such a big boy now! You're getting dressed all by yourself, just like Alex does!"

During the Beatlemania of the 1960s, many teenage boys began sporting "moppet" haircuts like those worn by the Beatles. Such haircuts were "in," at least in my high school, and none of us girls would have ever been caught dead with a boy who had hair shorter than Ringo Starr's. My friends and I were, in essence, reinforcing boys who modeled themselves after the Beatles. In earlier days, we would have reinforced anyone who could play the guitar and bat his eyelashes like Ricky Nelson.

The imitated behavior itself leads to reinforcing consequences. Many behaviors that we learn through observing others produce satisfying (reinforcing) results. For example, a French student who pronounces his "Comment allez vous?" correctly will have greater success communicating with a Parisian. An individual who can closely model a tennis instructor's body positions and arm movements is more likely to get the ball over the net.

Reinforcement of the model affects the observer's behavior as well. When people observe a model making a particular response, they may also observe the consequence of that response. If a model is reinforced for a response, chances are greater that the observer will also show an increase in that response, a phenomenon known as *vicarious reinforcement*. For example, if Jimmy sees Johnny gain popularity among the girls because he can play the guitar and bat his eyelashes in a come-hither fashion, Jimmy may very well buy a guitar and take a few lessons; he may also stand in front of the mirror practicing eyelash batting.

The power of vicarious reinforcement (and of *vicarious punishment* as well) was dramatically illustrated in a study by Bandura (1965b). Children watched a film of a model hitting and kicking an inflated punching doll. One group of children saw the model reinforced for such aggressive behavior, a second group saw the model punished, and a third group saw the

Reinforcement of the model affects the observer's behavior as well.

model receive no consequences for the aggression. When the children were then placed in a room with the doll, those children who had seen the model receive reinforcement for aggression displayed the most aggressive behavior toward the doll: they had been vicariously reinforced for aggression. Conversely, those children who had seen the model punished for aggression were the least aggressive of the three groups: they had been vicariously punished for such behavior.

Vicarious punishment indicates to the observer that a particular behavior will not be tolerated; vicarious reinforcement indicates that a behavior is acceptable. Apparently, a lack of punishment to the model may also be a form of vicarious reinforcement in that it conveys the message that a behavior will be tolerated (Bandura, 1973, 1977; Walters & Parke, 1964; Walters, Parke, & Cane, 1965). For example, in a study by Walters and Parke (1964), children in three different experimental groups watched a film in which a boy (the model) was told by an adult female not to play with a number of toys that lay on the table in front of him but instead to read a book that she had given him. As soon as the woman left the room, however, the boy began to play with the toys. At this point, the film was different for the three experimental groups, as follows:

1. Reward. The woman returned, handed the boy some toys, and played with him affectionately.

2. Punishment. The woman returned, snatched away the toys with which the boy was playing, shook him vigorously, and sat him back down with the book.

3. No consequence. The woman did not return to the room.

Children in these three groups, and children in a control group who did not view a film, were then taken to a room full of toys, told not to touch them, given a book to read, and left alone for fifteen minutes. Children in the "no consequence" group played with the toys (thus disobeying the experimenter's instructions) just as much as the "reward" group did. Children in the "punishment" group were more obedient, but the most obedient children were those in a control group who had not watched the disobedient model at all.

When individuals see other people misbehave without negative consequences, they are more likely to misbehave themselves. My daughter comes home almost daily with complaints about who has gotten away with what on the playground that day. When playground supervisors ignore transgressions day after day, their inaction not only perpetuates those misbehaviors but may even increase them. In the same way, I often wonder if individuals who see others quite literally get away with murder aren't more likely to engage in criminal activities themselves.

Thus, imitative behavior can be reinforced by the model, by other people, by consequences intrinsic to the imitative behavior itself, or by vicarious reinforcement. However, we encounter a number of problems if we try to explain modeling only from the operant conditioning paradigm. Let's look at some of these problems.

Problems with a Strict Operant Conditioning Analysis of Social Learning

One difficulty we encounter when using operant conditioning to explain imitated behavior is that completely new behaviors can be learned simply by watching others perform them (Bandura, 1977; Rosenthal, Alford, & Rasp, 1972). As you should recall, operant conditioning must start with an emitted response, a response that can then be modified through shaping. The learning of entirely novel responses—responses that an individual has seen but never previously emitted in any form—is difficult to explain from a Skinnerian perspective.

A second difficulty in explaining modeling through operant conditioning is the phenomenon of delayed imitation: some behaviors that are learned through observing others do not appear until much later. Remember, the operant conditioning paradigm looks like this:

$$(S+) R \rightarrow S_{Rf}$$

These three parts of the model—discriminative stimulus (S+), response (R), and reinforcement (S_{Rf})—follow one right after the other, with the response occurring in the presence of the discriminative stimulus. However, as Bandura (1977) has pointed out, the response and resultant reinforcement do not always appear immediately after the discriminative stimulus but are instead observed at a later time. For such delayed imitation to be exhibited, learning must actually take place when the discriminative stimulus is presented, despite the absence of reinforcement at that time.

Still a third problem lies in the powerful effect of vicarious reinforcement: individuals sometimes exhibit behaviors for which they themselves are *never* reinforced.

A Contemporary Social Learning Perspective of Reinforcement

Contemporary social learning theorists (e.g., Bandura, 1977; Rosenthal & Zimmerman, 1978) do not view direct reinforcement as essential in human learning. However, they believe that reinforcement does play at least two roles in learning and performance.

Reinforcement influences the extent to which an individual will exhibit a behavior that has been learned. Like Edward Tolman, social learning theorists believe that although a person may learn a behavior without any reinforcement present, the person will not demonstrate that behavior unless there is a reason (i.e., reinforcement) for doing so. For example, I learned many years ago that the capital of Alaska is Juneau. Yet I have never had a reason to demonstrate that knowledge, since I have never been tested on the capital of Alaska, nor have I ever been in Alaska desperately seeking a state capital. Now, of course, I do have a reason: I want to impress you with the fact that I know the capital of at least one of the fifty states.

Bandura (1977) has proposed that an individual forms hypotheses about what responses are most appropriate in different situations. These hypotheses are formed and modified with the feedback that reinforcement and punishment, either of one's own actions or those of others, provide. Although an individual may learn both appropriate and inappropriate behaviors equally well, the appropriate behaviors—those that will lead to reinforcement—are most likely to occur.

The expectation of reinforcement influences cognitive processes that promote learning. As an example of a cognitive process involved in learning, social learning theorists (e.g., Bandura, 1977) maintain that *atten-*

tion plays a critical role in learning. And attention is influenced by the expectation of reinforcement: people are more likely to pay attention to another's behavior when they believe they will be reinforced for modeling that behavior.

I have learned the hard way that when I tell my students they will not be held responsible for certain information, I am making a BIG MISTAKE. All I have to do is say something like: "Now I want you to listen carefully to what I have to say for the next five minutes, but *it won't be on your test*," and students put their pens down, settle back in their seats, and start to nod off. People are less likely to pay attention to information when they do not anticipate a payoff for learning it.

As you can see, social learning theorists stress the role of environmental factors in learning, but they acknowledge the importance of cognitive factors as well. Let's now turn our own attention to those cognitive factors.

COGNITIVE FACTORS IN SOCIAL LEARNING

The cognitive side of social learning theory is evident in several aspects of the theory: learning without performance, cognitive processing, expectations, awareness of response-reinforcement contingencies, and the self-regulation of behavior.

Learning without Performance

Bandura makes a distinction between learning through observation (something he calls *vicarious acquisition*) and imitation of what has been learned. People can learn by watching others without necessarily imitating the behaviors they have seen (Bandura, 1977; Rosenthal & Zimmerman, 1978). At least two sources of evidence indicate that this is so. For one thing, people can verbally describe behavior they have observed without actually performing it (Bandura, 1965a). Secondly, people who observe a model perform a behavior may not demonstrate that behavior until some later time when they have a reason to exhibit it. Earlier in the chapter, I described a study by Bandura (1965b) in which children watched a film of a model acting aggressively toward an inflated punching doll. As you may recall, the consequences of the aggression to the model (reinforcement, punishment, or no consequence) influenced the extent to which children themselves engaged in aggressive acts toward the doll. Later in the study, however, all the children were promised rewards (stickers and fruit juices) if they could imitate the model's behavior. At that point, differences among the three groups of children disappeared! Clearly they had all *learned* the model's behavior equally well; the consequences to the model apparently affected their earlier performance, but not their learning.

Cognitive Processing

Social learning theory incorporates a number of cognitive processes into its explanation of how people learn. For example, social learning theorists contend that *attention* is critical in learning. Furthermore, people are more likely to remember information when they mentally *rehearse* it and when they develop verbal and visual mental representations (*memory codes*) of this information. I will describe these processes in more detail when I present Bandura's four components of modeling later in the chapter.

Expectations

Social learning theorists share Edward Tolman's emphasis on the role of *expectations* in behavior (Bandura, 1977; Rosenthal & Zimmerman, 1978). People often have expectations of what is likely to happen in different situations; for example, they expect that certain behaviors will lead to reinforcement and that other behaviors will lead to punishment. The concept of *incentive*—anticipating that a particular reinforcement will occur if a particular behavior is performed—reflects this idea of expectation. Obviously, when people expect to be rewarded for imitating a behavior, they will be more likely to pay attention to that behavior and try to remember how it is performed. Furthermore, they will be motivated to demonstrate the behavior they have learned. You should notice a critical difference here between the role of reinforcement in operant conditioning and in social learning. In operant conditioning, reinforcement influences learning of the behavior it follows. In social learning, on the other hand, an expectation of reinforcement influences the learning of a behavior it precedes (Bandura, 1977).

The nonoccurrence of expected punishment can be reinforcing, and, conversely, the nonoccurrence of expected reinforcement is often a form of punishment (Bandura, 1977). Imagine yourself as a student in a class in which the teacher describes the criteria necessary to earn an A for the course. You work hard, and your performance meets the specified criteria, so you are naturally expecting an A. At the last minute, however, the teacher adds an additional requirement: to earn an A, students must write a twenty-page term paper. You are probably angry and frustrated (in a sense, feeling punished), because you had expected reinforcement based on the work you had already completed, and that reinforcement is now being withheld.

Awareness of Response-Reinforcement Contingencies

According to social learning theorists (e.g., Bandura, 1977; Rosenthal & Zimmerman, 1978), reinforcement and punishment have little effect on learning and behavior unless people are *aware* of the response-reinforcement and response-punishment contingencies (e.g., Bandura, 1977; Spielberger & DeNike, 1966). Reinforcement will increase a response only when an individual realizes which particular response has led to the reinforcement. Similarly, an individual must recognize what particular behavior is being punished before that behavior is likely to decrease. For example, consider a situation in which a student receives an F on a writing assignment with the comments "Poorly written" and "Disorganized." For many students, such feedback will be insufficient to bring about an improvement in writing because, among other things, it does not identify the specific parts of the assignment that are poorly written and disorganized.

Self-regulation of Behavior

As social learning theory has evolved over the years, it has increasingly emphasized the role of *self-regulation* of behavior (e.g., Bandura, 1977, 1982). Through both direct and vicarious reinforcement and punishment, people gradually learn which behaviors are acceptable and which are not. Eventually, they learn and adopt performance standards that become the basis for reinforcing themselves. For example, my son Alex's bedroom used to be a disaster area: getting from the door to the bed was a matter of wading through several layers of toy trucks, building blocks, and little plastic people. Now, however, Alex keeps his bedroom immaculate even without any parental nagging and prides himself on his tidiness. (Tina's and Jeff's rooms still resemble the city landfill, but that's another story.) Similarly, as students mature, they typically need less prodding to complete assignments and study for tests. Instead, they begin to talk about feeling good when assignments have been completed or feeling guilty when they are procrastinating.

The kinds of performance standards that people establish for their own behavior depend to some degree on the standards they see models set. In a study by Bandura and Kupers (1964), for example, children watched adult or child models reward themselves with M&M's candy and self-praise for their performance in a bowling game. Some of the children watched the models reward themselves only after achieving 20 points or more (reflecting very high performance); these models admonished themselves for lower performance. Other children observed models reward themselves after achieving as few as 10 points. The children were then given the opportunity to play the game and to help themselves to M&M's whenever they chose. Bandura and Kupers found that the children tended to reinforce themselves using performance standards very similar to what they had observed the models use.

People are most likely to adopt standards for their own performance like the standards of models similar to themselves in ability (Bandura, 1977). They are unlikely to adopt the standards of models who are much more competent (Bandura & Whalen, 1966) or who apply performance standards inconsistently (Bandura, 1977). For example, consider Jason, a student who perceives himself to have average intelligence; he is likely to form expectations for his own academic achievement that match the achievement of other "average" students. Jason is thus likely to pat himself on the back for B work. On the other hand, consider Joanna, a student whose close friends are the high achievers of the class. If Joanna believes she has ability similar to that of her friends, she is likely to adopt high standards for herself and to admonish herself for the very same B achievement of which Jason is so proud.

Once individuals have adopted standards of performance for themselves, they will apply those standards to new behaviors and new situations (Bandura, 1977): they will reinforce themselves when their performance meets those standards and punish themselves when their performance falls short. This self-praise and self-criticism can be as influential in altering behavior as the reinforcement and punishment administered by others.

It should be clear by now that social learning theory incorporates aspects of both behaviorism and cognitive psychology. We have examined some of the environmental and cognitive factors that, from a social learning perspective, are involved in the learning process. However, we must also consider how environment and cognition *interact* with each other. Let's turn next to that topic and to Bandura's concept of reciprocal determinism.

RECIPROCAL DETERMINISM

We have considered ways in which the environment influences behavior and the ways in which characteristics of the person (memory processes, expectations, etc.) influence behavior. But Bandura (1977) has proposed that behavior can also influence both the environment and the person. In fact, each of these variables—environment, person, and behavior—influences the other two, a phenomenon that Bandura calls *reciprocal determinism*. The interaction of environment (E), person (P), and behavior (B) can be depicted like this:

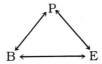

To illustrate, an individual's perceptions of the environment (a "person" variable) can influence behavior just as much as the environment itself can. I mentioned earlier that awareness of response-reinforcement contingencies influences the extent to which behavior is affected by them. Consider an experiment by Kaufman, Baron, and Kopp (1966) as a case in point. Subjects were all placed on a variable interval reinforcement schedule, with the average interval being one minute, and were told one of three different things about the schedule they were on. Subjects in Group 1 were told that they were on a one-minute variable interval schedule (i.e., they were told the truth). Group 2 subjects were told that they were on a one-minute *fixed*-interval schedule. Group 3 subjects were told that they were on a variable ratio schedule. The subjects' response patterns corresponded to the reinforcement schedules they *believed* they were on: Group 3 therefore showed the fastest response rate, and Group 2 showed the slowest response rate, consistent with the response patterns that are actually observed for these different reinforcement schedules.

Furthermore, while environment influences behavior, behavior can also influence the environment. For example, individuals typically behave in ways that increase reinforcement and decrease punishment (Bandura, 1974, 1977).

Behavior influences characteristics of the person—perceptions, attitudes, and self-concept—as well. By stumbling and falling frequently, a boy may learn that he is a klutz. By consistently performing well on mathematics assignments, a girl may begin to believe that she is a mathematics whiz.

And, of course, the environment also has an effect on the person. For instance, we have already seen how models (an environmental variable) can influence the expectations and performance standards that individuals set for their own behavior. Modeling, in fact, is a major influence that the environment exerts on both the person and behavior. We will now look more closely at the modeling process.

MODELING

According to Bandura (1977), many of the behaviors that people exhibit have been acquired through observing and modeling others. In this section, we will explore several topics related to the subject of modeling. We will first examine the processes involved in learning through modeling, then look at the characteristics of effective models and at the ways in which models can affect behavior. Finally, we will look at the effects of modeling in two specific forms of human behavior: aggression and morality.

Processes Involved in Learning Through Modeling

Bandura (1969, 1973, 1977) has proposed that four components are necessary for the modeling of behaviors that one observes. We will now examine each of these components.

Attention. For a behavior to be modeled, an individual must first pay attention to the model, and especially to significant aspects of the modeled behavior. For example, if Martha wishes to learn how to swing a golf club, she should watch how the golf pro stands, how her legs are placed, how her hands hold the club, and so on. Paying attention to the irrelevant parts of the model or her behavior—how she clears her throat or how her socks don't quite match—will of course not be helpful.

I still remember my first French teacher, a woman who came to my fifth-grade class for an hour one day a week. This woman always wore a dark green wool dress which, unfortunately, turned to a turquoise color in places where she perspired. I remember focusing on those turquoise spots, fascinated that a wool dress could actually change color just because of a little human sweat. Yes, I was paying attention to my model, but no, I did not learn any French, because I did not pay attention to the significant aspect of the behavior I was supposed to model—her voice.

Retention. The second step in learning from a model is to remember the behavior that has been observed. According to Bandura, people store both verbal representations (such as step-by-step instructions) and visual images of the behaviors they have seen. These verbal and visual *memory codes* serve as guides when people perform the observed behavior, whether it is performed immediately after the model has illustrated it or at some time in the future.

Considerable evidence indicates that learning from a model can be facilitated if learners are helped to form memory codes for the behaviors they observe (Alford & Rosenthal, 1973; Bandura & Jeffrey, 1973; Bandura, Jeffrey, & Bachicha, 1974; Coates & Hartup, 1969; Gerst, 1971; Rosenthal, Alford, & Rasp, 1972). For example, in a study by Gerst (1971), college students were asked to learn a number of words (hand signals) in sign language for the deaf. Three experimental groups were given instructions to encode the hand signals either by describing the signals to themselves or by forming mental images of the signals. All three groups showed better reproduction of the signals than a control group given a task that prevented encoding; the group that learned most successfully was one instructed to develop verbal labels descriptive of the hand movements. Teachers, too, can provide codes for learners. For example, in a study by Rosenthal, Alford, and Rasp (1972), second graders more effectively learned actions modeled by an adult when the adult described each action as well as demonstrating it.

The storage of information in memory and the different forms that such stored information can take is a topic that has been studied more extensively by information processing theorists than by social learning theorists. We will therefore return to this topic of memory storage again, in much greater detail, in Chapter 11.

Motor Reproduction. The third component in modeling is to replicate the behavior the model has demonstrated. When an individual lacks the ability to reproduce an observed behavior, perhaps because of physical immaturity, lack of strength, or disability, this third step obviously cannot occur. For example, a child with a speech impediment may never be able to say "sassafras" correctly, no matter how many times she has heard the word spoken. And a toddler who watches his teenage brother throw a football does not possess the muscular coordination to mimic that throw.

In my never-ending battle with the bulge, I turn on Jane Fonda's physical workout videocassette tape religiously every night (well, at least twice a month). Jane performs exercises in various pretzellike contortions that I in

Modeling cannot occur without the physical capability.

my wildest dreams would never be able to do. My body simply is not built to be folded in that many ways. Motor reproduction of everything I watch model Jane do is simply not possible.

Reproduction of an observed behavior at the time it is observed is often helpful because it provides an opportunity for learners to receive feedback about how to improve their reproduction of that behavior (Bandura, 1977; Schunk, 1981). For example, in teaching division to children having difficulty with mathematics, Schunk (1981) found that instruction that included an opportunity for practice and immediate feedback regarding correct and incorrect procedures and responses was clearly superior to instruction that provided no opportunity for such specific feedback.

Motivation. The final component of modeling is to be motivated to exhibit the modeled behavior: an individual must want to demonstrate what has been learned. For example, most people who have grown up in our society have seen numerous models on television point a gun in someone's ribs and say "Reach for the sky." Fortunately, very few people are motivated to model that behavior, at least with a real gun.

Although parents and teachers are often models for children, children do not model *all* the behaviors they observe their parents and teachers perform. For example, although my children model my ways of speaking to people on the telephone and my cookie-baking techniques, for some reason they don't seem to copy my broccoli cooking or my floor scrubbing. Children model behaviors only when they are motivated to do so.

To review, Bandura's four components of modeling are attention, retention, motor reproduction, and motivation. Because these components vary in different individuals, different people will model the same behavior differently. For example, Martha and Mary might pay attention to different aspects of their tennis instructor's tennis swing: Martha may focus on how the instructor is standing while Mary attends more to the way the instructor grips her racket. Or the two girls might store different visual images of the swing, Martha remembering that the instructor was facing the net and Mary remembering her standing with the left shoulder toward the net. Martha may be stronger, but Mary may be more motivated to play tennis well. The end result is that Martha and Mary will imitate the same tennis swing differently. Not only will the four components lead to individual differences in modeled behaviors, but the absence of any one of these components will make modeling unlikely to occur at all.

Characteristics of Effective Models

According to Bandura, people can learn from three different types of models. When we think of modeling, we most frequently think of a *live model*, an actual person demonstrating a particular behavior. However, we can also learn by observing a *symbolic model*, a person or character portrayed in a film, television show, book, or other medium. For example, many children model their behavior after football players or rock singers, or after such fictional characters as Superman, G.I. Joe, or Nancy Drew. And finally, we can learn from *verbal instructions*, descriptions of how to behave without an actual model being present at all.

People who are most likely to serve as live or symbolic models for others tend to have one or more characteristic traits.

The model is competent. People are more likely to be modeled if they are viewed as being competent, capable individuals. For example, a person trying to learn how to play tennis is more likely to model the techniques of a successful tennis player than those of a friend who cannot even get the ball over the net. And a student trying to learn how to write a better term paper is more likely to look at the work of someone who has consistently received high grades on term papers than at the work of a student who has been doing poorly.

The model has prestige and power. Individuals who have high status, respect, and power within their group, or within society as a whole, are more likely to be modeled (Bandura, 1977). A child is more likely to imitate the behaviors of a student leader or a famous rock star than the behaviors of a class dunce or a rock-and-roll "has-been." For example, Sasso and Rude

(1987) taught a number of nonhandicapped children (some of whom were popular with their peers and some of whom were not) methods of initiating appropriate social interactions with handicapped children. Other children who saw their more popular classmates interacting with handicapped children were likely to do so as well, but children who saw unpopular students modeling the same behavior were unlikely to follow suit.

The model is attractive. Models are usually physically attractive. For example, girls are more likely to imitate Cinderella than her ugly stepsisters. Boys will more often model Luke Skywalker than Yoda.

The model behaves in sex-appropriate ways. Males are more likely to model behavior that is consistent with male stereotypes; similarly, females are more likely to model behaviors that follow traditional female patterns.

Models are often competent, powerful, and attractive.

For example, in studies in which children watched adult models of both sexes being aggressive (Bandura, Ross, & Ross, 1961, 1963), boys were more likely than girls to imitate the aggressive behaviors, presumably because aggression is a trait more frequently associated with males than with females.

The model's behavior is relevant to the observer's situation. Individuals are more likely to model behaviors that have functional value within their own circumstances (Rosenthal & Bandura, 1978). For example, my daughter models many of my behaviors, but she definitely does not model the way I dress. She has told me, in so many words, that she would be laughed off the playground if she dressed the way I do.

Parents and teachers are among the people that children most often model, particularly when those parents and teachers are seen as competent, respected, powerful, and attractive. Children also frequently model their behaviors after famous personalities and fictional heroes. And children's peer groups—other children of the same sex and age—can be a source of powerful and influential models as well.

Effects of Modeling on Behavior

In what ways do models influence behavior? Social learning theorists (e.g., Bandura, 1969, 1973, 1977; Bandura & Walters, 1963; Rosenthal & Zimmerman, 1978) believe that modeling has at least three effects.

Modeling teaches new behaviors. Individuals can learn entirely new behaviors by observing others perform those behaviors (e.g., Bandura, Ross, & Ross, 1963). For example, by listening to and imitating the sounds made by others, a person learns to speak new words. And by watching how a parent swings a baseball bat and following the parent's verbal instructions ("Keep your eye on the ball!"), a child learns to hit a baseball.

Modeling inhibits and disinhibits previously learned behaviors. People are less likely to perform behaviors for which they have seen others punished; in other words, vicarious punishment has an *inhibition* effect. For instance, a child who observes another child being punished for chewing gum in class is less likely to display the same behavior.

Furthermore, people are more likely to perform behaviors when they have seen others reinforced for those behaviors; that is, vicarious reinforcement has a *disinhibition* effect. For example, in studies by Walters and his colleagues (Walters & Thomas, 1963; Walters, Thomas, & Acker, 1962), adults viewed either a film depicting aggression and violence (*Rebel Without a Cause*) or a nonaggressive film (*Picture Making by Teenagers,*) then were asked to administer "shocks" to other individuals. (These other individuals were confederates of the experimenter who did not really receive any shocks but behaved as if they did.) Subjects who had watched the violent, aggressive film administered more frequent and more intense "shocks" to the confederates. The film had apparently disinhibited previously learned aggressive behavior.

Modeling elicits similar behaviors. When a person observes a model performing a particular behavior, the observer may display similar rather than identical behavior. A boy who sees his older brother excel at basketball, but who lacks his brother's height advantage, may instead try to become a successful soccer player. As a high school student, I would have liked to become a "cool" cheerleader, but did not have the gymnastic skills necessary for cheerleading. Instead, I became a majorette in the marching band, an activity that was almost as cool.

Behaviors That Can Be Learned Through Modeling

Many behaviors can be learned through modeling: speech, motor skills, academic skills and habits, interpersonal skills, and attitudes are among them. In this section we will explore research regarding the impact of modeling in two particular areas: aggression and morality.

Aggression. I have already described several studies (e.g., Bandura, 1965b; Walters & Thomas, 1963; Walters et al., 1962) that demonstrate the influence of modeling on aggression. Other research studies (e.g., Bandura, Ross, & Ross, 1961, 1963; Mischel & Grusec, 1966; Steuer, Applefield, & Smith, 1971) also lead to the same conclusion: children become more aggressive when they observe aggressive or violent models. In the classic study in this area (Bandura, Ross, & Ross, 1961), preschoolers were taken, one at a time, to a playroom containing a variety of toys and seated at a table where they could draw pictures. Some of these children then observed an adult (an aggressive model) enter the room and engage in numerous aggressive behaviors toward an inflatable punching doll, including such behaviors as kicking the doll in the air, straddling it and hitting it over the head with a wooden mallet, and making statements like "Pow!" "Kick him," and "Punch him in the nose." Other children instead observed an adult (a nonaggressive model) come in and play in a constructive way with building blocks. Still other children saw no model while they were in the playroom. The children were then led to another room where they were mildly frustrated: just as they began to play with some very attractive, entertaining toys, the toys were taken away from them. They were then taken to a third room in which both nonaggressive and aggressive toys (including the inflatable punching doll and wooden mallet) were present; their behaviors were recorded and coded for aggressive content by observers on the other side of a one-way mirror. Children who had seen the aggressive model were clearly the most aggressive of the three groups, and in fact they mimicked many of the same behaviors they had seen the aggressive model display (e.g., straddling the doll and hitting it with the mallet). Children who had seen a nonaggressive model were even less aggressive than the no-model group. With regard to aggression, then, models can have an impact either way: aggressive models will lead to increased aggression in children, and nonaggressive models will lead to decreased aggression.

Children can also learn aggression from observing it in films or on television. In another study by Bandura and his colleagues (Bandura, Ross, & Ross, 1963), preschool children who had seen a film of either an adult or a cartoon character being aggressive showed just as much aggression toward an inflatable doll as did children who had seen a live adult model; all three of these groups were significantly more aggressive than children who had not observed a model at all. Modeled aggression is not limited to toys: in a study by Steuer, Applefield, and Smith (1971), children who watched cartoons depicting aggressive and violent behavior were significantly more aggressive toward other children than children who had not seen the cartoons.

The fact that children model aggressive behavior depicted in the media has obvious implications for television and movie violence. Not only do children model aggression, but they also tend to model the same *forms* of aggression that they observe (Bandura, Ross, and Ross, 1963; Mischel & Grusec, 1966). Even cartoons that display violent behaviors, including such classics as "Tom and Jerry" and "Roadrunner," may not be as harmless as they appear.

Morality. A growing body of literature indicates that many aspects of moral thinking and moral behavior can be influenced by observation and modeling. Research has demonstrated the importance of social learning for such behaviors as generosity (Elliott & Vasta, 1970; Radke-Yarrow, Zahn-Waxler, & Chapman, 1983; Rushton, 1975, 1982), self-control (Harter, 1983), and resistance to temptation (Wolf & Cheyne, 1972). Consider this study by Rushton (1975) as an example. Children first observed a model playing a bowling game and reinforcing himself with tokens for high performance. For some children, the model donated half of the earned tokens to a poor boy named Bobby pictured on a poster in the room; for other children, the model kept all his winnings for himself despite the presence of the poster. The children were then given the opportunity to play the game and to reward themselves with tokens. The more tokens they earned, the better prize they could purchase (therefore, donating to Bobby meant that they would have to purchase a lesser prize). Children who had watched generous models were more likely to donate some of their own tokens to Bobby than were children who had watched selfish models. This difference was true not only in the initial session but also in a follow-up session two months later.

Moral judgments regarding right and wrong may also be learned, at least in part, through social learning (Bandura & McDonald, 1963; Prentice, 1972; Schliefer & Douglas, 1973). For example, in a study by Bandura and McDonald (1963), children were presented with pairs of stories such as these:

1. John was in his room when his mother called him to dinner. John goes down, and opens the door to the dining room. But behind the door was a chair, and on the chair was a tray with fifteen cups on it. John did not know the cups were behind the door. He opens the door, the door hits the tray, bang go the fifteen cups, and they all get broken.

2. One day when Henry's mother was out, Henry tried to get some cookies out of the cupboard. He climbed up on a chair, but the cookie jar was still too high, and he couldn't reach it. But while he was trying to get the cookie jar, he knocked over a cup. The cup fell and broke (Bandura & McDonald, 1963, p. 276).

In each pair, one story portrayed one well-intended child (such as John) who caused major damage, and another child with malicious intent (such as Henry) who did minor damage. For each pair of stories, the children were asked which of the two children was the naughtier. Some children consistently picked the child with the bad intentions as being naughtier; these children were then exposed to an adult model who used amount of damage as the criterion for naughtiness. Other children had a pattern of judging the well-meaning but more destructive child as being naughtier; they were exposed to an adult model who used intentions as the criterion for naughtiness. Observing the model had a profound effect on the children's later moral judgments; children began to make moral decisions similar to those the model had made and opposite to their own previous judgments.

We have already seen that when models on film depict inappropriate behavior, that behavior is often imitated. But visual media can model appropriate behaviors as well. For example, in a study by Friedrich and Stein (1973), a group of preschool children watched "Mister Rogers' Neighborhood"—a television show that stresses such prosocial behaviors as cooperation, sympathy, and sharing—for thirty minutes each day over a four-week period. These children displayed more socially appropriate behavior and less aggression than children who instead watched shows with aggressive content ("Batman" and "Superman") during that same time period.

What about situations when a model preaches one set of moral values and practices another? A review of research by Bryan (1975) leads to a clear conclusion: when children hear a model say one thing and do something else, they are more likely to imitate what the model *does* than what the model *says*. In other words, to be effective, models must practice what they preach.

SOCIAL LEARNING IN THE CLASSROOM

Social learning theory has numerous implications for classroom practice. Let's take a look at some of them.

Observation alone is sufficient for learning. Behaviorists such as B. F. Skinner stress the necessity of active responding for learning to occur. But in this chapter I have presented examples of how learning can occur through observation alone. Not only can students learn information and academic skills through observing others, but they can learn moral values, performance standards, and appropriate and inappropriate modes of conducting themselves as well.

Modeling provides an alternative to shaping for teaching new behaviors. Operant conditioning provides one means through which a new response can be taught: the process of shaping. However, remember that shaping involves beginning with the reinforcement of existing behaviors and a gradual modification of those behaviors through differential reinforcement; for complex behaviors, this process can be time-consuming. With social learning theory, we now have a faster, more efficient means for teaching new behavior: the modeling process.

Teachers and parents should model appropriate behaviors. Teachers and parents often possess characteristics (e.g., competence, prestige, and power) that make them influential models for children. Adults must therefore be careful that they model appropriate behaviors for the children with whom they interact. I am delighted when I see teachers and adults show open-mindedness, empathy, and concern for physical fitness; I cringe when I see them express disdain for particular points of view, disregard the needs and concerns of other human beings, or smoke a cigarette.

A child I know recently tried out for a role in a Christmas pageant. Lisa went off to school on the morning of pageant tryouts, knowing that students could each try out for one part only and thinking that she had a good chance of winning the role of Mrs. Claus. Lisa was convinced that the teacher would award the role of Santa Claus to a girl named Ann; however, because Ann was late that morning and the teacher had announced that latecomers would not be allowed to try out, Lisa instead tried out for Santa himself. When Ann arrived ten minutes late, the teacher disregarded her rule about latecomers being ineligible, allowed Ann to try out for Santa Claus, and in fact awarded the role to Ann. In doing so, this teacher, one of the school's most visible role models, modeled both hypocrisy and favoritism.

As an educational psychologist who teaches teachers how to teach, my job is a particularly difficult one because I must practice what I preach. If I tell my students that immediate feedback, organization of information, vivid examples, hands-on experiences, and tests that match behavioral objectives are all important components of effective teaching, my students' learning will obviously be enhanced if I model all those things as well. To say one thing but do another would not only be hypocritical, it would also be counterproductive.

Teachers should expose students to a variety of exemplary models. Adult models do not need to be limited to children's teachers and parents. Other adults can be invited to visit classrooms on occasion (Bell-Gredler, 1986); for example, police officers, prominent city officials, business people, and doctors might demonstrate appropriate behaviors and attitudes related to safety, good citizenship, responsibility, and health. Symbolic models can also be effective; for example, studying the lives of such individuals as Helen Keller, Martin Luther King, Jr., and Eleanor Roosevelt is an alternative method of demonstrating many appropriate behaviors.

The four components of modeling—attention, retention, motor reproduction, and motivation—are critical to successful modeling. First of all, the teacher must make sure that students pay attention to the model and particularly to the relevant aspects of the model's behavior. Second, the teacher can help students' retention of what they observe by helping them form appropriate memory codes for those observations (ways in which teachers can do this will be discussed in Chapter 11). Third, giving students opportunities to practice the behaviors they see and giving them corrective feedback about their attempts will aid their motor reproduction of the responses they are modeling. Finally, remember that students will only display learned behaviors if they have the motivation to do so. Many children will be intrinsically motivated to perform, but others may require external incentives and reinforcers.

Vicarious reinforcement and vicarious punishment may influence student behaviors and misbehaviors. Students learn what behaviors are appropriate and what behaviors are inappropriate not only through the consequences of their own behaviors but through the consequences of other people's behaviors as well. Teachers and other school personnel must therefore be consistent in the rewards and punishments they administer, not only from time to time, but also from student to student.

Describing the consequences of behaviors can effectively increase appropriate behaviors and decrease inappropriate ones. As you will recall, social learning theorists propose that the awareness of response-consequence contingencies is an essential component of behavior control. Promises of rewards for good behaviors and threats of punishments for misdeeds can therefore be an effective means of improving student behavior. Conversely, administering reinforcement and punishment when students do not recognize the relationship between such consequences and particular responses they have made is unlikely to bring about behavior change.

Students should be helped to set realistic expectations for their own behavior. Modeling is a primary means through which students develop standards for their own performance. When a student's standards are unrealistically high, as might be true for a perfectionist, continual disappointment and frustration are likely to result. When a student's standards are too low, underachievement will result. Teachers can facilitate students' academic and social progress by helping them form self-expectations commensurate with their skills and ability.

Self-control techniques can be effective methods of modifying student behaviors. In Chapter 5, I described several techniques of self-control, including self-reinforcement, self-observation and measurement, and self-imposed stimulus control. Strictly speaking, because these methods involve self-regulation, they are probably best classified as being a blend of operant conditioning and social learning techniques. When students are intrinsically motivated to change their own behaviors, self-control can be an effective means of bringing about those desired behavior changes.

Clearly, the social context of the classroom cannot be ignored. Students can and do learn from the models—parents, teachers, and peers—that they see every day. And the social learning perspective has shown us that it is important to consider both environmental and cognitive factors in observational learning and modeling.

SUMMARY

Social learning theory focuses on the ways in which individuals learn from observing one another. This perspective reflects a blending of behaviorist concepts (e.g., reinforcement and punishment) with cognitive notions (e.g., expectation and awareness). Environmental and cognitive variables interact with one another and with behavior through a process known as reciprocal determinism. The concept of modeling is the focus of much social learning research and has numerous implications for classroom practice.

CHAPTER 9

Perception and Attention

Outline

Perception
Perception as Construction
Factors Influencing Perception
Expectations and the Perception of Ambiguous Stimuli

Attention
Factors Influencing Attention
Processes Underlying Attention
Attention as a Limited Capacity

Perception and Attention in Education
Perception and Interpretation in Learning
Attention in the Classroom
Attentional Processes in Reading and Spelling
Attention in Study Behavior

Summary

I MAGINE, for a minute, that your mind works like a videocassette recorder, that you have recorded everything you ever saw and heard. Your memory of an event would involve a simple process of finding and replaying the appropriate cassette, and you would be able to remember the event as completely and accurately as if you were reliving it. Studying for an exam would be easy, you might think—no need for reading the textbook more than once or for last-minute cramming or for mindless repetition of meaningless facts over and over again.

Unfortunately, our minds are not accurate recorders of life events. Our *perception* of events alters and distorts the information we learn and remember, so that, in a sense, what we see is not necessarily what we get. Our *attention* or nonattention to information also affects our learning: we are frequently in a position where many things compete for attention at the same time, and some of those things will not get the attention they deserve.

In this chapter, we will examine the various influences on what events we perceive and how we perceive them. We will look at the processes of perception and attention, with particular emphasis on their *constructive* nature. We will also explore a variety of implications that perceptual and attentional processes have for educational practice.

PERCEPTION

Let's begin our discussion by making a distinction between sensation and perception. *Sensation* refers to the reaction of your body—in particular, your sensory receptors—to environmental stimulation. *Perception*, on the other hand, refers to the meaning (the recognition and interpretation) that you give to that stimulation. For example, when something moves toward you, light waves bounce off it and hit the retinas of your eyes, giving you a certain visual sensation. But, in addition, you may perceive that object as a person walking in your direction. On a dark, cloudy afternoon, the sound waves resulting from a lightning bolt reach your ears, causing the sensation of sound that you perceive to be thunder. As you walk past a bakery, certain chemicals drift up your nostrils, and you perceive the aroma of freshly baked bread.

Sensation is a physiological process: the body responds to energy from the environment. Perception, on the other hand, is a psychological process: the mind interprets and recognizes what the body has sensed. But the process of perception does not always provide an accurate interpretation of the information being received from the receptors.

Curiously, perception is both less and more than sensation. Perception is *less* than sensation because people do not attempt to interpret all the sensations with which they are bombarded at any given moment. Right now, as you are looking at this book (and hopefully perceiving it), light waves are bouncing off the page and hitting the light-sensitive cells at the backs of your eyes. At the same time, you may also be receiving light waves from a table on which your book is resting, the carpet on the floor, and the pictures on the walls. Your ears are probably receiving numerous sound waves, maybe from a radio, a nearby conversation, an air conditioner, or traffic outside your window. Perhaps a certain smell is drifting through the air, or a certain taste from your last meal lingers in your mouth. It is neither necessary nor possible for you to interpret *all* these sensations, so you will attend to and perceive some of them and ignore the others.

But perception is also much *more* than sensation, because sensation alone provides insufficient information for an adequate interpretation of surrounding events. For example, eyes do not provide a continual report of visual stimulation; rather, they jump from one focal point to another, taking periodic "snapshots" of the visual field. These jumps in focus, or *saccades*, occur four or five times a second, with visual sensation occurring primarily during the rest periods between them. If we receive only four or five snapshots of visual information each second, our visual world should appear jerky and erratic, much as an old-time movie does. The fact that we instead see smooth-flowing motion is due in large part to the mental filling in that occurs as our minds interpret visual sensations.

Even if human eyes did function one hundred percent of the time, they would typically provide an incomplete picture of the environment, and we would have to fill in mentally the information that we did not sense. For example, imagine walking into a bookstore and seeing the store clerk behind the counter. You probably sense only the clerk's head and upper torso, yet you perceive an entire person. You assume that the clerk has a lower torso and two legs, and in fact would be quite surprised if the clerk's lower body looked any other way!

Consider the perception of spoken language. You may understand this sentence easily when you hear it:

I read a book.

while the identical sentence in Chinese gives you trouble:

Wǒkànshū.

In the first sentence, you probably "hear" four distinct, meaningful words, whereas in the second, you hear just one long nonsense word. To an individual fluent in Mandarin Chinese rather than English, the situation would be reversed; that person would hear this:

People often make assumptions about what they don't see.

Ireadabook.

and this:

Wǒ kàn shū.

In reality, most spoken language comes to us as one continuous stream of sound waves rather than as . . . separate . . . words . . . like . . . this. Only when you are familiar with the particular language spoken can you mentally divide the one long sound into separate words.

Perception as Construction

Many information processing theorists believe that perception involves a process of *construction*: people use the sensations they receive (sensations that typically provide an incomplete scenario of the event they are experiencing) to construct a perception of that event. For example, let's say that you are in a noisy room and hear someone say:

I —an't —ear a thing in this —lace!

While you haven't heard everything the person said, you may have enough information to perceive the sentence like so:

I can't hear a thing in this place!

In Figure 9–1 are three pictures first published by C. M. Mooney (1957). Most people perceive the picture on the left as being that of a woman, even though many of her features are missing. Enough features are visible—an eye, parts of the nose, mouth, chin, and hair—that you can construct a meaningful perception from them. Is there enough information in the other

Figure 9—1
Can you construct a person from each of these pictures?

(Reprinted from "Age in the Development of Closure Ability in Children" by C. M. Mooney, 1957, *Canadian Journal of Psychology, 11*, p. 220. Copyright 1957 by Canadian Psychological Association. Reprinted with permission.)

two figures for you to construct two more faces? Construction of a face from the figure on the right may take you a while, but it can be done.

Curiously, once you have constructed faces from the figures, they then seem obvious. Furthermore, you tend to perceive the same sensory information in the same way at a future time; a particular construction of sensory input tends to stick. For example, if you were to close this book now, and not pick it up again for a week or more, you would see the faces almost immediately, even if you had had difficulty perceiving them originally. (For a more detailed description of constructive processes in perception, see Neisser, 1967, or Ornstein, 1972.)

Factors Influencing Perception

Theoretically, it should be possible for people to construct their sensations into an infinite number of different perceptions. Yet most people tend to form similar, although not necessarily identical, perceptions of their environments. Several factors influence the ways in which people construct their perceptions, and these things affect everyone in more or less the same manner. Let's take a look at some of them.

Proximity. As you should recall from Chapter 7, Gestalt psychologists proposed that people organize information in certain predictable ways. According to Gestaltists, one of the dominant principles affecting how people organize information is proximity: people tend to perceive as a unit those things that are close together in space. For example, look at the dots in Figure 9—2.

Figure 9–2

Not only do you see nine dots, you probably also perceive an arrangement of three groups of three dots each; that is, you see those dots in closer proximity to one another as somehow belonging together. In the same way, notice how you read this phrase:

One very high way.

and this one:

On every highway.

In both phrases, the same letters appear in exactly the same sequence:

Oneveryhighway.

Yet because of the way the letters are grouped together, you read the phrases differently.

Similarity. Another organizational principle from Gestalt psychology is similarity: people tend to perceive as a unit those things that are similar to one another. For example, look at the dots in Figure 9–3.

Figure 9–3

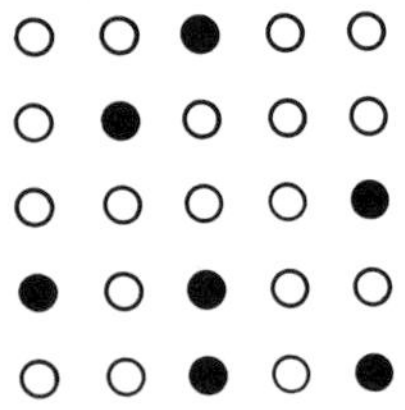

○ ○ ● ○ ○
○ ● ○ ○ ○
○ ○ ○ ○ ●
● ○ ● ○ ○
○ ○ ● ○ ●

Can you see a letter Y among them? Probably not. But now look at the dots in Figure 9–4.

Figure 9–4

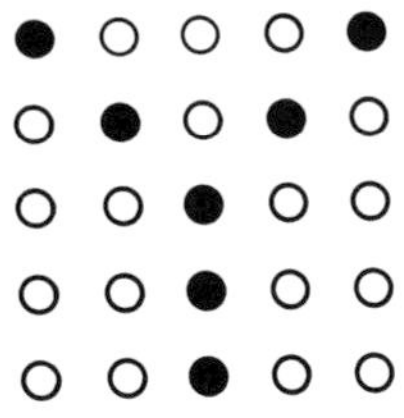

● ○ ○ ○ ●
○ ● ○ ● ○
○ ○ ● ○ ○
○ ○ ● ○ ○
○ ○ ● ○ ○

This time a letter Y is obvious. The arrangement of the dots in both cases is the same, but in the second case those dots forming a Y are all black, and you tend to perceive those similar black dots as a unit. Yet you probably haven't noticed other letters, such as the letter E, that are also formed by some of the dots.

Closure. Still another Gestaltist principle is closure: people tend to fill in missing pieces to form a complete picture. For example, what do you see in Figure 9–5?

Figure 9—5

You should have no difficulty recognizing the letter W, even though parts of it are missing. Can you also recognize the phrase in Figure 9–6?

Figure 9—6

Singing in the rain.

You are probably able to read "Singing in the rain," even though 50% of the print is missing. You simply fill in what is not there.

Context. In Figure 9–7 is something known as Benussi's ring. Both sides of the ring are an equal shade of gray, but many people perceive the right side as being a lighter shade than the left side. The appearance of the two sides of the ring is influenced by their context: the right side looks lighter against its black background.

Figure 9–8 shows another example of the effect of context (modeled after an example by Selfridge, 1955).

The word, of course, is *Matterhorn*. However, you may have noticed that the second and seventh "letters" are exactly the same figure. Whether you interpret the figure as an A or an H depends on its context within the other letters.

Past Experience. People are prone to perceive objects in ways that they have learned to perceive them in the past (e.g., Deregowski, 1972). For

Figure 9–7
Benussi's Ring

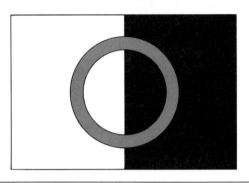

Figure 9–8

MATTERHORN

example, consider the picture in Figure 9–9. It is obviously a picture of a boy standing in a room. You probably did *not* perceive all the dotted portions of the picture as a unit, despite their proximity and similarity to one another; likewise, you did not perceive the striped parts as belonging together. You have learned from many previous experiences that heads, torsos, arms, and legs—at least when they appear in a certain arrangement—belong together, and in fact all belong to the same person.

When you see someone walking away from you, that person does not appear to shrink, even though the image on your retinas is in fact getting smaller. You have learned from your past experiences that people do not shrink just because they move away from you, and so you make certain mental adjustments regarding people's sizes. What would happen if you had no such prior experience with perceiving people at changing distances? The anthropologist Colin Turnbull (1961) observed exactly this situation while studying the Ba Mbuti pygmies, a tribe living in the thick jungle of the African Congo rain forest. With no open spaces in their environment, the Ba Mbuti never had the opportunity to see objects more than a few feet away from them. Turnbull described one particular incident in which a member of the tribe, a man named Kenge, traveled for the first time to an area of open grasslands. When Kenge spied a herd of buffalo grazing in the far distance, he asked, "What insects are those?" and dismissed as folly Turnbull's reply that they were actually buffalo that were very far away. A short time later, as the men approached the buffalo by car, Kenge grew

Figure 9—9

increasingly frightened as he watched the buffalo "grow" in size, fearful that a magic trick was being played on him.

People are surprisingly adaptable in their ability to learn to perceive in new ways. For example, in a series of experiments described by Kohler (1962), subjects wore special glasses that significantly distorted their vision. Some subjects wore prism glasses that made objects to the left look much thinner than they really were, while objects to the right appeared abnormally wide. After wearing such glasses continuously for several weeks, the wearers no longer perceived any distortions; they actually relearned to perceive the world normally. When they later removed their glasses, the original distortions were reversed: objects on the left looked fat and objects on the right looked thin. In another experiment, subjects wore glasses that horizontally reversed retinal images (objects actually on the left appeared to be on the right, and vice versa) and quickly adapted to them. Kohler described one individual who, after wearing the glasses for several weeks, could drive his motorcycle through the city streets without difficulty!

Expectation. Read the following sentence:

I pledge allegiance to the flag of the United Stetes of American, and to the Repulbic for which it stends, one nation, under God, indivsible, with liberty and justice for all.

You may have noticed one or two typographical errors in the passage. But did you catch them all? Altogether there were *five* mistakes, as shown below:

> I pledge allegiance to the flag of the United Stetes of American, and to the Repu*l*bic for which it stends, one nation, under God, indi*v*sible, with liberty and justice for all.

If you didn't notice all the errors—and many people don't—then your perception of the sentence was influenced by your expectation of what words *should* have been there. If you have seen and heard the United States Pledge of Allegiance as many times as I have, you know that the phrase "I pledge allegiance . . . " is usually followed by a certain sequence of words, and so you may have seen what you expected to see.

Expectation is one reason that people have difficulty with proofreading, especially when they are proofreading something they themselves have written. I have read countless student papers in which I have found obvious misspellings, despite the authors' insistences that they have proofread their work very carefully. The problem with proofreading your own work is that you as the writer know very well what *should* be written on the page, and so may read what you expect to be there rather than what actually *is* there.

Expectations are especially likely to influence perception when objects or events are ambiguous. It is to this topic—perceiving ambiguous stimuli—that we turn now.

Expectations and the Perception of Ambiguous Stimuli

Take a close look at the picture in Figure 9–10. Describe to yourself what you see. Notice the shape of the head, the eye, the nose, the mouth, the chin. But just what is it that you *do* see? Is this the picture of a man or of a mouse?

Figure 9–10

From "The Role of Frequency in Developing Perceptual Sets" by B. R. Bugelski & D. A. Alampy, 1961, *Canadian Journal of Psychology, 15*, p. 206. Copyright 1961 by Canadian Psychological Association. Reprinted by permission.

The man-mouse picture in Figure 9–10 is an example of an *ambiguous stimulus*, something that can be constructed into more than one perception. Some people perceive the figure as a bald man with an overbite and a backward tilt to his head. Others instead perceive a mouse or rat with a very short front leg and a long tail curling beneath its body.

Ambiguous stimuli are those most likely to be perceived in accordance with people's expectations. When I show the man-mouse picture to students in my classes, I consistently find that the great majority of students who have been led to expect a mouse—by previously viewing a similar picture that is clearly a mouse—*do* in fact see a mouse or rat. Those who are similarly led to expect a man see the baldheaded man. And notice how your expectations concerning how people typically behave influence your initial interpretation of the first statement below:

"We're going to have my grandmother for Thanksgiving dinner."
"You are? Well, we're going to have turkey" (Gleitman, 1985, p. 432).

In much the same way, human behaviors are often ambiguous, and individuals tend to interpret the behaviors of others in accordance with their own expectations (e.g., Nisbett & Bellows, 1977; Snyder & Swann, 1978). People expect positive behaviors from a person they like or admire and so are likely to perceive that person's behaviors in a positive light—a phenomenon referred to as the *halo effect*. In much the same way, they expect inappropriate behaviors from a person they dislike, and their perceptions of that person's behaviors are biased accordingly—we could call this the *horns effect*. For example, imagine that Mr. Brighteyes, a fifth-grade teacher, has one student, Mary, who consistently performs well in classwork, and another, Susan, who more typically turns in sloppy and incomplete work. Let's say that both girls turn in an assignment of marginal quality. Mr. Brighteyes is likely to *over*rate Mary's performance and *under*rate Susan's.

Many things affect people's expectations, and therefore their perceptions, of another's behaviors. For example, people often expect higher quality performance from people who are clean and well groomed than from people who are dirty and disheveled—hence the advice, "Dress for success." Socioeconomic status also appears to make a difference; consider this experiment by Darley and Gross (1983) as an example. Undergraduate students were told that they were participating in a study on teacher evaluation methods and were asked to view a videotape of a fourth-grade girl named Hannah. There were two versions of the videotape designed to give two different impressions about Hannah's socioeconomic status: Hannah's clothing, the kind of playground in which she played, and information about her parents' occupations indirectly conveyed to some students that she was from a low socioeconomic background and to others that she was from a high socioeconomic background. All students then watched Hannah taking an oral achievement test, on which she performed at grade level, and were asked to rate Hannah on a number of characteristics. Students who had been led to believe that Hannah came from wealthy surroundings rated her ability well above grade level, whereas students believing she lived in an impoverished environment evaluated her as being below grade level. The two groups of students also rated Hannah differently in terms of her work habits, motivation, social skills, and general maturity.

Individuals' expectations and perceptions may even be influenced by other people's names. In an experiment by Harari and McDavid (1973), elementary school teachers were asked to grade essays written by ten-year-old children. Teachers who read an essay supposedly written by Lisa gave it a better grade than teachers who read the same essay but thought it was written by Bertha. In the same way, David received better grades than Hubert. Perhaps we should think of student essays as being ambiguous stimuli, because the criteria for perceiving (grading) them are often somewhat subjective. Grading of such ambiguous stimuli may be especially influenced by teachers' past experiences with, and expectations for, their students.

Perception of an ambiguous stimulus is particularly susceptible to biases and expectations because some of the information necessary for an "accurate" perception (if such is possible) is simply not available. However, even when all the necessary information *is* present, people typically attend only to a small part of that information and ignore the rest. The kinds of information that people pay attention to, and the kinds that they ignore, are topics we will explore next.

ATTENTION

Attention is the process by which people select some of the environmental input they receive for further cognitive processing. For example, you are probably attending to only a small part of all the visual input that your eyes sense right now (I hope you are attending to the words on this page!). In the same way, you do not worry about all the sounds you hear at one time; you select only certain sounds to pay attention to.

As you will learn in the following chapter, attention plays a central role in learning and memory (e.g., Atkinson & Shiffrin, 1968; Kulhavy, Peterson, & Schwartz, 1986; Piontkowski & Calfee, 1979; Zelniker & Jeffrey, 1979). Because attention is such a critical component of the human information processing system, I would like to address several pertinent questions in the pages to follow: What kinds of stimuli are likely to capture our attention? What processes allow us to focus our attention on some stimuli and not others? How many different stimuli can we attend to at the same time? Let's explore each of these questions in turn.

Factors Influencing Attention

Certain kinds of stimuli tend to draw attention while other kinds do not. Let's take a look at some of the more critical factors affecting what people pay attention to.

Size. Which of the following letters first draw your eye?

A B c D

You probably noticed the B and D before the other letters because of their larger size. Attention tends to be drawn to large objects, a fact that newspaper publishers employ when they typeset front page headlines in large letters, and that advertisers use when they put potentially unenticing information in fine print.

Intensity. More intense stimuli—bright colors and loud noises, for instance—attract attention. Teachers will frequently speak more loudly than usual—"Be quiet!"—when they want to get their students' attention. Similarly, toy manufacturers emphasize bright colors in the toys they produce, knowing that children browsing store shelves will be more attracted to vivid reds and yellows than to muted pastels.

Novelty. Stimuli that are novel or unusual in some way will draw people's attention. For example, look at the women in Figure 9–11. You probably find yourself attending more to the woman on the right than to the others. A woman with two heads and three legs is not someone you see every day.

Incongruity. Objects that are incongruous—that don't make sense within their context—tend to capture people's attention. For example, read this sentence:

I took a walk to the rabbit this morning.

Figure 9–11
Novelty draws attention.

Did you spend more time looking at the word *rabbit* than at the other words? If so, it may have been because *rabbit* does not make much sense within the context of the sentence.

Emotion. Stimuli with strong emotional associations attract attention. A nude body flashing through a crowded room will usually draw the attention (and astonished expressions) of just about everyone present. Words such as *blood* and *murder* also are attention-getters because of their emotional overtones.

Personal Significance. Individuals tend to pay attention to stimuli that are important to them at a given time (e.g., Gibson & Rader, 1979; Vurpillot & Ball, 1979). When a student sits in front of a television set with an open textbook, the stimulus that the student will attend to—the television or the book—depends in large part on which stimulus is more closely related to the student's motives at that particular time. If the textbook is interesting or if an important examination is scheduled for the next day, the student will attend to the book. But if a popular situation comedy or a cliff-hanging soap opera is on, or if the textbook is dry and unenticing, the student may very well forget that the text is even in the same room!

Think, for a moment, about curriculum materials, including textbooks, that you have seen recently. Do they possess characteristics that are likely to catch a student's eye? Do important words and concepts stand out, perhaps because they are larger or more intense or unusual? Are certain topics likely to grab a student's interest because they are interesting and relevant to the age group? If your answer to these questions is no, then students are likely to have difficulty attending to and learning from those materials.

Processes Underlying Attention

What cognitive processes underlie people's ability to attend to certain aspects of the environment and ignore others? On the surface, the answer might appear simple: they just focus their eyes directly on what they want to pay attention to. Because more receptors are in the middle of the retinas than at the sides, visual perception is more accurate and more detailed for things in the center of the visual field. Yet you can probably think of many times when you have focused your eyes on an object yet not paid attention to that object at all: perhaps you were listening intently to a piece of music or were deep in thought about a particular problem.

Furthermore, people are able to focus the attention of other sensory modalities without having to orient their receptors in particular directions. Consider the case of auditory attention: you can go to a party at which numerous conversations are going on simultaneously and successfully attend to one conversation over the din of others, regardless of the direction your ears are "aimed." You may be listening to the person standing directly in front of you, or, if that person has been rambling on for more than an hour about the difficulty he has had cultivating rhubarb in his backyard, you may instead tune in to a more interesting conversation a few feet to your right or left. Even though you may be looking directly at the rhubarb-grower and nodding in mock agreement, your attention is somewhere else altogether!

The ability to attend to one spoken message while ignoring others—aptly called the *cocktail party phenomenon*—has been studied using a technique called shadowing: a research subject listens through earphones to two simultaneously spoken messages and tries to repeat the message presented by one of the speakers. By assessing the accuracy of the subject's repetition, researchers have been able to develop theories about cognitive processes underlying attention.

In pioneering research by Cherry (1953), subjects who listened simultaneously to two speeches (each consisting of numerous clichés strung together) spoken by the same individual were unable to attend to just one of the speeches: although the subjects were able to repeat entire clichés accurately, they sampled these clichés equally from the two speeches. On the other hand, when two messages on different topics were spoken simultaneously by different speakers with different voices coming from different directions, repetition of one of the messages was much more accurate.

Subjects who shadow one of two messages notice very little of the other message. They can seldom report any of the words included in that unattended message and typically do not even notice whether the language spoken is their native tongue. Superficial characteristics, such as a change from a man's voice to a woman's voice, are noticed, but the content of the message is not (Cherry, 1953). Because of Cherry's findings, an early theory of attention (Broadbent, 1958) likened auditory attention to a filter that allowed the selection of one message on the basis of physical characteristics and the screening out of others, much as a television tuner tunes in to one broadcast and shuts out the rest.

However, research subsequent to Broadbent's proposed filter theory has indicated that people do not totally filter out information from a supposedly unattended message. Subjects in shadowing experiments notice particularly meaningful words (such as their own names) in the unattended message (Treisman, 1964). They also hear words or phrases from that message if they fit meaningfully into the attended message (Gray & Wedderburn, 1960; Treisman, 1964). For example, suppose you hear these two sentences simultaneously and are asked to shadow only the first one:

Speaker 1: I bought candy at the plate today.

Speaker 2: Put the rhubarb on my store, please.

You might very well "hear" the first speaker say, "I bought candy at the store today" (borrowing the word *store* from the second speaker) because such a sentence makes more sense than what the speaker really did say.

Rather than thinking of attention as a filter, most psychologists now conceptualize attention as a result of cognitive processing and more specifically as another instance of construction (e.g., Neisser, 1967): depending on what stimulus they wish to pay attention to, people select certain pieces of information from among those they receive and construct a perception from them. For example, at a cocktail party they select the sounds that resemble a particular person's voice and that seem to fit into a meaningfully constructed sentence. However, if a word from another speaker seems to fit the meaning, it might very well be incorporated into what is "heard."

Attention as a Limited Capacity

Life might be much simpler if people didn't have to choose certain stimuli to pay attention to, but could just attend to *everything*. However, it turns out that people are incapable of attending to everything at once. For example, Figure 9–12 shows a figure sometimes called the Peter-Paul goblet. At first glance, you probably see a white goblet. But if you look at the black spaces on either side of the goblet, you should also be able to see two silhouettes ("Peter" and "Paul") staring at each other.

Now try this little exercise: See if you can focus on both the goblet and the two silhouettes at *exactly* the same time, so that you can clearly see the details of both. Can you do it? Most people are unable to attend to the goblet

Figure 9–12
The Peter-Paul goblet

and the faces at exactly the same time, although they may be able to shift their focus from the goblet to the faces and back again very quickly.

The Peter-Paul goblet illustrates the Gestalt principle of *figure-ground*: an individual can attend to one object (the *figure*) and notice the details of that object. Whatever the individual is not paying attention to (that is, the background, or *ground*) is not carefully inspected: some salient characteristics, such as color, may be noticed, but more specific information about unattended objects is overlooked. According to the Gestaltist notion of figure-ground, an individual can pay attention to only one thing at a time, hence the difficulty most people have in attending to both the goblet and the faces simultaneously. Several more recent theorists (e.g., Broadbent, 1958; Cherry, 1953; Treisman, 1964; Welford, 1977) have also supported such a *time-sharing* model of attention, proposing, as the Gestaltists did, that people can attend to only one meaningful source of information at a time. In situations where more than one stimulus requires attention, one's attention must be switched quickly back and forth from one to another.

But now consider a situation in which you are driving your car while also carrying on a conversation with a friend. Are you not attending to two things, the road and the conversation, at once? To account for such a situation, some theorists (e.g., Anderson, 1985; Kahneman, 1973; Norman & Bobrow, 1975) have begun to describe attention as involving a *limited processing capacity*, with the number of stimuli being attended to depending on how much cognitive processing is required for each stimulus. If you are engaging in a difficult task, such as learning to drive a car with a standard transmission, you may very well need to devote your full attention to that task. However, if you are doing something more habitual or automatic, such as driving a standard transmission after years of driving experience, you can easily devote some attention to another activity.

Regardless of how we view attention, one thing is clear: people's ability to attend is limited, such that they probably cannot attend to two *demanding* tasks at the same time (Anderson, 1985). Because of this, people must be very selective about the information they choose to process and must ignore a lot of the information they receive. Because attention plays a critical role in the human memory system, learning and memory are also affected by this limited capacity. Frustrating as it may seem, people simply cannot attend to, learn, and remember everything they encounter.

PERCEPTION AND ATTENTION IN EDUCATION

Perception and attention both play critical roles in the educational process. In this section, we will focus on several topics related to perception and attention in the classroom: perception and interpretation in learning, attention in the classroom, attentional processes in reading and spelling, and attention in study behavior.

Perception and Interpretation in Learning

Earlier in the chapter, we examined a number of influences on how people perceive the world. Two particular influences—past experience and expectations—will of course vary from one individual to the next. As a result, teachers should expect that different students will perceive their classroom experiences differently and will therefore learn different things from them.

Students' perceptions will probably show the greatest variability in situations involving ambiguous stimuli. For example, consider this situation. A teacher enters the classroom with a noticeable frown on her face. Sally might perceive her teacher as being sad about a recent event, George might think she is ill, Martha might believe she is angry with the class, and Paul might believe she is showing displeasure specifically with *his* behavior. Because a frown can reflect a number of different emotional and physical states, it is likely to be interpreted in many different ways.

Teachers must also remember that their own perceptions are subject to distortion as well. Students' behaviors can often be ambiguous enough that they are subject to a variety of interpretations; as an example, remember the case of Hannah that I described earlier in the chapter. Teachers' expectations for students influence their evaluations of those students (Good, 1987; Harari & McDavid, 1973). Furthermore, expectations also influence the ways in which teachers behave toward students, thus indirectly affecting students' achievement and classroom performance (Good, 1987). For example, teachers tend to treat low-achieving students differently from high-achieving students: low achievers are given less attention, criticized more often for their failures, and praised less frequently for their successes (Good, 1987). There does seem to be some truth to Rosenthal and Jacobson's (1968) notion of the *self-fulfilling prophecy*: how teachers expect students to perform to some degree affects how students actually *do* perform.

Attention in the Classroom

Classrooms are usually lively environments, with many stimuli competing for children's attention. Children are almost always attending to *something*, but that something may not be what their teacher wants them to attend to. For example, think of yourself in one of your college classes. Sometimes you pay attention to what the teacher is saying, but at other times your attention drifts to such things as the size of the instructor's nose, the style of another student's clothes, the doodles on your notebook, or the plans you have made for the upcoming weekend. If adults cannot pay attention during every minute of the class day, it is unreasonable to expect younger students to do so, either. But when students' attention wanders away from the topic of instruction, little learning of the kind the teacher desires is likely to occur.

How can teachers keep students' attention on the task at hand? Here are some suggestions.

Include variety in topics and presentation styles. Too many students see their classroom environments as dull and repetitious. For example, when my children come home from school and I ask them what exciting things have happened that day, their responses are usually "Nothing" or "Same old thing." Repetition of the same topics and the same procedures day after day can lead to boredom and reduced attention (Zirin, 1974). Variety and novelty in the subject matter and the mode of presentation will help keep students' attention focused on a lesson (Berlyne, 1960; Good & Brophy, 1984; Keele, 1973).

Minimize distractions when seatwork is assigned. As you well know, most students are better able to concentrate on seatwork assignments when the classroom is relatively quiet and subdued. Several "open classroom" schools in my region have recently acquired new walls for this very reason: too many different activities were occurring in the large, open classroom spaces, and students and teachers alike often found it difficult to focus their attention on any one thing for very long.

Monitor students' attention. Behaviors often provide a clue to whether students are paying attention. For example, students should direct their eyes at the teacher, workbook, or other appropriate stimulus and should be clearly working on the task at hand (Grabe, 1986; Piontkowski & Calfee, 1979; Samuels & Turnure, 1974).

Ask questions. Questions are an excellent way of maintaining students' attention that might otherwise wander away from a lesson (Grabe, 1986; Piontkowski & Calfee, 1979; Samuels & Turnure, 1974). By asking questions periodically, occasionally addressing questions to particular students, you can help students keep their attention where it should be.

Seat students near the teacher if they have difficulty paying attention. Research by Schwebel and Cherlin (1972) indicates that students are more likely to pay attention when they are placed at the front of the room and near the teacher. Front row seats may be particularly appropriate for students with a history of being easily distractible.

Attentional Processes in Reading and Spelling

Attention obviously influences how well students learn academic subjects. Its role is particularly important in reading and spelling, topics to which we turn now.

Reading. Reading is a cognitive process that can be at least partly understood in terms of the principles of perception and attention that we have discussed in this chapter. For example, as I showed you earlier, people tend to perceive groups of letters that appear close together as words. They also tend to see what they expect to see on a page: for example, the words *How are* . . . are frequently followed by the word *you*, and so that word may be *perceived* whether it appears on the page or not.

Beginning readers pay close attention to the letters on the page as they read and as a result often read slowly and without much comprehension. More mature readers tend not to look as carefully at the printed page. Instead, they rely on such things as context, sentence syntax, prior knowledge about a topic, and expectations about what the author is trying to communicate to jump to hasty, although usually accurate, conclusions about what is on the page. Precisely because mature readers *do* jump to conclusions about what is written, without taking time look at all the letters, can they read as quickly and efficiently as they do (Smith, 1988).

At the same time, mature readers run the risk of jumping to the *wrong* conclusions and therefore misinterpreting what they read. For example, my name—Jeanne Ormrod—is frequently misread as "Jeanne Orm*ond*," an error that I find quite annoying. But let's face it: Ormrod is an unusual name, while Ormond is more common. One can almost not blame readers who see *Orm* . . . and just assume that the rest of the word is . . . *ond*. (I blame them anyway.)

The design of reading materials themselves will also influence children's attentional processes. For example, an excessive number of pictures in a textbook, while possibly increasing the book's attractiveness, can distract a child's attention away from the more important part of the book—the text (Samuels, 1967). The presence of questions within a text (for example, questions at the beginning of a chapter) directs students' attention toward information that answers those questions, but sometimes away from information not related to those questions (e.g., Anderson & Biddle, 1975; Andre, 1979).

Spelling. I have long contended that students learn as much about spelling from their reading as they do from specific spelling instruction (e.g., Ormrod, 1986b, 1986c). By the time they reach college, students are expected to spell many words (e.g., *psychology* and *environment*) that probably were never included in their formal spelling lessons. If students know how to spell such words, it is generally because they have learned the spellings through repeated exposure to them in their reading assignments and recreational reading.

Several research studies (e.g., Frith, 1978, 1980; Ormrod, 1985, 1986a) indicate that spelling ability is probably related to reading style. Although it is quite possible to read without attending closely to the printed page, some students continue to pay close attention to the words they read even as their reading skills mature; these students are the good spellers. Mature readers with good verbal skills who are nevertheless poor spellers tend to be readers who rely more on context clues and their own expectations than on the specific letters on the page. Their attention to the page may be sufficient for them to identify words accurately but insufficient for them to learn how to spell those same words.

Attention in Study Behavior

Even when students are paying attention to the appropriate stimulus, they may be focusing on something very different from what the teacher thinks they are focusing on. The stimulus that the teacher presents to students—sometimes called the *nominal stimulus*—is not necessarily the stimulus that a student is actually attending to—the *effective stimulus*. For example, suppose a teacher teaching a phonics lesson presents a picture of a girl and asks for the first letter of the word it represents. Although the teacher is expecting the answer G, a student who focuses on the girl's dress may instead respond with D.

Once when I was teaching introductory psychology to college freshmen, a student who had failed my first two examinations approached me and expressed frustration about her lack of success in my class. When I asked her to describe how she went about completing the assigned readings in the textbook, she told me, "Well, I start looking through the chapter, and when I get to a page that looks important, I read it." I soon discovered that this young woman had been reading approximately one out of every three pages assigned! In this case, the effective stimulus was only one-third of the nominal stimulus.

As another example of how attention can influence students' studying and learning from curriculum materials, let's look at an experiment by Faust and Anderson (1967), in which students studied Russian vocabulary words under one of two conditions. Some students read single statements presenting an English word and its Russian equivalent, then were required to write the Russian word. Below is an example of the materials these students received:

A table is a stohl.
A table is a _____ .

Other students were shown short paragraphs, each containing several Russian words and their English equivalents, following which they wrote one of the Russian words. An example follows:

A rag is a tryapka. A bridge is a
mohst. A table is a stohl. A college
is a vooz. An onion is a look.
A table is a _____ .

Faust and Anderson found that students who were shown the paragraphs learned the English meanings of more Russian words than students who were given the single sentences, and reasoned that differences in attention explained the difference in achievement. To understand how attention might differ in the two situations, pretend for a moment that you are a student who wants to complete the Russian vocabulary task with a minimum of time and effort. Now look at the first set of stimulus materials. You don't have to read (attend to) the English word to answer correctly with *stohl*. If you know that the Russian word consistently appears at the last word of the sentence, then you only need to attend to that last word and copy it on the blank line. As a result, you may learn the Russian word but not connect it to its English meaning.

Now look at the second set of stimulus materials. Because several Russian words appear in the paragraph, you must determine which of them is the correct answer. At the very least, you must look at the English vocabulary word *table* in the incomplete statement at the bottom, then locate that word in the paragraph above. You find "A table is a *stohl*" and so write *stohl* in the blank. You may or may not have paid attention to other sentences in the paragraph, but at least you have attended to both the English word and its Russian equivalent. Hence, you are more likely to learn that *stohl* means "table."

As you have probably concluded, perception and attention can be idiosyncratic processes indeed: individuals attend to and perceive the world in their own unique ways, and all may arrive at different conclusions about what they have seen and heard. That different students perceive the same educational environment differently may be frustrating for teachers, for it will not be possible to control totally how students perceive instructional materials and events, or even what materials students pay attention to.

There is an old saying, "You can lead a horse to water, but you can't make him drink." Ormrod's corollary is: "The horse can't possibly drink if you don't at least lead him to the water." Drawing students' attention to important information is the first step in helping them learn information: it gets them to the water trough. Helping them drink up that information— that is, helping them store the information in their memory systems—is the next step, one that we will explore in the following chapters.

SUMMARY

Perception is a process of recognizing and interpreting one's sensations of environmental events. People do not perceive everything their bodies have sensed; at the same time, they also perceive things *beyond* their sensations (for example, by filling in an incomplete picture). Perception is a constructive process that is influenced by proximity, similarity, closure, context, past experience, and expectation. Attention involves the selection of certain stimuli from among many environmental events for further processing. Like perception, attention is constructive and is influenced by such stimulus characteristics as size, intensity, novelty, incongruity, emotion, and personal significance. Attentional capacity is limited; an individual can probably not pay attention to more than one demanding task at any given time. Accordingly, the individual must be selective about what events are attended to. Our understanding of perception and attention processes has numerous implications for classroom practice; attention plays a particularly important role in reading, spelling, and study skills.

Theories of Memory

I MAGINE yourself studying for an upcoming exam based on a complicated reading assignment. You understand most of the material and are confident that you will remember it. However, you have trouble learning one section of the assignment because it doesn't make much sense to you. In desperation, you try to memorize this section word for word, but your learning is slow and painful.

Now imagine yourself taking that exam. It was not as difficult as you had anticipated it would be, but you cannot remember the answer to a particularly trivial question: "What was Edward C. Tolman's middle name?" You know you studied the relevant section in the book, but you simply cannot remember the information called for. After considering all the names you can think of that begin with C, you finally give up and turn in your exam paper with the question unanswered.

Immediately afterward, you congregate with your classmates in the hall and rehash the questions. "What was Tolman's middle name?" you ask. Your friend Harry responds smugly, "It was Chace. I can remember that easily because my sister married a guy named Marvin Chace." And then your friend Carol adds, "I learned the name by imagining Tolman *chacing* his rats down their mazes." You grit your teeth, thinking it ridiculous that Harry and Carol would do better than you on a question because of a coincidental brother-in-law or a silly visual image. But let's face it, your classmates remembered and you did not.

Learning a piece of information does not guarantee that the information will be remembered later on. A number of variables determine what information gets into memory in the first place and what information stays there long enough to be remembered when it is needed. In this chapter, we will explore some models of how the human memory system works and how various factors influence its effectiveness.

Two major approaches are used in studying human cognition (Calfee, 1981). One approach focuses on the *structures* of the human mind, i.e., on its different components and their interrelationships. The second focuses on the mind's *functions*, i.e., on how the mind operates to process information. We will begin our examination of theories of memory with the *dual-store model*, one that focuses primarily on structure. Later in the chapter, we will turn to alternative views of memory that focus more on how memory functions and how information is processed.

THE DUAL-STORE MODEL OF MEMORY

In the latter part of the nineteenth century, the Harvard psychologist William James (1890) proposed that human memory has three components: an after-image, a primary memory, and a secondary memory. James's model was largely ignored during the behaviorism-dominated early decades of the twentieth century, but the advent of cognitivism in the 1960s brought a renewed interest in human memory, and in 1968, Richard Atkinson and Richard Shiffrin (1968, 1971) proposed a model of memory similar to that of James. Despite some weaknesses that I will describe later in the chapter, the Atkinson-Shiffrin dual-store model has become the most prevalent view of human memory.

The Atkinson-Shiffrin model of memory, simplified in Figure 10–1, has three components: *sensory register* (SR), *short-term memory* (STM), and *long-term memory* (LTM). Information from the environment—input—first enters the sensory register, where it is held for a short time (in the case of visual information, less than a second). If the information is processed in a particular way, it moves on to short-term memory. Information is held in short-term memory only for a few seconds, however, and must be processed further if it is to move on to long-term memory. The processing of information in short-term memory frequently involves the use of information from long-term memory as well (hence the two-way arrows between short-term and long-term memory in Figure 10–1). If a piece of information reaches sensory register or short-term memory but is not then processed sufficiently for its transference to the next component of the memory system, that information is assumed to be lost from the memory system—in other words, it is forgotten. Whether information can be lost from long-term memory as well (note the dotted arrow and question mark) is still an open question, one that we will address in Chapter 12.

The Atkinson-Shiffrin model of human memory can be likened to an information selection and storage system similar to what you might use to store important documents at home. You undoubtedly acquire numerous

Figure 10–1
A dual-store model of the human memory system

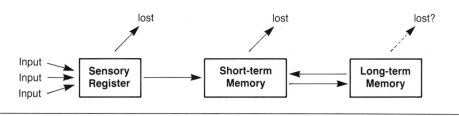

pieces of paper in your home over the course of a few months; among this mass of paper may be such items as newspapers, personal letters, bills, a driver's license, university transcripts, junk mail, and grocery store receipts. You probably discard some items (such as junk mail and grocery receipts) almost as soon as you get them; these things get no further than the sensory register of your storage system. Others (such as bills) need to be dealt with briefly (e.g., paid), then can be more or less forgotten; they are processed for a short time in your system's short-term storage. Still others (such as a driver's license and transcripts) may be important enough that you want to put them in a safe, organized place where you will be able to find them later; they end up in a long-term storage compartment such as a wallet, desk drawer, or safe deposit box.

In this chapter we will examine the characteristics of the three components of the Atkinson-Shiffrin model; we will also look at the various *control processes* that affect the movement of information from one component to another. However, as we proceed, we must remember that the language we will use in our discussion of human memory is largely metaphorical in nature (Roediger, 1980). For example, the three components of memory— sensory register, short-term memory, and long-term memory—are not necessarily three separate "places" in the brain. Furthermore, when we talk about memory processes, we are not necessarily saying anything about neurological events. Psychologists still know very little about how memory processes occur physiologically or how brain structure is related to psychological models of human memory.

SENSORY REGISTER

The first component of the Atkinson-Shiffrin model, the sensory register (also called sensory memory, sensory store, iconic memory, or echoic memory) holds incoming information long enough that it can undergo preliminary cognitive processing. All environmental information that we are capable of sensing probably stays with us in the sensory register for a *very* brief time. For example, if you have ever waved a flashlight or sparkler in the air on a dark night, you have probably noticed that the light leaves a trail behind it. This trail is not present in the air itself; it is the result of your sensory register holding the light you have seen for a short time after you saw it. As another example, when you sit in a classroom for an hour or more, your attention will almost inevitably wander away from the instructor at some point. You may have noticed that when you tune back in to what the instructor is saying, you can often recall two or three words that the instructor has said *before* your tuning in. Virtually everything the instructor has uttered has probably been recorded in your sensory register despite your mental absence from class, but, alas, only those last two or three words are still there when you decide to be present again.

Characteristics of Sensory Register

Researchers have examined three characteristics of sensory register: capacity, form of storage, and duration. Let's look at each of these in turn.

Capacity. The capacity of sensory register is, as far as psychologists can tell, unlimited. All the environmental information that human beings are capable of sensing is probably stored briefly in sensory register.

Form of Storage. Information appears to be stored in sensory register basically in the form in which it has been sensed: visual input is stored in a visual form, auditory input in an auditory form, and so on (Coltheart, Lea, & Thompson, 1974; Howard, 1983; Turvey & Kravetz, 1970). At this point, information has not yet been understood or interpreted by the individual. Sensory register holds information *before* it is processed.

Duration. As I have previously stated, information remains in sensory register for only a very brief time. But measuring its exact duration has been difficult. One problem in studying the characteristics of sensory register is that once people are asked to process the information stored there, it is automatically moved on to short-term memory, so is no longer in the place where we want to study it!

The classic experiment designed to assess the duration of sensory register was conducted by George Sperling (1960). Using adult subjects, Sperling presented displays of three rows of four letters and digits, like this:

$$
\begin{array}{cccc}
7 & 1 & V & F \\
X & L & 5 & 3 \\
B & 4 & W & 7 \\
\end{array}
$$

Each display was presented for a fraction of a second, following which the subjects were asked either to recall one particular row of symbols or else to recall all twelve symbols. When asked to recall a row, subjects were able to do so with seventy-six percent accuracy; because they were not told *which* row they would need to recall until after the display had disappeared, the subjects apparently remembered approximately seventy-six percent of the symbols they had seen. Yet when asked to recall all twelve symbols, they could do so with only thirty-six percent accuracy! Sperling's explanation of this result was that most of the symbols were stored initially but faded from memory before the subjects had a chance to write them all down. In a follow-up experiment, Sperling (1960) varied the amount of time that elapsed between the display and the signal indicating which row was to be remembered. Subjects could recall little of a display after a delay of more than a quarter second.

Estimating from research results such as those of Sperling, it appears that the duration of visual information in sensory register is probably less than a second (Loftus & Loftus, 1976; Wingfield & Byrnes, 1981). Auditory information, on the other hand, probably lasts longer, with a duration of two to four seconds (Conrad & Hull, 1964; Darwin, Turvey, & Crowder, 1972; Moray, Bates, & Barnett, 1965).

Why does auditory input last longer than visual input? One possible explanation (e.g., Wingfield & Byrnes, 1981) is that a major source of auditory input—human speech—can only be understood within its sequential context. For example, consider this often-heard sentence:

I scream for ice cream.

The sounds of the first two words can be interpreted either as *I scream* or *ice cream*. Only when you hear the third word—*for*—can you begin to interpret the first two words accurately. The task of understanding speech, which is often filled with temporarily ambiguous sounds, may be easier if you can hold those sounds in memory in an uninterpreted form until additional, clarifying information is received.

Probably two reasons account for the rapid disappearance of information from sensory register. First of all, *interference* may be a factor: new information coming in effectively erases the information already there (e.g., Breitmeyer & Ganz, 1976). Many psychologists also believe that, even without new input, existing information in sensory register simply fades away, or *decays*, over time (e.g., Loftus & Loftus, 1976; Wingfield & Byrnes, 1981). Regardless of the reasons for sensory register's short duration, in most instances people probably don't need to store information there for very long. Important information is probably going to be processed so that it enters short-term memory. Unimportant information, like junk mail, is probably best dealt with by throwing it away.

The Role of Attention

In Chapter 9, I indicated that attention is critical in human learning and memory. Now I can be more specific with regard to the role it plays. Attention is believed to be the process essential for moving information from sensory register to short-term memory. In essence, information to which one pays attention advances to short-term memory, whereas information that is not attended to may be lost from the memory system.

One reason that people don't learn, then, is their lack of attention to information in the first place. If you are sitting in class with your mind a thousand miles away from the professor's lecture, you might say that you forgot what the instructor said, or you might say that you never heard it in the first place. The reality of the situation is somewhere in between: the lecture reached your sensory register but was not sufficiently processed to move on to the next step in your memory system—short-term memory.

What happens to information that *does* enter short-term memory? Let's turn to that topic now.

SHORT-TERM MEMORY

Short-term memory is that component of the memory system in which the most active processing of information takes place. It is the component where thinking occurs and has often been likened to one's awareness or consciousness. Short-term memory selects what information will be attended to in sensory register and holds that information while it is being processed. In addition, short-term memory may also hold information retrieved from long-term memory—information that will help in the interpretation of newly received environmental input.

Characteristics of Short-term Memory

Just as we did for sensory register, let's look at three characteristics of short-term memory: capacity, form of storage, and duration.

Capacity. Unlike sensory register, short-term memory appears to have a limited capacity for storing information. After reviewing a number of studies related to short-term memory, George Miller (1956) proposed that the capacity of short-term memory can be characterized as the *magical number seven, plus or minus two*: that is, individuals can hold from five to nine units of information in short-term memory at one time, with the average number of memorable units being about seven.

Miller further proposed that although the *number* of information units in short-term memory cannot be increased beyond 7 ± 2, the *amount* of information in each unit can be increased. For example, consider this nine-digit string:

6 3 1 9 8 0 2 5 7

People are more successful in learning long strings of digits if they group the digits into larger numbers, perhaps storing them something like this:

6-3-1   9-8-0   2-5-7

This process of combining pieces of information, called *chunking,* increases the amount of information that can be stored in the limited space of short-term memory. To use Miller's analogy, if you can only hold seven coins, you're far richer holding seven quarters, or even seven gold pieces, than seven pennies.

More recent estimates of short-term memory vary from Miller's original assessment of 7 ± 2. It now appears that the number of chunks of information that can be stored depends on how much information is included in each chunk. For example, Simon (1974) found that, while he himself could remember a list of 7 one-syllable or two-syllable words, he could remember only 6 three-syllable words, 4 two-word phrases, and even fewer phrases of more than two words. In other words, the larger the chunks, the fewer of them that can be held in short-term memory at any one time.

Therefore, as Anderson (1985) has pointed out, it may be difficult to identify the true capacity of short-term memory, at least in terms of the number of discrete units of information that can be stored there at any given time. Furthermore, there may be a trade-off between how much processing is necessary and how much information can be held in short-term memory: cognitive processing may take up some of short-term memory's capacity, leaving less room for information storage. Nonetheless, one thing is clear: short-term memory can hold only a small amount of information at any one time.

Form of Storage. Regardless of the form in which information is received, it appears that much of the information stored in short-term memory is stored in an *auditory* form, at least when the information is language-based (Conrad, 1962, 1964, 1971). For example, in a study by Conrad (1964), adults were shown six-letter sequences, with letters being presented visually, one at a time, at three-fourth-second intervals. As soon as the last letter of each sequence had been presented, subjects wrote the letters down, guessing at any letters that they could not easily recall. When subjects made errors in their recollections, the letters they said they had seen were more likely to resemble the actual stimuli in terms of how they sounded than how they looked. For example, the letter F was remembered as the auditorially similar letter S 131 times, but as the visually similar letter P only 14 times. Similarly, the letter V was "remembered" as B 56 times, but as X only 5 times.

However, although auditory encoding of information in STM is common, it does not always occur. Deaf children, for example, probably store information in a visual form (Conrad, 1972). And young children (e.g., five-year-olds) are less likely to use an auditory code than older children (e.g., eleven-year-olds) (Conrad, 1971). Nevertheless, the auditory encoding of information provides a distinct advantage: it appears to improve the short-term memory of information (Conrad, 1971).

Duration. Short-term memory is exactly what its name implies: short. An experiment by Peterson and Peterson (1959), which I previously described in Chapter 7, gives us some idea of how long information in short-term memory lasts. In this experiment, adults were told three consonants (e.g., DXP), then immediately asked to count backward by threes from a three-digit number, which was different in each trial. At a signal that occurred anywhere from three to eighteen seconds after the three consonants had been presented, the subjects were asked to recall those letters. When their recall was delayed only three seconds, subjects were able to remember the letters with eighty percent accuracy; after an eighteen-second interval, however, their accuracy was only about ten percent.

Considering research results such as those of Peterson and Peterson, psychologists believe that the duration of short-term memory is probably somewhere between five and twenty seconds. As was true for sensory register, both decay and interference have been offered as explanations for this short time span. Some information stored in short-term memory may simply fade away if it is not processed further (Peterson & Peterson, 1959; Reitman, 1974; Shiffrin & Cook, 1978). Other information may be pushed out by new information (e.g., Keppel & Underwood, 1962; Melton, 1963; Reitman, 1974). For example, with a husband and three children in the house, I find myself frequently interrupted in the middle of tasks. If I have a batch of cookies in the oven, and Jeff asks me to make him a snack and Tina asks me to help her find her homework assignment, my cookies are very likely to be pushed from my short-term memory until I am confronted with new environmental input: the smell of something burning. My husband calls me absentminded, but I know better. My mind is definitely present, but the short-term component of it has a limited capacity, and new input interferes with the information already stored there.

Control Processes in Short-term Memory

Some processes in short-term memory—storing information in short-term memory, keeping it there, and retrieving it again so that it can be used—are related only to short-term memory itself. Still other processes are directed at moving information from short-term memory into long-term memory. At this point I will describe only the former processes, focusing on three in particular: organization, retrieval, and maintenance rehearsal. The processes that facilitate the transference of information into long-term memory will be discussed in the upcoming section on long-term memory.

Organization. Earlier, I described Miller's (1956) proposal that the process of chunking helps increase the amount of information that can be stored in short-term memory. As they develop, children show an increasing tendency to chunk information, thereby enhancing the capacity of their short-term memories (Farnham-Diggory, 1972).

Chunking is an organizational process, in that two or more pieces of information are combined. Information can be organized in a variety of ways. For example, consider again the 9-digit string I presented earlier:

6 3 1 9 8 0 2 5 7

I have already described one way of chunking this string: grouping it into three groups of three digits each. Another frequently observed organizational strategy is to impose a rhythm, or even a melody, to the numbers (Bower & Springston, 1970). Still another way of organizing the digits is to attach some meaning to them. For example, I can store the numbers as three meaningful pieces of information: my son Alex's birthday (the 6th month and 3rd day of 1980), a quarter (25 cents), and a week (7 days).

Retrieval. Retrieval of information from short-term memory depends largely on how much information is stored there, a point illustrated in a study by Sternberg (1966). In this experiment, college students were presented with a set of from one to six numbers (numbers that presumably were stored in short-term memory). Still another number was presented, and the students were asked whether that number had been among the original set. The time it took for subjects to answer the question almost entirely depended on the size of number set already stored in short-term memory, with each successively larger set yielding a reaction time of about forty milliseconds longer. Apparently, short-term memory retrieval is simply a process of scanning all of short-term memory, successively and exhaustively, until the desired information is found.

Maintenance Rehearsal. You look up a friend's telephone number and store that number in your short-term memory; its seven digits are about the limit of what your short-term memory can hold. But then you find that someone else is using the telephone, and so you must wait to place your call. How do you keep your friend's number in short-term memory? If you are like most people, you probably repeat it to yourself over and over again.

Repeating information to keep it alive in short-term memory is a process known as *maintenance rehearsal,* something that is perhaps a form of subvocal speech (e.g., Landauer, 1962; Sperling, 1967). Maintenance rehearsal provides a means by which information can be saved from the forgetting processes of decay and interference. You may recall that in Peterson and Peterson's (1959) examination of the duration of short-term memory that I described earlier, subjects were presented with three consonants, then asked to count backward by threes until the signal for recall. The backward counting kept subjects from rehearsing the three letters; otherwise, they might have kept them in short-term memory indefinitely simply by repeating them over and over as long as necessary.

Maintenance rehearsal is observed more frequently in older children and adults than in younger children (Conrad, 1971), so it may possibly be a learned skill. I myself used rehearsal frequently in high school and college whenever I had difficulty remembering a complicated piece of information I needed for an examination—a definition, a list, or a formula, for example. I would continue to repeat it to myself until I received the exam sheet, then would immediately write the information down in the margin so that it would be there for me if and when I needed it.

Although maintenance rehearsal can indeed be a useful strategy for keeping information in short-term memory, teachers must remember that information in short-term memory will disappear once rehearsal stops. If students are frequently observed using maintenance rehearsal, it should be an indication that they are having trouble storing that information in their *long*-term memories. Yet long-term memory is where important information should be stored, so let us turn now to that final component of the Atkinson-Shiffrin model.

LONG-TERM MEMORY

Long-term memory is clearly the most complicated component of the human memory system. As such, it has been studied more extensively than either sensory register or short-term memory, and theories about its characteristics and control processes abound. We will briefly examine the major characteristics of long-term memory here and explore them in more depth in the following two chapters.

Characteristics of Long-term Memory

As we did for both sensory register and short-term memory, we will look at the capacity, form of storage, and duration of long-term memory and then turn to control processes.

Capacity. As far as theorists can determine, the capacity of long-term memory is unlimited. In fact, as you will discover in Chapter 11, the more information that is already stored in long-term memory, the easier it is to store additional information there.

Form of Storage. Information is probably stored in long-term memory in a number of different ways. For example, language provides one basis of storing information, and visual imagery may provide another. However, most psychologists agree that the bulk of information in long-term memory is probably stored *semantically*—in terms of meanings.

Two characteristics of long-term memory storage should be mentioned here. First, information is rarely stored in long-term memory exactly as it was received. Individuals tend to remember the "gist" of what they see and hear rather than word-for-word sentences or precise mental images. Second, information stored in long-term memory is organized: related pieces of information tend to be associated together. Ultimately, probably every piece of information is either directly or indirectly connected with every other piece.

Duration. As you will learn in Chapter 12, theorists disagree with regard to the duration of long-term memory. Some theorists believe that information, once stored in long-term memory, remains there permanently. Others, however, believe that information can disappear from long-term memory through a variety of forgetting processes. In fact, although some information may remain in long-term memory for long periods of time, there is probably no way to show conclusively that *all* information stored there remains permanently. The question about the duration of long-term memory is still an open one, and the best we can say is that long-term memory's duration is indefinitely *long*.

Control Processes in Long-term Memory

We will now briefly consider what processes are involved in the storage of information in long-term memory and in the subsequent retrieval of stored information.

Storage. Storage processes in the first two components of memory are relatively straightforward; anything sensed is stored in sensory register, and anything attended to is stored in short-term memory. However, as we shall see in the following chapter, storage of information in long-term memory is not so easily accomplished. Although some information may be stored easily (visual images are an example), most information must be consciously and actively processed before it is stored. Information is most likely to be stored in long-term memory when it is understood, organized, and integrated with information already stored there.

Remember, the processing necessary for the storage of information in long-term memory is accomplished in short-term memory. And remember, too, that short-term memory has a limited capacity, such that it can only handle so much information at one time. The result is that long-term memory storage occurs slowly, and a great deal is lost from short-term memory along the way. In essence, short-term memory is the bottleneck in the memory system: it prevents most information from ever getting into long-term memory.

Retrieval. Retrieval of information from sensory register and short-term memory is relatively simple: if the information is still there, it will probably be found. Retrieval of information from long-term memory is more difficult: long-term memory has much more information than an individual can realistically search through at one time, and so the success of retrieval depends largely on whether the individual searches in the right "location." Furthermore, retrieval from long-term memory is closely tied to storage processes: the more completely information has been understood, the better it has been organized, and the more closely it has been integrated with previously stored concepts, the more easily that information can be remembered.

Speaking of retrieval from long-term memory, what was Edward C. Tolman's middle name? Did you perhaps remember your friend Harry's brother-in-law, Marvin *Chace*? Or did you think of Tolman *chacing* his rats down their mazes? The more ways individuals store a piece of information in long-term memory, the more likely it is that the information will be retrieved when it is needed.

ARE SHORT-TERM MEMORY AND
LONG-TERM MEMORY REALLY DIFFERENT?

Up to this point, we have been talking about short-term memory and long-term memory as two distinctly different components of memory; in other words, we have been talking about a *dual-store* model. Some psychologists, however, have proposed that short-term and long-term memory are really a single entity. Let's look at the evidence both in favor of and against the short-term memory/long-term memory distinction.

Evidence Supporting the Distinction

Several research findings have been cited as evidence for the distinction between short-term and long-term memory. For one thing, the major form of storage in the two memories appears to be different, short-term memory being primarily acoustic and long-term memory being primarily semantic.

Secondly, you may recall the serial learning curve described in Chapter 7. Given a list of items to remember, individuals more often remember the first few items in the list (a *primacy effect*) and the last few items (a *recency effect*) than they remember the middle items. The serial learning curve has frequently been explained in terms of a dual-store model (e.g., Glanzer & Cunitz, 1966; Norman, 1969). The first few items in the list can be processed sufficiently for their storage in long-term memory, and the last few items are still stored in short-term memory. The middle items, however, cannot be processed into long-term memory (presumably because the rate of item presentation does not allow adequate time for processing), and they have been pushed out of short-term memory by later items. In support of the view that early items in the list are stored in long-term memory is the finding that when the presentation rate is slowed down (thus allowing for more processing), the primacy effect is increased (Glanzer & Cunitz, 1966). Conversely, when processing of list items is prevented, the primacy effect disappears; that is, items early in the list are remembered no better than items in the middle of the list (Peterson & Peterson, 1962). On the other hand, the recency effect seems to be more affected by the recall interval: the longer that recall of the list is delayed, the less individuals are able to remember items at the end of the list, a finding consistent with the notion that these items are stored in the short-lived short-term memory (Glanzer & Cunitz, 1966; Postman & Phillips, 1965).

Third, studies of individuals who have undergone certain brain injuries or neurosurgical procedures sometimes show an impairment of one memory without a corresponding loss of function in the other (Atkinson & Shiffrin, 1968; Scoville & Milner, 1957). For example, some individuals can recall events experienced before the brain trauma but are unable to retain new experiences, indicating a possible problem with short-term memory while long-term memory remains intact. Other individuals can recall new experiences long enough to talk briefly about them but cannot remember them a few minutes later; here are cases where short-term memory is functioning, but new information seemingly cannot be transferred into long-term memory.

Evidence Against the Distinction

Other research findings indicate that short-term memory and long-term memory may not be as distinctly different as I have described them. For example, although information is frequently stored acoustically in short-term memory and semantically in long-term memory, there is also evidence for *semantic* storage in short-term memory (Shulman, 1971, 1972) and for *acoustic* storage in long-term memory (Nelson & Rothbart, 1972).

Furthermore, some of the evidence to support the dual-store model can also be explained without resorting to a short-term/long-term distinction. Wickelgren (1973), for instance, has proposed that the serial learning curve can be explained as easily by a single-store model as by a dual-store model. He has described forgetting as occurring rapidly at first and then slowly tapering off. From this perspective, the recency effect may be due simply to the fact that the last items of a list have not yet undergone that rapid decay.

Alternative explanations also exist for the impairments in memory observed in individuals who have undergone brain traumas (e.g., Glass, Holyoak, & Santa, 1979; Zechmeister & Nyberg, 1982). These impairments may reflect specific difficulties in storage or retrieval processes rather than in short-term or long-term memory per se.

The debate regarding dual-store and single-store models is by no means resolved; more complete discussions of the issue are presented elsewhere (e.g., Adams, 1980; Ellis & Hunt, 1983; Hintzman 1978; Loftus & Loftus, 1976; Travers, 1982; Wickelgren, 1973). In the meantime, recent memory research has shifted away from a focus on the components of memory to a focus instead on how information is processed. The alternative views I present next are examples of such functional theories.

FUNCTIONAL THEORIES OF HUMAN MEMORY

At least three alternatives to the Atkinson-Shiffrin model of memory have been proposed: levels of processing, working memory, and activation. These models emphasize the cognitive processes involved in human memory rather than its structure. Let's look briefly at each theory.

Levels of Processing

The *levels of processing* model of human memory (Cermak & Craik, 1979; Craik & Lockhart, 1972) was the first major theoretical alternative to the Atkinson-Shiffrin model. According to this view, incoming information is processed by a *central processor* at any one of a number of different levels of complexity. This central processor has a limited capacity, in that it can only hold so much at one time; the information temporarily held there is what we are aware of at any given time.

How long and how well information is remembered after it leaves the central processor is a function of how thoroughly it has been processed. Information that has not been processed at all leaves only a very brief impression (much as it does in Atkinson and Shiffrin's sensory register). Information that has been rehearsed in a meaningless fashion may last a few seconds (much as it does in Atkinson and Shiffrin's short-term memory). Only when information has undergone deep processing—that is, when it has been interpreted, understood, and related to previously learned information—is it remembered for any length of time.

An experiment by Turnure, Buium, and Thurlow (1976) illustrates how different levels of processing lead to different degrees of retention. Four- and five-year-old children were given the task of remembering pairs of common objects (for example, remembering that *soap* and *jacket* go together). Children processed the information in one of five different ways, as follows:

1. Labels. They repeated the names of the objects.
2. Sentence generation. They made up sentences that included both objects in a pair.
3. Sentence repetition. They repeated experimenter-generated sentences in which a relationship between the two objects was stated (e.g., "The soap is hiding in the jacket").
4. "What" question. They answered a question about a relationship between the objects (e.g., "What is the soap doing in the jacket?").
5. "Why" question. They answered a question concerning why a particular relationship existed between the objects (e.g., "Why is the soap hiding in the jacket?").

In this experiment, children learned most effectively when they were forced to think about (i.e., to process) a relationship between the objects: the question-answering conditions (Conditions 4 and 5) led to the greatest recall of the word pairs. Repeating a sentence that expressed such a relationship (Condition 3) led to some recall; presumably repetition led to some processing of the association between each pair. Least effective for learning were the first two conditions. In the labeling condition (Condition 1), no relationship between objects was processed, and children in the sentence generation condition (Condition 2) often constructed sentences that did not effectively connect the two objects (an example might be "I have some soap and a jacket").

One element that frequently arises as important in learning is *intention to learn*: people who intend to learn something are more likely to learn and remember it than people who do not specifically try to learn that information. Proponents of the levels of processing model have argued that people process information more thoroughly when they are intending to learn it and that the depth of processing, rather than the intention to learn per se, affects the success of learning. In fact, research supports this point: when material is processed deeply, it will be successfully learned even when individuals are not specifically trying to learn that material (Postman, 1964). In other words, nonintentional learning (often called *incidental learning*) is just as effective as intentional learning if the degree of processing is equal in the two situations.

A study by Hyde and Jenkins (1969) provides an example of successful incidental learning due to deep processing. College students listened to a list of twenty-four words presented at a rate of one word every two seconds. Some students (a control group) were merely told to learn the words; thus, they would be intentionally learning the words. Different experimental groups received different instructions, as follows:

1. Pleasantness rating. Students were told to rate each word for its degree of pleasantness; for example, a word such as *love* might be rated as relatively pleasant, while *hate* might be rated as less pleasant.
2. Counting letters. Students were told to count the number of letters in each word.
3. Counting letter E's. Students were told to count the number of letter E's in each word.

At the same time, some of the students receiving each of the different instructions (intentional learning subjects) were told to learn the words as they went along. Other students (incidental learning subjects) were not told to learn the words.

The different tasks used in the Hyde and Jenkins study should lead to different levels of processing. In counting all the letters in a word or the number of E's, one needs to look only at the superficial characteristics of the word and does not have to interpret the word's meaning; thus, a counting task should lead to relatively shallow processing. In rating a word's pleasantness, one must examine the word's meaning; hence, deeper, semantic processing of the word should result. Consistent with levels of processing theory, subjects who rated words for their pleasantness remembered more words than subjects who counted letters. More interesting, however, is the fact that incidental learning students who rated the words for their pleasantness generally remembered as many words as any of the intentional learning groups (in fact, they did better than the intentional counting groups). Here was a case where learning was facilitated simply by virtue of the fact that students had to focus on the underlying meaning of the material to be learned. Depth of processing, not intention to learn, was the critical factor affecting the degree of learning.

Despite such convincing evidence, however, weaknesses of the levels of processing model have begun to surface. Research has mounted to indicate that degree of learning is not always a function of the degree of processing in the way that the model predicts. For example, the more frequently information is repeated, the better it can be remembered *regardless* of the depth of processing it has undergone (Nelson, 1977). Even more damaging, however, is the finding that, in some cases, superficial processing actually leads to *better* recall than deeper processing. In an experiment by Morris, Bransford, and Franks (1977), college students were given a series of words and asked (1) whether each word fit appropriately into a sentence (a task involving deep semantic processing) or (2) whether the word rhymed with another word (a task involving superficial phonetic processing). Students recalled more words on an unexpected recall test when they had processed them semantically; however, they were more successful at identifying rhymes of the original words when they had processed them phonetically. Similar results have been reported by Stein (1978).

More recent thinking related to the levels of processing approach is that information processing is most effective not necessarily when it is semantic, but rather when it is *elaborative*—that is, when the learner adds information to the to-be-learned material in such a way that the new material is encoded more precisely, more meaningfully, and more completely (Craik & Tulving, 1975; Ellis & Hunt, 1983). We will examine the process of elaboration in more detail in the next chapter.

Working Memory

A term sometimes used as an alternative to short-term memory is *working memory* (e.g., Baddeley, 1978; Baddeley & Hitch, 1974; Daneman & Carpenter, 1980). The concept of working memory is similar to short-term memory but with a greater emphasis on its processing as well as its storage functions.

As an example of the storage and processing functions of working memory, try figuring this long division problem in your head, *without* referring back to the page until you have solved it:

$$37\overline{)4281}$$

Almost impossible, isn't it? You may have found that while you were dividing 37 into 42, you forgot what the last two digits of the dividend were. Although you probably had no trouble holding six numbers in your working memory, you may not have been able to hold all six and still process those numbers at the same time.

Short-term memory and working memory, although not identical concepts, both refer to the limited capacity storage and processing center that we often think of as consciousness or awareness. As a result, many psychologists use the two terms almost interchangeably. In later chapters, I will refer to this storage/processing center as short-term memory, but you should keep in mind the "working," processing aspect of it.

Memory Activation

Some psychologists (e.g., Anderson, 1984; Collins, & Loftus, 1975) propose that short-term and long-term memory are not separate components but instead simply reflect different *activation* states of a single memory. According to this view, all information stored in memory is in either an active or inactive state. Information that is currently active, which may include both incoming information and information previously stored in memory, is the information that individuals are paying attention to and processing—information that I have previously described as being in short-term memory. As attention shifts, other pieces of information in memory become activated, and the previously activated information gradually becomes inactive. The bulk of the information stored in memory is in an inactive state, so that we are not consciously aware of it—this is information that I have previously described as being in long-term memory. The activation theory of memory is particularly useful in understanding how individuals retrieve information from long-term memory. Accordingly, we will encounter this theory again in Chapter 12.

Clearly, not all theorists agree about exactly how memory is structured or how it functions. However, they do agree about a number of general principles with regard to human memory. Before we conclude this chapter,

The author activates part of her memory.

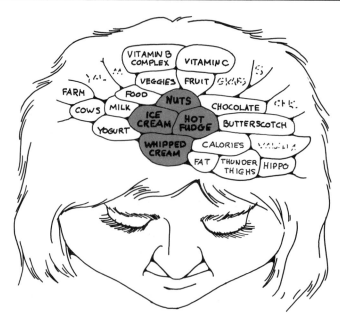

let's turn our attention to those principles and their educational applications.

GENERAL PRINCIPLES OF MEMORY AND THEIR EDUCATIONAL IMPLICATIONS

At least four general principles of memory have particular relevance to educational practice.

Attention is essential for learning. As we have seen, attention is considered the process through which information moves from sensory register into short-term memory. Although there is no guarantee that attended-to information will be stored in long-term memory (it must be processed further for that to happen), information that is *not* attended to will clearly *not* be learned. Teachers must always keep in mind the fact that students are going to learn information only when they are paying attention to it.

Short-term memory is the bottleneck in the human memory system. Short-term memory can hold only so much information and can process it only so fast. Accordingly, getting information into long-term memory will be a slow process. Educators must remember this point in pacing their lectures and choosing their instructional materials. When too much information is presented too fast, students simply cannot store it all in long-term memory.

Memory is selective. Because of the bottleneck nature of short-term memory, learners must continually make choices about what information to focus on and what information to ignore. The limited capacity of short-term memory to hold and process information is often forgotten by educators, who load students up with more details than they can possibly remember (Calfee, 1981). In such situations, students will select the information that they think is probably most important, but, as many teachers have found, students are not always the best judges of what is important and what is not.

Details are often important means of illustrating, clarifying, and elaborating upon the main points of a lecture or textbook. In this sense, they are indispensable. At the same time, students must be helped to sort through essential and nonessential information so that they don't lose sight of the forest because of the trees.

The limited capacity of short-term memory is not necessarily a bad thing. Because of the STM bottleneck, learners are forced to condense, organize, and synthesize the information they receive (Gagné & Driscoll, 1988). As you will discover in the following chapter, these processes are beneficial: they enable students to store information in their long-term memories in an efficient and meaningful way.

SUMMARY

The most prevalent view of human memory, the Atkinson-Shiffrin model, proposes that memory has three distinct components. The first component, sensory register (SR), holds information for a short period of time (a fraction of a second for visual information, two–four seconds for auditory information). Information that is attended to moves on to the second component, short-term memory (STM), which holds a small amount of information for five–twenty seconds. Information that undergoes further processing (e.g., comprehension, organization, and integration with previously stored information) moves on the third component, long-term memory (LTM). Theorists disagree as to whether short-term memory and long-term memory are really distinct entities, and at least three alternatives to the Atkinson-Shiffrin model have been proposed.

CHAPTER 11

Long-Term Memory I: Storage

A T least once a semester, a student will appear at my office door after receiving a low score on one of my exams. "But I studied so *hard!*" the student will whine, displaying a look of frustrated desperation. "I studied twice as long as my roommate did, yet my roommate only missed one question and I missed seventeen!"

Storing information in long-term memory and retrieving it later can be a tricky business. If the two roommates are equally motivated to achieve in my class, the difference between them may well be due to their storage and retrieval processes. After more than a decade of talking with students about how they typically study, I have come to the conclusion that most students are sadly uninformed about how best to learn and remember information.

Even when students do store information in their long-term memories, they don't always learn what their teachers *think* they are learning. For example, when my daughter Tina was in fourth grade, she came home one day complaining about a song she was learning in her elementary school choir. "It has bad words in it, Mom," she told me. I was quite surprised to learn that she was talking about "America the Beautiful," but then she recited the guilty line from the second verse:

all the bastard cities gleam.

After shuddering about the richness of my daughter's vocabulary, I patiently explained to her that the line in question was actually "alabaster cities gleam." Two weeks later the rest of the family went to hear Tina's choir performing in concert. As the children began to sing "America the Beautiful," six-year-old Alex turned to me and whispered, "Why are they singing about spaceship skies?"

Long-term memory provides a mechanism for storing information over a relatively long period of time. It also provides a knowledge base from which to interpret new information. As we shall see, the storage of incoming information in long-term memory is most effectively accomplished when that information can be related to what one already knows, that is, to information already residing in long-term memory. As a result, the same information will be stored differently by different individuals because the information already stored in their respective long-term memories is different. Alex had never heard the word *spacious* before, but *spaceship* was a frequent word in his world of science fiction cartoons. Similarly, Tina was unfamiliar with *alabaster*, but . . . well, never mind.

In this chapter, we will explore the complicated process of storing information in long-term memory. We will examine three aspects of storage: the variety of ways in which information can be encoded, the organization of that encoded information, and specific storage processes. In the following chapter, we will look at the processes involved in retrieving information from long-term memory and also at some possible reasons that some of that information may be forgotten.

ENCODING: HOW INFORMATION IS STORED IN LONG-TERM MEMORY

Take a minute and think about a rose. What things come to mind? Perhaps words like *flower, red, beautiful,* or *expensive* pop into your head. Perhaps you can picture what a rose looks like or imagine its smell. Perhaps you can even feel a thorn prick your finger as you reach out to clip a rose from its bush.

Information is probably encoded in long-term memory in a number of different ways. For one thing, it may be encoded *verbally,* represented in memory by words; for example, "Roses are red, violets are blue." Sometimes input is stored as an *image* that retains some of its physical characteristics; for example, a rose has a certain look and a particular smell. Input may also be represented as one or more *propositions,* so that its underlying abstract meaning is stored; for example, the fact that "A rose is a flower" may be stored as an abstract idea. Still another way in which information can be stored in long-term memory is *productions*—the procedures involved in performing a particular task. For example, one learns the procedure necessary for clipping a rose from a rose bush. These four forms of information storage—verbal codes, imagery, propositions, and productions—appear frequently in long-term memory theory, and so we will examine each of them in more detail.

Verbal Codes

There is no question that a good deal of information is stored in terms of words (e.g., Bower, 1972; Paivio, 1971). First of all, people store verbal labels for most of the objects and events in their lives; for example, this thing you are reading is called a *book.* Secondly, people sometimes learn information in a verbatim fashion; Hamlet's soliloquy ("To be or not to be . . . ") and the Preamble to the U.S. Constitution are examples of things that are typically learned word for word (Rubin, 1977). On still other occasions people use language to help them learn to associate things. For example, the French word for "dog" is *chien;* I usually remember this word by thinking "dog chain." Many of the principles that emerged from verbal learning research (e.g., the serial learning curve) probably apply primarily to information stored in a verbal code.

Imagery

Can you imagine your mother's face? The melody of a favorite song? The smell of a rose? If so, then you are probably using mental imagery. Many psychologists believe that individuals store images in several modalities, including visual, auditory, and olfactory ("smelling") modes. However, research and theory have emphasized visual imagery, so that is what we will focus on here.

Introspective reports have frequently been cited as support for the existence of visual imagery: people often say that they see pictures in their minds. However, given an inherent weakness of introspection—the fact that people cannot always describe their own cognitive processes accurately (Nisbett & Wilson, 1977; Zuriff, 1985)—psychologists have devised other research methods for demonstrating the existence of visual imagery. An ingenious example can be found in an experiment by Shepard and Metzler (1971) involving pictures of three-dimensional block configurations similar to those shown in Figure 11–1. In this experiment, adult subjects compared pairs of these pictures and determined whether they represented the same three-dimensional configuration. For example, (a) and (b) in Figure 11–1 constitute a "match": if (b) were rotated ninety degrees clockwise, it would be identical to (a). However, (a) and (c) are not a match: if (c) were rotated ninety degrees counterclockwise, it would be apparent that one of its top branches points in a different direction from (a).

Shepard and Metzler measured subjects' reaction time to each pair of figures, assuming that more extensive cognitive processing would be reflected in longer reaction times. Results were quite dramatic: reaction times were almost totally a function of how much a figure would have to be rotated for it to be lined up with another figure. In other words, subjects were responding as if they were mentally rotating images: more rotation resulted in a longer reaction time. Similar results were obtained when subjects compared rotated letters (Cooper & Shepard, 1973).

Figure 11–1
Figures similar to those used by Shepard and Metzler (1971)

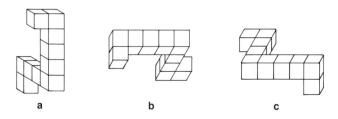

      a   b   c

Although some theorists (e.g., Pylyshyn, 1973) have argued against the existence of visual imagery, most psychologists believe that it is a distinct form of information storage (e.g., Bower, 1972; Kosslyn & Pomerantz, 1977; Paivio, 1971). The exact nature of visual imagery is still an open question, but one thing is clear: a visual image is probably *not* a mental snapshot. Visual images tend to be imprecise representations of external objects, with many details omitted or altered. Furthermore, individuals can construct mental images of things they have never seen; for example, you can probably visualize a rhinoceros with a pumpkin stuck on its horn even though you have never seen a rhino in that predicament. Psychologists are now beginning to think of imagery as being an *abstract analog* of visual input (e.g., Anderson, 1985; Glass et al., 1979).

Regardless of its exact nature, psychologists have learned a couple things about visual imagery that have implications for educators. First of all, imagery can be an extremely powerful means of storing information. Numerous studies have shown that people have a remarkably accurate memory for visual information (e.g., Bower, 1972; Mandler & Ritchey, 1977; Shepard, 1967; Standing, 1973; Standing, Conezio, & Haber, 1970). For example, in an experiment by Shepard (1967), college students looked at more than 600 pictures (color photos and illustrations from magazines), with an average inspection time of fewer than six seconds per picture. Subjects were then given pairs of dissimilar pictures and asked to identify which picture in each pair they had seen; subjects were able to do so with ninety-eight percent accuracy. (Their accuracy on a similar task using words was only eighty-eight percent.) Furthermore, images may be relatively enduring: in a study by Mandler and Ritchey (1977), subjects' memory for meaningfully organized pictures showed little decline over a four-month period.

Another thing that psychologists have learned about visual imagery is that it does not always provide a complete and accurate representation of initial input. Images tend to be fuzzy and less detailed than the original environmental input (Anderson, 1985). They can also be distorted by an individual's general knowledge. An early study by Carmichael, Hogan, and Walters (1932) illustrates the point. In this experiment, adults were asked to remember simple pictures like the ones shown on the left-hand side of Figure 11–2. Two different groups of subjects were given two different sets of labels for these pictures. Subjects tended to remember the pictures in ways that more closely fit the labels. For example, as you can see in Figure 11–2, the first picture was reproduced differently depending on whether it had been labeled as eyeglasses or dumbbells. Similarly, recall of the second picture was influenced by its identity as a kidney bean or a canoe.

Because images tend to be incomplete and inaccurate, they may not be helpful when precise, detailed information must be stored. For example, many educators have advocated the use of visual imagery in learning to spell (e.g., Fitzsimmons & Loomer, 1977; Harris, 1985; Hildreth, 1955;

Figure 11–2

Experimental stimuli and examples of subjects' reproductions, from Carmichael, Hogan, and Walters (1932)

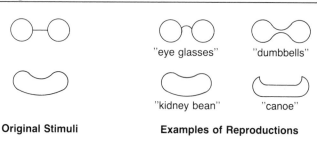

"eye glasses"　　"dumbbells"

"kidney bean"　　"canoe"

Original Stimuli　　**Examples of Reproductions**

Hillerich, 1976; Horn, 1919; Radebaugh, 1985; Walker, 1974), and research by Roberts and Ehri (1983) has provided some support for this practice. However, although imagery may help spelling, we should remember that one's visual image of a word will not necessarily include *all* of its letters (Ormrod & Jenkins, 1988). To illustrate, my mental image of the word *silhouette*, until I looked it up in the dictionary just now, is approximated in Figure 11–3. I had an image of *silhouette* that was sufficient for my recognizing the word when I read it, but not sufficiently detailed for spelling the word correctly.

Despite this drawback to visual imagery, its increased use in the classroom has been widely recommended. Visual images can be stored quickly and retained over long periods of time. For this reason, visual aids in the classroom are likely to provide a beneficial supplement to verbally presented information (Bower & Hilgard, 1981), and, in fact, when pictures and diagrams support and supplement ideas presented verbally, learning and retention of that information are enhanced (Kulhavy, Schwartz, & Shaha, 1983; Mayer, 1983a; Waddill, McDaniel, & Einstein, in press; Wagner, 1988, 1989).

Encouraging students to form their own mental images of information can also be an effective instructional technique. For example, when students are instructed to form visual images connecting object pairs, memory for those pairs is enhanced (e.g., Bower, 1972). Accordingly, imagery provides the foundation for a number of memory strategies called *mnemonics*, strategies that we will explore in Chapter 13.

Figure 11–3

sil·⋯·ette

Meanings and Propositions

People are more likely to remember the meaning of what they see or hear than precise, word-for-word detail. For example, think about the section you just read on imagery. What do you remember about it? You probably do not remember the specific words that you read, but you should be able to recall the general ideas of the section. (If you cannot, go back and read the section again!)

Many learning theorists (e.g., Anderson, 1976, 1983a, 1985; Ellis & Hunt, 1983; E. Gagné, 1985) believe that meanings are stored as *propositions*, that is, as small units of knowledge concerning relationships among objects or events. More specifically, to paraphrase John Anderson's (1985) definition, a proposition is a unit of knowledge that can stand as a separate statement or assertion, and can be judged as being either true or false.

To illustrate, consider the following sentence:

Mary's uncle, whom she adores, owns a red Ferrari.

This complex sentence can be broken up into four smaller assertions, each containing part of its meaning:

1. Mary has an uncle.
2. Mary adores the uncle.
3. The uncle owns a Ferrari.
4. The Ferrari is red.

Each assertion is either true or false; if any one of them is false, then the entire sentence is false. The four assertions are rough verbal analogs of the abstract propositions that may be stored in memory when the sentence itself is encountered.

Any proposition has two components. First, it includes one or more *arguments*—objects or events that are the topics of the proposition. Second, it involves a single *relation*—a description of an argument or a relationship among two or more arguments. For example, the assertion "Mary has an uncle" contains two arguments ("Mary" and "uncle") and one relation ("has"). Arguments are usually reflected by nouns and pronouns in a sentence, whereas relations are more typically reflected by verbs, adjectives, and adverbs.

Propositions provide a theoretical model of how meanings are stored. It is becoming increasingly clear that a great deal of the information individuals receive is stored primarily in terms of underlying meanings. For example, in studies by Sachs (1967) and Reder (1982), subjects could easily remember information verbatim if asked to do so immediately after that information had been presented. When recall was delayed, their ability to remember the exact input declined rapidly, yet they continued to remember its *meaning* fairly accurately.

Nonverbal visual information also appears to be stored at least partly in terms of meanings (e.g., Mandler & Johnson, 1976; Mandler & Parker, 1976; Mandler & Ritchey, 1977). An experiment by Mandler and Johnson (1976) illustrates this point well. In the experiment, college students looked at line drawings that included a number of different objects; for instance, one picture was a classroom scene that included a teacher, student, desk, bookshelf, flag, clock, globe, and large map. The students were then shown another set of pictures and asked whether each of the pictures was identical to a previous picture or had been changed in some way. Changes in the pictures were far more likely to be noticed if they reflected a change in the meaning (e.g., the teacher was pointing to a child's drawing instead of a world map) than if they reflected a nonmeaningful change (e.g., the teacher's skirt and hairstyle were different).

According to Anderson (1985), the meaning of the information people receive endures far longer than either verbal or visual information. If this is so, then educators who are concerned that their students remember information over long periods of time should help students focus on the underlying meaning of that information. This idea of *meaningful learning* is one that we will explore in considerable detail a little later in the chapter.

Productions

Up to this point, we have been talking about storing information related to how things are. In other words, we have been talking about ways of storing what psychologists call *declarative* knowledge. But individuals have another kind of knowledge as well: they know "how to do things." For example, you probably know how to ride a bicycle, wrap a gift, and add the numbers 57 and 94. This other kind of knowledge—*procedural* knowledge—may be partly stored in terms of verbal codes, images, and propositions. However, to perform behaviors successfully, you must be able to adapt your behaviors to changing conditions. Codes that allow responsiveness to different situations are known as *productions* (e.g., Anderson, 1976, 1985; E. Gagné, 1985).

Productions can best be described as a set of IF-THEN rules. For example, productions for riding a bicycle would include rules such as these:

1. IF I want to speed up, THEN I pedal at a faster rate.
2. IF I want to slow down, THEN I pedal at a slower rate.
3. IF my route turns to the right, THEN I turn the handlebars in a clockwise direction.
4. IF my route turns to the left, THEN I turn the handlebars in a counterclockwise direction.

5. IF an object is directly in front of me, THEN I must turn either right or left.

6. IF I want to stop, THEN I squeeze the brakes on the handlebars.

Similarly, productions for adding two two-digit numbers would include these rules:

1. IF the digits in the "ones" column equal nine or less, THEN I write their sum in the "ones" column of the answer space.

2. IF the digits in the "ones" column equal ten or more, THEN I write the digit that appears in the "ones" column of that total in the "ones" column of the answer space, and carry the "1" to the "tens" column of the problem.

3. IF the digits in the "tens" column equal nine or less, THEN I write their sum in the "tens" column of the answer space.

4. IF the digits in the "tens" column equal ten or more, THEN I write the digit that appears in the "ones" column of that total in the "tens" column of the answer space, and write the "1" in the "hundreds" column of the answer space.

As you can see, the "if" part of a production specifies the condition under which a particular behavior will occur, and the "then" part specifies what that behavior will be. Productions provide a means through which individuals can be responsive to different conditions in their environments. They are especially relevant to discussions of problem solving; accordingly, we will return to them in Chapter 15.

Any one of these four different codes—verbal codes, images, propositions, and productions—may be the form in which new information is encoded. Furthermore, the same information may be encoded simultaneously in two or more different ways. In support of this idea, college students in an experiment by Pezdek (1977) confused information they had seen in pictures with information they had read in sentences. For example, some subjects first saw a picture of a car parked by a tree, then read the sentence, "The car by the tree had ski racks on it." These subjects tended to recognize a picture of a car with ski racks as being one they had seen before, even though the original picture had not included a rack; hence, they were probably storing the same information in both visual and verbal form. Similarly, in the study by Carmichael et al. (1932) that I described previously, subjects probably stored the stimulus figures both as images (e.g., two balls connected by a line) and as words (e.g., eyeglasses or dumbbells).

When the same information is coded in different ways, those different codes are apparently associated together in long-term memory. It also appears that different but related pieces of information are frequently stored in connection with one another. It is time now to look more closely at the interconnections in long-term memory—in other words, at the organization of long-term memory.

THE ORGANIZATION OF LONG-TERM MEMORY

Contemporary views of long-term memory are *associationistic*: they incorporate the idea that pieces of information stored in long-term memory are associated, or connected, with one another. To show you what I mean, get a piece of paper and try this exercise. In just a minute, you will read a common, everyday word. As soon as you read it, write down the first word that comes into your head. Then write down the first word of which *that* word reminds you. Continue writing down the first word that each successive word brings to mind until you have a list of ten words.

Ready? Here is the word to get your mind rolling:

beach

Once you have completed your list of ten words, examine it carefully. It should give you an idea of what ideas are associated with what other ideas in your long-term memory.

Here is the list that I constructed using the same procedure and my own long-term memory:

sand

castle

king

queen

Elizabeth

England

London

theater

Hair

nude

Some of my associations might be similar to ones you also have. For example, beach-sand and king-queen are common associates. Others might be unique to me. For instance, the last five items on my list reflect my trip to London many years ago when I attended a different play every night. The most memorable of the plays I saw was the musical *Hair*, in which several actors briefly appeared nude.

Psychologists believe that virtually all pieces of information stored in long-term memory are directly or indirectly related to one another. Different individuals relate and organize their long-term memories somewhat idiosyncratically because their past experiences have been different. Nevertheless, the organizational schemes that people use may share some common features. At least two models of long-term memory organization have been proposed: the hierarchy and the propositional network.

Long-term Memory as a Hierarchy

An early view of long-term memory organization was that information was stored in a hierarchical arrangement, with more general, superordinate information at the top of the hierarchy, and more specific, subordinate information below it (Ausubel, 1963, 1968; Ausubel & Robinson, 1969; Collins & Quillian, 1969, 1972). An example of such a hierarchy is my own knowledge of the animal kingdom, part of which is reflected in Figure 11–4. Notice how the most general category—animals—is at the top of the hierarchy. Next are two major categories of animals—vertebrates and invertebrates—followed by more and more subordinate categories, until finally specific instances of a category (Rin Tin Tin, Tippy, and Anna are all German shepherds) are reached. As you can see, part of my hierarchy would resemble that of a biologist (my classes of vertebrates, for instance), but other parts are uniquely my own.

In a classic study, Collins and Quillian (1969) demonstrated how long-term memory might be organized hierarchically. Subjects were given a num-

Figure 11–4

The author's hierarchial knowledge of the animal kingdom

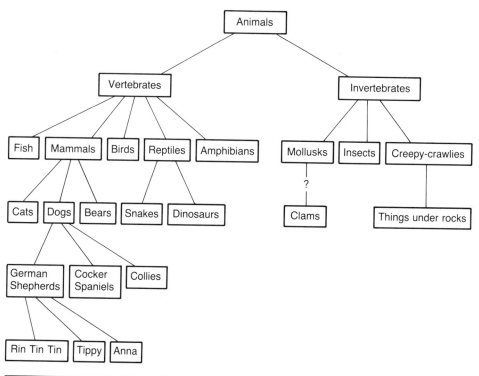

ber of statements (e.g., "A canary can sing") and asked to indicate whether they were true or false; subjects' reaction times to verify or reject the statements were recorded. Here are some examples of true statements and approximate reaction times to them:

Statements About Category Membership	Reaction Times (msec)
A canary is a canary.	1000
A canary is a bird.	1160
A canary is an animal.	1240

Statements About Characteristic	Reaction Times (msec)
A canary can sing.	1300
A canary can fly.	1380
A canary has skin.	1470

Notice how the reaction times increased for the three sentences regarding category membership: subjects most quickly verified that a canary is a canary and least quickly verified that a canary is an animal. Now notice the different reaction times for the three statements concerning a canary's characteristics: subjects found the statement about singing easiest and that about having skin most difficult. Collins and Quillian argued that the two sets of sentences are actually parallel, because most people associate singing directly with canaries, while they associate flying with birds and having skin with animals.

Collins and Quillian suggested that an individual's knowledge about categories and category characteristics is arranged in a hierarchical fashion similar to what is depicted in Figure 11–5. To verify the statements, subjects had to locate the two components of the statement (e.g., "canary" and

Figure 11–5
A simplified version of the Collins and Quillian (1969) knowledge hierarchy

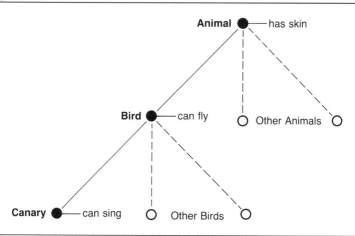

"skin") within their long-term memories and determine if they were associated together, either directly or indirectly. The farther apart the two components were in the hierarchy, the longer it would take to verify a statement (hence, the longer the reaction times).

Strictly hierarchical models of long-term memory have been the object of considerable criticism (e.g., Bourne, Dominowski, Loftus, & Healy, 1986; Loftus & Loftus, 1976; Wingfield & Byrnes, 1981). First of all, information is not always hierarchical in nature. Second, predictions consistent with hierarchically arranged information are not always confirmed. For example, just as people verify that a canary is a bird faster than they verify that a canary is an animal, we should expect that people would agree with the statement, "A collie is a mammal" faster than the statement, "A collie is an animal" because "collie" is closer to "mammal" than it is to "animal" in a logical hierarchy of animals. Yet the opposite holds true: people more quickly agree that a collie is an animal than that it is a mammal (Rips, Shoben, & Smith, 1973).

At this point, it appears that some information in long-term memory may be arranged hierarchically but that most information is probably organized less systematically. An alternative view of long-term memory, the propositional network, may provide a more useful and flexible theoretical model.

Long-term Memory as a Propositional Network

A *network* model portrays memory as consisting of many pieces of information interconnected through a variety of associations. For example, let's return again to my own previous list of successive associations resulting from the word beach: sand, castle, king, queen, Elizabeth, England, London, theater, *Hair*, nude. Such a list might have been generated from a long-term memory network such as the one in Figure 11–6.

Different individuals should have networks with somewhat different associations and so should generate different lists. Some individuals, depending on their past experiences at the beach, might even associate beach and nude directly with each other!

Currently, the most popular model of long-term memory organization is the *propositional network* (e.g., Anderson, 1976, 1983a, 1983b, 1985; Anderson & Bower, 1973; E. Gagné, 1985; Lindsay & Norman, 1977; Norman & Rumelhart, 1975; Rumelhart, Lindsay, & Norman, 1972). A propositional network is one in which propositions and their interrelationships are stored in a networklike fashion. To illustrate, let's return to a sentence we considered earlier:

Mary's uncle, whom she adores, owns a red Ferrari.

and to the four assertions contained within it:

1. Mary has an uncle.
2. Mary adores the uncle.

Figure 11—6

A hypothetical network of information in long-term memory

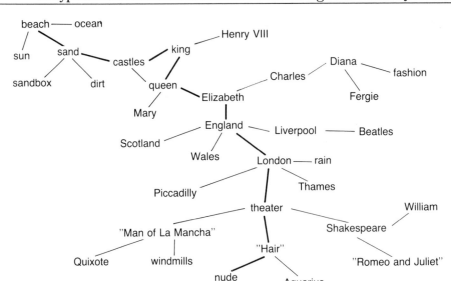

3. The uncle owns a Ferrari.

4. The Ferrari is red.

The four assertions can be diagramed as propositions, as shown in Figure 11—7. These diagrams, using Anderson's (1985) symbols, each show a proposition (symbolized by an oval) that encompasses one relation and one or more arguments.

As you should notice, the four diagrams in Figure 11—7 share several objects, or arguments; in particular, Mary, uncle, and Ferrari each appear in two or more propositions. Such commonalities allow the propositions to be linked in a network; an example is shown in Figure 11—8. A propositional network model of long-term memory is obviously more flexible than a hierarchical model. A hierarchy includes only superordinate-subordinate relationships; a network, on the other hand, can easily include a wide variety of relationships (e.g., possession, location, opposition).

Propositional networks are often conceptualized as including not only propositions (meanings), but other memory codes (such as imagery and productions) as well (e.g., E. Gagné, 1985; Glass et al., 1979). For example, you might have a visual image of a Ferrari stored in association with the information about Mary's uncle and his red sportscar. Perhaps not too far away in the same propositional network are productions related to how you drive a car.

As you will see shortly, the organization of long-term memory becomes a critical factor in how information is stored there in the first place. Let's turn now to that topic—long-term memory storage processes.

Figure 11–7
Diagrams of separate propositions

1. Mary has an uncle.

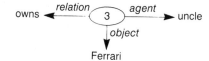

2. Mary adores the uncle.

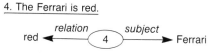

3. The uncle owns a Ferrari.

4. The Ferrari is red.

Figure 11–8
A propositional network

Mary's uncle, whom she adores, owns a red Ferrari.

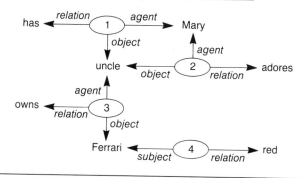

STORAGE PROCESSES

Before we begin our discussion of long-term memory storage, try this exercise. Here is a short story entitled "The War of the Ghosts" (Bartlett, 1932, p. 65). Read it silently one time only, then cover the page and write down as much of the story as you can remember.

The War of the Ghosts

One night two young men from Egulac went down to the river to hunt seals, and while they were there it became foggy and calm. Then they heard war-cries, and they thought, "Maybe this is a war-party." They escaped to the shore, and hid behind a log. Now canoes came up, and they heard the noise of paddles, and saw one canoe coming up to them. There were five men in the canoe, and they said:

"What do you think?" We wish to take you along. We are going up the river to make war on the people."

One of the young men said: "I have no arrows."

"Arrows are in the canoe," they said.

"I will not go along. I might be killed. My relatives do not know where I have gone. But you," he said, turning to the other, "may go with them."

So one of the young men went, but the other returned home.

And the warriors went on up the river to a town on the other side of Kalama. The people came down to the water, and they began to fight, and many were killed. But presently the young man heard one of the warriors say, "Quick, let us go home: that Indian has been hit." Now he thought: "Oh, they are ghosts." He did not feel sick, but they said he had been shot.

So the canoes went back to Egulac, and the young man went ashore to his house, and made a fire. And he told everybody and said, "Behold I accompanied the ghosts, and we went to fight. Many of our fellows were killed, and many of those who attacked us were killed. They said I was hit, and I did not feel sick."

He told it all, and then he became quiet. When the sun rose he fell down. Something black came out of his mouth. His face became contorted. The people jumped up and cried.

He was dead.

Now cover the story and write down what you can recall of it.

Once you have finished, compare your reproduction with the original. What differences do you notice? Your reproduction is probably shorter than the original. Some details are almost certainly omitted. Perhaps you even added some things. But you probably maintained the gist of the story: you included its main ideas and events, mostly in their proper sequence.

Using this Native American ghost story, Frederic Bartlett (1932) conducted one of the earliest studies of the long-term memory of meaningful verbal information. Bartlett asked his students at Cambridge University to read the story two times, then to recall it at various times later on. Students' recalled stories differed from the actual story in a number of ways.

The words themselves were changed. In other words, recall was not verbatim.

The gist of the story, including the major sequence of events, was usually retained. Some details, especially ones that were either essential to the story or particularly striking, were retained. Unimportant details and meaningless information, however, were omitted. For example, such details as "something black came out of his mouth" and "he was dead" were likely to be remembered; such details as "the young man . . . made a fire" and "a town on the other side of Kalama" were frequently forgotten.

Parts of the story were distorted and other information was added so that the story was more logical and consistent with English culture. For example, people rarely go "to the river to hunt seals," because seals are saltwater animals. Students might therefore say that the men went to the river to *fish*. Similarly, the supernatural element did not fit comfortably with the religious beliefs of most Cambridge students and was often altered. In the recollection below, written by a student six months after he had read the original story, several additions and distortions are evident:

> Four men came down to the water. They were told to get into a boat and to take arms with them. They inquired, "What arms?" and were answered "Arms for battle." When they came to the battle-field they heard a great noise and shouting, and a voice said: "The black man is dead." And he was brought to the place where they were, and laid on the ground. And he foamed at the mouth (Bartlett, 1932, pp. 71–72).

The main idea of the story—a battle—is retained. But after six months, the story has been so distorted that it is barely recognizable!

There was a tendency to explain the story's events in addition to describing them. For example, one student insisted on explaining events in parentheses:

> The young man did not feel sick (i.e., wounded), but nevertheless they proceeded home (evidently the opposing forces were quite willing to stop fighting). (Bartlett, 1932, p. 86)

Bartlett's findings illustrate several principles of long-term memory storage. First, individuals select some pieces of information to store and exclude others. Second, they are more likely to store underlying meanings (perhaps in the form of propositions) than verbatim input. Third, they use their existing knowledge about the world (i.e., information they have already stored in long-term memory) to help them understand the new information. And, fourth, some of that existing knowledge may be added to the new information, such that what is learned may be more than, or at least different from, the information actually presented.

In this section, we will look at five processes related to long-term memory storage. We will look at selection, the process of determining which information is stored and which is not. We will also examine rehearsal, a means of processing information in a relatively nonmeaningful, rote manner. We will then turn to three processes that involve encoding information in terms of its meanings: meaningful learning, internal organization, and elaboration.

Selection

As you learned in the previous chapter, short-term memory is a bottleneck in the human memory system. Only a fraction of what enters the sensory register can be held in short-term memory. Furthermore, information in short-term memory must undergo additional processing before it can be stored in long-term memory. Individuals must be extremely selective in the information they choose to process and must therefore have a means of determining what is important and what is not.

Long-term memory plays a critical role in the selection of information for processing through the memory system. Individuals' knowledge about the world, their priorities, and their predictions about what environmental input is likely to be useful affects what they pay attention to, hence also affecting what information moves from sensory register into short-term memory. A student who has learned that a teacher's lecture content will probably reappear on an exam is likely to pay attention to what the teacher is saying. A student who has learned that a teacher's exams are taken totally from reading assignments or has decided that an active social life is more important than classroom achievement may instead attend to something more relevant: the flattering new hairstyle being displayed by the student on the right.

In some cases, once information has been attended to, it is automatically stored in long-term memory (Hasher & Zacks, 1984; Zacks, Hasher, & Hock, 1986). For example, consider this question:

Which word occurs more frequently in English—*bacon* or *pastrami*?

You probably had no difficulty answering correctly that bacon is the more frequent word. Hasher and Zacks (1984) found that people could easily answer such questions about the frequency of events even though they had never bothered to count them. Similarly, they could answer questions about the spatial and temporal locations of events without having intentionally processed such information.

However, more meaningful information apparently must be encoded as well as attended to if it is to be effectively stored in long-term memory. Such encoding takes time. For example, Simon (1974) has estimated that each new piece of information takes about ten seconds to encode. Using this estimate and her own estimate that thirty new propositions may be presented in a minute of a typical classroom lecture, Ellen Gagné (1985) has estimated that students can process only six propositions per minute—*one-fifth* of lecture content!

Given the capacity and time constraints of human memory, how can teachers help students select important information? An obvious way is simply to tell students what information is important and what is not; when students are told *not* to remember certain information, that information is less likely to go further than short-term memory (Bjork, 1972). Another way is to build redundancy into lectures and instructional materials so that important points are repeated several times. For example, when I am presenting an important idea to my students, I typically present it several different times. I state the idea once and then state it again using different words. I then illustrate it with at least two examples (often as many as five), and I present the idea itself once again. Notice the redundancy in the last four sentences—it should have been very difficult not to process my meaning at least once!

Rehearsal

You should recall from the previous chapter that rehearsal provides a means of maintaining information in short-term memory indefinitely. Atkinson and Shiffrin (1971) proposed that rehearsal is also a method of storing information in long-term memory, and there is some evidence that they were right. Several studies have shown that more frequently rehearsed items are better remembered than less frequently rehearsed ones (Nelson, 1977; Rundus, 1971; Rundus & Atkinson, 1971).

However, a number of theorists (e.g., Craik & Watkins, 1973; Klatzky, 1975; Watkins & Watkins, 1974) have argued that rehearsal only leads to storage in long-term memory if that rehearsal facilitates the association of the new information with existing information. From their perspective, mere repetition of the information—*maintenance rehearsal*—is sufficient to keep the information in short-term memory but *in*sufficient to move it into long-term memory. Rehearsal through which the information is better understood and made more meaningful—*elaborative rehearsal*—does facilitate storage in long-term memory. For example, in a study by Craik and Watkins (1973), college students were asked to perform two tasks simultaneously: they had to keep one word in their short-term memories (by rehearsing it) while at the same time examining additional words to see if they met certain criteria. In this situation, the amount of rehearsal did *not* influence the extent to which the subjects were able to recall the words they had rehearsed; apparently the second task kept them busy enough that they were unable to make associations with the rehearsed words. However, when the additional words were presented at a slower rate, recall of the rehearsed words improved, presumably because the subjects could devote more short-term memory capacity to forming associations with those words.

Learning information primarily through repetition is sometimes called *rote learning* (e.g., Ausubel, 1963, 1968; Ausubel, Novak, & Hanesian, 1978; Ausubel & Robinson, 1969). In rote learning, there is little or no attempt to make the information meaningful or to understand it in terms of things one already knows. If such information is stored in long-term memory at all, it is not stored in association with similar information but instead is relatively unconnected and isolated. As you will see in the following chapter, information stored in this unorganized fashion becomes difficult to retrieve.

So many times I have seen students engage in what appears to be maintenance rehearsal (mere repetition) as a means of trying to learn new information. This process, often referred to as memorizing, emphasizes the learning of verbatim information rather than the learning of underlying meanings. Although rehearsal is probably used most frequently by younger children (Cuvo, 1975), I have observed it being used by high school and college students as well. Students must be helped to understand that mere repetition is an inefficient means of storing information for the long run, if in fact it even works at all! The three processes we turn to now—meaningful learning, organization, and elaboration—are clearly more effective methods of long-term memory storage.

Meaningful Learning

Look at this list of fifteen letters:

MAIGUWRSENNFLOD

And now look at this list:

MEANINGFULWORDS

Both lists are the same length, and both contain exactly the same letters. Which list is easier to learn? No doubt you will agree that the second list is easier, because it can be related to common words that people already know. In the same way, my daughter related a phrase from "America the Beautiful" to her existing knowledge about the world, which unfortunately included *bastard* but not *alabaster*, as did my son, who heard *spaceship skies* instead of *spacious skies*. By relating new information to knowledge already stored in their long-term memories, people find a *meaning* in that information. Hence, this process is most frequently known as *meaningful learning*; it is also what we are referring to when we talk about understanding or comprehension.

When information is learned meaningfully, it is stored in long-term memory in association with similar, related pieces of information. Meaningful learning appears to facilitate both storage and retrieval: the information goes in more quickly and is remembered more easily (e.g., Ausubel et al., 1978). To illustrate, consider this passage from an experiment by Bransford and Johnson (1972):

> The procedure is actually quite simple. First you arrange things into different groups. Of course, one pile may be sufficient depending on how much there is to do. If you have to go somewhere else due to lack of facilities that is the next step, otherwise you are pretty well set. It is important not to overdo things. That is, it is better to do too few things at once than too many. In the short run this may not seem important, but complications can easily arise. A mistake can be expensive as well. At first the whole procedure will seem complicated. Soon, however, it will become just another facet of life. It is difficult to foresee any end to the necessity for this task in the

immediate future, but then one never can tell. After the procedure is completed one arranges the materials into different groups again. Then they can be put into their appropriate places. Eventually they will be used once more and the whole cycle will then have to be repeated. However, that is part of life (Bransford & Johnson, 1972, p. 722).

All the words in this passage were undoubtedly familiar to you, yet you may have had some difficulty understanding what you were reading, because you did not know what the passage was about, so you could not relate it to your existing long-term memory. But now try reading it again, this time thinking of it as a passage about washing clothes. Bransford and Johnson found that college students who knew the topic of the passage remembered twice as much as those who had no topic with which to connect it.

Nonverbal material is also more easily stored when it can be meaningfully understood. For example, in a study by Bower, Karlin, and Dueck (1975), students were asked to remember somewhat meaningless line drawings; examples of these "droodles" appear in Figure 11–9. Students who were given meaningful labels for such pictures, such as "a midget playing a trombone in a telephone booth" or "an early bird who caught a very strong worm" were more likely to remember them correctly a week later than students who were not given labels.

As I have said, meaningful learning is a process of associating new information with existing information in long-term memory. Exactly how is this associational process accomplished? Using a hierarchical model of long-term memory organization, we can describe meaningful learning as being a process of placing, or *subsuming*, new information under an appropriate superordinate category (Ausubel, 1963, 1968; Ausubel et al., 1978; Ausubel & Robinson, 1969). For example, students are more likely to learn meaningful information about an animal known as a skink if they

Figure 11–9
Droodles from Bower, Karlin, and Dueck (1975)

From "Comprehension and Memory for Pictures" by G. H. Bower, M. B. Karlin, and A. Dueck, 1975, *Memory and Cognition, 3*, p. 217. Reprinted by permission of Psychonomic Society, Inc.

are told that it is "a kind of lizard that looks like a snake" than if they are told that it is "brightly colored" or "a shy, seldom-seen creature."

Using a propositional network model of long-term memory, meaningful learning can be characterized as a process of storing new propositions with related propositions in the network. For example, let's assume that you have already stored some propositions concerning Mary's uncle and his red Ferrari in a form similar to what I depicted earlier in Figure 11–8. You then read the following sentence:

The uncle is named Charles.

You might connect this proposition to your existing propositions about the uncle and perhaps to propositions concerning another Charles that you know, as illustrated in Figure 11–10.

Regardless of whether we use a hierarchical or a network model of long-term memory, the basic principle is the same: in meaningful learning, new ideas are connected to old ones.

When is meaningful learning most likely to occur? Let's look at three factors that seem to make a difference.

The learner must have a meaningful learning set. The learner must approach new information with the attitude that it can be meaningfully understood, something that Ausubel calls a *meaningful learning set* (Ausubel et al., 1978). This attitude is more likely to be present in students when teachers emphasize meanings rather than verbatim recitation (Ausubel et al., 1978); for example, students are more apt to learn material meaningfully when they know they will be expected to explain it in their own words than

Figure 11–10
Meaningful learning in a propositional network

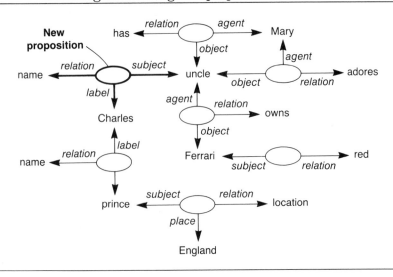

when they will have to reproduce textbook definitions. A meaningful learning set is also more likely to occur when students are confident that new material *can* be understood. Students who have learned through past experiences that a certain subject matter (e.g., mathematics) is confusing are more likely to resort to a rote-learning approach (Ausubel, 1963, 1968; Ausubel & Robinson, 1969).

The learner has previous knowledge to which the new information can be related. Meaningful learning can only occur if the new information can be associated with existing information (e.g., Ellis & Hunt, 1983; Johnson, 1975). In other words, one of the most important factors affecting long-term memory storage is what the individual already knows (Ausubel et al., 1978; Ausubel & Robinson, 1969). Individuals who have a large body of information already stored in long-term memory have more ideas to which they can relate their new experiences and so can more easily learn at a meaningful level. Individuals who lack relevant knowledge must resort to inefficient rote-learning strategies. (This is probably one reason that older children and adults usually learn most things more quickly than younger children.) To put it bluntly, the rich (in knowledge) get richer, and the poor stay relatively poor.

The importance of previous knowledge for learning new information has been illustrated in numerous studies (e.g., Chase & Simon, 1973; Chiesi, Spilich, & Voss, 1979; deGroot, 1965; Ormrod, Ormrod, Wagner, & McCallin, 1988; Saxe, 1988; Spilich, Vesonder, Chiesi, & Voss, 1979). For example, some of my colleagues and I recently conducted a study of how well people from different disciplines learn and remember maps (Ormrod et al., 1988). We asked faculty members and students in three disciplines—geography, sociology, and education—to study two maps and then reproduce them from memory. The first of these maps, shown in Figure 11–11, depicts a city arranged in accordance with usual "citylike" patterns—that is, its arrangement is *logical*. Notice how the downtown business district is located at a point where it can be easily reached from different directions (this is typical), and the mills, lumberyard, and low-income housing are situated near the railroad tracks (also typical). The second map, shown in Figure 11–12, is on a larger scale and depicts several political regions (countries, perhaps). Several things about this map make no sense—that is, its arrangement is *illogical*. Notice how a river originates in the plains and runs *up* into the mountains, transportation networks do not interconnect, and towns are not located at transportation junctions. My colleagues and I predicted that geographers would remember more of the logical city map than either sociologists or educators because they could use their knowledge of typical urban patterns to learn the map meaningfully. We also predicted that the geographers would have no advantage over the other disciplines on the illogical "countries" map because geographic principles were largely inapplicable in making sense out of the map. Our predictions were confirmed: geographers showed better recall than the other two groups

Figure 11–11

The logical city map from Ormrod *et al.* (1988)

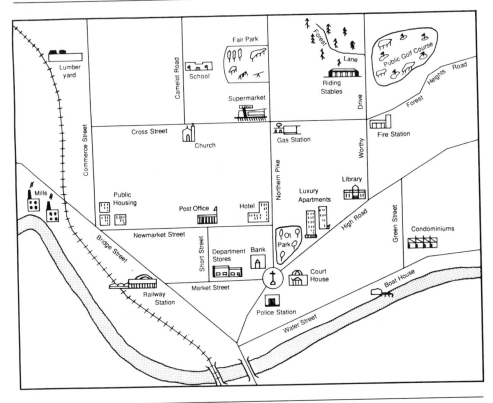

Reprinted from "Reconceptualizing Map Learning" by J. E. Ormrod, R. K. Ormrod, E. D. Wagner, & R. C. McCallin, 1988, *American Journal of Psychology, 101*, p. 428. Reprinted with permission of the University of Illinois Press.

for the logical city map but not for the illogical countries map. Because we had asked our subjects to think aloud as they studied the maps, we were also able to examine the strategies they employed; as we expected, the geographers learned the maps more meaningfully than the other groups, and the city map was learned more meaningfully than the countries map. Our nongeographers used primarily rote-learning strategies, mostly in the form of repetition.

Other studies have yielded similar results. For example, people who know a lot about baseball can remember more about the specific events of a baseball game than people relatively uninformed about the sport (Spilich et al., 1979). Experts at the game of chess can remember the locations of chess pieces on a chessboard more accurately than chess novices, but only when the placement of pieces is logical within the framework of an actual game (Chase & Simon, 1973; deGroot, 1965). Second-grade students in

Brazil who have experience as street vendors learn basic arithmetic more easily than students without street-vending experience (Saxe, 1988).

Relating new information to one's self can have a particularly dramatic effect on learning. This point was clearly illustrated in a study by Rogers and colleagues (Rogers, Kuiper, & Kirker, 1977). College students were given a list of forty adjectives (some words were printed in large type and some in small type) and asked to respond to one of four questions about each word.

Figure 11—12
The illogical country map from Ormrod *et al.* (1988)

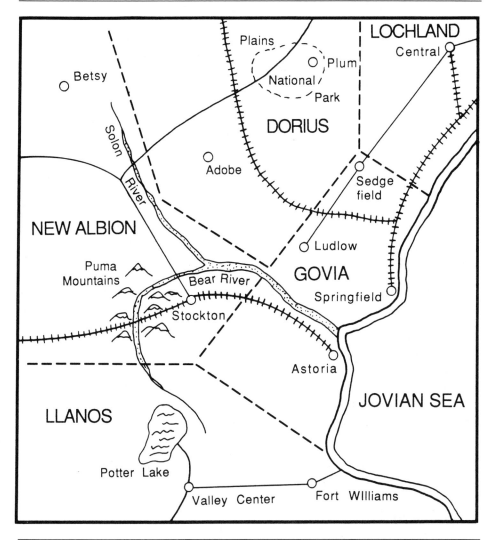

Reprinted from "Reconceptualizing Map Learning" by J. E. Ormrod, R. K. Ormrod, E. D. Wagner, & R. C. McCallin, 1988, *American Journal of Psychology, 101*, p. 429. Reprinted with permission of the University of Illinois Press.

They were then unexpectedly asked to remember as many of the forty adjectives as they could. Below are the four questions asked about different adjectives, and the percentage of incidental learning that resulted from answering them:

Question	Percent Recalled
1. Does it have big letters?	3%
2. Does it rhyme with _____?	7%
3. Does it mean the same as _____?	13%
4. Does it describe you?	30%

When subjects were required to relate the word to something they already knew (question 3), they remembered more than when they were asked to deal with superficial characteristics of the word (questions 1 and 2). But when they were asked to relate the word to themselves (question 4), incidental learning was more than twice what it was for meaningful but not self-related processing.

I repeat an important point: The more closely learners can relate new material not only to previously learned information but also to themselves and their own personal experiences, the more effective meaningful learning is likely to be.

The learner is aware that a piece of previously learned information is related to a new piece of information and has both pieces in short-term memory at the same time. The individual must know that the new information is related to something already in long-term memory (Ausubel, 1963, 1968; Ausubel & Robinson, 1969). The relevant information in long-term memory must also be retrieved to short-term memory to allow for the integration of the new information with it (Gagné & Driscoll, 1988).

An experiment by Hayes-Roth and Thorndyke (1979) illustrates the latter principle. In this experiment, students read one of two passages describing a fictional country; the same pieces of information appeared in both passages, but in a somewhat different order. In one passage, related pieces of information appeared in sequential sentences, while in the other, they appeared in separate paragraphs. Students more frequently made the connection between the two related pieces of information (and thus could draw an inference from them) when those pieces of information were presented one right after the other, presumably because they were more likely to be stored in short-term memory at the same time.

Teachers can facilitate students' learning by pointing out the kinds of knowledge they can use to understand new material. For example, in an experiment by Royer and Cable (1976), students read passages concerning principles of either electrical conductivity or heat flow. Some students were given information that showed how they could relate the physical principles to ideas with which they were already familiar; for example, they were shown how the process of heat flow was similar to falling dominoes. Students given such connections learned more about electrical conductivity and heat flow than students not given those connections.

There should be no question in your mind at this point about the benefits of meaningful learning over rote learning. In essence, meaningful learning allows new information to be organized with previously learned information; the process is therefore sometimes referred to as *external organization* (e.g., E. Gagné, 1985). Another equally important process is the organization of a new body of information within itself—that is, *internal organization*. We turn now to this form of organization.

Internal Organization

A body of new information to be learned is stored more effectively and remembered more completely when it is organized. In fact, people seem to have a natural tendency to organize and integrate the information they receive. As an example, you may recall the Bransford and Franks (1971) study described in Chapter 7, in which you learned how "The ants in the kitchen ate the sweet jelly which was on the table."

You have undoubtedly had teachers whose lectures were unorganized, with one point following another in an unpredictable order. As you might expect, material that is presented in such an unorganized fashion is more difficult to learn than clearly organized material. An experiment by Bower and colleagues (Bower, Clark, Lesgold, & Winzenz, 1969) demonstrates just how significant organization can be. College students were given four study trials in which to learn 112 words that fell into four categories (minerals, plants, etc.). For some of the students, the words were arranged randomly,

Figure 11–13
Example of a conceptual hierarchy from Bower *et al.* (1969)

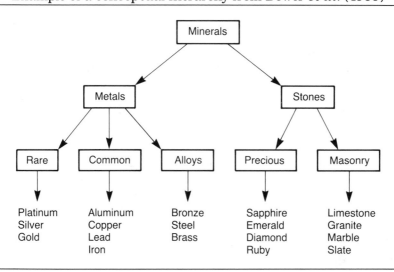

(From "Hierarchial Retrieval Schemes in Recall of Categorized Word Lists" by G. H. Bower, M. C. Clark, A. M. Lesgold, and D. Winzenz, 1969, *Journal of Verbal Learning and Verbal Behavior, 8*, p. 324. Copyright 1969 by Academic Press. Reprinted by permission.)

while for other students the words were arranged in four conceptual hierarchies (the minerals hierarchy in Figure 11–13 is an example). After one study trial, students who had studied the organized words could remember more than three times as many words as those who had studied the randomized words. After four study trials, the students in the organized group remembered all 112, while those in the random group remembered only 70.

Many good students organize information spontaneously as they learn it, and such student-generated organization can in fact be very effective (Mandler & Pearlstone, 1966; Tulving, 1962). Furthermore, providing students with specific organizational schemes can dramatically affect student learning and retrieval (DuBois, 1987; DuBois, Kiewra, & Fraley, 1988; Kiewra, DuBois, Christian, McShane, Meyerhoffer, & Roskelly, 1988). We will explore ways of facilitating students' organizational processes in Chapter 13.

Elaboration

Suffering from cold symptoms? Consider this:

> Aren't you tired of sniffles and runny noses all winter? Tired of always feeling less than your best? Get through a whole winter without colds. Take Eradicold Pills as directed (Harris, 1977, p. 605).

Do Eradicold Pills prevent colds? If you believe that they do, then you are the unwitting victim of *elaboration*: you added your own information to the passage you read, and "learned" that information along with what you had actually read. In a study by Harris (1977), subjects who read the above passage asserted that Eradicold Pills prevented colds almost as frequently as those who read an explicit statement to that effect.

When individuals receive new information, they often use what they have already learned about the world to help them understand that information—that is, to learn it meaningfully. Sometimes the new information is incomplete: missing pieces need to be filled in. When new information resembles previously experienced events, then assumptions, interpretations, and inferences drawn from those previous events are likely to be imposed on the new information and learned right along with it. Elaboration, then, is a process of learning more than the information actually presented. I call it learning between the lines.

In recent years, the elaboration process has been investigated in numerous studies (e.g., Bower, Black, & Turner, 1979; Harris, 1977; Johnson, Bransford, & Solomon, 1973; Owens, Bower, & Black, 1979; Reder, 1982; Reder & Ross, 1983). The results of these studies all point to the same conclusion: individuals frequently elaborate on the information they receive and later have difficulty distinguishing between the actual "truth" and their elaborations of it.

To illustrate, below is a passage from an experiment by Owens et al. (1979). Read it *once*.

Nancy woke up feeling sick again and she wondered if she really were pregnant. How would she tell the professor she had been seeing? And the money was another problem.

Nancy went to the doctor. She arrived at the office and checked in with the receptionist. She went to see the nurse, who went through the usual procedures. Then Nancy stepped on the scale and the nurse recorded her weight. The doctor entered the room and examined the results. He smiled at Nancy and said, "Well, it seems my expectations have been confirmed." When the examination was finished, Nancy left the office (Owens, Bower, & Black, 1979, pp. 185–186).

Did the doctor tell Nancy she was pregnant? The fact is, he did not. Yet in the study conducted by Owens and his colleagues, when students read the passage and then were asked a day later to recall information about it, they "remembered" considerably more than they had actually read. Many of their recalled elaborations were directly related to Nancy's suspected condition. Other students in the experiment read only the second paragraph of the passage, so were unaware that Nancy thought she was pregnant; these students added far fewer elaborations.

Learning theorists have come to several conclusions about the factors involved in elaboration, and about the role of elaboration in long-term memory.

Elaboration is a form of construction. In Chapter 9, I described perception as a constructive process: people use the sensations they receive to construct a perception of that event. Elaboration is constructive as well (e.g., Ellis & Hunt, 1983; Kulhavy, Peterson, & Schwartz, 1986; Spiro, 1980a, 1980b). It is a process of using both new information and one's existing knowledge about the world to construct a meaningful interpretation of that new information. If you thought that Eradicold Pills prevent colds, or that Nancy was pregnant, then you constructed those conclusions yourself.

Elaboration frequently involves the use of schemas. Jean Piaget used the concept of schema to refer to a mental unit representing a class of similar actions or thoughts. More recently, psychologists have been using the same term in a somewhat different sense. In contemporary cognitive theory, the term *schema* usually refers to an organized body of knowledge about a specific topic (e.g., Anderson, 1985; Bartlett, 1932; Posner, 1978; Rumelhart & Ortony, 1977).

For example, suppose you went to see a faculty member at your university. What objects would you expect to find in that faculty member's office? Probably at least a desk, a chair, shelves, and books. Your schema of a faculty office might then color your later memory of what the office was actually like. In a study by Brewer and Treyens (1981), thirty students were brought to a room they believed to be the experimenter's office. After waiting in the office for less than a minute, they were taken to another room and asked to write down everything they could remember about the room. Most students correctly remembered things that one would expect to find in an office (e.g., a desk, a chair, and shelves). Relatively few of them remembered items not likely to be part of an office schema (e.g., a skull, a clown-shaped light switch, and a tennis racket). And nine of the thirty "remembered" books that hadn't actually been there at all!

People often form schemas about events as well as objects; such event schemas are sometimes called *scripts* (e.g., Bower, Black, & Turner, 1979; Schank, 1975; Schank & Abelson, 1977). For example, what things usually happen when people go to a doctor's office? In a study by Bower et al. (1979), most individuals agreed that this series of activities is typical of a visit to the doctor:

They check in with the receptionist.

They sit down.

They read a magazine.

The nurse performs tests.

The doctor examines them.

They leave the office.

An individual's mental script of an event will influence what information is "learned" from a given instance of that event. For example, in another study by Bower et al. (1979), college students read this passage:

> John was feeling bad today so he decided to go see the family doctor. He checked in with the doctor's receptionist, and then looked through several medical magazines that were on the table by his chair. Finally the nurse came and asked him to take off his clothes. The doctor was very nice to him. He eventually prescribed some pills for John. Then John left the doctor's office and headed home (Bower, Black, & Turner, 1979, p. 190).

The students in the experiment "remembered" reading about many activities that were likely to be part of a visit to the doctor (e.g., arriving at the doctor's office), but that they had in fact *not* read.

Remember, the human memory system is typically confronted with more information than it can possibly handle. A schema provides a means by which this information overload can be reduced: it helps people focus their attention on information that is likely to be important and to ignore what is probably unimportant (Posner, 1978). For example, when going to see the doctor, it is more important that you check in with the receptionist than that you attend to the styles of clothing worn by other people in the waiting room. Schemas also enable people to make sense out of an incomplete set of information (Posner, 1978). For example, if you hear someone describe an experience at the doctor's office, you can assume that the person entered the examination room, even if that statement is not explicitly stated. In the above passage about John visiting the doctor's office, it highly unlikely that the nurse asked John to take off his clothes in the waiting room, although that is in fact what the passage implies!

Different individuals elaborate the same information in different ways and accordingly learn different things. Consider the following passage from research by Anderson, Reynolds, Schallert, and Goetz (1977):

> Rocky slowly got up from the mat, planning his escape. He hesitated a moment and thought. Things were not going well. What bothered him most was being held, especially since the charge against him had been weak. He considered his present situation. The lock that held him was strong but he thought he could break it. He knew, however, that his timing would have to be perfect. Rocky was aware that it was because of his early roughness that he had been penalized so severely—much too severely from his point of view. The situation was becoming frustrating; the pressure had been grinding on him for too long. He was being ridden unmercifully. Rocky was getting angry now. He felt he was ready to make his move. He knew that his success or failure would depend on what he did in the next few seconds (Anderson et al., 1977, p. 372).

Is this story about a wrestling match? Or is it about a prison escape? Read the passage again, and you should notice that it could be about either one. Anderson and his colleagues found that students' interpretations of the story depended on their background: physical education majors more frequently viewed it as a wrestling match, while music education majors (most of whom had little or no knowledge of wrestling) were more likely to interpret it as a prison escape. Obviously, people elaborate the same information in different ways depending on their previous experience and their expectations about the new information.

Elaboration sometimes leads to the storage of distorted or erroneous information. As you should recall, Bartlett (1932) found that many of his students recalled distorted versions of "The War of the Ghosts." When people use previously acquired facts and beliefs to elaborate on new information, they may alter the new information erroneously. For example, in a study by Eaton, Anderson, and Smith (1984), fifth graders spent several weeks studying a unit on light in their science curriculum. A pretest before the unit had shown that many students had a particular misconception about light: they believed that people see things because the light shines on them and makes them brighter. During the unit, the correct explanation of human sight was presented: because light reflects off objects and travels to the eye, people are able to see those objects. Despite their reading and hearing this information, a posttest revealed that most students had retained their misconceptions about seeing. Only twenty-four–thirty percent of them correctly indicated in their answers that light must travel not only from the light source to the object but also from the object to the eye.

Similar results have been reported by Champagne, Klopfer, and Gunstone (1982) for students studying physics. Many children have misconceptions about basic principles of physics that then interfere with their learning in a physics class. To illustrate, a misconception held by many students is that objects float on water because they are light rather than heavy, when in fact an object's relative weight (compared to water of equal volume) determines whether the object floats or sinks. Even when students correctly recite physics principles, they may continue to apply their earlier misconceptions when asked to explain real-world situations (Champagne et al., 1982). Hence, a student may accurately use the relative weight principle in describing how objects float on water yet have difficulty using that principle to explain why a heavy metal battleship doesn't immediately sink to the bottom of the ocean.

Teachers often present information to students thinking that students' erroneous beliefs will be corrected. What may happen instead is that, through the processes of meaningful learning and elaboration, the new information will be related to, and altered to fit, students' preconceived notions about the world. As a result, students learn inaccurate rather than accurate information.

Elaboration usually leads to better retention of information. Although elaboration can sometimes lead to distortions and errors in what is learned, generally, elaborated information is more effectively learned and remembered than nonelaborated information (Anderson, 1985; Bobrow & Bower, 1969; Craik & Tulving, 1975; Stein & Bransford, 1979). As Anderson (1985) has pointed out, most elaborations reflect correct assumptions and interpretations of an event, not incorrect ones.

Accordingly, students should be instructed about the benefits of elaboration when they study. In a study of reading comprehension (Linden & Wittrock, 1981), fifth graders in an experimental group were taught a number of elaboration strategies to employ when they read, including summaries, inferences, analogies, and mental images. These students showed higher levels of reading comprehension than students in a control group. We will be looking at a variety of specific elaboration strategies that students can be taught when we examine mnemonics and study skills in Chapter 13.

Elaboration appears to be especially effective when it helps to tie new information together. For example, in studies by Stein, Bransford, and their colleagues (Stein & Bransford, 1979; Stein, Bransford, Franks, Owings, Vye, & McGraw, 1982), fifth graders and college students were instructed to learn a series of sentences. Each sentence involved a particular kind of man and a particular activity; below are some examples:

The fat man read the sign.

The hungry man got into the car.

The sentences were elaborated with phrases added on to them, elaborations generated either by the experimenters or by the subjects themselves. Some of the elaborative phrases (*precise* elaborations) explained the connection between a man's characteristic and his activity, like so:

The fat man read the sign warning about the thin ice.

The hungry man got into the car to go to the restaurant.

Other elaborative phrases (*imprecise* elaborations) did not tie the characteristic and activity together; here are some examples:

The fat man read the sign that was two feet high.

The hungry man got into the car and drove away.

Precise elaborations were far more effective than imprecise ones in helping subjects learn the original sentences.

Elaboration facilitates long-term memory for several reasons. First, elaborated information may be less likely to be confused with other, similar information stored in long-term memory (Ellis & Hunt, 1983). Second, elaboration may provide additional means through which the information can later be retrieved (Anderson, 1985); in a sense, it provides more places to "look" for the information. And, third, elaboration may help with inferences about what the information was *likely* to have been when the information itself cannot be accurately recalled (Anderson, 1985).

I suspect that many students try to learn information strictly at face value, without trying to understand it, organize it, or elaborate upon it. (Perhaps teachers' frequent overreliance on achievement measures of verbatim knowledge encourages such an ineffective approach to learning.) Students should instead be instructed in study strategies that use meaningful learning, organization, and elaboration processes. For instance, they can be taught to state ideas in their own words, generate their own examples of ideas, make connections between new concepts and their own past experiences, and draw logical inferences from the data they are given. As we will see in Chapter 13, students don't always know how best to learn and stand to benefit from specific instruction in studying techniques.

Some Final Remarks About Long-term Memory Storage

Before we leave our discussion of storage processes, a few final points should be made about storage in long-term memory.

One piece of information may be stored in more than one form and in more than one place (e.g., Anderson & Bower, 1973). For example, the same information may be stored both as an image and as a proposition and may be connected to a variety of other pieces of information.

The more frequently a piece of information is used, the more different pieces of information it is likely to be connected with (e.g., Calfee, 1981). When an individual uses the same information in many different situations, the information becomes associated with a variety of other pieces of information in long-term memory. As you will learn in the next chapter, the more associations you have with a piece of information, the more easily you can retrieve that information. Hence, more frequently used information is more quickly and easily remembered.

The storage of new information may affect previously stored information. A new piece of information may help an individual recognize that something stored earlier was inaccurate or that two other pieces of information are related in a way not previously realized.

Information tends to be stored in ways that are convenient rather than logical. Earlier in the chapter I mentioned a finding by Rips et al. (1973) that people can verify that "A collie is an animal" more quickly than they can verify that "A collie is a mammal." It is probably a more economical use of long-term memory "space" to remember that a collie is a mammal and that a mammal is an animal; one can then easily infer that a collie must be an animal. Yet it appears from these researchers' results that individuals store the fact that a collie is an animal as well, a fact that is redundant with other knowledge in long-term memory but probably convenient for the owner of that long-term memory.

Long-term memory is idiosyncratic. Any two people store different information from the same situation. First of all, they attend to different aspects of the situation, so that different information is placed in their short-term memories. Second, they encode that information differently; for example, some people use visual imagery more than others. And, third, they bring their own unique background experiences to the situation so that the interpretations of what they observe are truly their own.

The way in which information is stored in memory determines the ease with which it can be retrieved. Long-term memory storage and retrieval processes are closely related. In the next chapter, we will turn to the topic of long-term memory retrieval, including its relation to storage processes.

SUMMARY

Information is probably encoded in long-term memory in a number of different forms, including verbal codes, imagery, meanings (e.g., propositions), and productions. Information in long-term memory is interconnected in an organized fashion (possibly hierarchically or as a network), so that related pieces of information are associated with one another. Rote learning (learning material through repetition, without relating it to previous learned information) is a relatively inefficient method of storing information in long-term memory; furthermore, rote-learned material is difficult to retrieve. Three more effective processes for LTM storage are meaningful learning (relating new material to information already stored), organization (integrating pieces of information together in a logical fashion), and elaboration (adding one's own ideas to the material to be learned).

C H A P T E R 12

Long-Term Memory II: Retrieval and Forgetting

H ERE are some definitions of words in the English language. Can you identify the specific words to which they refer?

- The fluid part of blood
- A picture form of writing used in ancient Egypt
- A game whose object is to snap small plastic disks into a container
- A zigzag trim used to decorate clothing
- A small, hard-shelled, ocean-dwelling animal that attaches itself to rocks and ships

You probably identified some of these words almost without thinking. But there is a good chance that you could not retrieve all five instantaneously. For one or more of them, you may have found yourself looking around in your long-term memory, perhaps for a lengthy period of time, in "places" where a word might be located. (In case you could not retrieve all five words, they are plasma, hieroglyphics, tiddlywinks, rickrack, and barnacle.)

Retrieving information from long-term memory is sometimes easy and automatic, at other times slow and strenuous, and at still other times virtually impossible. Frequently used information tends to be remembered without conscious effort; for instance, people usually retrieve the locations of their homes and the names of close friends with ease. When information is seldom used, however, its retrieval may be difficult. For example, people often have trouble remembering rarely used words: they may even feel that the words are on the tip of their tongues, yet cannot recall them (Brown & McNeill, 1966). Similarly, people may experience difficulty in identifying people whom they have not seen recently or frequently (Yarmey, 1973).

In this chapter, we will focus on the retrieval of information from long-term memory and on various explanations for why information cannot always be retrieved (i.e., theories of forgetting). We will first look at how memory theorists believe retrieval works and at how retrieval is related to storage. We will examine the concept of retrieval cue, a type of hint that helps us locate desired information in long-term memory. Next, we will return to a process we have encountered before—construction—this time looking at it as an integral part of long-term memory retrieval. After considering some ways to facilitate retrieval of information, we will explore some explanations of why forgetting occurs. Finally, we will apply principles of long-term memory storage and retrieval to classroom practice.

HOW RETRIEVAL WORKS

How easily something is retrieved from long-term memory depends to a great extent on how well it was stored in the first place. Unlike short-term memory, which is apparently quite small, long-term memory is so large that an exhaustive exploration of it all is probably impossible. A search of long-term memory must therefore be selective; only certain sections of it will be explored (e.g., Hopkins & Atkinson, 1968). If the sought-for information is not stored in one of those sections, it will not be retrieved.

Retrieval of information from long-term memory depends to some extent on whether the information was well organized when first stored. To understand the role that organization plays in retrieval, let's first look at an analogous situation—your great grandmother's attic. (I am going back three generations, because young families tend to have homes without much attic space, and many grandparents seem to live in condominiums.) Granny probably kept many items in her attic: furniture, books, old clothes, seldom used cooking utensils, and holiday decorations. Granny may have been a very organized woman, one who stored all the books in one place, all the clothes in another, and all the holiday decorations someplace else. On the other hand, she may have been haphazard, throwing things up there any old place, so that some cooking utensils were with books, others were with clothes, and still others were stuffed in an old dresser or on the top shelf of a dilapidated armoire. How Granny stored items in her attic undoubtedly affected her ability to find those items again. If she stored things systematically (e.g., books with books and cooking utensils with cooking utensils), she would have been able to find them easily when she needed them. But if she stored things in a helter-skelter fashion, she may have had to purchase new canning jars every summer because she couldn't locate her jars from any of the previous thirteen years.

So it is with long-term memory. Retrieval is more effective when related pieces of information are stored in close association with one another, because the individual then has a good idea about where to find a certain piece of information. To illustrate, try answering this quick quiz item testing your memory of an earlier chapter:

What is a discriminative stimulus?

You may be able to answer the question quickly and easily, or you may have to search your long-term memory for a while. Your ability to retrieve the answer will depend to some extent on how well you have organized the information you acquired from previous chapters. The word *stimulus* should of course lead you to look among the information you have stored about behaviorist learning theories. The word *discriminative* might suggest to you that you look more specifically in your information about discrimination. If your knowledge about discrimination is stored with what you know about stimulus control (and it should be, because the two con-

Things are more easily retrieved when long-term memory is organized.

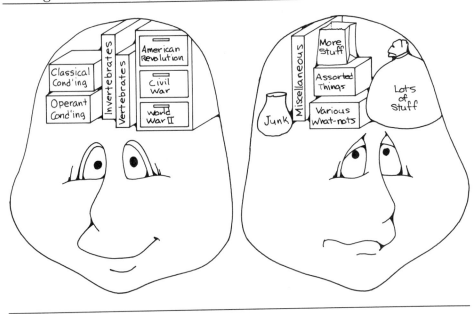

cepts are related), then you should find the answer to the question. A discriminative stimulus sets the occasion in which a response is reinforced.

Lindsay and Norman (1977) have characterized long-term memory retrieval as similar to looking for something in a large, dark room with just a small flashlight. Imagine that the electricity goes off in Granny's house on a dark, moonless night. Because Granny can no longer use either her electric can opener or her electric lights, she takes a flashlight up to the attic to find the manual opener she stored there last October. She switches on her flashlight and begins her search. Unfortunately, the flashlight cannot illuminate the whole attic at once. Instead, she must aim the light first at one spot, then at another, until eventually she finds the can opener. This necessity to search the attic one spot at a time will not be a problem if Granny knows exactly where the can opener is located (e.g., in a drawer with other small cooking utensils), but if she has no idea where she might have put it, she may search all night without success. In much the same way, retrieval from long-term memory is a process of looking in various small "locations" of memory, just one location at a time. Information that has been stored in a logical place (i.e., associated with similar ideas) will probably be found quickly. Information that has been stored haphazardly, in a rote-learning fashion, will be found only after a great deal of searching or possibly not at all.

An experiment by Bower and Holyoak (1973) illustrates this dependence of retrieval on earlier storage. Some college students in this study listened to a set of tape-recorded sounds and identified something that the sound might be (for example, chirping crickets or soldiers clumping down stairs). Two weeks later, the students listened to a second set of sounds, including some of the sounds they had heard previously and some new sounds as well. Once again they were asked to identify what the sound might be and to indicate whether they had heard that exact sound during the first session. When students labeled a sound in the same way in the second session as they had in the first session, they were likely to recognize the sound as being one they had heard before. When they labeled it in a different way in the two sessions (for example, once as a bouncing ball and once as a heartbeat), they were less likely to recognize it as being a familiar one. Other students, who had labels provided for them by the experimenter, showed similar results. By using a label that they had used before, subjects apparently were more likely to search that part of long-term memory where the previous sound was stored.

You may recall the activation model of memory that I described in Chapter 10. According to this model, all information stored in memory is in either an active or an inactive state. Information in an active state is what we might think of as short-term memory, whereas inactive information is in long-term memory. This model lends itself particularly well to an understanding of how long-term memory retrieval might work. From this perspective, retrieval can be viewed as a process of *spreading activation*, with the activation flowing through connected propositions within the propositional network (e.g., Anderson, 1985; Collins & Loftus, 1975; E. Gagné, 1985). Only a small part of the network can be activated at once, thus accounting for the limited capacity, "flashlight" quality of retrieval. If the activation eventually spreads to that part of the network in which the information is located—something more likely to happen if similar ideas are closely associated in that network—the individual will retrieve the desired information.

Retrieval is obviously easier when people know more or less where to look in their long-term memories; that is, when they know which part of long-term memory to activate. Therefore, hints about where a certain piece of information can be found are helpful. It is to these hints—these *retrieval cues*—that we turn now.

RETRIEVAL CUES

Can you fill in the blank in this sentence from "The War of the Ghosts"?

The warriors went on up the river to a town on the other side of _____ .

See if you can remember the name of the town before you continue reading.

Any luck? If not, then perhaps you will recognize the town from among these four choices: (1) Bisantri, (2) Dormro, (3) Muckaruck, (4) Kalama. Is it any easier to fill in the blank now? It should be. I hope you have now identified (4) as the correct answer. In this question, I gave you a type of retrieval cue known as an *identity cue* (e.g., Bourne et al., 1986), because it was identical to the information you were trying to retrieve. Recognition tests, such as multiple choice, are often easier than recall tests because of the identity cues they provide.

Now try this exercise. Read the list of twenty-four words below once through only. I will ask you to recall them as soon as you have finished.

tulip	pencil	spoon	bed	baker	ruby
hat	mountain	doctor	paper	daisy	shirt
chair	fork	diamond	canyon	knife	table
hill	soldier	rose	pen	shoe	emerald

Now that you have read all twenty-four words, cover the page and write as many of them as you can remember. *Do not peek back at the list just yet.*

If you cannot remember all twenty-four, see if these words and phrases help you:

clothing	professions
eating utensils	writing supplies
gemstones	furniture
flowers	landforms

These category names should help you remember more of the words, because all of the twenty-four words fall into one of those categories. Such *associate cues* are related to the words you were searching for; as such, they should direct your search toward relevant parts of your long-term memory.

Still a third kind of retrieval cue is an organizational structure, or *frame*, that guides the retrieval process systematically through long-term memory (e.g., Calfee, 1981). For example, in the previous chapter I described an experiment by Bower and his colleagues (Bower, Clark, Lesgold, & Winzenz, 1969) in which presenting words in an organized, hierarchical format (e.g., the minerals hierarchy shown in Figure 11–13) rather than in a random order facilitated learning. The effectiveness of an organizational structure probably lies partly in the fact that it provides one or more retrieval cues (e.g., "Hmm, now that I've remembered the rare and common metals, I need to remember the alloys").

Consider this sentence that science education students often tell me they use to remember the biological classification system:

King Philip comes over for good spaghetti.

The students use the first letter of each word in the sentence to help them remember this list of terms in its correct order: *kingdom, phylum, class, order, family, genus, species.* Each word in the sentence provides a retrieval cue, that is, search one's knowledge of the biological classification to find a word that begins with the correct letter.

Retrieval cues definitely aid recall of information (e.g., Tulving & Thomson, 1973). They are likely to be most effective when they have been associated frequently with information an individual is trying to remember (Ellis & Hunt, 1983; Tulving, 1968, 1975; Tulving & Thomson, 1971; Underwood, 1983). For example, in retrieving the list of twenty-four words I gave you earlier, once you remembered *table,* you should have had little trouble remembering *chair* as well (or vice versa), because they are frequently associated words.

The environmental context in which information was originally learned can often provide an effective retrieval cue: retrieval is easier when conducted in the same environment as the original learning (Godden & Baddeley, 1975; Smith, Glenberg, & Bjork, 1978). In an unusual demonstration of this principle, Godden and Baddeley (1975) had scuba divers learn thirty-six unrelated words in either of two environments: on shore or twenty feet below the water's surface. They were then asked to remember the words in either the same or a different environment. On a free recall task, the divers were able to recall more words when they were in the same environment in which they had learned the words than when they were in the other environment.

Although retrieval cues usually facilitate the recall of information, they can hinder it when they direct the individual's search to a part of long-term memory *other* than that in which the information is located. For example, in a study by Brown (1968), an experimental group of college students was given a list of twenty-five U.S. states to read, while a control group had no such list. Both groups were then asked to recall as many of the fifty states as they could. Compared to the control group, the experimental group remembered more of the states they had previously read, but *fewer* of the states they had not read. Thus, retrieval cues are helpful only to the extent that they direct an individual to that part of long-term memory in which the desired information is likely to be found.

CONSTRUCTION PROCESSES IN RETRIEVAL

Consider this passage used in an experiment by Sulin and Dooling (1974):

Carol Harris' Need for Professional Help

Carol Harris was a problem child from birth. She was wild, stubborn, and violent. By the time Carol turned eight, she was still unmanageable. Her parents were very concerned about her mental health. There was no good institution for her problem in her state. Her parents finally decided to take some action. They hired a private teacher for Carol (Sulin & Dooling, 1974).

Now cover the passage and answer this question: Did you read the statement, "She was deaf, dumb, and blind," anywhere in the passage?

You probably answered no to my question, just as subjects in Sulin and Dooling's study did. However, another group of subjects read the same passage, with one exception: the name Helen Keller was substituted for Carol Harris. Immediately after reading the passage, twenty percent of these subjects stated that the passage *had* included a statement about Helen being "deaf, dumb, and blind" (none of the subjects in the "Carol Harris" group made that mistake). One week later, the number asserting they had read such a statement rose to fifty percent for the Helen Keller group, but only to five percent for the "Carol Harris" group. In a follow-up study using the same passage, Dooling and Christiaansen (1977) found that subjects who read about Carol Harris, but who were told at recall a week later that the passage was really about Helen Keller, were also likely to "remember" the statement about her being "deaf, dumb, and blind." Apparently, the subjects in the two studies were using their prior knowledge about Helen Keller as well as their actual memory of what they had read at the time of retrieval. The longer the time interval between storage and retrieval time, the greater the impact that prior knowledge had.

Results such as those of Sulin and Dooling (1974), Dooling and Christiaansen (1977), and others (e.g., Neisser, 1981; Spiro, 1980a, 1980b) indicate that long-term memory retrieval, like LTM storage, may involve constructive processes. Individuals frequently retrieve only a portion of the information that has been presented to them; on such occasions, they may fill in the holes in their memory based on what is logical or consistent with their knowledge about the world.

Construction can occur in the retrieval of nonverbal information as well as verbal material. For example, in the previous chapter, I described research by Carmichael, Hogan, and Walters (1932), in which subjects' reproductions of line drawings were influenced by the labels (e.g., eyeglasses or dumbbells) assigned to them. The subjects probably remembered only parts of those drawings and filled in the rest based on what they knew about the objects that the labels identified. Another example of constructive retrieval of nonverbal material can be found in the recall of a crime one has witnessed. Eyewitness testimony is sometimes an inaccurate representation of what actually happened (e.g., Buckhout, 1974; Wells & Loftus, 1984). People's descriptions of the crime may vary considerably, depending on prior knowledge about the individuals involved, expectations about what typically happens in such a situation, and additional information presented at a later time.

As an illustration of constructive processes in eyewitness retrieval, consider an experiment by Loftus and Palmer (1974). Subjects in five groups watched a film depicting a car accident, then individuals in each group were asked one of five questions about how fast the car was going. Subjects' estimates of the speed varied significantly, depending on how the question was worded. Italics highlight the variations in wording:

Questions Asked	Estimated Speed (mph)
About how fast were the cars going when they *contacted* each other?	31.8
About how fast were the cars going when they *hit* each other?	34.0
About how fast were the cars going when they *bumped* into each other?	38.1
About how fast were the cars going when they *collided* into each other?	39.3
About how fast were the cars going when they *smashed* into each other?	40.8

As you can see, the subjects' reconstructions of the accident were influenced to some extent by the severity of the crash implied in the questions they were asked.

Constructive processes may be responsible for many errors in what is "remembered." More frequently, however, construction is a useful component of long-term memory retrieval. When memory of an event is incomplete, you can fill in details based on what makes sense (e.g., Glass et al., 1979; Kintsch, Mandel, & Kozminsky, 1977). A student may not immediately remember which general surrendered at Appomattox but can reason that because the South lost the Civil War and General Robert E. Lee commanded the Southern troops, then it was probably General Lee who surrendered at Appomattox. A student who is trying to remember how to spell the word *ascertain* may surmise that, because the word is related in meaning to the word *certain*, it should be spelled similarly.

In some cases, retrieval is almost entirely constructive, in that an individual is asked to provide information that has never actually been stored. For example, consider this arithmetic problem:

$$1/2 \times 0 = ?$$

You may never have been given the answer to this specific problem, yet you no doubt learned long ago that anything times zero equals zero. Hence you are able to construct the correct answer:

$$1/2 \times 0 = 0$$

Constructive retrieval enables individuals to produce information beyond what they have specifically stored. At the same time, it must be recognized that such construction takes time (Anderson, 1985). In a study by Stazyk, Ashcraft, and Hamann (1982), students easily retrieved multiplication facts they had practiced many times over so that they quickly answered such problems as 2×3 and 4×6. On the other hand, they were slower to answer "zero" problems such as 2×0 and 0×6. Many students probably store a general rule for such problems (i.e., that anything times zero is zero) rather than specific answers to each problem and must therefore construct their answer from the rule each time such a problem is presented. In cases where fast reaction times are essential (e.g., when numerous basic math facts are needed to solve complex problems), it is probably to a student's advantage to learn the specific information rather than a more general rule from which it can be deduced.

FACILITATING RETRIEVAL FROM LONG-TERM MEMORY

As we have seen, retrieval from long-term memory, although often easy and automatic, can sometimes be slow, effortful, and even unsuccessful. Let's consider some helpful hints to facilitate the retrieval process.

Meaningfully learned information is more easily retrieved than information learned in a rote fashion. Although I made this point earlier in the chapter, it is important enough to repeat here. When information is stored in association with similar information—that is, it is stored in a logical "place"—it is more easily retrieved when needed.

The more ideas a given piece of information has been associated with in long-term memory, the more easily that information can be retrieved. Associative networks provide "routes" from one piece of information to another. The more routes to a particular piece of information, the more likely it is that the information will be discovered.

Practice and overlearning increase both the likelihood that information will be retrieved and the speed with which it will be retrieved. The more frequently information is used and practiced, the more pieces of information it will be associated with in long-term memory and the stronger those associations will be (Anderson, 1985). In other words, practice makes perfect, at least in terms of retrieval.

Retrieval is more likely when you are relaxed. Think about what happens when you are looking for your car keys, and you are desperate to find them *immediately* because you are already late for an appointment. As you begin to panic, your search strategies become less and less efficient. You begin to look in the same places over and over again, rather than thinking creatively about the wide variety of places in which the keys might be lurking. So, too, is retrieval adversely affected by anxiety: long-term memory is not searched in an "open-minded" manner, and the chances of the desired information being found are reduced.

If you anticipate needing to retrieve information within a particular context, you should store the information within that context. Information relevant to a situation is likely to be retrieved if you have stored it in close association with other aspects of that situation. If you have stored it elsewhere, you are much less likely to stumble on it at times when it will be useful. Thus, information should be stored with retrieval in mind. This point is particularly important when we are talking about using learned information in new situations. We will therefore return to it again in Chapter 15 on transfer and problem-solving.

Let's now turn our attention to situations in which attempts at retrieval have proven fruitless—in other words, situations in which information has been forgotten.

THEORIES OF FORGETTING

As you should recall from the Chapter 10, most information loss from sensory register and short-term memory is believed to be due to processes of decay and interference. Information is probably "forgotten" from long-term memory in a number of ways. Let's look at several possibilities.

Decay

Theorists disagree about the permanence of information stored in long-term memory (Loftus & Loftus, 1980). Some theorists believe that information, once stored in long-term memory, remains permanently; they attribute information "loss" to such factors as interference or an inability to retrieve (Loftus & Loftus, 1980). Others, however, believe that information can fade, or *decay*, from long-term memory, particularly when that information is not used.

Some evidence indicates that information may indeed remain in long-term memory for a long time. For example, in a study by Bahrick (1984), individuals remembered a considerable amount of the Spanish they had learned in high school or college as many as fifty years before, even if they had not spoken Spanish since that time. Other evidence is provided by experiments in which subjects are asked to *re*learn information they have previously learned but can no longer recall or recognize: these subjects nonetheless learn the information more quickly than subjects who have not previously learned the same material (Nelson, 1971, 1978).

The observations of neurosurgeon Wilder Penfield (e.g., Penfield, 1958, 1959; Penfield & Roberts, 1959) are widely cited as evidence for the permanence of long-term memory. Penfield sometimes operated on locally anesthetized but otherwise conscious patients. In doing so, he discovered that by stimulating portions of the brain with a weak electric current, he could produce vivid sensations in his patients. Patients would describe hearing a song, delivering a baby, or going to a circus as if the experience were actually happening to them at that very moment. They acted almost as if they were reliving previous events in their lives.

Unfortunately, none of these research studies provides conclusive evidence for the permanence of long-term memory: they do not demonstrate that *all* information stored in long-term memory remains there for the life of the individual. Penfield's work has been additionally criticized: Penfield never determined whether the events his patients "remembered" had actually occurred. Ultimately, it may be impossible to determine whether long-term memory is subject to decay over time.

Obliterative Subsumption

A variation of the decay theory is Ausubel's notion of *obliterative subsumption* (Ausubel, 1963, 1968; Ausubel et al., 1978; Ausubel & Robinson, 1969). According to Ausubel, meaningful learning is a process of subsuming new pieces of information into long-term memory under more general, superordinate pieces of information. Over time, these specific pieces of information may be absorbed by their superordinates: that is, they are obliteratively subsumed. For example, a teacher may present a general concept and then illustrate that concept with a number of examples; the student probably subsumes the examples under the concept. Over time, however, some of the examples may lose their distinctiveness, or *dissociability*, from the concept itself, and eventually blend in with the subsuming concept. At that point, the concept continues to be remembered, but the examples are forgotten.

As evidence for his theory, Ausubel has pointed out that general ideas are more likely to be remembered than specific details. Furthermore, details that are distinctive in some way are remembered, while less distinctive ones are forgotten. To illustrate, when I think back to my early lessons in American history, I remember the general idea behind the American Revolution: the Americans were fighting for independence from British rule. I also remember certain distinctive details: for example, the Battle of Bunker Hill is commemorated by a monument I visited frequently as a child, and the Boston Tea Party was a unique and colorful illustration of American dissatisfaction with British taxation policies. However, I have forgotten the details of many other events, because, to my young mind, they consisted of undistinctive places and people.

The notion of obliterative subsumption is certainly consistent with what we commonly observe to be true regarding the kinds of information we remember and the kinds we forget. However, as is true regarding decay theory, to date little evidence either supports or refutes its validity as a major, distinct factor in forgetting.

Interference

In Chapter 7, I described the phenomena of proactive and retroactive inhibition: in both situations the learning of one set of verbal material interferes with ability to recall another set. Verbal learning theorists (e.g., McGeoch, 1942; Melton & Irwin, 1940; Postman & Underwood, 1973; Underwood, 1948) proposed that such *interference* is a major cause of forgetting verbal information. In support of this idea, recall of word lists can be as high as

85% when sources of interference are removed from a serial learning task (Underwood, 1957).

Imagine that you have to learn a list of twenty words. You are then asked to learn another list of twenty more words. Now try to remember the first list. Learning the second list has probably made it more difficult to recall the first list; to some extent, you have forgotten which words are in which list! The interference theory of forgetting might best be described as a theory of confusion: an individual has learned numerous responses and gets them mixed up. Using more conventional behaviorist terminology, verbal learning theorists called this phenomenon *response competition* (e.g., Melton & Irwin, 1940).

An experiment by Anderson (1974) helps to place interference within a contemporary cognitive framework. Undergraduates learned a long list of propositions, each of which involved a person and place; these are some examples:

A hippie is in the park.

A hippie is in the church.

A policeman is in the park.

A sailor is in the park.

The people and places appeared in varying numbers of propositions; some items appeared in only one proposition (e.g., the policeman), whereas others appeared several times (e.g., the park). The subjects studied the sentences until they knew them very well—that is, until they could respond to a long list of questions (e.g., "Who is in the park?" "Where are the hippies?") with one-hundred percent accuracy. At that point, they were given a new set of propositions and asked to indicate whether these had been among the previous set. The more frequently the person and the place had appeared in the previous set of propositions, the longer it took the subjects to determine whether the person and place had appeared *together* in that first set. Anderson (1974, 1976, 1985) has explained these results as being a function of the numerous associations the subjects developed to the frequently appearing people and places. For example, the more frequently that places had been associated with the word *hippie* in the original set of propositions, the longer subjects would take to search among their associations with *hippie* to determine if a new proposition about a hippie had been among the previous set. Thus, multiple associations with a concept can slow down retrieval time for information connected with that concept, a phenomenon that Anderson calls the *fan effect*.

Interference is probably more relevant in the forgetting of rote-learned information than in meaningfully learned information (Good & Brophy, 1986). Response competition and confusion are more likely to be a problem when associations between pieces of information are arbitrary rather than logical.

Failure to Retrieve

Inability to retrieve information clearly affects "forgetting" from long-term memory. The fact that an individual can have difficulty remembering a piece of information at one time but remember it later indicates that the information did not disappear from memory but rather remained unfound when first sought.

Inability to retrieve is most likely to be a cause of forgetting when you neglect to search that part of long-term memory in which the desired information is located. Given appropriate retrieval cues, the information may eventually be found (Tulving, 1975; Tulving & Psotka, 1971; Underwood, 1983).

Repression

Yet another explanation of forgetting is one first introduced by Sigmund Freud (e.g., Freud, 1922). *Repression* occurs when a piece of information is emotionally painful; a traumatic accident, for example, might be too distressing to remember. To describe repression in contemporary memory terminology, painful information begins to produce anxiety whenever the relevant part of long-term memory is approached. Because anxiety itself is unpleasant, the memory search will tend to steer clear of the anxiety-arousing part of long-term memory. Thus, the painful memory, as well as any other information stored in close association with it, will remain forgotten.

Evidence for repression to explain forgetting can be found in an experiment by Zeller (1950). Two groups of college students studied fifteen nonsense syllable pairs until they could recite them without error. They were then asked to perform a task involving the tapping of four blocks in a particular order. Control subjects were asked to follow an easy sequence (tap the blocks in this order: 1, 3, 2, 4). Experimental subjects were asked to remember and reproduce a longer and more difficult sequence, one that was virtually impossible to remember. When these subjects failed the task, they were told that they had poor memories and minimal chances of being successful in the world. Immediately afterward, the two groups were once again asked to practice the original nonsense syllable pairs until they knew them perfectly. At this point, the control subjects relearned the pairs far more quickly than the experimental subjects; this difference was still evident three days later. Zeller's interpretation of the results was that the anxiety-arousing block-tapping task had caused subjects to repress all aspects of the experimental situation, including the paired associates.

Construction Error

We have already seen how construction can lead to errors in recall. Construction may occur either at storage (learner-invented information is stored) or at retrieval (the learner "remembers" information that was never presented).

Construction at retrieval time is particularly likely when there are holes in the information retrieved—holes possibly due to decay, interference, or unsuccessful retrieval.

Failure to Store

A final explanation of "forgetting" is that some information may never have been learned in the first place (e.g., Bourne et al., 1986; Ellis & Hunt, 1983). Perhaps you didn't pay attention to the information, so it never entered short-term memory. Or perhaps you didn't process it sufficiently to store it in long-term memory. Simply being in the right place at the right time does not mean that information will be assimilated by the memory system.

Probably all the considerations I have described are partly responsible for the universal human problem of "forgetting." The problem is particularly evident in the classroom, where oftentimes students seem to lose information almost as soon as they have acquired it. I hope this chapter has given you some ideas on how to facilitate students' retrieval of information and how to minimize their forgetting.

To sum up these two chapters on long-term memory, let's look at some general principles of facilitating long-term memory storage and retrieval in classroom learning situations.

FACILITATING STORAGE AND RETRIEVAL IN THE CLASSROOM

Some principles related to long-term memory storage and retrieval processes are particularly applicable to classroom learning.

Meaningful learning should be emphasized over rote learning. As we have seen, meaningful learning leads to more rapid storage and more successful retrieval than rote learning. Teachers should stress the importance of learning for understanding, not only in their lectures and classroom discussions but in their assignments and examinations as well.

Unfortunately, educators forget this basic principle all too often. For example, Beck and McKeown (1988) recently examined a number of elementary school social studies textbooks and found them often lacking a meaningful presentation of concepts and events. Beck and McKeown illustrated their point by describing how four widely used history texts describe the events leading to the American Revolution. In these books, events are frequently described as isolated incidents (thus promoting a disorganized, rote learning of them) rather than as having any significant cause-effect relationships to one another or to the revolution. Beck and McKeown have argued that history texts should instead help students to make sense of history; for example, the French and Indian Wars, the Boston Tea Party, and the Intolerable Acts all contributed to the colonists' eventual rebellion against Britain and should be learned within that context.

To learn new material meaningfully, students must have knowledge and experiences to which that material can be related, and they must see how that material relates to what they already know. Teaching subject matter that does not overlap with students' existing knowledge is likely to be a slow and, in the long run, futile effort. When students are observed processing material in a rote fashion (e.g., rehearsing it), they probably either lack the appropriate background knowledge for learning that material effectively (hence the need for identifying prerequisites in many cases) or are unaware that the material can in fact be understood in terms of that background knowledge. Beck and McKeown (1988) observed that history textbooks frequently refer to American distress over Britain's "taxation without representation" policy, without always providing an adequate explanation of why this policy was so upsetting to the colonists. Many adults can easily relate the idea of taxation without representation to their own frustrations with high taxes. Most fifth graders, however, have little if any experience upon which to draw in understanding the colonists' situation as it must have been.

New material should be appropriately organized. When material is presented in an organized fashion, students are more likely to store it in a similar organizational network. And when information in long-term memory is organized, it can be more easily retrieved.

Students should be encouraged to elaborate on new information, but their elaborations should be monitored for appropriateness and accuracy. The more the new material is elaborated, the more completely and precisely it will be stored. At the same time, teachers must monitor students' elaborations to be sure that students' previous misconceptions do not result in the learning of *mis*information.

Students should store information with retrieval in mind. As they learn new material, students should relate it to the various situations in which its retrieval is likely to be required. For example, a student is more likely to retrieve mathematical ideas relevant to accounting, surveying, or engineering if the mathematics instructor includes some simple problems in accounting, surveying, and engineering. Similarly, a student studying for a psychology test stressing application becomes better prepared by using study time to consider numerous situations in which psychological principles can be applied.

Students' memories will probably never be totally reliable records of information. Long-term memory storage and retrieval are both constructive processes and therefore will always be fallible. Memory can undoubtedly be improved but probably never perfected.

In addition to the general principles I have just listed, contemporary memory theory has yielded numerous specific educational applications. We will examine these in the following chapter.

SUMMARY

Retrieval of information from long-term memory appears to be a process of searching, in one "location" at a time, until the desired information is found. Retrieval is easier when information has previously been stored in a meaningful and organized fashion and when retrieval cues are present. Retrieval often appears to be a partially constructive process, in that some pieces of information may be retrieved and others filled in so that an event is remembered completely, albeit sometimes inaccurately. Numerous factors may be involved in "forgetting" information, including decay, obliterative subsumption, interference, failure to retrieve, repression, construction error, and failure to store the information in the first place. Our understanding of storage and retrieval processes in long-term memory has numerous implications for classroom practice.

CHAPTER 13

Educational Applications of Human Information Processing Theory

U NQUESTIONABLY, human information processing theory is relevant to students' learning strategies and teachers' instructional methods. As cognitive psychologists develop a better understanding of how the information processing system operates, they are beginning to turn their attention to the question of how student learning and performance can be facilitated. Five areas of theory and research are particularly applicable to educational settings: automaticity, expository teaching, mnemonics, metacognition, and study skills. In this chapter, we will explore work that has been done in each of these areas.

AUTOMATICITY

Walter Schneider and Richard Shiffrin (Schneider & Shiffrin, 1977; Shiffrin & Schneider, 1977) have distinguished between two types of information processing: controlled processing and automatic processing. *Controlled processing* requires much of an individual's attention and is likely to use most (possibly all) of the individual's short-term or working memory capacity. In other words, controlled processing requires conscious thought and effort. An example is the cognitive processing necessary for learning to drive a car. I still remember the summer evening in 1966 that my father tried to teach me to drive a standard shift in our 1951 Ford convertible. Trying to steer the car in appropriate directions while monitoring the speed and negotiating the stick shift and clutch pedal consumed all my attention and short-term memory capacity. In fact, my short-term memory must have been overflowing, because I kept forgetting to step on the clutch, thus jerking the car forward and almost catapulting my father into outer space. (Dad enrolled me in driver education the following morning.)

On the other hand, *automatic processing,* also known as *automaticity,* occurs with little or no conscious attention or effort and requires little short-term memory capacity; it is, in a sense, "thoughtless." For example, my driving today, more than twenty years after that jerky start, is accomplished with little thought on my part and with few mistakes. I do not have to remind myself to step on the clutch every time I want to shift gears or to remove my foot from the brake when I want to increase speed. Except under difficult conditions such as heavy traffic or inclement weather, I can make the hour's drive to Denver while drinking coffee, harmonizing with the radio, talking to a friend, or shouting at the kids to keep their hands to themselves. Even though I still drive a standard shift, driving is an automatic activity for me.

Controlled processes become increasingly automatic through repetition and practice (Cheng, 1985; Fisk, 1986; Norman, 1976; Piontkowski & Calfee, 1979; Schneider & Shiffrin, 1977; Shiffrin & Schneider, 1977). As I continued to drive that 1951 Ford, I not only became more proficient, I was also able to devote less and less mental effort to the task of driving itself. Within several months of persistent practice, I was cruising Main Street with my friends, tapping my fingers to Beatles' music on the car radio, munching McDonald's French fries (twelve cents a bag in those days), and perusing the sidewalk for classmates of particular interest.

As you should recall from Chapter 9, people can usually attend to only one demanding task—a task that requires conscious, controlled processing—at a time. On the other hand, they can probably attend to several tasks simultaneously when each of them involves only automatic processing. How many mental activities can be conducted at the same time, then, depends on how automatically each of them can be performed. Remember, short-term memory has a limited capacity; people can perform as many activities simultaneously as that capacity will allow.

Many academic tasks, such as reading, writing, and mathematics, require performing a number of "subtasks" at more or less the same time. If these tasks are to be performed successfully, some of those subtasks should probably be automatic. For example, consider the case of reading. Comprehending what one reads is often a difficult task involving controlled, conscious effort. If students are going to understand what they read, more basic reading processes, such as letter and word identification, must occur automatically. In fact, research is clear on this point: the more effort a student must devote to identifying the words of a passage, the lower the student's comprehension of that passage will be (LaBerge & Samuels, 1974; Perfetti & Hogaboam, 1975; Perfetti & Lesgold, 1979).

In research on the writing process, Birnbaum (1982) and Pianko (1979) found that good writers paid attention primarily to the communicative aspect of writing (expressing one's thoughts in a clear, logical, and organized fashion). Apparently, these individuals had already learned the mechanics of writing (e.g., spelling, grammar, punctuation) thoroughly enough to apply them automatically. Less skilled writers, on the other hand, paid more attention to mechanics and less to communicating their ideas. Poor writers can possibly be helped to become better writers through the automatization of the mechanical aspects of writing. They should be able to attend more carefully to the task of clear self-expression if they are not so bogged down in concerns about subject-verb agreement or the correct spelling of *psychology*.

So, too, do some aspects of mathematics—in particular, the basic math facts—need to become second nature (e.g., Gagné, 1983). For example, in my course on educational testing, students must be able to solve problems like this one before they can learn to interpret intelligence test (IQ) scores:

$$\frac{70 - 100}{15} = ?$$

To solve such a problem easily, my students must have certain arithmetic facts at their fingertips; they must be able to subtract 100 from 70 quickly and must automatically know that -30 divided by 15 equals -2. I have frequently observed that when my students must consciously and effortfully calculate a simple arithmetic problem, they lose sight of the overall task they are trying to accomplish.

In the previous two chapters, I emphasized the importance of meaningful learning: by understanding the information that they store in long-term memory, students can more easily retrieve it. At the same time, in the case of many basic skills, understanding is not enough, because the retrieval of these skills must be fast and automatic. Such skills must be repeated and practiced, perhaps at a rote level, often enough that they become second nature to students, so that students can then perform them essentially without thinking.

EXPOSITORY TEACHING

The lecture method has often been criticized as being a relatively ineffective instructional technique. For example, B. F. Skinner has proposed that learning can occur only when the individual makes an active response; because the typical classroom lecture does not allow much active responding, it is unlikely to be an effective pedagogical practice. Similarly opposed to the lecture method is Jerome Bruner (e.g., 1961a, 1961b), who has proposed that students can better understand ideas when they are first allowed hands-on experiences related to those ideas. Bruner has argued that a discovery approach to teaching—in which students discover various properties of the environment through manipulation of concrete objects—would be more effective than a traditional lecture.

Nevertheless, the lecture method has some strong advocates, including many human information processing theorists. David Ausubel (e.g., Ausubel, 1963; Ausubel et al., 1978; Ausubel & Robinson, 1969) has argued that students listening to a lecture are not necessarily the passive nonresponders that Skinner portrays. Instead, students, although perhaps not overtly active, are nevertheless *cognitively* active, in that they busily attend to and meaningfully interpret the information they hear. Furthermore, although students at Piaget's concrete operational stage may well require the concrete experiences that discovery learning provides, formal operational students are quite capable of understanding concepts presented at an abstract level. For the latter group of students, a concise, organized lecture is often the most rapid and efficient means of presenting a body of information.

The lecture is one form of *expository teaching*—teaching in which the instructional material is given to students more or less in the form in which it is to be learned. The other common form of expository teaching is the textbook; there again, virtually all the information that needs to be learned is explicitly presented. Let's take a look at some recommended components of this approach to instruction.

The information should be presented in an organized fashion. Expository teaching should present new information in the basic organizational format in which students should store it in memory. In fact, Tennyson and his colleagues (e.g., Tennyson & Cocchiarella, 1986; Tennyson, Tennyson, & Rothen, 1980) have argued that the structure of knowledge should be a critical consideration in designing instructional materials. How information is presented to students (for example, the order in which different concepts are introduced) influences the way students store that information and therefore also affects their success in retrieving it. The organization of information may be particularly important for low-ability students; apparently, high-ability students can sometimes organize poorly sequenced information themselves (Buckland, 1968).

The information should overlap with what students already know. Too often, teachers assume that students know more than they really do and begin instruction at a point beyond what students can comprehend. Before any instructional unit, students' existing levels of knowledge should be ascertained through either formal pretesting or informal questioning. Instruction is clearly more effective when it begins with what students know (e.g., Bobango, 1988).

Students should be shown how instructional material is organized and how it relates to what they have previously learned. In Chapter 11, I distinguished between two forms of information organization, internal organization—the relationship of the various information pieces to one another—and external organization—the relationship of that material to what the student already knows. One means of facilitating both forms of organization is through the use of *advance organizers* (e.g., Ausubel et al., 1978). An advance organizer is an abstract, general introduction to a new body of information (e.g., a new topic in a lecture or a new chapter in a textbook) that is typically designed to accomplish either or both of two purposes. An *expository organizer* provides a rough overview or outline of the new unit, describing the general topics (superordinate concepts) that will be included and their relationship to one another; thus, it provides the beginnings of an internal organizational scheme. (The outlines and introductory paragraphs appearing at the beginning of each chapter in this text are examples of expository organizers.) A *comparative organizer* shows how the new unit relates to students' previous experiences, to information they have previously learned in school, or possibly to their own purpose for studying the material; it furthermore points out the similarities between the new information and the old. In this way, the organizer facilitates external organization. An additional advantage of a comparative organizer, as Ausubel has pointed out, is that it establishes a meaningful learning set: the student anticipates being able to understand the new material at a meaningful level and thus approaches the learning task with meaningful learning in mind.

Research consistently demonstrates the effectiveness of advance organizers in facilitating student learning, particularly when students have difficulty organizing on their own or when the organization of material is not clear (Ausubel et al., 1978; Mayer, 1979a, 1979b). Advance organizers also appear to promote more meaningful learning and consequently to facilitate the application of learned information to new situations (Mayer, 1987). A variety of formats of advance organizers (e.g., overviews, outlines, analogies) all appear to be effective (Alexander, Frankiewicz, & Williams, 1979; Glynn & DiVesta, 1977; Mayer, 1984). For example, here is an example of how a lesson on radar might be introduced by means of an analogy—a comparative advance organizer:

> Radar means the detection and location of remote objects by reflection of radio waves. The phenomenon of acoustic echoes is familiar. Sound waves reflected from a building or cliff are received back at the observer after a lapse of a short interval. The effect is similar to you shouting in a canyon and, seconds later, hearing a nearly exact replication of your voice. Radar uses exactly the same principle except that the waves involved are radio waves, not sound waves. These travel very much faster than sound waves, 186,000 miles per second, and can cover much longer distances. Thus, radar involves simply measuring the time between transmission of the waves and their subsequent return or echo, and then converting that to a distance measure (Mayer, 1984, p. 30).

Advance organizers sometimes appear as one or more questions presented at the beginning of a unit (e.g., Frase, 1975). Recently, most of the questions that appear in textbooks have been criticized for focusing primarily on information gathering rather than on more sophisticated objectives (Allington, 1988; Armbruster, 1988; Winograd, 1988). Teachers and textbook writers should probably include other types of introductory questions as well. Questions asking students to apply, synthesize, draw inferences, and think about where they might go for additional information may facilitate students' processing of expository material in a more meaningful and elaborative manner (Allington, 1988; Armbruster, 1988; Winograd, 1988).

Basic principles of meaningful learning should be observed. When an expository teaching approach is used, students should be encouraged to process the information so that they learn it meaningfully. Such techniques as familiar examples, in-class activities, and small group discussions about particular aspects of the instructional material may help students to understand information within the context of their own experience. And, of course, teachers should evaluate students on the basis of demonstrated comprehension of that information rather than rote memorization of it.

When expository teaching is approached from the perspective of the meaningful storage of information, it can serve as an efficient, organized means of providing information to a large number of students. On the other hand, when it is approached without regard for how students will learn it meaningfully, organize it, or elaborate upon it, expository teaching may lead to disappointing results in student achievement. Ausubel and his colleagues (Ausubel et al., 1978) have identified some particularly inept practices in expository teaching:

1. Premature use of pure verbal techniques with cognitively immature pupils [e.g., preoperational or concrete operational students].

2. Arbitrary presentation of unrelated facts without any organizing or explanatory principles.

3. Failure to integrate new learning tasks with previously presented materials.

4. The use of evaluation procedures that merely measure ability to recognize discrete facts or to reproduce ideas in the same words or in the identical context as originally encountered (Ausubel et al., 1978, p. 124).

In expository teaching, learning will be maximized when information is presented with meaningful, organized learning in mind. But what do teachers do in situations when, for whatever reasons, information must be learned that students either cannot learn meaningfully or cannot organize logically? In such situations, mnemonic devices provide a workable alternative.

MNEMONICS

Looking back on your own educational experiences, you can no doubt recall many situations when you had difficulty learning important information. Perhaps the troublesome material consisted of long lists of items or unfamiliar vocabulary words in a foreign language or particular rules of grammar, spelling, or mathematics. *Mnemonics* are devices that facilitate the learning and recall of many such forms of difficult material. In this section we will look at four different types of mnemonics—verbal mediation, visual imagery, superimposed meaningful structures, and external retrieval cues—and will then examine some of the reasons that mnemonics are so effective.

Verbal Mediation

Imagine that you are trying to learn that the German word *Handschuh* means "glove." You might remember this word by thinking of a glove as a "shoe for the hand." Such a mnemonic is an example of the use of *verbal mediation,* in which two words or ideas are associated by a word or phrase (the verbal mediator) that connects them together. Here are some examples of verbal mediators for other German vocabulary words:

German Word	English Meaning	Mediator
der Hund	dog	hound
das Schwein	pig	swine
die Gans	goose	gander
der Stier	bull	steer

Notice that in every case, the verbal mediator bridges the gap between the German word and its English equivalent. By storing the mediator, you can make a connection between the two words.

Verbal mediators clearly facilitate learning (e.g., Bugelski, 1962), and their use is not necessarily restricted to the learning of foreign vocabulary words. For example, here is a mnemonic sometimes seen in spelling instruction:

The principal is my pal.

Remembering this sentence will enable a student to remember that the correct spelling for a school administrator is "princi*pal*" rather than "princi*ple*." As another example, my daughter remembers the chemical symbol for gold—Au—by thinking, "*Ay, you* stole my *gold* watch!"

Visual Imagery

As you learned in Chapter 11, a visual image is a powerful storage code that can be formed quickly and retained for a relatively long period of time (e.g., Shepard, 1967; Standing, 1973; Standing, Conezio, & Haber, 1970). Accordingly, visual imagery forms the basis for a number of effective mnemonic devices. I will describe three of them: the method of loci, the pegword method, and the keyword method.

Method of Loci. In the days of the Greek and Roman empires, orators used a particular technique to help them remember the major ideas they wished to include in their hours-long harangues at the local forum (lecture notes were apparently not acceptable in those days). These orators would think about a familiar route that they walked frequently—the route from home to the forum, for example—and about the significant landmarks along the way—perhaps a bridge, a large tree, and a brothel, in that order. Then, when planning a speech, they would translate each key point into some sort of concrete, observable object and form a visual image of each successive key point located at each landmark along the familiar route. For example, let's say that an orator's first three points in his speech were the frequent traffic jams near the forum, the importance of a mass transit system in downtown Rome, and the consequent necessity for a tax increase. He might store images such as these: (1) numerous horses and pedestrians entangled in a traffic jam on the bridge (first landmark), (2) a gigantic, 30-person chariot perched among the branches of the large tree (second landmark), and (3) several toga-clad prostitutes pitching coins at a tax collector from the up-stairs window of the brothel (third landmark). Later, when pontificating at the forum, the orator would take a mental walk along his familiar route; as he passed each landmark, he would readily retrieve the image of that land-mark and the object symbolizing the next major point of his speech. In this manner, he could easily remember all the main ideas of the oration and their correct order. By the way, in case you are unaware of the fact, *loci* is the Latin word for "places."

The *method of loci* is clearly an effective mnemonic technique (Christen & Bjork, 1976; Groninger, 1971; Snowman, 1986) and lends itself readily to the storage and retention of lists of items. For example, in a study by Gron-inger (1971), some subjects learned a list of twenty-five words using the method of loci while others learned the words simply by grouping them. Subjects using the method of loci learned the words faster and remembered more of them on a free recall task 5 weeks later. However, both groups of subjects performed equally well when asked to recognize the words; thus, it appears that the benefit of the method of loci may lie in the imagery-based retrieval cues it provides.

Pegword Method. The *pegword method* is another technique through which a list of items and their relative positions can be learned effectively (Bower, 1972; Bugelski, Kidd, & Segmen, 1968; Higbee, 1976). This method consists of using a well-known or easily learned list of items that then serves as a series of "pegs" on which another list is hung through visual imagery.

Here is a poem that is frequently used as a pegboard:

One is a bun.
Two is a shoe.
Three is a tree.
Four is a door.
Five is a hive.
Six is sticks.
Seven is heaven.
Eight is a gate.
Nine is a line; and
Ten is a hen.
(Miller, Galanter, & Pribram, 1960, p. 135).

This poem should be an easy one to remember because its lines are com-posed of the numbers one through ten in conjunction with rhyming nouns. Now suppose you need to remember a list of items in a certain order. You take the first item on the list and form a visual image of it interacting with the noun that rhymes with *one* (in this case, *bun*), then take the second list item and imagine it interacting with the noun that rhymes with *two* (*shoe*), and so on. Images can be formed quickly and typically do not need to be rehearsed in order to be remembered.

Consider this food chain (Ebert, Loewy, Miller, & Schneiderman, 1973) as an example of a list to be learned using the "One is a bun" poem:

Algae in a lake are eaten by

Water fleas, which are eaten by

Minnows, which are eaten by

Larger fish, which are eaten by

Eagles.

Using the pegword method, the learner forms an image of algae and a bun together: a hamburger bun is covered with green algae. Similarly, water fleas are visualized in conjunction with a shoe: a shoe is filled with water, and several water fleas are doing the backstroke across the surface. For the last three items of the food chain, the learner might form images of a tree with minnows hanging down like fruit, a door with a large fish stuffed through the keyhole, and an eagle wearing a beehive for a hat. Remembering the food chain, then, is simply a matter of thinking, "One is a bun," conjuring up the image of the bun with algae, then thinking, "Two is a shoe," retrieving the shoe image, and so on.

Keyword Method. I have already described the use of verbal mediation in learning foreign language vocabulary words. But you may have noticed that the German words I chose closely resembled English words. More often, however, words in a foreign language are not so obviously related to their English meanings. In such situations, the *keyword method* is an effective alternative. This technique, which is actually a combination of verbal mediation and visual imagery, involves two steps, like so: identify an English word or phrase (the keyword) that sounds similar to the foreign word; then form a visual image of the English sound-alike word with the English meaning. For example, consider how we might remember these German words:

German Word	English Meaning	Keyword(s)	Visual Image
das Pferd	horse	Ford	a *horse* driving a *Ford*
der Fuchs	fox	forks	a *fox* holding *forks*
das Kaninchen	rabbit	can on chin	a *rabbit* with a *can on* its *chin*
der Waschbär	raccoon	wash bar	a *raccoon wash*ing with a *bar* of soap

The keyword method has been shown to be an effective instructional device in teaching both English and foreign language vocabulary words; it is also useful in teaching such paired associates as states and their capitals and cities and their products (Atkinson, 1975; Levin, 1981; Levin, McCormick, Miller, Berry, & Pressley, 1982; Pressley, Levin, & McCormick, 1980; Raugh & Atkinson, 1975). Furthermore, older students (such as eighth

Using a keyword to remember that a horse is a "pferd"

graders) often spontaneously apply the mnemonic to new learning tasks (Jones & Hall, 1982). Although only concrete objects can actually be visualized, the technique can be used with more abstract words as well, provided that they can be adequately represented by a concrete object. For example, consider the Spanish word for "love": *el amor*. This word might be learned by picturing a heart (symbolizing "love") wearing a suit of armor (the keyword).

In any mnemonics based on visual imagery, three precautions must be kept in mind. First, many young children cannot generate effective images on their own, so probably need to have pictures provided for them (Mayer, 1987). Second, for imagery to be an effective means of remembering a connection between two items (e.g., between a bridge and mass transit, or between love and *amor*), the two items must be incorporated into the same image in an *interacting* fashion (Bower, 1972; Dempster & Rohwer, 1974). Thus, while an image of a heart wearing armor is an effective way of remembering the Spanish word for "love," an image of a heart standing beside a suit of armor probably is not. Third, as I indicated in Chapter 11, imagery does not preserve details very effectively (Anderson, 1985); therefore, it may not help one remember such specific information as the exact shape of a heart or the number of dents on a suit of armor.

Superimposed Meaningful Structure

One of my most vivid memories from my years as an undergraduate psychology major is being required to learn the twelve cranial nerves: olfactory, optic, oculomotor, trochlear, trigeminal, abducens, facial, auditory, glossopharyngeal, vagus, spinal accessory, and hypoglossal. It is not the nerves themselves that I remember, but rather how painfully difficult it was to learn them all in their correct order. I had little luck drilling the list into my thick skull (I was using the tried-and-not-so-true method of rote memorization) until a friend passed along this mnemonic:

On old Olympus' towering top, a Finn and German viewed some hops.

Notice that the first letters of the words in the sentence correspond with the first letters of the twelve cranial nerves: just as in the list of nerves, the first three words in the sentence begin with O, the next two begin with T, and so on. And the sentence, while a bit strange, is fairly easy to remember because of the structure provided by its rhythm and rhyme.

"On old Olympus" is an example of a mnemonic I call a *superimposed meaningful structure* (sometimes also known as *semantic elaboration*). The technique is simple: one imposes a familiar structure on the body of information to be learned. That structure can be a sentence, story, poem, acronym, or anything else already meaningful to the learner. Some examples are shown in Figure 13–1.

To illustrate just how effective such superimposed structures can be, let's look at an experiment by Bower and Clark (1969). Two groups of college students learned twelve lists of ten nouns: Group 1 learned each list through repetition, while Group 2 composed narrative stories that included all ten

Figure 13–1
Examples of superimposed meaningful structures

The Mnemonic	What It Represents
ROY G. BIV	The spectrum: red, orange, yellow, green, blue, indigo, violet.
HOMES	The five Great Lakes: Huron, Ontario, Michigan, Erie, Superior.
Every good boy does fine.	The lines on the treble clef: E G B D F.
When the "mites" go up, the "tites" go down.	The distinction between stalagmites and stalactites.
A "boot"	The shape of Italy.
A "bearskin rug."	The shape of France.
George Ellen's old grandmother rode a pig home yesterday.	The correct spelling of "geography."
I before *E*, except after *C*.	The correct spelling of words like "receive."
Thirty days has September. . . .	The number of days in each month.

words of each list. Here is an example of such a Group 2 story (the nouns to be remembered are in capital letters):

A LUMBERJACK DARTed out of a forest, SKATEd around a HEDGE past a COLONY of DUCKS. He tripped on some FURNITURE, tearing his STOCK-ING while hastening toward the PILLOW where his MISTRESS lay (Bower & Clark, 1969, p. 182).

After the students had learned each of the twelve lists perfectly, they were then asked to recall all 120 words (the first word of each list was given as a retrieval cue). Students in Group 1 (repetition) recalled only thirteen percent of the words; in contrast, students in Group 2 (stories) recalled ninety-three percent!

External Retrieval Cues

One of my own memory problems is remembering to remember. I forget to turn off my car lights after driving to work on a foggy morning. I occasionally forget important meetings. Sometimes I forget to bring crucial handouts or overheads to class. Yes, yes, I know what you're thinking: I'm suffering from the absentminded professor syndrome.

It's not that I really forget information. When I go to the parking lot at the end of the day and find that my car has a dead battery, I readily remember the fact that I turned on my car lights that morning. When I am reminded of the important meeting I've just missed, I think, "Of course!" My problem is that I forget to retrieve important information at the appropriate time. Given the number of my students who sometimes forget homework assignments (or even that they have class!), I know my problem is not an unusual one.

When you need to remember to retrieve, an *external retrieval cue* can be helpful. The classic example is the proverbial string around the finger: the string is tied in a spot impossible to overlook and serves as a reminder that something needs to be remembered. Finger strings are terribly unfashionable, but other external retrieval cues can be equally effective. Appointment books, to-do lists, and little self-reminder notes increase the likelihood that students remember important assignments and engagements and also help them learn to be responsible for their retrieval.

Why Mnemonics Work

It should be clear by now that mnemonics can be extremely helpful learning aids. As you may have noticed, their effectiveness lies in their conformity with a few critical principles of storage and retrieval. First, they often impose a structure or organization on the material to be learned. Second, they help the learner relate the new material to information already stored in long-term memory (e.g., the number system or a familiar poetic meter).

And, third, they provide retrieval cues that help the learner find the information at a later time.

Yet students, and people in general, rarely use mnemonics (Morris, 1977), perhaps because they are unaware of their existence or their benefits. Teachers can obviously help students learn difficult information if they identify or develop mnemonics for that information. Furthermore, teachers can help students become more independent learners by showing them how to develop effective mnemonics on their own.

METACOGNITION

As you have been reading this book, I hope you have been learning a great deal about how you yourself learn and remember; perhaps you have also been modifying your approach to your learning tasks. For example, you may now be trying to pay closer attention to what you read in textbooks and what you hear in class. You may also be focusing more on understanding, organizing, and elaborating on your course material.

People's knowledge of their own learning and cognitive processes, and their consequent regulation of those processes to enhance learning and memory, are known as *metacognition* (e.g., Brown, 1978; Duell, 1986; Flavell, 1976; Flavell & Wellman, 1977; Siegler, 1986). Metacognition includes such skills as these:

1. Being aware of one's own learning and memory capabilities, and of what learning tasks can realistically be accomplished
2. Knowing which learning strategies are effective and which are not
3. Planning an approach to a learning task that is likely to be successful
4. Using effective learning strategies
5. Monitoring one's present knowledge state; knowing when information has been successfully learned and when it has not
6. Knowing effective strategies for retrieval of previously stored information

As you might expect, students' metacognitive awareness is significantly related to their school learning (Peterson, 1988). Yet many people, including students, are sadly unaware of, or misinformed about, their own learning and memory processes. Metacognitive skills do improve with age, however (Duell, 1986; Flavell, 1985; Siegler, 1986). Let's look at three developmental trends in metacognition.

Children become increasingly realistic about their memory capabilities and limitations (Cavanaugh & Perlmutter, 1982; Duell, 1986; Flavell, Friedrichs, & Hoyt, 1970). Young children typically overestimate how much they can remember. For example, in a study by Flavell et al. (1970), four age groups of children (ranging from nursery school to fourth grade) were shown strips of paper picturing from one to ten objects and asked to predict how many objects they thought they could remember at a time (a short-term memory task). The children were then tested to determine how many objects they actually could remember. All four groups of children tended to overestimate their short-term memory capacities, but the estimates of the older children were more realistic. For example, kindergarten children predicted that they could remember an average of 8.0 objects, but in fact remembered only 3.6. The fourth graders, on the other hand, estimated that they could remember 6.1 objects, and actually recalled 5.5.

As they grow, children develop an increasing ability to use effective learning and memory strategies. In a study by Masur, McIntyre, and Flavell (1973), three age groups of subjects (first and third graders and college students) were given a series of trials in which they studied thirty-six drawings of common objects (e.g., a bell, a flag, a wagon) and then recalled as many of them as they could. After each recall, the subjects were allowed to pick half of the drawings for further study. The third graders and college students used a logical strategy: they chose to study those items they had failed to remember on the previous trial. The first graders, however, chose their study items randomly, without consideration of past memory failures.

Older children apparently know better what learning strategies are effective in different situations; for example, they more frequently use organization and elaboration than younger children do (Siegler, 1986). Furthermore, although even kindergartners possess some rudimentary retrieval skills (Kreutzer, Leonard, & Flavell, 1975), older children are more adept in their attempts at retrieval and are more likely to use effective retrieval cues (Ritter, Kaprove, Fitch, & Flavell, 1973). Even when young children can verbally describe which learning and memory strategies are effective and which are not, when left to their own devices they will often use relatively ineffective strategies (Strage, Christopoulos, Rohwer, Thomas, Delucchi, & Curley, 1988).

Children become increasingly able to determine when they actually know something. In the previously described study by Flavell et al. (1970), children of different ages were also asked to study a series of pictures until they were certain they could recall all of them in the correct order. Older children (second and fourth graders) were relatively accurate in ascertaining their own knowledge levels and were able to recall most of the pictures after their self-terminated study periods. On the other hand, younger children (those in nursery school and kindergarten) terminated their study sessions before they were able to recall the pictures accurately.

Despite these developmental improvements in metacognitive knowledge and skills, many upper-level elementary school students are sadly uninformed about effective learning strategies (e.g., Knight, 1988). Even high school and college students are often metacognitively naive (e.g., Ormrod

& Jenkins, 1988). For example, when I present a unit on cognitive psychology to my junior-level educational psychology class, my description of such basic strategies as organizing information and relating it to familiar concepts and experiences appears to be a major revelation to about half of my students. Sadly, too many of these students have viewed learning as being best approached through rote memorization throughout their many years in school.

In addition, students are often ignorant about what they know and what they don't know, a phenomenon known as *secondary ignorance* (Sieber, 1968, cited in Brown, 1978). For example, students often think they know how to spell words that they actually do not (Adams & Adams, 1960; Johnson, Langford, & Quorn, 1981; Ormrod & Wagner, 1987). And I frequently have students appear at my office confused about why they have done so poorly on an exam when they "knew" the information so well. When I ask these students specific questions about the material, I usually find that they don't really have a good grasp of it at all!

Can metacognitive knowledge be taught? Many psychologists believe that it can, and furthermore that it *should* be taught. Instruction in study skills can make a difference, sometimes a dramatic one, in student achievement. Therefore, we turn next to an examination of effective study skills and of how they can be improved.

STUDY SKILLS

Clearly, students develop better metacognitive knowledge and skills as they progress through the grades. Yet they continue to be somewhat uninformed about their own learning and memory processes as they reach high school, college, and even graduate school. Many teachers assume that students will use appropriate study strategies (for example, that they will try to organize new material, make sense of it, and find its main ideas), an assumption that is probably unsubstantiated in many cases. Compounding the problem, the learning process itself becomes more difficult as the material to be learned becomes more difficult (Howe, 1980).

But before we can help students improve their study skills, we must determine which strategies are in fact effective. This issue underlies a major focus in educational research at present. We will look first at some of the findings regarding specific study techniques and then examine research on the effectiveness of study skills training programs.

The Effectiveness of Different Study Techniques

In this section, we will survey research related to seven study techniques: selection of important information, summarizing, organizing, note taking, underlining, self-questioning, and elaborative processing.

Selection of Important Information. Students are often confronted with more information than they can possibly store in their long-term memories, at least within a reasonable period. Accordingly, they are frequently instructed to select important information (e.g., main ideas), a technique that Mayer (1984) has called focusing attention. Unfortunately, students often have trouble identifying the main points of a lecture or reading assignment. For example, many students use relatively inadequate methods of selecting information, such as focusing on first sentences of paragraphs and on distinctive pieces of information (e.g., definitions and formulas); they miss some critical ideas as a result (Mayer, 1984). Even graduate students are fallible in this respect, because they are often distracted away from central information by relatively unimportant but interesting details (Gillingham, Garner, & Wright, 1988).

Summarizing. Students are often encouraged to summarize the information they read and hear. After reviewing research on the effectiveness of summarizing for learning and remembering information, Snowman (1986) concluded that summaries are only effective when students have some idea about how they are going to be evaluated and can therefore tailor their summaries toward the evaluation criteria. Concerns about selecting important information apply here as well: students who have difficulty identifying main ideas will certainly have difficulty combining those main ideas into a summary.

Organizing. In Chapter 11, we saw evidence for the importance of organization on long-term memory storage. Nevertheless, students often fail to develop appropriate organizational schemes for the information presented in lectures and written materials. Rather than recognizing and using the overall structure of information to organize it, students frequently "organize" information merely as a list of facts (Meyer, Brandt, & Bluth, 1980). Furthermore, students are less likely to organize information as the material becomes more difficult for them (Kletzien, 1988).

Note Taking. In general, taking notes on information presented in lectures and textbooks is positively correlated with student learning (e.g., Hale, 1983; Howe, 1970). To some extent, the notes that students take probably reflect what parts of a lecture or text they are attending to and encoding (Howe, 1970; Weinstein & Mayer, 1986). For example, in a study by Howe (1970), undergraduate students listened to a recorded passage and took notes about what they heard; immediately afterward, their notes were taken away from them. A week later the students were asked to recall as much as they could about the passage. Information was far more likely to be remembered if it had appeared in students' notes, even though the students had had no opportunity to study those notes.

In my own classes, I have often observed how very different the notes of different students can be, even though all the students have sat through the same lecture. Some students write extensively, others write very little. Some students try to capture all the main ideas of a lecture, whether I have written them down or not, whereas others only copy the specific words I write on the board—mostly terms and their definitions. Some students include details and examples in their notes, others do not.

Not surprisingly, just how effective note taking is depends on the type of notes taken (Snowman, 1986). For example, notes are more likely to promote learning when they represent an encoding of the information that is consistent with the objectives of the instructional unit; hence, those objectives should be clear to students (Snowman, 1986). Notes are also more likely to be effective when they summarize main ideas (Brown, Campione, & Day, 1981; Doctorow, Wittrock, & Marks, 1978; Kiewra, 1985; Taylor, 1982) and include details that support those main ideas (Kiewra, 1985).

Another technique that appears to be effective is reorganizing and elaborating on notes after a lecture has been attended or a reading assignment has been completed (DuBois et al., 1988; Kiewra, 1985; Kiewra et al., 1988; Shimmerlick & Nolan, 1976). Particularly in a lecture situation, students do not have control over the rate at which information is presented and may not have time to process everything meaningfully. In such a case, students may need to focus merely on writing information during class and then encoding it appropriately afterward.

Underlining. Students commonly underline or highlight information in purchased textbooks. With my own students, I advocate underlining for two reasons: (1) it is less time-consuming than taking notes on a book's content, and (2) it keeps specific information within the context of the entire reading assignment. However, underlining is probably only effective when used sparingly, so that main ideas and essential details are emphasized (Snowman, 1986). Underlining and highlighting should help the student focus attention; highlighting the entire page, as if with a paint roller, is not likely to be beneficial.

Self-questioning. Study skills manuals frequently advise students to ask themselves questions about what they are about to read (e.g., Bragstad & Stumpf, 1982; Robinson, 1961; Thomas & Robinson, 1972). For example, Robinson (1961) has suggested that a student turn each heading and subheading into a question to be answered and then read sections of text with the intention of finding answers to those questions. A possible advantage of asking oneself questions about material to be learned is that it facilitates meaningful and elaborative processing of that material. However, in reviewing research on the effectiveness of self-questioning, Snowman (1986) concluded that positive effects are limited to the acquisition of facts, without any noticeable impact on more sophisticated behaviors such as application or evaluation of those facts. I suspect that students may be asking themselves fact-based questions (e.g., "When did Columbus reach the New

World?") rather than higher-level questions (e.g., "Why did Columbus risk his life to find a new route to India?") partly because they have learned to expect mostly fact-based questions on their classroom examinations.

Elaborative Processing. In Chapter 11, I defined the process of elaboration: the addition of information from long-term memory to new material so that the new material can be better interpreted and understood. I also provided some evidence for the fact that elaboration facilitates long-term memory storage and retrieval. Let's now look at how elaboration enters into students' study behaviors.

In a study by Van Rossum and Schenk (1984), college students studied and took notes on a historical passage, then took a test on the contents of the passage and answered questions about how they had studied. Approximately half the students described rote-learning approaches to studying; they interpreted the objective of the assignment as one of memorizing facts (as one student described it, "learning everything by heart"). The other half described meaningful learning approaches to the study process: they attempted to understand, interpret, abstract meaning, and apply what they read. One student's self-report illustrates this meaningful learning approach:

First I read the text roughly through and try to form a picture of the content. The second time I read more accurately and try through the structure of the text to make the small connections in and between the paragraphs. The third or fourth time I try to repeat to myself, without looking at the text, the main lines of the argument, emphasizing reasonings. This is my usual way to study texts (Van Rossum & Schenk, 1984, p. 77).

There were no differences between the two groups of students in their performance on multiple choice questions that tested their knowledge of the passage. However, students who used meaningful learning strategies performed better on multiple choice questions that required drawing inferences and produced better integrated and qualitatively superior responses to an essay test over the same material.

Students also appear to interpret information differently depending on whether they are trying to remember facts or generate applications. In a recent dissertation by one of my doctoral students (McCallin, 1988), undergraduate education majors enrolled in two educational psychology classes completed a questionnaire that assessed their approach to learning the course material. Some students described themselves as preferring to be given specific procedures for classroom teachers (i.e., they wanted to be told what to do). Other students described themselves as preferring to understand psychological principles of human learning and behavior so that they could develop their own procedures. Following the course's unit on educational testing and measurement, McCallin used a procedure known as *cognitive mapping*: she gave the students a list of basic concepts in educational testing and asked them to write the concepts on a piece of paper in such a way that the interrelationships among them were indicated. Students with a tell-me-what-to-do attitude tended to describe relationships among concepts that were simplistically factual or procedural (e.g., "*Raw scores* are used to compute a *mean*"). On the other hand, students with a let-me-apply-it-myself attitude described conceptual interrelationships that reflected more sophisticated processing, including hierarchical structures, cause-effect relationships, and deductive reasoning (e.g., "*Reliability* affects the *standard error of measurement*").

Clearly, then, some study techniques are more effective than others, and to some extent different techniques lead to different kinds of learning. Can study skills be improved with training? We turn to this question next.

The Effectiveness of Study Skills Training

Some efforts at training study skills have been successful, although others have not (Siegler, 1986). In this section, we will look at examples of successful programs in two areas: reading instruction and college study skills training.

Reading Instruction. Several studies have demonstrated the positive effects of teaching upper elementary and junior high school students how to learn from what they read (Hansen & Pearson, 1983; Palincsar & Brown, 1984; Paris, Cross, & Lipson, 1984). A problem of such training programs is that they teach numerous skills at the same time, so it is not always clear which specific skills are effective and which are not. Given this limitation, let me list typical components of successful reading strategies programs:

1. Awareness of the purpose of reading
2. Activation of background information and experiences relevant to the topic
3. Attention to main ideas
4. Drawing inferences from the information presented (elaboration)
5. Monitoring one's own comprehension of what one has read

Reading instruction that focuses on strategies such as these appears to improve reading comprehension (Palincsar & Brown, 1984; Paris, et al., 1984), especially for poor readers (Hansen & Pearson, 1983). Furthermore, when students develop these skills, they may transfer them to other classroom learning tasks (Palincsar & Brown, 1984).

College Study Skills Training. College students can also be taught more effective study strategies, with training being especially useful to low-ability students (e.g., Dansereau, Collins, McDonald, Holley, Garland, Diekhoff, & Evans, 1979; DuBois, 1987; DuBois et al., 1988; Holley & Dansereau, 1984; Holley, Dansereau, McDonald, Garland, & Collins, 1979). As is the case for the reading programs I have just described, such training tends to be multifaceted. For instance, in a study by Dansereau and colleagues (Dansereau et al., 1979), students who were taught methods for learning and remembering information (e.g., meaningful learning, mnemonics) and were also taught how to set goals for themselves and monitor their comprehension later performed better than a control group on both multiple choice and short answer tests.

At the State University of New York in Oneonta, Nelson DuBois (e.g., DuBois, 1987; DuBois et al., 1988) offers an undergraduate course in study skills. Among other things, students are taught about the importance of interpretation, organization, and elaboration of course information. They are also taught how to recognize the various *structures* underlying bodies of knowledge (e.g., hierarchies, cause-effect sequences, two-way matrices) and to fit pieces of information to these structures as a means of organizing course material. Results of a pilot study have been quite dramatic: one year after the study skills course, sixty-seven percent of students who had taken the study skills course had a mean grade point average of 3.0 or higher, whereas only thirty-two percent of students in a matched control group had attained a 3.0 GPA. Cook (1983) has reported success with a similar program: students are better able to learn complex information and apply it to new situations and problem-solving tasks.

Clearly, then, learning and study skills can be taught, with resulting improvement in school achievement. When teaching these skills, however, some main points should be kept in mind.

Sophisticated learning strategies can only be employed if students have a relevant knowledge base to which new material can be related (Brown, Campione, & Day, 1981; Weinstein & Mayer, 1986). Such processes as meaningful learning and elaboration can only occur if students can relate new information to what they already know.

Students must understand why the skills they are taught are helpful. For example, in a study by Paris, Newman, and McVey (1982), first and second graders were taught a variety of strategies for learning and remembering lists of items. Students who were also taught the *reasons* that these strategies were beneficial were more likely to use them, both at the time of training and later.

Students must recognize that school achievement consists of more than just learning facts. As we have seen in this chapter, many students focus on rote learning of isolated pieces of factual information at the expense of more meaningful processing. Their emphasis may be partly due to the fact that many standardized and teacher-made achievement tests also emphasize this factual knowledge. However, as you now know, learning is most effective when it is processed in more interpretive and elaborative ways. Students should be taught that it is desirable to understand, apply, analyze, and evaluate what they read and hear in the classroom.

SUMMARY

Human information processing theory is now being translated into a variety of educational applications. Because individuals can only attend to a limited amount of information at once and can only hold a small amount of information in short-term memory, many basic skills need to be learned to a level of automaticity, so they can be performed with little conscious effort. Expository teaching, the presentation of information in the form in which it is to be learned (as is done in lectures and textbooks), provides a means by which information can be organized and explained in a meaningful fashion. Mnemonics facilitate learning through the use of verbal mediation, visual imagery, or organization; they provide a number of methods for effectively learning what is otherwise rote-level material. People's knowledge of their own learning and cognitive processes and their regulation of these processes to enhance learning are known as metacognition. People are frequently ignorant about how best to learn information, but research indicates that training in effective study skills can significantly enhance classroom achievement.

PART FOUR

COMPLEX LEARNING
AND COGNITION

C H A P T E R 14

Learning Concepts

Outline

The Nature of Concepts
Defining a Concept
Advantages of Concepts
A Potential Disadvantage of Concepts

Basic Concepts in Concept Learning
Positive and Negative Instances
Features
Rules

Factors Affecting Concept Learning
Salience of Defining Features
Redundancy of Defining and Correlational Features
Number of Irrelevant Features
Complexity of Rules
Positive Instances vs. Negative Instances
Sequential vs. Simultaneous Presentation of Instances

Theories of Concept Learning
Buildup of Habit Strength
Mediation
Hypothesis Testing
Prototypes
Feature Lists

Relating Concepts to Other Forms of Learning: Robert Gagné's Analysis
Learning Associations
Learning Intellectual Skills

Concept Learning in the Classroom

Summary

O NE night in late May, my son Jeff and I had a discussion about the seasons. It went something like this:

Jeff: When are spring and summer coming?

Mom: Spring is already here. Haven't you noticed how warm it is, and how the leaves are back on the trees, and how the birds are singing again?

Jeff: Oh. Then when is summer coming?

Mom: Well, you only have one more week of school, and then a couple weeks after that, summer will be here.

Jeff: Summer is when we go swimming, right?

Mom: (I pause and think about how to answer.) Right.

As a four-year-old, Jeff had not precisely defined the concepts of spring and summer yet. When I myself was a child, summer was a season of heat, humidity, and no school. As an adult, I define it more formally as the three-month period between the summer solstice and the autumn equinox. To Jeff, however, summer is simply the time when he can swim.

Much of our cognitive growth involves the learning and refinement of concepts. Some concepts are defined by readily observable characteristics, so are fairly easy to learn. For example, the word milk refers to a white liquid with a particular taste. Similarly, the word red refers to a certain range of light wavelengths (although people disagree about exactly where "red" ends and "orange" begins). Other concepts are defined by less salient attributes, so are more slowly learned and more easily misconstrued. For instance, the four seasons of the year are "officially" designated by the occurrences of solstices and equinoxes that go virtually unnoticed by most individuals, so many people erroneously define them in terms of different weather conditions. Still other concepts may be even harder to grasp, because they are based on abstract, relativistic, or even elusive criteria. For example, psychologists have wrestled with the concept of intelligence for many years and still do not agree on what the term means.

In this chapter, we will examine the multifaceted process of learning concepts. We will first define the term *concept* and examine how concepts affect learning and information processing. We will also see how concept learning relates to other forms of learning, as is reflected in Robert Gagné's theory. Finally, we will apply current views of concept learning to classroom practice.

THE NATURE OF CONCEPTS

Before we explore theories of concept learning, we must first address three basic issues: the meaning of the term *concept*, the benefits of concepts for human learning and information processing, and a possible difficulty that concepts may create.

Defining a Concept

Ironically, psychologists have not agreed on how to define the concept of *concept*. Behaviorists (e.g., Hunt, 1962; Kendler, 1961) have frequently defined a concept as the same response to different stimuli, as illustrated here:

$$S_1 \searrow$$
$$S_2 \rightarrow R$$
$$S_3 \nearrow$$

Cognitivists, on the other hand, are more likely to define a concept as a mental phenomenon, a category of objects or events that share one or more common properties.

Most concepts are identified by a label—a word that symbolizes the concept and represents it in both thought and communication. For example, you have probably formed a concept that encompasses the many items you have seen with the following characteristics:

- Shorter and wider than adult humans
- Covered with a short, bristly substance
- Appended at one end by an object similar in appearance to a paintbrush
- Appended at the other end by a lumpy thing with four pointy objects sticking upward (two soft and floppy, two hard and curved around)
- Held up from the ground by four spindly sticks, two at each end
- Usually observed in pastures or barns
- Almost always eating

You have no doubt attached a particular label to these similar looking objects: cow.

Robert Gagné (e.g., 1985) has distinguished between two different kinds of concepts. *Concrete concepts* are concepts that can be identified by their physical appearance; cow, red, and round are examples. *Defined concepts* are instead identified by a rule or formal definition; for example, biologists define mammal as a particular form of vertebrate that gives birth to and suckles live offspring. In many cases, people first learn a concept in a concrete form, then later acquire a more abstract definition of it. When I was a child, summer was a concrete concept for me: heat, humidity, and no school were easily observable characteristics. I later acquired a defined concept of summer as I learned how the seasons are determined by the tilt of the earth in relation to the sun. In a similar way, children first learn about a circle as a concrete concept (i.e., a "roundish" thing); later, perhaps in high school geometry class, they may develop a defined concept of circle (i.e., all points on a plane equidistant from a single other point). As you will learn later in the chapter, the processes by which concrete and defined concepts are learned may be somewhat different.

Advantages of Concepts

As people develop and learn, they acquire an ever increasing number of concepts. Concepts have several advantages.

Concepts reduce the world's complexity (Bruner, 1957; Bruner, Goodnow, & Austin, 1956; Sokal, 1977). Classifying similar objects and events makes life simpler and easier to understand. For example, when you drive along a country road, it is easier to think to yourself, "There are some cows," than to think, "There is a brown object, covered with bristly stuff, appended by a paintbrush and a lumpy thing, and held up by four sticks. Ah, yes, and I also see a black-and-white spotted object, covered with bristly stuff, appended by a paintbrush and a lumpy thing, and held up by four sticks. And over there is a brown-and-white spotted object . . . " In other words, concepts condense and summarize information.

Concepts facilitate generalization to new situations (Bruner, 1957; Bruner et al., 1956; Ellis, 1978; Johnson-Laird & Wason, 1977). When people learn a concept, they associate certain characteristics with it. Then, when they encounter a new instance of the concept, they can draw on their knowledge of associated characteristics to form assumptions and inferences about the new instance. For example, if you see a herd of cattle as you drive through the countryside, you can assume that you are passing through either dairy or beef country—depending on whether you see large udders hanging down between two of the spindly sticks. If you purchase a potted flower, you know that you must water it regularly because of something you have learned about the concept *flower*: it needs water to live. Thanks to concepts, people don't have to learn from scratch in each new situation.

Concepts allow abstraction of the environment (Bruner, 1966). An object covered with bristly stuff, appended by a paintbrush and a lumpy thing, and held up by four sticks is a very concrete thing. The concept of *cow*, however, can be more abstract: it incorporates such characteristics as "female," "supplier of milk," and, to the dairy farmer, "economic asset." Concepts and their labels allow individuals to think about their experiences without necessarily having to consider all their concrete, perceptual aspects. In fact, many defined concepts, such as *intelligence*, do not have easily identifiable real-world referents at all.

Concepts enhance the power of thought (Bruner, 1966). When you are thinking about an object covered with bristly stuff, appended by a paintbrush and a lumpy thing, held up by four sticks, and so on, you can think of little else; to express this point in terms of contemporary memory theory, short-term memory capacity is exhausted. On the other hand, when you simply think *cow*, you can also think about *horse*, *dog*, *goat*, and *pig* at the same time.

Interrelationships among concepts can be established (Bruner, 1957; Bruner et al., 1956). Once information has been condensed and abstracted into concepts, those concepts can be associated and interrelated in long-term memory. For instance, the concept *cow* is related to the concepts *bull* and *calf* in a familial sort of way and to *mammal*, *animal*, and *living thing* in a hierarchical fashion.

A Potential Disadvantage of Concepts

By identifying a new stimulus as being an instance of a certain concept, people are likely to react to that stimulus as they would to any other instance of the concept. In the process, they may lose sight of the unique qualities of that particular stimulus. Furthermore, if they have identified the stimulus incorrectly, their response to it may be inappropriate. I remember as a young child trying to make a vehicle using square pieces of wood for wheels. Calling those pieces of wood *wheels* was an inaccurate identification, and, as you can imagine, my car didn't move very far.

BASIC CONCEPTS IN CONCEPT LEARNING

Before we examine theories of concept learning, we must first define some concepts related to it. In particular, we need to distinguish between positive instances and negative instances and to specify what is meant by the terms *features* and *rules*.

Positive and Negative Instances

A *positive instance* is a particular example of a concept. To illustrate, you and I are positive instances of the concept person, and this thing you are reading is a positive instance of the concept book. A *negative instance* is a nonexample of the concept. You and I are negative instances of the concept cow, and this book is a negative instance of the concept pencil.

One sign that individuals have truly learned a concept is that they correctly identify all positive and negative instances of that concept. A child who vehemently denies that a chihuahua is a dog has not completely learned the concept of dog; neither has the child who calls the neighbor's cow "doggie." Denying that a chihuahua is a dog—*undergeneralization*—reflects an inability to recognize all positive instances. Identifying a cow as a dog—*overgeneralization*—reflects an inability to reject all negative instances.

Features

Features (some theorists instead use the term *attributes*) are the characteristics of a concept's positive instances. For example, consider my dog Anna. She has numerous features worthy of note, including these:

- Hairy
- At one time physiologically equipped to give birth to live young
- Likely to bark loudly at any negative instance of an Ormrod
- Wearing a chain collar
- Presently located on my office floor

Some features are important for identifying positive instances of a concept, while others are not. *Defining features* (also known as critical or criterial features) are characteristics that must be present in all positive instances. For example, to be a dog, Anna must have hair and, as a female, must have (or once have had) the capability of giving birth to live young. *Correlational features* are frequently found in positive instances but are not essential for concept membership. For example, most dogs bark and many dogs wear collars, but neither of these features is a characteristic of *all* dogs. *Irrelevant features* are characteristics that are unrelated to membership in the concept. Anna's location on my office floor is totally irrelevant to her dogness.

Let's pause here for a brief exercise. In Figure 14–1, I have presented eight positive instances and eight negative instances of the concept *gudge*. Can you identify one or more defining features of a gudge?

As you may have surmised, the two defining features of a gudge are that it be gray and square. A large black dot is a correlational feature: black dots are found on six of the eight gudges, but on only one nongudge. White dots and topside "whiskers" are irrelevant features, because they are found equally often on gudges and nongudges.

Concept learning is a process of learning what features are important for identifying positive instances of that concept. In essence, one must learn that certain features are an essential component of the concept and that other features are frequently present but unessential. Learning to differentiate between a concept's defining and correlational features takes time and experience, often many years' worth. For example, consider this question that Saltz (1971) posed to children:

> A father goes to work. On the way home from work in the evening he stops at a bar to have a drink. His friends there are drunkards and he becomes a drunkard too. Is he still a father? (Saltz, 1971, p. 28).

Figure 14–1
Positive and negative instances of a *gudge*

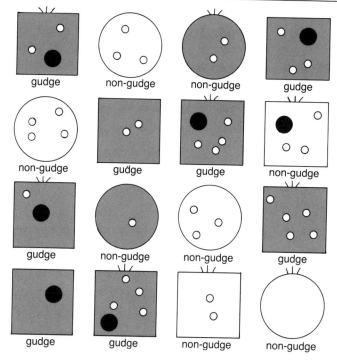

Saltz found that, even at the age of eight, most children denied that a drunkard could still be a father. Apparently, many young children believe that "goodness" defines fatherhood rather than correlating with it, a belief that they are likely to discard only when they encounter enough "bad" positive instances of a father.

Rules

The concept red has one defining feature: a particular range of wavelengths. The concept gudge has two that must both be present: square and gray. The concept out in baseball is an example of a concept in which no single defining feature is always present: it can be three strikes while a player is at bat, the tagging of a player who is running from base to base, or a fly ball caught before it touches the ground.

Concept *rules* specify how defining features are combined to define those concepts. Theorists (e.g., Bourne, 1967; Bruner et al., 1956; Dodd &

White, 1980; Klein, 1987; Saltz, 1971) have identified a number of different concept rules; four rules are most commonly described:

1. Simple. Only one particular feature must be present; for example, red is a specific wavelength.
2. Conjunctive. Two or more features must all be present; for example, a circle must be two-dimensional and must have all points equidistant from a center point.
3. Disjunctive. Two or more defining features are not all present at the same time; for example, an out in baseball occurs in any one of several different situations.
4. Relational. The relationship between two or more features determines the concept; for example, the concept *between* requires three objects, two located on opposite sides of a third.

As you might guess, the nature of a concept's features and rules influence the ease with which the concept is learned. Let's now look at these and other factors that affect the speed with which concepts are acquired.

FACTORS AFFECTING CONCEPT LEARNING

Numerous factors affect the ease and rapidity of concept learning: the salience, redundancy, and number of features, the complexity of rules, the frequency and nature of positive and negative instances, and the timing with which these instances are presented.

Salience of Defining Features

The more salient, or obvious, the defining features are, the more easily a concept is learned. For example, my son Jeff easily learned the correct meanings of milk, hot, and television, presumably because the features that define these concepts are readily observable. However, he is still struggling with spring and summer and is only beginning to comprehend such words as work and university.

Because the attention of young children is typically drawn to obvious features, their early concepts are likely to be based (sometimes erroneously) on such features. For example, in a study by DeVries (1969), children ranging in age from three to six played for a short time with a good-natured cat named Maynard. Then, as they looked on, the experimenter placed a ferocious-looking dog mask on Maynard and asked them, "What is this animal now?" Many of the three-year-olds asserted that Maynard was now a dog and refused to pet him. The six-year-olds, on the other hand, could overlook the dog mask, recognizing that it did not change Maynard's "catness." As children grow older, they begin to attend less to perceptually salient features, and focus more on abstract qualities (Anglin, 1977; Ausubel, Novak, & Hanesian, 1978).

Redundancy of Defining and Correlational Features

As defining and correlational features become increasingly redundant with one another, positive instances of a concept become easier to identify (Good & Brophy, 1986). For example, the concept *bird* is relatively easy to learn, because many characteristics—feathers, wings, beak, small size, scrawny legs and feet—are either defining or correlational features. On the other hand, the concept *weed* is more difficult, because it has only two defining features, and one of them is fairly abstract: it is a plant, and it is in the wrong place at the wrong time.

Number of Irrelevant Features

The more irrelevant features present, the more difficult a concept is to learn (Good & Brophy, 1986). For instance, the concept animal is a difficult one for many children, because most of the salient features—body covering, nature and number of limbs, facial features, shape, and size—are irrelevant. Although my son Jeff quite accurately identifies positive instances of birds, he continues to have trouble identifying positive instances of animals: he adamantly rejects any suggestion that people, fish, or insects fall into this category.

Complexity of Rules

The rules that specify how defining features are combined influence the ease with which concepts are learned (Bourne, 1967; Haygood & Bourne, 1965; Neisser & Weene, 1962). Simple rules are typically the easiest to learn, conjunctive and disjunctive are moderately difficult, and relational are most difficult. Young children often have trouble understanding such common relational concepts as under, over, more, and less; for example, children as old as seven years often do not fully understand what the concept less means (Palermo, 1973).

Positive Instances vs. Negative Instances

Generally speaking, the presentation of positive instances leads to faster concept learning than the presentation of negative instances, although exceptions to this rule have been observed (Ausubel et al., 1978; Barringer & Gholson, 1979). In other words, it is generally more helpful to see what a concept is than what it is not.

However, for accurate concept learning, both positive and negative instances are desirable if they are carefully chosen. Positive instances should illustrate the full range of the concept, so that it will not be undergeneralized. For example, to learn an accurate concept of dog, one should see chihuahuas and Great Danes as well as cocker spaniels and Irish setters. Negative instances can illustrate "near misses," so that the concept will not be overgeneralized (Winston, 1973). For example, one must be informed that such creatures as cats, goats, and cows are nondogs to learn just where to draw the line on dogness.

Sequential vs. Simultaneous Presentation of Instances

In their everyday lives, individuals typically learn concepts through *sequential presentation*: they encounter a series of positive and negative instances, one at a time over a period of weeks, months, or years, and receive feedback about what is and is not an example of the concept. A faster way to learn concepts is *simultaneous presentation*, in which people are given a number of positive and negative instances all at once (Bourne, Ekstrand, & Dominowski, 1971). One likely reason for the difference in effectiveness of the two presentation methods is that, in sequential presentation, a person must store in memory what is learned from each instance, and that information can be forgotten from one instance to the next. In simultaneous presentation, on the other hand, the information to be gleaned from positive and negative instances is available all at once, so demands on memory are not as great.

What exactly *is* learned in concept learning? It is to this topic—to theories of concept learning—that we turn next.

THEORIES OF CONCEPT LEARNING

Here we will examine five different theories of concept learning. We will look first at a strictly behaviorist perspective based on the notion of habit

Concepts are best learned through a simultaneous presentation of both positive and negative instances.

Each of these is a dog.

None of these is a dog.

strength. We will begin to see signs of cognitivism in the second theory, a neo-behaviorist model incorporating mediation. We will then examine three cognitive theories of concept learning, based on the notions of hypothesis testing, prototypes, and feature lists.

Buildup of Habit Strength

An early theory of concept learning was proposed by Clark Hull in 1920. To use contemporary terminology, Hull's theory was that any instance of a concept has both defining and irrelevant features, and that an organism that correctly identifies a stimulus as being a positive instance is reinforced for responding to both its defining and irrelevant features. When correctly identifying a second positive instance, it is again reinforced for responding to the defining and irrelevant features. In repeated trials with the same concept, the defining features are always the same; however, the irrelevant features differ from one occasion to the next. Thus, the individual is *always* reinforced for responding to the defining features, but only *occasionally* reinforced for responding to various irrelevant features. Thus, the habit strength of a response to defining features is greater than that of a response to irrelevant features, and the organism learns to respond in the same way to the same (defining) features of different positive instances.

A demonstration exercise, in which you will learn the concept *mudge*, illustrates Hull's theory. Take a piece of paper and cover Figure 14–2, exposing only the top section above the dotted line. In the top section you should see two objects, one of which is a mudge. Take a wild guess and see if you can pick the mudge. Once you have made your selection, move your paper down to the next dotted line, revealing the correct answer. In this section you will see two more objects; pick the one you think is the mudge. Continue moving your paper down the page, one section at a time, on each occasion getting your feedback and then selecting a likely mudge from the next pair of objects.

You have presumably learned that *mudge* is "large." Let's analyze this concept learning task from a Hullian perspective. You were reinforced every time you chose a large square, you were never reinforced for choosing a small square, and you were reinforced for choosing black, white, left, or right squares only about half of the time. Thus, the occurrence of reinforcement for choosing boxes with different characteristics was as follows:

Characteristic	Amount of Reinforcement
large	100%
small	0%
black	50%
white	50%
left	50%
right	50%

Figure 14–2
Pick the mudge in each section

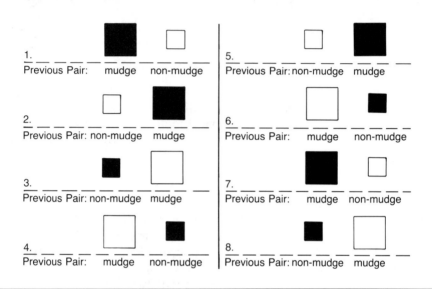

Therefore, the response of selecting "large" should be the strongest habit, and you should be most likely to choose a large square again, regardless of its color and position.

Mediation

A problem with viewing concept learning simply as a buildup of habit strength was identified by Kendler and Kendler (1959, 1961, 1962). Their series of experiments were similar to my "mudge" example: subjects were shown numerous pairs of different-sized black and white boxes and asked to choose the "correct" one in each pair; they were reinforced for choosing the large square each time, regardless of its color or position. Once subjects were consistently choosing the large square in each pair, without warning or explanation there was a shift in the characteristic that was reinforced. Some subjects were now reinforced for choosing the small square in each pair; the Kendlers called this a *reversal shift* (the opposite, or reverse, characteristic was being reinforced). Other subjects were instead reinforced for choosing the black square of each pair—the Kendlers called this a *non-reversal shift*.

Which group of subjects should learn the new concept more quickly? Let's look at this situation from the perspective of habit strength buildup. Just as was true when you were learning *mudge*, subjects who have been reinforced for choosing a large square were also reinforced for choosing a black square fifty percent of the time, but were *never* reinforced for choosing a small square. Because the habit strength of a "black" response was greater than the habit strength of a "small" response, a nonreversal shift should have been an easier shift for subjects to make than a reversal shift.

In fact, the Kendlers found the opposite result, at least for children over five years old. Reversal shifts—learning to choose small boxes after previously being reinforced for choosing large ones—were easier than nonreversal shifts. They proposed that subjects *mediated* their overt responses (i.e., their choices) by first making internal, mental responses, as illustrated here. The following figure illustrates the process that the Kendlers proposed, with uppercase letters indicating observable stimuli and responses and lower case letters indicating mental stimuli and responses.

$$S \rightarrow r_{size} \rightarrow s_{size} \nearrow R_{large} \atop \searrow R_{small}$$

Subjects may have thought something along the line of "It's the size that matters," and then chosen the large one in response to that mental stimulus. In the case of a reversal shift, the mediating response and stimulus ("size") would be the same, and only the overt response would have to change. However, for a nonreversal shift, the mediating response would have to be changed as well as the overt response, a learning task that should take more time. Curiously, however, the Kendlers found that children below the age of five, and animals as well, learned the nonreversal shift more easily; hence the learning of these subjects may have been more a process of forming various S-R habits.

Hypothesis Testing

In their discussion of mediation, Kendler and Kendler proposed that mental responses were involved in how people learn concepts. A few years earlier, Jerome Bruner and his colleagues (Bruner, Goodnow, & Austin, 1956) had proposed a theory of concept learning that was even more clearly cognitive in nature. Before I describe their theory, however, take a minute to learn the concept *studge*. In Figure 14–3, I have provided numerous positive and negative instances of a studge. As you did in learning about mudges, use a piece of paper to reveal one section at a time and try to guess whether each object is a studge or nonstudge.

I hope you have learned that the concept *studge* is "two or three circles." Shape and number are defining features for the concept; color is irrelevant to studgeness. In learning about studges, you may have found yourself forming different hypotheses about what is a studge and what is not. For instance, the first example was a studge. You may have used that positive instance to generate one or more hypotheses such as these:

- A studge is anything gray.
- A studge is round.
- A studge is three of something.
- A studge is three gray circles.

Figure 14–3
Positive and negative instance of a *studge*

Which of the examples below are studges?

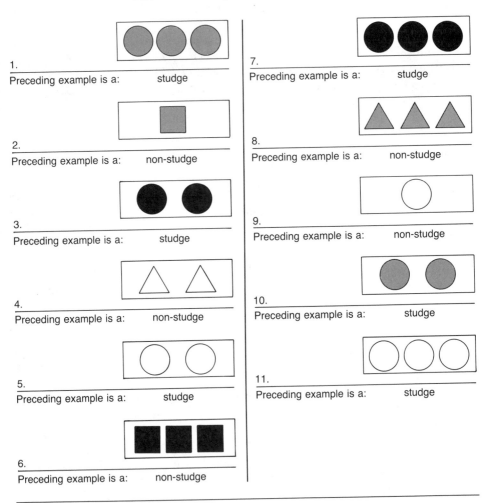

1. Preceding example is a: studge

2. Preceding example is a: non-studge

3. Preceding example is a: studge

4. Preceding example is a: non-studge

5. Preceding example is a: studge

6. Preceding example is a: non-studge

7. Preceding example is a: studge

8. Preceding example is a: non-studge

9. Preceding example is a: non-studge

10. Preceding example is a: studge

11. Preceding example is a: studge

The second example in Figure 14–3 was a nonstudge, so, had you held the hypothesis that a studge is gray, you would have eliminated that particular hypothesis at that point. A hypothesis such as "three of something," however, would have been confirmed with the second example, but disconfirmed with the third. Eventually you may have ended up with the correct hypothesis: a studge is two or three circles.

Bruner, Goodnow, and Austin (1956) proposed that concept learning is a process of forming various hypotheses about the features and rules that define a concept and then using positive and negative instances to confirm or reject those hypotheses. To illustrate their theory, they used stimuli similar to my positive and negative instances of studges to study concept learning in adults. They gave their subjects one positive instance of the concept and then asked them to try to select other positive instances from among an array of stimuli varying on four dimensions (shape, color, number of objects, and number of borders around the objects). By noting the selections that subjects made, Bruner and his colleagues observed several different approaches that subjects used in formulating and testing their hypotheses. Some subjects appeared to test one hypothesis at a time, choosing stimuli that varied on only one feature from a previous positive instance. If they received feedback that confirmed their hypothesis, they continued to test it; if they received contradictory feedback, they would form a different hypothesis and begin to test that one. Other subjects appeared to hold several hypotheses in mind at the same time and eliminate them simultaneously with their selection of different stimuli. This latter strategy would of course be faster, but it would also place greater demands on memory, hence leading to more errors. This tendency to test several hypotheses simultaneously has also been observed by Levine (1966).

Although some hypothesis testing may well occur when people learn concepts, hypothesis testing is probably not the only process involved in concept learning. Experiments in which hypothesis testing has been observed, such as those of Bruner et al. (1956) and Levine (1966), have been criticized for being artificial and not resembling real-world concept learning conditions (e.g., Glass, Holyoak & Santa, 1979; Rosch, 1973a). People are rarely given a situation in which they can pick possible examples of a concept in any systematic fashion; more typically, they encounter a positive instance here, a negative instance there, and so on, in a somewhat haphazard fashion over a period of time. Furthermore, in several experiments (Brooks, 1978; Reber & Allen, 1978; Reber, Kassin, Lewis, & Cantor, 1980), subjects who were instructed to find the rules underlying certain classification schemes (i.e., to form hypotheses) actually performed more poorly in identifying examples of a concept than subjects who were not so instructed. In these cases, the more successful subjects were the less analytic ones: they simply remembered early positive instances and compared new examples to them. A different theory of concept learning—one involving the formation of *prototypes*—better explains such data.

Prototypes

Eleanor Rosch (1973a, 1973b, 1977a; Rosch, Mervis, Gray, Johnson, & Boyes-Braem, 1976) has argued that many real-world concepts are difficult to delineate in terms of defining features and precise rules. Objects can lack important features, yet still be recognized as positive instances of a particular concept. For example, a salient feature of human beings is that they have two legs, yet you can still recognize a human who has no legs at all. Similarly, although birds typically fly, most people correctly identify nonflying penguins and ostriches as birds. Thus, it appears that people often use correlational features rather than defining features to identify positive instances of a concept.

Furthermore, concepts often have fuzzy boundaries, so that in certain borderline cases correct identification of positive and negative instances is difficult (Rosch, 1973a, 1978; Zazdeh, Fu, Tanak, & Shimura, 1975). For example, is a stroke a disease? In a study by McCloskey and Glucksberg (1978), some people believed that it was and others did not. Is turquoise a shade of blue or a shade of green? My husband insists that turquoise is green, but I know better: it's blue.

Instead, Rosch (1973a, 1973b, 1975, 1977a, 1977b, 1978; Rosch et al., 1976) and others (Attneave, 1957; Tennyson & Cocchiarella, 1986) have proposed that people form concepts by developing a *prototype*, or representative example, of a typical member of that category. To illustrate, form an image in your mind of a bird. What probably comes to mind is a small creature, perhaps about the shape and size of a robin or sparrow. It is unlikely that you would instead imagine a penguin or an ostrich because these animals, while birds, are not as typically birdlike in appearance as robins and sparrows. Similarly, imagine a vehicle. Your image probably resembles a car or a truck rather than a canoe or hot-air balloon because cars and trucks are more commonly observed instances of vehicles. Now imagine red. You probably picture a color similar to that red crayon you had when you were five, rather than pink or maroon.

A prototype is likely to incorporate features of the most typical and commonly observed positive instances of the concept. For instance, your prototype of a human being probably has two arms and two legs, stands upright, and is slightly less than two meters tall. Your prototype of a table is likely to be a rectangular flat surface held up by four legs, one at each of the four corners. New objects are identified as positive instances of a particular concept when they are compared to the concept prototype and found to be sufficiently similar. A positive identification does not require that all features be present, however; a legless person can still be recognized as a human being, and a three-legged object can still be recognized as a table.

At least two sources of evidence support the idea that concepts are represented in memory in the form of prototypes. First of all, people easily identify positive instances of a concept that closely resemble the prototype but have difficulty identifying positive instances that do not (e.g., Glass, Holyoak, & O'Dell, 1974; Posner & Keele, 1968, 1970; Rips, Shoben, & Smith, 1973; Rosch, 1973b, 1978; Rosch & Mervis, 1975; Rosch, Simpson, & Miller, 1976; Wilkins, 1971). In one experiment by Rosch (1973b), elementary school and undergraduate students identified as birds creatures that looked particularly "birdlike" (e.g., robins and sparrows) more quickly than they identified creatures less similar to the prototype (e.g., chickens and ducks).

A second source of evidence for prototypes is the fact that people sometimes recognize positive instances they have never encountered before when those instances closely resemble the prototype. In fact, subjects recognize them more easily than positive instances they *have* encountered that do not closely match the prototype (Franks & Bransford, 1971; Posner, Goldsmith, & Welton, 1967; Posner & Keele, 1968). For example, in an experiment by Franks and Bransford (1971), college students viewed a series of geometric patterns that involved one or more variations from a particular base pattern; the base pattern itself was not presented. Subjects were then shown another series of patterns and asked to identify which ones they had previously seen (they had actually seen none of them before). Subjects were most likely to "recognize" patterns that closely resembled the base pattern; subjects were most confident that they had seen the base pattern itself. Presumably, the base pattern represented the single best example of the various stimuli that had originally been viewed and thus most closely approximated the pattern prototype that subjects had formed.

Possibly, prototypes are used to identify positive instances in clear-cut situations, and more formal definitions are used in other, more ambiguous ones (Andre, 1986; Glass & Holyoak, 1975; Glass et al., 1979). For example, I mentioned earlier that my son Jeff denies that animals include people, fish, and insects. His rejection of these groups as nonanimals is a common phenomenon among young children, who often restrict their conception of animals to four-legged mammals (Saltz, 1971). I suspect that Jeff's animal prototype may resemble the family dog or the cows he sees in the surrounding countryside. When he begins studying the animal kingdom in school, he will probably learn a biology-based definition of an animal that incorporates some of its major features: a form of life that derives its food from other organisms, responds immediately to its environment, and can move its entire body. At that point he will presumably acknowledge that people, fish, and creepy-crawlies are legitimate animals. (If he takes college biology at a later date, however, he may learn that biologists do not really agree on a definition of *animal*, and that true defining features of the concept are difficult to identify.)

Feature Lists

Much of the research supporting prototype theory can just as easily be explained by a *feature list* theory of concept learning (e.g., Bourne, 1982; Bourne et al., 1986; Neumann, 1974, 1977). This theory is similar to prototype theory but focuses more on a concept's defining and correlational features. From this perspective, learning a concept involves learning the following:

1. Its *relevant* features, both defining and correlational
2. The probability that each of these features is likely to be present in any specific instance; that is, the frequency with which each feature occurs
3. The relationships among the features; that is, the rules for their combination

Recognizing an object as a positive instance of a concept, then, is a matter of determining whether the object possesses enough relevant features. Prototypes are recognized more quickly than other positive instances only because they encompass most or all of the concept's relevant features.

A prediction from feature list theory is that negative instances will be erroneously identified as positive instances if a sufficient number of relevant features are present. Bourne (1982) confirmed this prediction in an experiment involving an *exclusive disjunctive* concept. Earlier in the chapter, I described a disjunctive concept as being one with two or more defining features that did not all have to be present at once (the example I presented was an out in baseball). An exclusive disjunctive concept is a sub-form of this kind of concept: an item possessing any of the defining features is a positive instance, but an item possessing all of them is not. (For example, a pludge is anything that is red *or* square, but things that are *both* red and square are nonpludges.) In an experiment involving undergraduate students, Bourne presented numerous positive and negative instances of an exclusive disjunctive concept that had two relevant features; an item that had one, but not both, of the features was a positive instance. Despite their training, when subjects were later asked to identify examples of the concept, they were more likely to "recognize" those stimuli possessing both relevant features than those possessing only one of the two features.

Regardless of which theory of concept learning may eventually be found to model human behavior most closely, two factors emerge as essential for the learning of concepts. First, individuals must learn the defining and correlational features that distinguish concept membership (and learn which of those features, if any, are truly definitive). Second, individuals must develop a realization of the degree of acceptable variation from best examples of the concept. For example, an ostrich is a bird even though it is much larger than the prototypic bird; however, a certain other creature that is the same size and also walks on two legs—a human being—falls outside the bird category. In other words, to learn a concept completely, one must eventually learn the boundaries of that concept.

Now that we have looked at behaviorist and cognitive explanations of how concept learning occurs, it is time to turn to a related topic: how concept learning relates to other forms of learning. Robert Gagné has offered a theory of human learning in which concept learning depends on some forms of learning and is a prerequisite to other forms.

RELATING CONCEPTS TO OTHER FORMS OF LEARNING: ROBERT GAGNÉ'S ANALYSIS

Robert Gagné (e.g., R. Gagné, 1985; Gagné, Briggs, & Wager, 1988; Gagné & Driscoll, 1988) has incorporated concept learning into a sequence of eight types of learning of increasing complexity. Gagné has proposed four basic forms of learning—classical conditioning, operant learning, chaining, and verbal association—that can be explained in terms of simple principles of S-R association. Four more complex forms—learning discriminations, concepts, rules, and higher-order rules—involve the use of *symbols* (i.e., mental representations of various objects, events, and ideas) to interact with the environment; Gagné refers to these four as *intellectual skills*.

According to Gagné, simple forms of learning are usually necessary before other, more complex forms can occur. For example, concept learning can occur only after basic associations and discriminations have been learned. At the same time, concept formation is a prerequisite to learning rules and higher-order rules, things necessary for problem solving. Let's look at each of Gagné's eight forms of learning, and at how they are interrelated.

Learning Associations

Gagné has identified four forms of learning that can be understood in terms of simple stimulus-response associations: classical conditioning, operant learning, chaining, and verbal association.

Classical Conditioning. As you should recall from Chapter 3, classical conditioning is a process whereby one learns an involuntary response to a particular stimulus. Classical conditioning occurs when one stimulus that already elicits a response (i.e., an unconditioned stimulus eliciting an unconditioned response) is paired with a stimulus that does not initially elicit a response. This second, "neutral" stimulus begins to elicit a response as well, hence becoming a conditioned stimulus that elicits a conditioned (learned) response.

Operant Learning. Gagné's description of operant learning is similar to B. F. Skinner's model of operant conditioning in that a voluntary response is learned. However, whereas Skinner focuses more on the response-reinforcement ($R \rightarrow S_{Rf}$) connection, Gagné emphasizes the formation of a single stimulus-response ($S \rightarrow R$) association. Nevertheless, Gagné does point out that immediate reinforcement of a response is a necessary condition for operant learning to occur.

Chaining. Chaining is the formation of a series of nonverbal stimulus-response ($S \rightarrow R$) associations, such that a sequence of behaviors is learned. For example, using a pair of scissors involves a number of responses that typically occur in the same order: putting the forefinger through one hole, putting the thumb through the other hole, spreading the forefinger and thumb apart (thus opening the scissors), placing the open scissors against the edge of the paper to be cut, squeezing the thumb and forefinger together (thus cutting the paper), and so on.

Depicted graphically, chaining looks like this:

$$S \rightarrow R \longrightarrow S \rightarrow R \longrightarrow S \rightarrow R \longrightarrow S \rightarrow R$$

Each response provides a new stimulus situation to which a new response is made. For example, when a child using scissors has made one cut, the cut serves as a stimulus for the next response of opening the scissors. The open scissors in turn provide a stimulus for the response of moving the scissors to the spot where additional cutting must occur.

Verbal Association. Verbal association involves the chaining of verbal S-R connections. An example of verbal association is uttering a typically invariant sequence of words, such as "How are you?" or "I pledge allegiance to the flag. . . . " In such cases, each word is considered a response, and responses are performed in a particular order.

Verbal association differs from chaining in that not all stimuli and responses are necessarily observable; some of them may be mental events within the individual. For example, a French teacher might teach students how to remember that *le chien* means "dog" in this way:

> When I say *le chien*, that can remind you of the word *chain*, because *chien* sounds very much like *chain*. A chain can remind you of a leash, and a leash should make you think of *dog*.

The teacher is asking students to form a verbal association like this one:

$$\text{LE CHIEN} \longrightarrow \text{chain} \longrightarrow \text{leash} \longrightarrow \text{DOG}$$
$$\text{S} \longrightarrow \quad \text{r} \to \text{s} \longrightarrow \text{r} \to \text{s} \longrightarrow \quad \text{R}$$

Notice that some of the words, and some of the S's and R's, are capitalized, while others are lowercase. Capitalized words and letters indicate *observed* stimuli and responses; lowercase words and letters indicate internal, and therefore unobservable, stimuli and responses. The teacher presents the word *le chien* (an observable stimulus), and the students learn the mental response of *chain*. *Chain* in turn serves as a stimulus for the mental response *leash*, which in turn becomes the internal stimulus for the observable response of saying *dog*.

According to Gagné, the learning of chains and verbal associations can only occur after individual S→R connections have already been mastered; hence, classical and/or operant conditioning are prerequisites.

Learning Intellectual Skills

Gagné has identified four intellectual skills that cannot be easily reduced to simple S-R associations: discrimination learning, concept learning, rule learning, and the learning of higher-order rule.

Discrimination Learning. In Chapter 4, I described stimulus discrimination, a situation in which a response is reinforced in the presence of one stimulus (S+) but not in the presence of another stimulus (S−). Gagné's discrimination learning is similar: an individual learns to respond to one stimulus, but not to another, perhaps very similar, stimulus. Discrimination learning can be depicted graphically like this:

$$S_1 \rightarrow R_1$$
$$S_2 \rightarrow \varnothing \text{ (no response)}$$

Discrimination learning is essentially a process of learning to distinguish among objects on the basis of their physical appearances. For example, a child might learn to say "bee" when seeing the letter b, but not when seeing such similar looking letters as d, p, or q. Similarly, a child might begin to hear the difference between two musical notes, or to feel the difference in texture of two different types of fabric.

Concept Learning. As I mentioned earlier in the chapter, Gagné has distinguished between two kinds of concepts, *concrete concepts* (those identified by their physical appearance) and *defined concepts* (those identified by a definition). He restricts his view of concept learning to concrete concepts, arguing that defined concepts actually reflect a form of rule learning. Gagné describes the learning of concrete concepts as a process of putting different stimuli into the same *class* and then responding to any member of that class in the same way. For example, a child who is learning the letter A must learn that many different stimuli, such as:

$$\text{A} \quad \textbf{A} \quad \text{A} \quad \mathscr{A} \quad \text{A}$$

must all be responded to in the same way:

$$\text{"ay"}$$

When an individual makes the same response to all members of a class, then the individual has formed a concept.

A prerequisite condition for the successful learning of concrete concepts is that discriminations among stimuli belonging to different concept classifications must already have been learned. For example, before students can form a concept of the letter A, they must be able to discriminate between such letters as these:

$$\text{A vs. B} \qquad \mathscr{A} \text{ vs. } \mathscr{D} \qquad \text{A vs. X}$$

Because concept learning often involves learning which stimuli are examples of the concept and which stimuli are not, an individual must first be able to discriminate between examples and non-examples.

Rule Learning. Gagné defines a *rule* this way:

> A rule . . . is an inferred capability that enables the individual to respond to any instance of a class of stimulus situations with an appropriate instance of a class of performances (R. Gagné, 1985, p. 118).

One cannot learn defined concepts through physical examination.

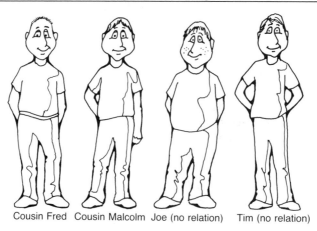

Cousin Fred   Cousin Malcolm   Joe (no relation)   Tim (no relation)

According to Gagné, rules organize human behavior and allow people to respond effectively to a wide variety of stimulus situations. Rules can be thought of as a chain of two or more concepts. For example, consider this common, everyday rule:

Balls roll.

This rule includes two concepts, *ball* and *roll*, as well as the relationship between them: one (ball) accomplishes the other (roll). Here is another example of a rule, in this case from physics:

$$v = a \times t$$

This rule includes the interrelationships among five concepts: velocity (v), equality ($=$), acceleration (a), multiplication ($\times$), and time (t).

As I indicated earlier, defined concepts are a type of rule. Unlike concrete concepts, they cannot be learned through an examination of the physical appearance of stimuli. For example, there is no way to learn the concept of *cousin* simply by looking at examples of cousins and noncousins; all will have one head, two arms, two legs, and so on. Instead, defined concepts must be learned through definitions—through statements expressing rules for classification. An individual can only learn the concept of *cousin* by learning that a cousin is an offspring of a parent's sibling. To learn the rule, one must previously have learned the concepts contained within it: *offspring, parent,* and *sibling.*

Rules form the basis for many intellectual skills. People cannot write, read, compute, create, or even speak without applying numerous rules. For instance, rules used in writing include the following:

1. Each sentence should have a subject and a predicate.

2. Each sentence should begin with a capital letter.

3. Each sentence should end with a period, question mark, or exclamation point.

4. Each word should be spelled correctly.

Because rules include concepts, they obviously cannot be learned until those concepts have already been learned. For example, a young child can learn that *balls roll* only after already learning about balls and rolling. And a physics student must master the concepts of velocity, equality, acceleration, multiplication, and time before learning that "velocity equals acceleration times time."

Learning Higher-order Rules. Sometimes two or more rules are combined to form higher-order rules. According to Gagné, problem solving typically occurs through the formation of such higher-order rules. For example, consider this problem (R. Gagné, 1985):

$$24\frac{1}{8} - 22\frac{3}{16} = ?$$

Students who have not been taught to solve this kind of problem may be able to do so if they have learned simpler rules—for example, how to form equivalent fractions and how to subtract one fraction from another—that can be combined to solve the problem.

The topic of problem solving will be addressed more thoroughly in the following chapter. But here I want to emphasize an important point. Because higher-order rules comprise rules that in turn include concepts, they cannot be effectively learned until all the concepts and rules contained within them have already been mastered. In fact, all of Gagné's more complex forms of learning depend heavily on lower forms of learning. Basic associations are necessary for discrimination learning, discriminations are necessary for concept learning, concepts are necessary for rule learning, and rules are necessary for forming higher-order rules. Gagné's theory, then, can provide guidance to teachers and instructional designers regarding the order in which different intellectual skills should be taught.

Now that we have explored theories of how people learn concepts, and of how concepts relate to other forms of learning, it is time to look at how these theories can affect classroom practice.

CONCEPT LEARNING IN THE CLASSROOM

Theories and research related to concept learning yield a number of implications for educational practice. Here are some things that teachers can do to facilitate concept learning in the classroom.

Provide a definition of the concept (R. Gagné, 1985; Merrill & Tennyson, 1977; Owen, Blount, & Moscow, 1978; Tennyson & Cocchiarella, 1986).

Defining features and any rules related to them (e.g., "all defining features must be present") should be specified. Teachers must also remember that a definition should be presented only in terms of other concepts with which students are already familiar (R. Gagné, 1985).

Provide numerous and varied positive instances to illustrate the concept (Clark, 1971; R. Gagné, 1985; Merrill & Tennyson, 1977, 1978; Owen, Blount, & Moscow, 1978; Tennyson & Cocchiarella, 1986). Through encountering many instances of concepts, people may form prototypes of those concepts. In fact, in some situations providing a "best example" is more helpful than a definition. To illustrate, in a study by Park (1984), two instructional methods were used to teach basic psychology concepts (e.g., positive and negative reinforcement) to high school students. For some students, instruction focused on the defining features of the concepts; for others, instruction focused on illustrative examples of the concepts. Students for whom defining features were emphasized were better able to classify new examples during instruction. However, students who had been given examples of the concepts remembered more of what they had learned after instruction was completed. Ideally, of course, definitions and examples should be presented hand in hand, and in fact this combination of methods leads to more effective concept learning than either method alone (Dunn, 1983; Tennyson, Youngers, & Suebsonthi, 1983).

Concepts are better learned with many examples than with only one or two (Tennyson & Park, 1980; Tennyson & Tennyson, 1975). First examples should be simple and straightforward, with as few irrelevant features as possible (Clark, 1971; Merrill & Tennyson, 1977, 1978). Line drawings of concepts are often helpful because defining features can be emphasized and irrelevant features deemphasized or omitted. Later examples should be more difficult, with more irrelevant features present (Clark, 1971; Merrill & Tennyson, 1977). Ultimately, examples should illustrate the full range of the concept so that students do not undergeneralize (Merrill & Tennyson, 1978; Tennyson & Cocchiarella, 1986); for example, the concept *mammal* should be illustrated by whales and platypuses as well as by cats and dogs.

Provide negative instances to show what the concept is not (Clark, 1971; Freiburgs & Tulving, 1961; R. Gagné, 1985; Merrill & Tennyson, 1977; Owen et al., 1978; Tennyson & Cocchiarella, 1986; Winston, 1973). Although negative instances were viewed as relatively unimportant by early theorists (Hovland & Weiss, 1953; Smoke, 1932), their importance has more recently been recognized. Negative instances, particularly when they are "near misses" to the concept, are helpful in defining the concept's limits and in preventing overgeneralization (Merrill & Tennyson, 1977; Winston, 1973). For example, in learning about mammals, students can be shown such similar-looking nonmammals as lizards and frogs.

Present positive and negative instances simultaneously (Ellis & Hunt, 1983; R. Gagné, 1985). Research consistently indicates that people learn concepts more easily when they see examples and nonexamples simultaneously rather than sequentially (Bourne et al., 1971).

Test students' understanding of concepts by asking them to classify new examples (Merrill & Tennyson, 1977; Owen et al., 1978; Tennyson & Cocchiarella, 1986). Students sometimes learn a concept's definition at a rote level only; in such cases of meaning*less* learning, students may not be able to use the definition to identify positive and negative instances accurately. A study by Wilson (1988) illustrates this point. Sixth and eighth graders were asked to define the concept of *rectangle*: many of them defined a rectangle in such a way that squares were (appropriately) included. Yet, when shown a variety of shapes and asked to identify the rectangles, the great majority of the students who had correctly defined the concept of *rectangle* nevertheless did *not* identify any squares as being positive instances.

Correct recitation of a concept's definition does not necessarily indicate that a student has a meaningful understanding of that concept. Inaccuracy in identifying positive and negative instances of a concept will reflect misconceptions that a student has about a concept, particularly about borderline cases. For instance, my son Jeff shows his limited understanding of the concept *animal* when he denies that people and fish are positive instances.

Ask students to generate their own examples and applications of concepts (Ellis & Hunt, 1983; Watts & Anderson, 1971). Such a practice will help students to test and refine their own understanding of the concept. The benefits of self-generated examples and applications are illustrated in an experiment in which high school students received instruction in basic psychological concepts (Watts & Anderson, 1971). Students who were asked to *apply* those concepts to new situations remembered more of the material than students who were asked merely to recall certain facts.

Identify skills and associations that are prerequisite to understanding concepts and their definitions, and sequence instruction accordingly. Robert Gagné's theory of the interrelationships among associations and intellectual skills points out the necessity for learning relevant associations and discriminations prior to concept learning. Furthermore, the learning of concrete concepts must precede the learning of concept definitions (rules) that incorporate those concrete concepts. Finally, the formation of higher-order rules that can be used to solve problems can occur only when concrete and defined concepts contained within them have already been mastered. We will examine the process of problem solving, as well as the related phenomenon of transfer, in the next chapter.

SUMMARY

A concept can be defined either as the same response to different stimuli (a behaviorist perspective) or as a category of objects or events that share one or more common properties (a cognitive perspective). Concepts facilitate thought and behavior in a number of ways, for example by reducing the complexity of the environment and by facilitating generalization to new situations. Learning a concept involves learning the features and rules that determine which objects and events are members of that concept (i.e., positive instances) and which are nonmembers (i.e., negative instances). Numerous factors affect the ease with which concepts are learned, including the salience and redundancy of defining and correlational features, the number of irrelevant features, the complexity of the rules determining the combination of features, and the frequency and timing with which positive and negative instances are presented. Several theories of concept learning have been proposed, including habit strength buildup, mediation, hypothesis testing, prototypes, and feature lists; Robert Gagné has also proposed a theory that incorporates concept learning into a list of eight interrelated forms of learning. Our understanding of how concepts are learned should affect classroom practice.

C H A P T E R   15

Transfer and Problem Solving

THREE days a week, I teach a course in educational psychology to undergraduate education majors. In various class sessions, I talk about operant conditioning, memory theory, meaningful learning, motivation, discipline, and educational testing. Many of my students seem to learn the material well: they carry on informed discussions in class and demonstrate comprehension and application on examinations. But I always wonder about what happens to these students when they finish my course. Does the information they have learned in educational psychology make a difference in the way they eventually teach their own students? Do they really apply the things I have taught them? Does educational psychology help them solve classroom problems?

When something you learn in one situation affects how you learn or perform in another situation, *transfer* has occurred. Sometimes people transfer knowledge and skills they have previously learned to solve a problem; hence, *problem solving* is a form of transfer.

Ideally, the major goals of our educational system are transfer and problem solving. Schools at all levels, from preschools to doctoral programs, teach knowledge and skills with the implicit assumption that students will then apply what they have learned to the "real world." But the things people learn in school do not always seem to be transferred to new situations and new problems. Many adults cannot use basic addition and subtraction procedures to balance their own checkbooks. Many teachers reinforce inappropriate behaviors in their classrooms, ignoring the basic operant conditioning principles they learned in their undergraduate education classes. There are people of all ages who know right from wrong, yet cannot relate that knowledge to their own behaviors.

In this chapter, we will examine the processes of transfer and problem solving in some depth. We will examine concepts, theories, and research in both areas and will consider a variety of factors that facilitate, as well as interfere with, successful transfer and problem solving. At the end of the chapter, we will look at implications for educational practice.

TRANSFER

Transfer is a part of everyday life: individuals continually encounter new situations and draw on their previously acquired knowledge and skills to deal with them. In fact, transfer is an essential component of human functioning. Without it, people would have to learn from scratch about how to behave in every new circumstance and would spend most of their time in trial-and-error learning.

In this section, we will explore various aspects of transfer. We will consider several different types of transfer, then examine theories of transfer, looking first at early theories and subsequently moving to more contemporary views. We will also look at what affects the likelihood that transfer will occur.

Types of Transfer

The concept of transfer refers to many different, although related, phenomena. Theorists distinguish among types of transfer in terms of at least three dimensions: positive vs. negative, vertical vs. lateral, and specific vs. general.

Positive vs. Negative Transfer. When learning in one situation facilitates learning or performance in another situation, we say that *positive transfer* has occurred. Learning basic mathematics procedures should facilitate one's ability to balance a checkbook. Learning principles of reinforcement should improve a teacher's ability to modify student behavior. Knowing the difference between right and wrong should have a positive impact on moral and ethical behavior.

In a sense, meaningful learning involves positive transfer, because previously learned information is used to help learning of new information (Ausubel, Novak, & Hanesian, 1978; Brooks & Dansereau, 1987). "Old" information can help new learning in a variety of ways: for instance, it can serve as a conceptual framework to which new material is attached, facilitate the elaboration of the new information, or provide an analogy through which new material is better understood (Brooks & Dansereau, 1987). Many of the examples of meaningful learning and mnemonics that I described in Chapters 11 and 13 were forms of positive transfer because old information was being applied to help the learning of new information.

On the other hand, when something learned in one situation hinders one's ability to learn or perform in a second situation, then *negative transfer* has occurred. For example, when I play tennis after having played racquetball the day before, I find myself missing the ball a lot: I keep positioning myself too close to the ball because I am accustomed to a short racquetball racquet rather than to the much longer tennis racket. Individuals accustomed to driving a standard transmission who then find themselves behind the wheel of an automatic transmission often step on a clutch that isn't there. People who learn a second language typically apply patterns of speech production characteristic of their native tongue, thus giving them a foreign accent (Schmidt & Young, 1987). Students who are accustomed to memorizing facts in other college courses often don't perform well on my own application-oriented examinations.

An example of a situation in which negative transfer frequently rears its ugly head is in work with decimals: students often erroneously apply mathematical rules they have learned for whole numbers. For example, when asked to compare two decimals such as these:

$$2.34 \text{ vs. } 2.8$$

students sometimes apply the rule that "more digits mean a larger number," thus concluding that 2.34 is the larger of the two decimal numbers (Behr & Harel, 1988). Another rule that is inappropriately transferred to decimals is this whole-number rule: "When a number is divided, the result is a smaller number." Even college students show negative transfer of this rule; for instance, many assert that the answer to this problem:

$$5 \div 0.65$$

is a number *smaller* than 5 (Tirosh & Graeber, 1988). The answer is actually 7.69, a *larger* number.

As you can see, transfer is not always a desirable occurrence. At the end of the chapter, we will look at ways to maximize positive transfer while minimizing negative transfer.

Vertical vs. Lateral Transfer. In some subject areas, topics build on one another in a hierarchical fashion, so that an individual must almost certainly know one topic before moving to the next. For example, a student should probably master principles of addition before moving on to multiplication, because multiplication is an extension of addition. Similarly, a medical student must have expertise in human anatomy before studying surgical techniques: it is difficult to perform an appendectomy when you can't find the appendix. *Vertical transfer* refers to such situations—one acquires new knowledge or skills by building on more basic information and procedures.

In other situations, knowledge of one topic may affect learning a second topic even though the first is not a prerequisite to the second. Knowledge of French is not essential for learning Spanish, yet knowing French should facilitate one's learning of Spanish because many words are similar in the two languages. When knowledge of that first topic is not essential to learning the second one but has an impact nevertheless, we say that *lateral transfer* is occurring.

Specific vs. General Transfer. In *specific transfer,* the original learning task and the transfer task overlap in content. For example, having knowledge about the anatomy of a human should help a veterinary student learn the anatomy of a dog, because the two species have many parallel anatomical features. A student who knows Spanish should easily learn Portuguese, because the two languages share much in common.

In *general transfer*, the original task and the transfer task are different in content. For example, if knowledge of Latin helps a student learn physics, or if the study habits a student develops in a physics course facilitate the learning of sociology, then general transfer is occurring.

Research clearly shows that specific transfer is more common than general transfer (Gray & Orasanu, 1987). In fact, the question of whether general transfer can occur at all has been the subject of much debate over the years. We turn now to early and contemporary theories of transfer, which vary considerably in their perspectives of what things transfer, and when.

Theories of Transfer

How does transfer occur? Let's look first at an early view of transfer—one that predates twentieth-century learning theories—and then examine both behaviorist and cognitive views.

A Historical Perspective: Formal Discipline.   In days of yore, serious scholars studied many rigorous and difficult topics—for instance, Latin, Greek, calculus, and formal logic—that are not as frequently studied today. Although these subject areas may have had no specific applicability to an individual's day-to-day functioning, scholars believed that learning such subjects would nevertheless improve learning and performance in many other aspects of their lives. As recently as the middle of the twentieth century, students were given frequent practice in memorizing poems, apparently as a method of improving their general learning capabilities. Such practices reflect the notion of *formal discipline*: just as you exercise muscles to develop strength, you exercise your mind to learn more quickly and deal with new situations more effectively.

The theory of formal discipline, a predominant view in educational circles until the turn of the century, emphasized the importance and likelihood of general transfer, the idea being that learning in one situation improves learning and performance in another situation, regardless of how different the two situations might be. However, as human learning began to be studied empirically, this notion of "mind as muscle" was soon discarded. For example, William James (1890) memorized a new poem each day over the course of several weeks, assuming that he would begin to learn poems more quickly with practice. However, he soon found that his poem-learning did not improve; if anything, he learned his later poems more *slowly* than his early ones. The consensus of contemporary learning theorists is that general transfer, in the extreme sense portrayed by the formal discipline perspective, probably does not occur.

An Early Behaviorist Theory: Thorndike's Identical Elements. Edward Thorndike (1903, 1924; Thorndike & Woodworth, 1901) proposed a theory of transfer that emphasized specific transfer: transfer occurs only to the extent that the original and transfer tasks have *identical elements*. In an early study supporting Thorndike's theory (Thorndike & Woodworth, 1901), subjects were given extensive training in estimating the areas of rectangles. This training improved their subsequent ability to estimate the areas of rectangles and other two-dimensional forms (e.g., triangles and circles) as well. However, training had less of an impact on the judgment of nonrectangular shapes, presumably because nonrectangles had elements both similar and dissimilar to the elements of rectangles. In a later study, Thorndike (1924) examined the interrelationships of high school students' academic achievement in different curricular areas. Achievement in one subject matter appeared to facilitate students' achievement in another only when there was some commonality between the two subject matters. For example, arithmetic achievement was related to performance in a bookkeeping course, but Latin proficiency was not. Thorndike concluded that the value of studying specific topics was due not to the benefits of mental exercise, but to "the special information, habits, interests, attitudes, and ideals which they demonstrably produce" (Thorndike, 1924, p. 98).

A Later Behaviorist Perspective: Similarity of Stimuli and Responses. Since Thorndike's work, behaviorist views of transfer have focused on how transfer is affected by stimulus and response characteristics in the original and transfer situations. As an illustration, consider these four lists of paired associates:

List 1	List 2	List 3	List 4
lamp—shoe	lamp—sock	rain—shoe	lamp—goat
boat—fork	boat—spoon	bear—fork	boat—shop
wall—lawn	wall—yard	sofa—lawn	wall—rice
corn—road	corn—lane	book—road	corn—fish

Imagine that you first learn List 1, then are asked to learn List 2. Will your knowledge of the pairs in List 1 help you learn the pairs in List 2? Based on the results of verbal learning studies (Hall, 1966, 1971), the answer is yes: the stimulus words are identical in the two situations and the responses are similar, so positive transfer from one list to the other is likely to occur.

Now, however, imagine that you have to learn List 1 and then List 3. Will prior learning of List 1 help with List 3? The answer again is yes (Hall, 1966, 1971). Even though the stimulus words are very different, the responses in List 3 are identical to those of List 1 (hence they have already been learned), and only need to be attached to new stimuli.

On the other hand, let's now suppose that, after learning List 1, you need to learn List 4. Here is a case in which very different responses from those of List 1 must be learned to the very same stimuli. Learning List 1 is likely to make learning List 4 more difficult because you will sometimes remember the List 1 response instead of the List 4 response, (Hall, 1966, 1971), and negative transfer will result.

In general, principles of transfer which have emerged from behaviorist literature (e.g., Osgood, 1949; Thyne, 1963) include the following:

1. When stimuli and responses are similar in the two situations, maximal positive transfer will occur.
2. When stimuli are different and responses are similar, some positive transfer will occur.
3. When stimuli are similar and responses are different, negative transfer will occur.

As an example of this last point, I remember one year as a high school student when my class schedule included second-period Latin and third-period French. The word for "and" (*et*) is spelled the same in both languages, but is pronounced very differently ("et" in Latin and "ay" in French), hence meeting the conditions for negative transfer (similar stimuli, different responses). On several occasions I blurted out an "et" in my French class, a response that inevitably evoked a disgusted scowl from my French teacher.

Human Information Processing Theory. Cognitive psychologists have become increasingly interested in transfer in recent years (Fleishman, 1987) and are beginning to develop their own views of how and when transfer occurs. A currently prominent view of transfer is this one: relevant information and skills are transferred to a new situation only when they are retrieved to short-term memory within the context of that new situation (Brooks & Dansereau, 1987; Cormier, 1987; Gick & Holyoak, 1987). Given the low probability that any particular piece of information will be retrieved, as well as the limited capacity of short-term memory, many potentially relevant pieces of information may very well *not* be transferred in situations in which they would be helpful.

The presence or absence of retrieval cues in the transfer situation determines what relevant information, if any, is retrieved from long-term memory. A new situation is more likely to call to mind previously learned information if the situation and the relevant information are closely associated in memory. This will happen, for instance, if the new situation was previously anticipated when the new information was stored, so that the situation and information relevant to it were stored in association with each other. To illustrate, when students are learning basic arithmetic principles, they should be given practice using those principles in as many different problem situations as possible: for example, determining best buys at a grocery store, dividing items fairly among friends, running a lemonade stand, and so on. Arithmetic will then be associated in long-term memory with all of those situations, and when the need arises to determine which of two grocery products yields the most for the money, relevant arithmetic procedures should be readily retrieved.

Current Views on General Transfer. We have already seen two extreme perspectives regarding general transfer. Advocates of formal discipline argued that learning rigorous and demanding subject matter was beneficial to later learning situations because it "disciplined" the mind. Thorndike, on the other hand, argued that one task would transfer to another only to the extent that the two tasks had identical elements. Current views concerning general transfer are somewhere in between: general transfer is not as common as specific transfer (Gray & Orasanu, 1987), but learning occurring at one time *can* facilitate learning at another time if, in the process, the individual *learns how to learn*.

In several early studies of learning to learn, Harry Harlow (1949, 1950, 1959) found that monkeys and young children became progressively faster at discrimination-learning tasks. More recently, studies have emphasized the transfer value of metacognitive skills such as those I described in Chapter 13. Many theorists believe that the development of effective study methods and habits (finding main ideas, learning for meaning, organizing, etc.) will transfer readily from one subject matter to another (e.g., Brooks & Dansereau, 1987; Brown, 1978; Pressley, Snyder, & Cariglia-Bull, 1987).

As long as there is a "common something" among tasks, the possibility of transfer between one task and another exists (Gray & Orasanu, 1987). But the existence of "common somethings" does not guarantee transfer. When is transfer likely to occur? Let's look at some things that appear to affect the transfer process.

Factors Affecting Transfer

A number of variables are related to the occurrence of transfer. We will consider several of them.

Meaningful learning promotes better transfer than rote learning. In Chapters 11 and 12, I explained that meaningfully learned information is more easily stored and retrieved than information learned at a rote level. Now we see an additional advantage of meaningful learning: it leads to better positive transfer (Ausubel et al., 1978; Brooks & Dansereau, 1987; Mayer, 1987). For example, in a study by Brownell and Moser (1949, cited in Mayer, 1977), third-grade students were taught the idea of borrowing in subtraction in a presumably meaningful manner: two-digit numbers were represented by individual sticks and groups of ten sticks bundled together, with borrowing represented by the untying of one group of ten. These students solved a variety of subtraction problems more successfully than students taught the same information simply through verbally presented rules. Along a similar vein, in an experiment by Mayer and Greeno (1972), two groups of undergraduate students received one of two methods of instruction on a formula related to basic probability theory. Group 1 received instruction that focused on the formula itself, whereas Group 2 received instruction that emphasized the relationship of the formula to subjects' general knowledge. Group 1 subjects were better able to apply the formula to problems similar to those they had studied during instruction, but Group 2 subjects were better able to use the formula in ways that had not specifically been covered in instruction—that is, they could transfer the formula to a wider variety of situations. Apparently, Group 2 subjects had made more connections between the new material and existing information in their long-term memories, and those connections enabled the subjects to transfer probability theory in ways that Group 1 subjects could not.

The more thoroughly something is learned, the more likely it is to be transferred to a new situation. There is often a trade-off between instructional time and transfer; the more quickly a topic is covered, the less likely it is to be transferred (Cormier & Hagman, 1987; Ellis, 1978; Gick & Holyoak, 1987). The implications of this finding for educational practice are clear: students should demonstrate thorough mastery of material if they will be expected to apply that information in future situations.

Principles are more easily transferred than knowledge. General principles and rules are more applicable than specific facts and information (Cheng, Holyoak, Nisbett, & Oliver, 1986; Fong, Krantz, & Nisbett, 1986; Gick & Holyoak, 1983, 1987; Judd, 1932). For example, if you have read Chapter 4 on operant conditioning, then you probably remember the general principle about reinforcement: a reinforcer is a stimulus that increases the later frequency of a response it follows. This principle is easily transferable to a wide variety of situations, whereas specific facts that I identified in the same chapter (e.g., who wrote what, and when) are not. Similarly, in trying to understand such current events as revolutions and international wars, general principles from history—for example, two groups of people will engage in battle when other attempts at reaching a mutually satisfying state of affairs have failed—are probably more applicable than knowledge about specific battles of World War II.

The more similar two situations are, the more likely it is that what is learned in one situation will be applied to the other situation. Behaviorists have argued that similarity of either stimuli or responses is necessary for transfer to occur. Cognitivists have proposed instead that because transfer depends on retrieval of relevant information at the appropriate time, the *perceived* similarity rather than actual similarity of the two situations is important (Gick & Holyoak, 1987). Either way, one thing is clear: similarity between two situations affects transfer.

Transfer to a new task is more likely when retrieval of relevant information and skills is facilitated. Previously acquired knowledge can be applied in a new situation only if it is retrieved to short-term memory at that time. People are therefore more likely to transfer if they are given hints (potential retrieval cues) about relevant items in their long-term memories than if they are left to their own devices (Gick & Holyoak, 1987).

Numerous and varied examples and opportunities for practice increase the extent to which information and skills will be applied in new situations. Individuals are more likely to transfer something they have learned if they have encountered a wide variety of examples and practice situations (Cheng et al., 1986; Cormier, 1987; Fong et al., 1986; Gick & Holyoak, 1987; Schmidt & Young, 1987). Individuals trained in this fashion store what they have learned in association with many different contexts and will therefore be more likely to retrieve information when they again encounter one of those contexts.

I have kept this principle in mind as I have written this book. You may have noticed that the book has many more examples than most textbooks, and in fact you may be feeling "exampled" to death. But I am trying to write this book so that you will *use* principles of human learning, something that is more likely to happen if you can see those principles in action in many different situations.

The probability of transfer decreases as the time interval between the original task and the transfer task increases. Research on transfer has focused on very short delays between the original task and the transfer task (Gick & Holyoak, 1987). Yet transfer decreases as the time interval between the original and transfer situations increases (Gick & Holyoak, 1987). Here is another principle that is probably due to retrieval: information that has been learned recently is more likely, and more able, to be retrieved than information acquired further back in time.

How and when do people transfer information they have learned to find solutions to problems? It is to this topic—problem solving—that we turn next.

PROBLEM SOLVING

Can you solve these three problems?

1. What number is obtained when 3354 is divided by 43?

2. How can a forty-year-old educational psychologist be helped to control her junk food habit?

3. How can two large countries of differing political persuasions and a mutual lack of trust be convinced to reduce their military defense spending and instead work toward cooperation and peaceful coexistence?

The world presents us with many different kinds of problems. Some, such as Problem 1, are straightforward: all the information necessary for a solution is presented, and the solution is definitely right or wrong. Others, such as Problem 2, may require seeking out some additional information (e.g., Does the educational psychologist keep physically active, or does she sit around the house all day watching television game shows?), and there may be two or more solutions to the problem (self-reinforcement for altered eating habits, six months on a deserted island, etc.). Still others, such as Problem 3, may be so complicated that, even after considerable research and creative thought, no easy solution emerges. Different kinds of problems require different procedures and different solutions; this multifaceted nature of problem solving has made the theoretical study of problem solving a very challenging endeavor indeed.

In the following pages, we will explore a number of topics related to the complex activity of human problem solving. We will first define some basic concepts used in problem-solving literature, then examine both behaviorist and cognitive theories of problem solving. Because cognitive views are predominant at the present time, we will look in depth at memory factors and cognitive strategies involved in problem solving; we will also examine how the cognitive processes of expert problem solvers and novices differ.

Basic Concepts in Problem Solving

Among the more basic concepts appearing in problem-solving literature are problem components, algorithms, heuristics, and well-defined problems vs. ill-defined problems.

Components of a Problem. Any problem has at least three components (Glass, Holyoak, & Santa, 1979; Wickelgren, 1974):

1. Givens. Pieces of information that are provided when the problem is presented.
2. Goal. The desired end state—what a solution to a problem should accomplish.
3. Operations. Actions that can be performed to approach or reach the goal.

Operations are frequently described in terms of *productions*, "if-then" conditional actions described in Chapter 11. When one or more operations can be applied so that the goal state is reached, then the problem is successfully solved.

Algorithms and Heuristics. Some problems can be approached using a set of specified operations that always lead to a correct solution. For example, the problem of dividing 3354 by 43 can be solved using either of two procedures: (1) applying prescribed methods of long division, or (2) pushing the appropriate series of buttons on a calculator. Either way, the correct answer—78—is obtained. Similarly, a cherry pie recipe, if followed to the letter in terms of ingredients, measurements, and oven temperatures, provides a series of steps that guarantees a successful dessert. Such specific, step-by-step procedures for solving problems are called *algorithms*.

Unfortunately, not all problems can be solved with algorithms. No algorithm can establish world peace or eliminate a junk food addiction. In such situations, people use other approaches to problem solving—approaches that may or may not work. These approaches, known collectively as *heuristics*, comprise general problem-solving strategies, rules of thumb, and "best guesses" based on past experiences with similar problems. For example, in helping an educational psychologist reduce her junk food intake, one heuristic is to think of as many different solutions as possible (a technique known as *brainstorming*), in hopes that one of them will be acceptable. The problem of disarmament of two large countries can perhaps be solved by analogy: if two coworkers can resolve their differences when they sit down and talk about them, maybe the same strategy will be effective with political leaders (hence the frequent summit conferences between leaders of the United States and the USSR).

Heuristics are also used when algorithms are impractical or timeconsuming. For example, I recently coordinated a chili supper for the Parent-Teacher Association of the local elementary school and needed numerous volunteers to assist me. The PTA board suggested an algorithm for me to use: contact the more than 200 individuals who had indicated on a questionnaire several months earlier that they would help at PTA functions.

Being pressed for time, I instead chose a heuristic: contact people I knew personally, aware that I could shame many of them into helping out. Similarly, although an algorithm exists for determining the best move in a game of checkers, people tend not to use it because of its impracticality. This algorithm, as Samuel (1963) has described it, is as follows: consider every possible move, then consider every possible next move that the opponent could make in response to each of those moves, then consider every follow-up move that could be made in response to each of *those* moves, and so on, until the winner is projected for every conceivable series of moves. Such an algorithm would take either a sophisticated computer programmer or several lifetimes of complete dedication to a single game of checkers.

Well-defined vs. Ill-defined Problems. Problems vary greatly in terms of how well they are structured or defined. Many theorists have found it helpful to distinguish between well-defined and ill-defined problems (e.g., Frederiksen, 1984; Reitman, 1964, 1965; Simon, 1973, 1978), a distinction that probably reflects a continuum of problem structure rather than a rigid dichotomy (Frederiksen, 1984). At one extreme is the *well-defined* problem, one for which goals and givens are clearly stated, all the necessary information for solving the problem is presented, and an algorithm exists that will lead to a correct solution. At the other extreme is the *ill-defined* problem, one in which the desired goal is ambiguous, some information necessary for problem solution is lacking, and no relevant algorithm for problem solution exists. Well-defined problems often have only one right solution, whereas ill-defined problems often have several possible solutions that vary in terms of their relative "rightness" or acceptability. The problem of dividing 3354 by 43 is well-defined, while that of military disarmament is ill-defined (for example, the goal of "cooperation and peaceful coexistence" is ambiguous). As you might guess, ill-defined problems are typically more difficult to solve and require more complex problem-solving strategies than well-defined ones.

Theories of Problem Solving

Since Edward Thorndike's early work with the cat in the puzzle box, several theories of problem solving have emerged from both the behaviorist and cognitive perspectives. We will first look at two behaviorist views: trial and error and the response hierarchy. We will then examine three more cognitive approaches: Gestalt psychology, stages of problem solving, and human information processing.

Trial-and-Error Learning. In Chapter 2, you encountered Thorndike's (1898) classic work with a cat in a puzzle box. The cat needed to solve a problem: how to get out of a confining situation. It explored the box, manipulating the box's various parts, and eventually triggered the mechanism that opened the door. Once again it was put back in the box, and once again it tried different behaviors until it triggered the release mechanism. In each succeeding trial, escape from the box took less time than in the previous trial. The cat's approach to the problem situation appeared to be one of trial and error, with the correct solution being followed by a positive consequence (escape from the box).

A trial-and-error approach is often observed in the problem-solving behavior of children. For example, consider how many young children assemble jigsaw puzzles: they try to fit different pieces into the same spot, often without considering each piece's shape and appearance, until eventually they find a piece that fits.

Response Hierarchy. Another concept that you encountered in Chapter 2 was Clark Hull's notion of a habit family hierarchy, now more generally known as a *response hierarchy*: an organism learns several different responses to the same stimulus, each of which is associated with that stimulus with a different degree of habit strength. When a stimulus is presented, an organism will, if possible, make the response for which the habit strength is the strongest. If that response fails or is prevented from occurring, the organism will make the second response, and so on down the hierarchy (e.g., Hull, 1934, 1937, 1938). A response hierarchy can be graphically depicted like this:

$$\begin{array}{c} \nearrow R_1 \\ S \rightarrow R_2 \\ \searrow R_3 \end{array}$$

In this case, three responses have been learned to the same stimulus, with stronger stimulus-response associations being indicated by thicker arrows. The organism first emits the response with the strongest association to the stimulus (R_1). If that response fails to achieve its goal, the response with the second strongest association (R_2) is emitted, then the third strongest response (R_3), and so on, until eventually the goal is achieved.

A number of behaviorists (e.g., Davis, 1966; Mayzner & Tresselt, 1958, 1966; Skinner, 1966a) have applied the notion of response hierarchy to a problem-solving situation. Stimuli in the problem situation will undoubtedly evoke a number of different responses, and those responses will be produced, one at a time and in order of their strength, until either the problem is solved or the organism exhausts its repertoire of responses. To illustrate, my daughter Tina is often confronted with the same problem: getting permission from her parents to do something we may not want her to do. Given this problem, she tries three different responses, usually in the same order. First she smiles sweetly and describes how much she would like to engage in that forbidden activity (such a response, apparently, is associated most strongly with this particular problem situation). If that tactic is unproductive, she speaks indignantly about how her parents never let her do anything. As a last resort, she runs off to her room, slamming her door and shouting that her parents hate her. Unfortunately, Tina has not yet learned that some problems, such as engaging in forbidden activities, will be solved over her parents' dead bodies.

In their emphasis on trial-and-error learning and habit strength, behaviorists have obviously focused on the role that stimulus-response connections play in problem solving. Although such an approach can often be used to explain problem-solving behavior, contemporary theorists have largely abandoned it in favor of an increased focus on the mental processes involved in problem solving. Consistent with this trend, we too will abandon behaviorism at this point and embrace a more cognitively oriented perspective for the remainder of the chapter.

An Early Cognitive View: Gestalt Psychology. In Chapter 7, I described Wolfgang Köhler's (1925) observations of chimpanzee behavior in problem-solving situations. Köhler observed little trial-and-error behavior of the form that Thorndike had described. Rather, it appeared to him that the chimpanzees carefully examined the components of a problem situation (sizing things up, so to speak), and mentally combined and recombined those components until they eventually found a winning combination. At this point of *insight*, the chimps would immediately move into action, performing the required responses in a deliberate manner until the problem was solved. From such observations, Köhler (1925, 1929) concluded that problem solving was a process of mentally *restructuring* a problem situation until insight into the problem's solution was reached.

Stages of Problem Solving. In addition to the Gestaltist view, another early cognitive approach to problem solving was to identify the cognitive processes involved in problem solving in the form of steps to be followed (e.g., Polya, 1957; Wallas, 1926). For example, Wallas (1926) identified four steps in problem solving:

1. Preparation. Defining the problem and gathering information relevant to its solution.
2. Incubation. Thinking about the problem at a subconscious level while engaging in other activities.
3. Inspiration. Having a sudden insight into the solution of the problem.
4. Verification. Checking to be certain that the solution is correct.

Similarly, Polya (1957) listed these four steps:

1. Understanding the problem. Identifying the problem's knowns (givens) and unknowns, and, if appropriate, using suitable notation, such as mathematical symbols, to represent the problem.

2. Devising a plan. Determining appropriate actions to take to solve the problem.

3. Carrying out the plan. Executing the actions that have been determined to solve the problem and checking their effectiveness.

4. Looking backward. Evaluating the overall effectiveness of the approach to the problem, with the intention of learning something about how similar problems may be solved on future occasions.

Unfortunately, both Wallas and Polya were rather evasive about how all these steps could be accomplished. For example, Wallas's notion of incubation revealed little about how to behave to facilitate the occurrence of inspiration. Similarly, Polya recommended devising a plan with little consideration of just how one would go about doing that. In this sense, then, early "stage" theories were of limited use in helping psychologists determine what specific cognitive processes are involved in solving problems successfully.

Human Information Processing Theory. Most contemporary theories focus less on the steps people follow in solving problems and more on the nature of the various mental processes employed to reach problem solutions. These information processing theories (e.g., Andre, 1986) emphasize the role of short-term memory capacity, meaningful learning, organization of long-term memory, retrieval of relevant information, and specific cognitive strategies. The bulk of current research in problem solving reflects inquiry into the nature of these cognitive processes; in the following pages we will look at them in detail.

Cognitive Factors in Problem Solving

Ability to solve problems successfully depends on a number of factors related to the human information processing system. Here we will focus on three of them: short-term memory capacity, encoding and storage in long-term memory, and long-term memory retrieval.

Short-term Memory Capacity. As you should recall, short-term memory is the component of memory in which active, conscious processing of information occurs. Yet this component has a limited capacity: it can hold and process only a small amount of information at a time. If the information and processes necessary to solve a problem exceed short-term memory capacity, the problem cannot be solved. For example, you may remember from Chapter 11 how difficult it can be to solve long division problems in your head.

The short-term memory limitation can be overcome in problem-solving situations in at least two ways. First of all, some of the information necessary to solve the problem can be written down (i.e., stored externally). This is the method typically used in solving complicated arithmetic problems. Second, as I indicated in Chapter 13, some skills involved in problem solving should be learned well enough that they become automatic, thus requiring only minimal short-term memory capacity (Anderson, 1982; Gagné, 1982).

Encoding and Storage of the Problem. Consider this classic children's riddle:

> As I was going to St. Ives,
> I met a man with seven wives.
> Every wife had seven sacks.
> Every sack had seven cats.
> Every cat had seven kits.
> Kits, cats, sacks, wives.
> How many were going to St. Ives?

Many people take this logical approach to the problem: 1 traveler plus 1 man with 7 wives plus 7^2 sacks (49) plus 7^3 cats (343) plus 7^4 kits (2401) equal a total of 2802 going to St. Ives. People who solve the problem in this manner have encoded the problem incorrectly. In particular, they have overlooked the first line of the riddle: "As *I* was going to St. Ives." The problem statement doesn't tell us where the polygamist was taking his harem and menagerie (perhaps to St. Ives, perhaps not).

Following is a passage containing some information you will need to solve a mathematical problem. Read the information, then, after you have finished, turn the page to read the problem:

I went to a store and made the following purchases:

- A roasting chicken for $4
- A dozen eggs for $1 per dozen
- Three avocados for 50¢ each
- Two cans of tomato sauce for 25¢ each
- Five apples for 20¢ each

Now for the problem:

How many items did I buy?

Did you find that you stored the wrong information? You may have been expecting the problem "How much did I spend?" If so, then you probably determined the total amount spent in each line of the problem and added the amounts together for a grand total. Using this approach, however, you would not have stored the information actually necessary for solving the problem: the number of items mentioned in each line.

One critical factor in problem solving is what information is stored in memory. A difficulty you may have had with the grocery shopping problem is that some irrelevant information was presented (i.e., the prices of items), and you may have stored that information instead of more essential data. Irrelevant information can be distracting, thus interfering with successful problem solving. For example, when I give examinations to my own students, I often present more information than is necessary to solve a problem, and some students have difficulty sorting through it all. Similarly, I have noticed that my daughter has trouble with mathematics problems in which super-fluous information is presented. My students and my daughter behave al-most as if they have learned that they need to use *all* the information they are given. This attitude may be the result of their own prior school experi-ences: most problems presented in the classroom (especially mathematics problems) present only the information needed to solve the problem—no more, no less.

A second critical factor related to long-term storage is how a problem is encoded in memory (e.g., Bourne et al, 1986; Matlin, 1983; Mayer, 1982; Ormrod, 1979; Schwartz, 1971). For example, Mayer (1982) examined un-dergraduate students' ability to recall problems such as this one:

> A truck leaves Los Angeles en route to San Francisco at 1 p.m. A second truck leaves San Francisco at 2 p.m. en route to Los Angeles going along the same route. Assume the two cities are 465 miles apart and that the trucks meet at 6 p.m.. If the second truck travels at 15 mph faster than the first truck, how fast does each truck go? (Mayer, 1982, p. 202).

Mayer's subjects had considerable difficulty encoding relational information (e.g., one truck traveling *15 mph faster* than another). They made three times as many errors in recalling relational aspects of problems as they did in recalling basic assertions (e.g., two cities being 465 miles apart), reflect-ing greater difficulty in storing relational information.

Wertheimer (1945) has provided another example of the importance of encoding in problem solving: calculating the area of a parallelogram. As you probably know, the area of a rectangle is determined by multiplying its height by its width. But how is the area of a parallelogram determined? Problem solution is easier once you realize that the extra "triangle" at one end of the parallelogram is identical to the missing triangle at the other end, as illustrated in Figure 15–1.

Figure 15–1
Finding the area of a parallelogram

1. Take one parallelogram:

2. Cut off the extra triangle at one end, like so:

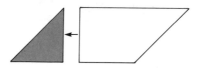

3. Attach it to the other end, like so:

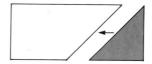

4. Multiply the height by the width, like so:

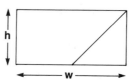

The area of a parallelogram = height × width:

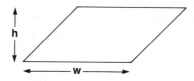

Individuals are often predisposed to approach and encode problems in particular ways, a phenomenon known as *set* (Gestalt psychologists called it *Einstellung*). Here is a problem in which people are often the victims of a mental set:

How can you throw a tennis ball so that it goes a short distance, comes to a complete stop, then reverses its direction? You may not bounce the ball against a surface, nor may you attach any other object (such as a string) to it (Adapted from Gardner, 1978).

I once gave this problem to a masters level learning class, and only a handful of the 35 students was able to solve it. Most of them worked on the assumption that the ball had to be thrown horizontally (some may even have encoded the problem as a visual image of a pitcher). Once you break this mental set, the answer is quite simple: you throw the ball *up*.

As another example of set, consider this "candle" problem adapted from a similar one used by Duncker (1945):

> You are in a room with a bulletin board firmly affixed to the wall. Your task is to stand a candle upright beside the bulletin board about 4 feet above the floor. You do not want the candle touching the bulletin board, because the candle's flame must not singe the bulletin board. Instead, you need to place the candle about a centimeter away. How can you accomplish the task, given the following materials:
>
> - A small candle (birthday-cake size)
> - A match
> - A box of thumbtacks
> - A twelve-inch wooden ruler
> - A metal knitting needle

Develop a solution for the problem before you continue reading.

When I have brought these materials into my graduate classes, students typically identify three different solutions. One solution is to stab the knitting needle through the candle and into the bulletin board; this action inevitably splits the candle and gouges the bulletin board. A second solution is to form a flat surface for the candle with the ruler, propping it against the bulletin board with thumbtacks; however, the precariously placed ruler usually falls to the floor. Only a third solution works: one must take the thumbtacks out of the box, use the tacks to attach the box to the bulletin board, then affix the candle to the top side of the box (with either melted wax or a tack). The solution is obvious once you think about it, but many people have difficulty with the problem because they encode the box as a container and overlook its other possible functions.

The tendency to think of objects as having only one function, thereby overlooking other possible uses, is a form of set known as *functional fixedness* (e.g., Birch & Rabinowitz, 1951; Duncker, 1945; Maier & Janzen, 1968). The degree to which individuals experience functional fixedness is at least partly influenced by situational conditions. For instance, when trying to solve the candle problem, subjects more easily solve the problem if the tacks are presented *outside* the box, presumably because the box is then less likely to be thought of as a container (Duncker, 1945). The problem is also more easily solved if the box itself is labeled "box" (Glucksberg & Weisberg, 1966), possibly because the label draws attention to the box as something that can be used in problem solution.

Set and functional fixedness are at least partly the result of past experiences: if a particular approach to a problem has been successful in the past, an individual is likely to continue using that same approach even in situations where it is inappropriate or unnecessarily cumbersome. Luchins's experiments with water jar problems (Luchins, 1942; Luchins & Luchins, 1950) illustrate just how strongly one's past experiences can influence problem solving. Imagine, if you will, that you have three jars of three different sizes, like so:

Jar A holds 20 ounces of water.

Jar B holds 59 ounces of water.

Jar C holds 4 ounces of water.

You need exactly 31 ounces of water. Assuming that you have an unlimited amount of water, how can you get the exact amount of water using only the three jars that you have? Try to find a solution before you read further.

The solution to the water jar problem is as follows:

1. Fill Jar B. This gives you 59 ounces of water.

2. Pour water from Jar B into Jar A until A is full. This leaves 39 ounces in Jar B.

3. Pour water from Jar B into Jar C until C is full. This leaves 35 ounces in Jar B.

4. Pour the water out of Jar C.

5. Once again pour water from B into C. At this point you have 31 ounces in Jar B, the exact amount that you need.

Mathematically speaking, the solution to the problem is

$$B - A - 2C$$

Luchins (1942) gave his subjects a series of such problems, with the answer always being the same: $B - A - 2C$. He then presented these three problems:

Jar A holds:	Jar B holds:	Jar C holds:	Obtain this amount:
23	49	3	20
15	39	3	18
28	76	3	25

Virtually everyone solved the first two of these using the same formula as before: $B - A - 2C$. They had difficulty solving the third problem because the standard formula did not apply. But notice that all three can be solved quite easily: the solution for the first and third problems is $A - C$, and that for the second problem is $A + C$. Luchins's subjects (who in fact were professors and graduate students!) were victims of a problem-solving set established through prior experience.

In most situations, one's predisposition to approach similar problems in similar ways is beneficial in that it facilitates successful problem solving

(Maier, 1945). However, a mental set does influence the way in which a problem is encoded in memory, and this encoding in turn influences the parts of long-term memory that are searched for information potentially relevant to the problem (Glass et al., 1979). If a problem's encoding steers an individual in the wrong direction in terms of a long-term memory search, then problem solving performance is hindered. Let's turn now to this next cognitive factor in problem solving: retrieval from long-term memory.

Retrieval from Long-term Memory. To use previously learned information to solve a problem, the information must be retrieved at the time the problem is being considered. Thus, the factors that facilitate long-term memory retrieval—for example, meaningful learning and organized storage—facilitate problem-solving success as well (e.g., Ausubel et al., 1978).

In searching long-term memory for information relevant to a problem, individuals begin by looking in logical "places." People tend to retrieve familiar ideas first; original and unusual problem solutions tend to be retrieved later in the process, if at all (Bourne et al., 1986). People also tend to retrieve information closely associated with aspects of the problem situation; for example, subjects more easily solve the candle problem when they have previously learned a paired-associate list that includes the pair candle—box (Weisberg, DiCamillo, & Phillips, 1979). Hints that provide important retrieval cues can be helpful, at least if individuals perceive their relevance (Bourne et al., 1986). For example, the solution of anagrams such as this one:

Unscramble these letters to form a real word: NEEPLATH

is easier when subjects know that the solution belongs to a particular category such as animals (Safren, 1962). (The solution, by the way, is *elephant.*)

As I mentioned in Chapter 12, anxiety interferes with retrieval by restricting the part of long-term memory that is searched. Anxious individuals are therefore likely to have difficulty solving problems whose solutions are not readily apparent. For example, Glucksberg (1962) asked four groups of subjects to solve the candle problem. For two groups of subjects, the tacks were out of the box (the easy version of the problem), and for the other two groups, the tacks were in the box (the difficult version). Two groups were given no reason to be anxious about solving the problem; their success or failure in finding a solution had no consequences. The other two groups were given an incentive to make them more eager and anxious about finding a solution: the fastest twenty-five percent of the problem solvers would receive $5, and the fastest individual would receive $25 (a tidy sum back in 1962). Below are the mean reaction times (in minutes) for the four groups of problem solvers; larger numbers indicate greater difficulty in solving the problem:

	Easy Version	**Difficult Version**
High Anxiety	3.67	11.08
Low Anxiety	4.99	7.41

When the box was empty, its use as a platform for the candle was obvious, and anxiety facilitated problem solution. But when the box was already being used as a container, anxiety made the problem even more difficult to solve than it already was!

The effects of anxiety on problem solving seem to be reduced or eliminated when individuals know where to search in long-term memory. Although high-anxious individuals typically perform more poorly on problem-solving tasks than low-anxious individuals, the problem-solving performance of the two groups is equivalent when memory aids that promote appropriate retrieval are provided (Gross & Mastenbrook, 1980; Leherissey, O'Neil, & Hansen, 1971).

In addition to looking for relevant information, individuals must also search their long-term memories for relevant *strategies* that can be applied to solving a problem. We next explore the strategies—effective and ineffective alike—that people use to solve problems.

Problem-Solving Strategies

Some types of problems (e.g., long division problems) have specific algorithms associated with them—algorithms that always produce a correct solution. But what do people do to solve problems for which algorithms are impractical or nonexistent? Researchers have identified numerous problem-solving strategies that people use.

Combining Algorithms. Sometimes, when a problem cannot be solved by a single algorithm, it can instead be solved by using several algorithms in combination; Robert Gagné's (1985) notion of a higher-order rule, in which two or more simple rules are incorporated, reflects this idea. Mathematics problems (e.g., algebraic equations, geometric proofs) are frequently solved through a combination of algorithms.

In some cases, individuals may have to learn, through either formal classroom instruction or informal experiences, the process of combining algorithms. A study by Scandura (1974) illustrates this point. Elementary school children were taught trading rules such as these:

n caramels $= n + 1$ toy soldiers

n toy soldiers $= n + 2$ pencils

They were then asked to make trades that involved combining two of these rules (e.g., trading caramels for pencils). Children who were unable to combine rules successfully were identified, and half of them were given specific instruction on how to combine the rules. Subsequently, all of these instructed children effectively combined the trading rules (one of them first required additional instruction), while none of the children in an untrained control group were able to do so.

In addition to the occasional beneficial effects of instruction, people are also more likely to combine algorithms when they have learned those algorithms in a meaningful fashion—in other words, when they understand *why* those algorithms produce positive results (e.g., Ausubel et al, 1978). Furthermore, when algorithms are followed blindly, without any understanding of them, problem solving can actually be hampered (Brown, 1978; Resnick & Glaser, 1976).

Hill Climbing. *Hill climbing* (Andre, 1986; Mayer, 1983b; Wickelgren, 1974) is a problem-solving strategy in which individuals make any move that brings them closer to the problem goal. For example, consider this problem:

> You have a pile of 24 coins. Twenty-three of these coins have the same weight, and one is heavier. Your task is to determine which coin is heavier and to do so in the minimum number of weighings. You are given a beam balance (scale), which will compare the weight of any two sets of coins out of the total set of 24 coins (Wickelgren, 1974, p. 34).

Stop to figure out a solution before you continue.

You undoubtedly used hill climbing to solve the problem, weighing different groups of coins against one another and gradually eliminating some of them, until eventually only the single heavier coin remained. How many weighings did you use? In fact, the heavy coin can be identified with only *three* weighings, like so:

1. Divide the 24 coins into three groups of 8 coins each. Whichever of the three groups is heavier than the other two must contain the heavy coin. Weigh one group against a second; if one group tips the scale, it must contain the heavy coin. If the two groups balance each other, the third group must contain the heavy coin.

2. Divide the 8-coin group containing the heavy coin into three smaller groups, with two groups of 3 coins and one group of 2 coins. Weigh the two 3-coin groups against each other. As before, the scale will tell you if one group is heavier (in which case it contains the heavy coin). If the two groups balance each other, the group of 2 coins must contain the heavy coin.

3. Using the same reasoning as in the previous two steps, the heavy coin can be identified from the group of 2 or 3 coins with only one additional weighing.

Hill climbing is often a very effective problem-solving technique. However, it will be ineffective in situations in which the problem solution requires one or more temporary steps *backward*. To illustrate, consider this problem:

> A zookeeper must transport three lions and three giraffes across a river. She has a barge that can hold only herself and two other animals, so she will have to make several trips and leave some of the animals unattended some of the time. However, whenever she leaves a group of animals, the giraffes must outnumber the lions; otherwise, the lions will gang up on one of the giraffes and kill it. How can the zookeeper transport all six animals safely across the river?

Try to solve the zookeeper's problem before you read any further.

The zookeeper can transport the animals across the river in this manner:

1. She takes two lions to the other side, leaving three giraffes and one lion behind (since the giraffes outnumber the lion, they will be safe).
2. She comes back alone.
3. She takes one giraffe to the other side, leaving two giraffes and one lion behind.
4. She *brings back* the two lions, leaving one giraffe alone on the other side.
5. She takes the two giraffes to the other side, leaving the three lions behind.
6. She comes back alone, leaving the three giraffes behind.
7. She takes two lions to the other side, leaving one lion behind.
8. She comes back alone, leaving three giraffes and two lions behind.
9. She takes the last lion across the river.

Problem solution, then, requires a step backward: the zookeeper must bring two of the lions back to the first side of the river (Step 4). A person using a hill climbing strategy would not consider such a step and would be unable to solve the problem.

Means-Ends Analysis. *Means-ends analysis* (e.g., Newell & Simon, 1972; Restle & Davis, 1962; Resnick & Glaser, 1976) is a process whereby an individual breaks a problem down into two or more subgoals and then works successively on each of those subgoals. To illustrate, consider this situation:

> I have just had a brick barbecue built in my backyard. I have had it built with metric dimensions: the grill is 1 meter wide and 1.5 meters long. Rich and Marcy Jones look over from their yard next door and say, "Oooo, nice barbecue, almost as big as ours."
> "Mine is bigger," I reply.
> "Can't be," they say. "Our grill is 3.5 feet by 5 feet."

The question: Have I kept up with the Jones family by buying a bigger barbecue grill? I can solve this problem by breaking it down into four subgoals and solving each one in turn:

1. Convert the dimensions of the Jones's grill into metric units. One foot equals approximately 0.30 meters; multiplying the "feet" dimensions by 0.30 yields dimensions of 1.05 by 1.5 meters.

2. Compute the area of the Jones's grill. Multiplying 1.05 by 1.5 equals 1.575 square meters.

3. Compute the area of my grill: Multiplying 1 by 1.5 equals 1.5 square meters.

4. Compare the areas of the two grills: Rich and Marcy's grill is still larger than mine. I have not kept up with the Joneses.

Means-ends analysis appears to be a relatively common method of solving problems (Greeno, 1973; Newell & Simon, 1972), and is most likely to be used when the goal is clearly specified (Sweller & Levine, 1982). However, a potential disadvantage of this approach is that, by attending to only one subgoal at a time, one may lose sight of the problem as a whole (Sweller & Levine, 1982).

Working Backward. Consider this game, similar to one described by Wickelgren (1974):

> There are 21 pennies on a table. Two players, Mary and Susan, take turns removing pennies from the table; in any given turn, a player must take one, two, or three pennies. The player who removes the last penny from the table wins the game and keeps all 21 pennies. Mary begins by taking two pennies. What strategy can Susan use to be sure that she wins the game?

See if you can solve the problem before reading further.

The problem is solved by beginning at the *end* of the game, at the point where Susan removes the last penny, and then going backward to the first move. In what situation will Mary be in the position of allowing Susan to win? Remember, each player can remove one, two, or three pennies on a turn. Let's look at the solution as a series of steps:

1. Mary must be forced into the situation where she has to leave one, two, or three pennies on the table. Susan can then take them all, and victory is hers.

2. If, on the preceding turn, Susan leaves 4 pennies, then Mary's options are such that she must leave one to three pennies on her turn.

3. For Susan to leave four pennies, Mary must, on the previous turn, leave five, six, or seven pennies.

4. For Mary to leave five to seven pennies, Susan must leave eight pennies for Mary to choose from.

If the steps are continued in this manner, then a pattern emerges: Susan must always leave a number divisible by four. Therefore, when Mary removes two pennies, leaving nineteen on the table, Susan should take 3 pennies.

The method I used to help Susan figure out how to win the game every time illustrates the process of *working backward* (e.g., Matlin, 1983; Newell, Shaw, & Simon, 1958; Wickelgren, 1974). This strategy is one of beginning at the problem goal and then working backward, one step at a time, toward the initial problem state. In each step backward, the individual identifies one or more conditions that would produce the present condition. In a sense, working backward is the opposite approach to that of means-ends analysis.

Working backward is frequently used in solving algebra and geometry proofs. Students are given an initial situation—a formula or a geometric configuration with certain characteristics—then are asked to prove how another formula or another characteristic (the goal) must also be true through a series of mathematically logical steps. Sometimes it is easier to move logically from the goal backward to the initial state, and, mathematically speaking, this approach is just as valid.

Drawing Analogies. See if you can solve this problem originally used by Duncker (1945) and adapted by Gick and Holyoak (1980):

> Suppose you are a doctor faced with a patient who has a malignant tumor in his stomach. It is impossible to operate on the patient, but unless the tumor is destroyed the patient will die. There is a kind of ray that can be used to destroy the tumor. If the rays reach the tumor all at once at a sufficiently high intensity, the tumor will be destroyed. Unfortunately, at this intensity the healthy tissue that the rays pass through on the way to the tumor will also be destroyed. At lower intensities the rays are harmless to healthy tissue, but they will not affect the tumor either. What type of procedure might be used to destroy the tumor with the rays, and at the same time avoid destroying the healthy tissue? (Gick & Holyoak, 1980, p. 307–308).

If you are having difficulty with the problem, then consider this situation:

> A general wishes to capture a fortress located in the center of a country. There are many roads radiating outward from the fortress. All have been mined so that, while small groups of men can pass over the roads safely, any large force will detonate the mines. A full-scale direct attack is therefore impossible. The general's solution is to divide his army into small groups, send each group to the head of a different road, and have the groups converge simultaneously on the fortress (Gick & Holyoak, 1980, p. 309).

Now go back to the tumor problem. Perhaps the general's strategy in capturing the fortress has given you an idea about how to destroy the tumor. It can be destroyed by shooting a number of low-intensity rays from different directions, such that they all converge on the tumor simultaneously. Gick and Holyoak found that subjects were much more likely to solve the tumor problem when they had first read the solution to the fortress problem, because the two problems can be solved in analogous ways.

Drawing an analogy between a problem situation and another situation sometimes provides insights into how a problem can be solved. As another example, consider this problem presented to the Greek scientist Archimedes sometime around 250 B.C. (Bendick, 1962):

> King Hiero had ordered a crown of pure gold from the local goldsmith. He suspected that the goldsmith had cheated him by replacing some of the gold with silver, a cheaper metal. The only way to determine the goldsmith's honesty was to compare the crown's weight against its volume. Any metal has a particular volume for any given weight, and that ratio is different for each metal. The crown could be weighed easily enough. But how could its volume be measured?

Archimedes was pondering the problem one day as he stepped into his bathtub. He watched the bathwater rise and, through analogy, immediately identified a solution to the king's problem: the crown's volume could be determined by placing it in a container of water and measuring the amount of water that was displaced.

The major drawback to using analogies as a problem-solving strategy is that analogous situations are seldom retrieved when individuals are in a particular problem situation. The fact is, people rarely use analogies in solving problems (Reed, Ernst, & Banerji, 1974). When they do, it is often because they serendipitously encounter both the problem and the analogous situation at the same time. In other words, it may often be a matter of luck, of just happening to think of the right thing at the right time.

Shortcut Heuristics: Representativeness and Availability. Klein (1987) has described two shortcut problem-solving strategies that are executed quickly and simply; unfortunately, they often lead to inaccurate solutions. *Representativeness* (also described by Kahneman & Tversky, 1972, 1973) involves jumping to conclusions about a solution based on obvious characteristics of the problem. Let me illustrate by adapting a problem used by Kahneman and Tversky (1973). Imagine that I have a stack of one-hundred personality profiles on thirty engineers and seventy lawyers, all of whom are successful in their careers. I pull this description randomly from the pile:

> Jack is a forty-five-year-old man. He is married and has four children. He is generally conservative, careful, and ambitious. He shows no interest in political and social issues and spends most of his free time on his many hobbies, which include home carpentry, sailing, and mathematical puzzles (Kahneman & Tversky, 1973, p. 241).

Now for the problem: What is the probability that this man is one of the thirty engineers?

The probability that the man is an engineer is thirty percent, because there were thirty engineers among the stack of one-hundred individuals. Yet many subjects in the Kahneman and Tversky study gave a higher figure; they jumped to a conclusion based on obvious characteristics about Jack that many people associate stereotypically with engineers (e.g., conservatism and enjoyment of mathematical puzzles).

A second short-cut heuristic, *availability,* is a strategy wherein a problem is solved based only on information that comes immediately to mind (i.e., is retrieved from long-term memory) when the problem is encountered. Typically, the problem will be solved using recently acquired information rather than information acquired in the distant past, because recent experiences are more likely to be retrieved than ones from long ago. For example, imagine that you are trying to decide whether to go to California or Florida for a sunny March vacation at the beach. You learned many years ago that Florida has more rainfall than California. In February, just as you are about to make your choice, you hear on the news that California has just been drenched in a heavy rainstorm. You may easily book a flight to Florida, retrieving the available information about the California rainstorm rather than the overall frequency of rainfall in the two states.

At this point, we have surveyed a variety of different problem-solving strategies. Because many problems have no right or wrong solutions, there may be no single "best" strategy that can be applied in solving them. Obviously, different strategies are appropriate in different situations. But one way of discovering which strategies are most effective is to observe how experts solve problems in their fields of expertise. We turn now to differences in problem-solving behavior of *experts* and of nonexperts (*novices*).

Expert/Novice Differences in Problem Solving

Numerous instances have been observed in which experts and novices solve problems in qualitatively different ways. At least two generalizations can be made about the factors that lead to the more successful problem-solving performance of experts.

First of all, how individuals approach a problem—how they encode it and what strategy they choose in trying to solve it—depends on how they classify the problem. Experts and novices seems to classify problems differently (Anderson, 1985; Chi, Feltovich, & Glaser, 1981; Larkin, 1980; Schoenfeld & Herrmann, 1982). Experts generally classify a problem on the basis of abstract concepts, principles, patterns, and schemas that can be applied to its solution. Novices, on the other hand, tend to focus on specific parts of a problem and to retrieve information related only to those aspects. To illustrate, Schoenfeld and Herrmann (1982) compared the ways in which mathematics professors and students classified a variety of mathematical problems. Professors classified the problems on the basis of abstract principles related to their solution: for example, those solved by analogy were grouped together, as were those solved by contradiction, and so on. Students, on the other hand, classified the problems on the basis of more superficial characteristics, such as whether they contained polynomial expressions or whether they included figures from plane geometry. After a course in mathematics, the students were asked to repeat the classification task; at this point, they began to classify the problems more like their professors, that is, on the basis of principles involved in problem solution.

This difference between experts and novices in classifying problems is undoubtedly related to a second difference: experts have a more complete and better organized knowledge base for the problems they solve (Anderson, 1985; Cochran, 1988; Good & Brophy, 1986; Voss, Greene, Post, & Penner, 1983). For example, Cochran (1988) examined the achievement (much of which involved problem solving) of high school physics students studying a unit on electricity. The higher achievers were students who had better organized information about concepts in electricity in their long-term memories; not only did they know better which concepts should be associated with which, but they also knew the particular relationships that different concepts had with one another. Low achievers were often uncertain about just how the different aspects of electricity fit together and were more often wrong about how the concepts interrelated.

How can educators help students become more expert at both transfer and problem solving? Let's turn now to the topic of facilitating transfer and problem solving in educational settings.

FACILITATING TRANSFER AND PROBLEM SOLVING IN THE CLASSROOM

Unfortunately, students often do not see the relevance of what they have learned in school to new school tasks or to real-life problems (Gick & Holyoak, 1987). Thus, a major objective of our educational system is probably not being achieved. At the same time, students sometimes erroneously apply what they have learned to situations in which it is not appropriate—a case of negative transfer.

Learning theorists are only beginning to understand the complex activities of transfer and problem solving. Nevertheless, theories and research in both areas provide numerous suggestions for educational practice.

Students need to learn information meaningfully and thoroughly. Theorists agree that a solid knowledge base is a prerequisite for successful transfer and problem solving (Ausubel et al., 1978; Frederiksen, 1984; Greeno, 1973; Mayer, 1975; Norman, 1980; Reif & Heller, 1982; Simon, 1980; Simon & Hayes, 1976). My daughter struggles through homework problems involving the equivalence of fractions because she still has not mastered the basic idea of what fractions *are*. I encourage her to persevere only because such work with fractions is a required part of the school curriculum, but I would be very surprised if she could apply the procedures to any real-world situations. And so, in the back of my mind, I have to wonder: what's the point?

Oftentimes our classrooms have long lists of topics that must be taught, and as a result no single topic is taught very thoroughly. Breadth of coverage occurs at the expense of depth of coverage—and at the expense of successful transfer and problem solving as well.

Some prerequisite skills should be learned to the point of automaticity (Frederiksen, 1984; Gagné, 1982). Remember that problem solving occurs in a component of memory that has a limited capacity, such that only so much information can be held and only so much processing can occur at any single point in time. To the extent that students can process more basic aspects of a problem automatically, thereby using only a minimal amount of short-term memory capacity in processing those aspects, greater capacity can be devoted to the more novel and difficult parts of the problem.

Numerous and varied examples and opportunities for practicing transfer and problem solving should be provided (Bourne et al., 1986; Chase & Chi, 1980; Cormier, 1987; Ellis, 1978; Frederiksen, 1984; Gagné & Driscoll, 1988). Experience with many practice examples promotes associations in long-term memory between newly learned information and a variety of relevant situations; hence, that information is more likely to be retrieved when it is needed later on. For example, in an experiment by Pepper (1981), students studied computer programming techniques from one of three instructional booklets. Two booklets were taken from actual programming textbooks. The third was a modified text in which simple examples were inserted to illustrate all major points and most minor ones; it was therefore longer and wordier than either of the other booklets. Despite its length, the example-filled booklet was liked most by students and led to the highest performance on an examination (eighty-three percent for the example-filled booklet, vs. fifty-eight percent to sixty-seven percent for the other two booklets).

To minimize negative transfer, differences between two tasks should be emphasized. Insects and spiders are similar stimuli—they are both small arthropods with exoskeletons and a generally creepy-crawly nature—and so students may inappropriately transfer what they know about one group of creepy-crawlies to the other. For similar stimuli, negative transfer can be reduced if differences are emphasized rather than similarities. For instance, there are numerous differences between insects and spiders (e.g., six legs vs. eight legs, three body parts vs. two, antennae vs. no antennae) that, if emphasized, could reduce negative transfer from one group to the other. Additionally, if negative transfer between two tasks is anticipated, it can be reduced by teaching the two tasks in different environments (Bilodeau & Schlosberg, 1951; Greenspoon & Ranyard, 1957)—for example, by teaching students about insects while sitting in the classroom, and teaching them about spiders while on a field trip to the natural history museum.

Problem-solving skills are sometimes better learned through a discovery approach. Although expository teaching is in many cases the most efficient means of transmitting information to students in an organized fashion, instructional approaches that emphasize guided discovery learning may facilitate better transfer of problem-solving skills to new situations (Gagné & Brown, 1961; Mayer, 1974; Roughead & Scandura, 1968). Discovery is probably most appropriate when problems are ill-structured and students have a solid knowledge base (Doyle, 1983; Frederiksen, 1984). However, for well-structured problems that can be solved by a specific algorithm (e.g., long division problems), and for students relatively unsophisticated about a particular topic, direct instruction of the algorithm may be preferable (Frederiksen, 1984; R. Gagné, 1985).

Teaching general learning and problem-solving skills may be helpful. As I indicated in Chapter 13, training in study skills can be effective and appears to improve achievement in a variety of areas. At the same time, remember that not everything will apply to everything else: Latin will help a student learn physics only to the extent that, while studying Latin, the student develops better learning strategies that are also applicable to the study of physics.

Many theorists believe that teaching general problem-solving strategies can be useful (e.g., E. Gagné, 1985; Glaser, 1979; Herrnstein, Nickerson, de Sánchez, & Swets, 1986; Mayer, 1987; Resnick, 1976; Schoenfeld, 1979; Simon, 1980). A recent study by Herrnstein et al. (1986) has provided some optimism about the effectiveness of training problem-solving skills. Seventh-grade Venezuelan students who took a year-long course in reasoning, problem solving, and decision-making skills showed greater improvement in both the specific skills taught and general intellectual ability than did students in an untrained control group.

Several problem-solving strategies may be transferable to a wide variety of problem situations. One helpful strategy is talking aloud about the problem (Gagné & Smith, 1962; Stinessen, 1975); a second is using paper and pencil to diagram a problem or list its components (Ellis & Hunt, 1983; Wickelgren, 1974). Still a third is brainstorming (e.g., Osborn, 1963), a technique that involves thinking of as many hypothetical problem solutions as possible without initially evaluating any of them. The absence of evaluation when generating ideas can potentially facilitate a broader search of long-term memory for unusual and creative possibilities. After a long and seemingly exhaustive list of problem solutions has been generated, the individual critically examines the various solutions for workable and unworkable ones.

Some theorists (e.g., Anderson, 1985; Ellis & Hunt, 1983; Wallas, 1926) have suggested that the incubation of a problem—letting it remain unsolved in memory for a period of time—can be a helpful strategy, although there are mixed reviews on its effectiveness (Anderson, 1985; Bourne et al., 1986; Dominowski & Jenrick, 1972). The benefits of an incubation period are more likely to be evident for difficult problems than for easy ones. For one thing, some of the factors that interfere with problem solving, such as fatigue and anxiety, may diminish during the incubation period (Ellis & Hunt, 1983). In addition, the individual may find more appropriate mental sets or more relevant information in long-term memory after leaving the problem alone for a time (Anderson, 1985; Ellis & Hunt, 1983).

Students need to learn strategies for defining ill-defined problems. As Frederiksen (1984) has pointed out, most problems presented in the classroom are well-defined. Students are asked to identify the protagonist and antagonist in a story, use a dictionary to find two different pronunciations of the word *wind*, or calculate how many candy bars six boys can each have if there are eighteen bars altogether. On the other hand, most real-world problems are ill-defined. People need to find viable means of home financing, decide what life insurance policy to purchase (if any), and maintain friendly and productive relationships with obnoxious work associates.

Ill-defined problems often require an individual to search outside sources to find relevant and potentially helpful information (Simon, 1978). Students should therefore be well versed in techniques for finding information through such resources as libraries, computer data bases, and government agencies. Students should also be taught techniques for more precisely defining ill-defined problems; for example, one helpful technique is to break a larger problem into a number of subproblems, and to define and impose constraints on each of those subproblems (Reitman, 1965; Simon, 1973). Finally, to the extent that students possess a solid knowledge base, they will be better able to define the problems they encounter (Frederiksen, 1984).

If transfer and problem solving are instructional objectives, then students' ability to apply what they have learned should be evaluated. Too many classroom tests emphasize the learning of specific facts. Basic knowledge and skills are important and form the foundation for more sophisticated academic behaviors, but students should also be asked to demonstrate their ability to apply what they have learned to a variety of situations, so that successful transfer and problem solving become common phenomena rather than rare occurrences.

Educators must always remember that teaching for effective transfer and problem solving takes time. Too often, schools seem to rush through the curriculum at the expense of providing sufficient practice at any one point along the way. Educators should probably slow down and give children time to use and apply the information and skills they learn. Students are likely to accomplish more over the long run.

SUMMARY

Transfer is the process of applying what has been learned in one situation to one's learning or performance in another situation. Several theories of transfer have been proposed; current views incorporate basic notions of information processing theory. Among the factors that facilitate transfer are meaningful learning, degree of learning, situation similarity, and retrieval of relevant information in the transfer situation.

Problem solving is a form of transfer, in that previously learned information is applied to resolve a problem situation. Problems can be solved through either algorithms (procedures that guarantee correct solutions) or heuristics (shortcuts without guaranteed outcomes). Both behaviorist and cognitive theories of problem solving have been proposed, with information processing theory being predominant at present; such cognitive factors as short-term memory capacity, encoding, and retrieval influence problem solving success. People employ numerous problem-solving strategies that are differentially applicable to different kinds of problems; experts often use different strategies than novices. Our understanding of how transfer and problem-solving occur should influence classroom practice.

R E F E R E N C E S

Adams, J. A. (1980). *Learning and memory* (rev. ed.). Homewood, IL: Dorsey.

Adams, P. A., & Adams, J. K. (1960). Confidence in the recognition and reproduction of words difficult to spell. *American Journal of Psychology, 73,* 544–552.

Alexander, L., Frankiewicz, R., & Williams, R. (1979). Facilitation of learning and retention of oral instruction using advance and post organizers. *Journal of Educational Psychology, 71,* 701–707.

Alford, G. S., & Rosenthal, T. L. (1973). Process and products of modeling in observational concept attainment. *Child Development, 44,* 714–720.

Allington, R. (1988, April). Questions as a learning device. In R. Peterson (Chair), *What do we know about learning from textbooks? Part I.* Symposium conducted at the American Educational Research Association, New Orleans, LA.

Anderson, J. R. (1974). Retrieval of propositional information from long-term memory. *Cognitive Psychology, 6,* 451–474.

Anderson, J. R. (1976). *Language, memory, and thought.* Hillsdale, NJ: Erlbaum.

Anderson, J. R. (1982). Acquisition of cognitive skill. *Psychological Review, 89,* 369–406.

Anderson, J. R. (1983a). *The architecture of cognition.* Cambridge, MA: Harvard University Press.

Anderson, J. R. (1983b). A spreading activation theory of memory. *Journal of Verbal Learning and Verbal Behavior, 22,* 261–295.

Anderson, J. R. (1984). Spreading activation. In J. R. Anderson & S. M. Kosslyn (Eds.), *Tutorials in learning and memory.* San Francisco: Freeman.

Anderson, J. R. (1985). *Cognitive psychology and its implications* (2nd ed.). New York: Freeman.

Anderson, J. R., & Bower, G. H. (1973). *Human associative memory.* Washington, DC: Winston.

Anderson, R. C., & Biddle, B. (1975). On asking people questions about what they are reading. In G. H. Bower (Ed.), *Psychology of learning and motivation* (Vol. 9). New York: Academic Press.

Anderson, R. C., Reynolds, R. E., Schallert, D. L., & Goetz, E. T. (1977). Frameworks for comprehending discourse. *American Educational Research Journal, 14,* 367–381.

Andre, T. (1979). Does answering higher-level questions while reading facilitate productive learning? *Review of Educational Research, 49,* 280–318.

Andre, T. (1986). Problem solving and education. In G. D. Phye & T. Andre (Eds.), *Cognitive classroom learning: Understanding, thinking, and problem solving.* Orlando, FL: Academic Press.

Anglin, J. M. (1977). *Word, object, and conceptual development.* New York: Norton.

Anker, A. L., & Crowley, T. J. (1982). Use of contingency contracts in specialty clinics for cocaine abuse. *National Institute on Drug Abuse: Research Monograph Series, 4,* 452–459.

Appel, J. B., & Peterson, N. J. (1965). Punishment: Effects of shock intensity on response suppression. *Psychological Reports, 16,* 721–730.

Armbruster, B. (1988, April). Questions in content area textbooks: Do they function? In R. Peterson (Chair), *What do we know about learning from textbooks? Part I.* Symposium conducted at the American Educational Research Association, New Orleans, LA.

Atkinson, J. W. (1958). *Motives in fantasy, action, and sobriety.* Princeton, NJ: Van Nostrand.

Atkinson, R. C. (1975). Mnemotechnics in second-language learning. *American Psychologist, 30,* 821–828.

Atkinson, R. C., & Shiffrin, R. M. (1968). Human memory: A proposed system and its control processes. In K. W. Spence & J. T. Spence (Eds.), *The psychology of learning and motivation: Advances in research and theory,* (Vol. 2). New York: Academic Press.

Atkinson, R. C., & Shiffrin, R. M. (1971). The control of short-term memory. *Scientific American, 225* (2), 82–90.

Attneave, A. (1957). Transfer of experience with a class schema to identification learning of patterns and shapes. *Journal of Experimental Psychology, 54,* 81–88.

Ausubel, D. P. (1963). *The psychology of meaningful verbal learning.* New York: Grune & Stratton.

Ausubel, D. P. (1968). *Educational psychology: A cognitive view.* New York: Holt, Rinehart & Winston.

Ausubel, D. P., Novak, J. D., & Hanesian, H. (1978). Educational psychology: A cognitive view (2nd ed.). New York: Holt, Rinehart & Winston.

Ausubel, D. P., & Robinson, F. G. (1969). *School learning: An introduction to educational psychology.* New York: Holt, Rinehart & Winston.

Ayllon, T., Layman, D., & Kandel, H. J. (1975). A behavioral-educational alternative to drug control of hyperactive children. *Journal of Applied Behavior Analysis, 8,* 137–146.

Azrin, N. H. (1960). Effects of punishment intensity during variable-interval reinforcement. *Journal of the Experimental Analysis of Behavior, 3,* 123–142.

Azrin, N. H. (1967, May). Pain and aggression. *Psychology Today, 1,* 27–33.

Azrin, N. H., & Holz, W. C. (1966). Punishment. In W. K. Honig (Ed.), *Operant behavior: Areas of research and application.* New York: Appleton-Century-Crofts.

Baddeley, A. D. (1978). The trouble with levels: A reexamination of Craik and Lockhart's framework for memory research. *Psychological Review, 85,* 139–152.

Baddeley, A. D., & Hitch, G. (1974). Working memory. In G. H. Bower (Ed.), *The psychology of learning and motivation* (Vol. 8). New York: Academic Press.

Bahrick, H. P. (1984). Semantic memory content in permastore: Fifty years of memory for Spanish learned in school. *Journal of Experimental Psychology: General, 113,* 1–29.

Bandura, A. (1965a). Behavioral modification through modeling practices. In L. Krasner & L. Ullman (Eds.), *Research in behavior modification*. New York: Holt, Rinehart & Winston.

Bandura, A. (1965b). Influence of models' reinforcement contingencies on the acquisition of imitative responses. *Journal of Personality and Social Psychology, 1*, 589–595.

Bandura, A. (1969). *Principles of behavior modification*. New York: Holt, Rinehart, & Winston.

Bandura, A. (1973). *Aggression: A social learning analysis*. Englewood Cliffs, NJ: Prentice-Hall.

Bandura, A. (1974). Behavior theory and the models of man. *American Psychologist, 33*, 859–869.

Bandura, A. (1977). *Social learning theory*. Englewood Cliffs, NJ: Prentice-Hall.

Bandura, A. (1982). Self-efficacy mechanism in human agency. *American Psychologist, 37*, 122–147.

Bandura, A. (1986). *Social foundations of thought and action*. Englewood Cliffs, NJ: Prentice-Hall.

Bandura, A., Grusec, J. E., & Menlove, F. L. (1966). Observational learning as a function of symbolization and incentive set. *Child Development, 37*, 499–506.

Bandura, A., & Jeffery, R. W. (1973). Role of symbolic coding and rehearsal processes in observational learning. *Journal of Personality and Social Psychology, 26*, 122–130.

Bandura, A., Jeffery, R. W., & Bachicha, D. L. (1974). Analysis of memory codes and cumulative rehearsal in observational learning. *Journal of Research in Personality, 7*, 295–305.

Bandura, A., & Kupers, C. J. (1964). Transmission of patterns of self-reinforcement through modeling. *Journal of Abnormal and Social Psychology, 69*, 1–9.

Bandura, A., & McDonald, F. J. (1963). Influences of social reinforcement and the behavior of models in shaping children's moral judgments. *Journal of Abnormal and Social Psychology, 67*, 274–281.

Bandura, A., & Perloff, B. (1967). Relative efficacy of self-monitored and externally imposed reinforcement systems. *Journal of Personality and Social Psychology, 7*, 111–116.

Bandura, A., Ross, D., & Ross, S. A. (1961) Transmission of aggression through imitation of aggressive models. *Journal of Abnormal and Social Psychology, 63*, 575–582.

Bandura, A., Ross, D., & Ross, S. A. (1963). Imitation of film-mediated aggressive models. *Journal of Abnormal and Social Psychology, 66*, 3–11.

Bandura, A., & Walters, R. H. (1963). *Social learning and personality development*. New York: Holt, Rinehart & Winston.

Bandura, A., & Whalen, C. K. (1966). The influence of antecedent reinforcement and divergent modeling cues on patterns of self-reward. *Journal of Personality and Social Psychology, 3*, 373–382.

Barringer, C., & Gholson, B. (1979). Effects of type and combination of feedback upon conceptual learning by children: Implications for research in academic learning. *Review of Educational Research, 49*, 459–478.

Barrish, H. H., Saunders, M., & Wolf, M. M. (1969). Good behavior game: Effects of individual contingencies for group consequences on disruptive behavior in a classroom. *Journal of Applied Behavior Analysis, 2*, 119–124.

Barth, R. (1979). Home-based reinforcement of school behavior: A review and analysis. *Review of Educational Research, 49*, 436–458.

Bartlett, F. C. (1932). *Remembering: A study in experimental and social psychology.* Cambridge, England: Cambridge University Press.

Baumrind, D. (1983). Rejoinder to Lewis's reinterpretation of parental firm control effects: Are authoritative families really harmonious? *Psychological Bulletin, 94*, 132–142.

Bechterev, V. M. (1913). *The psychologie objective.* Paris: Alcan.

Beck, I. L., & McKeown, M. G. (1988). Toward meaningful accounts in history texts for young learners. *Educational Researcher, 47* (6), 31–39.

Becker, W. C. (1971). *Parents are teachers.* Champaign, IL: Research Press.

Becker, W. C., Madsen, C. H., Arnold, C. R., & Thomas, D. R. (1967). The contingent use of teacher attention and praise in reducing classroom behavior problems. *Journal of Special Education, 1*, 287–307.

Bee, H. (1985). *The developing child* (4th ed.). New York: Harper & Row.

Behr, M., & Harel, G. (1988, April). Cognitive conflict in procedure applications. In D. Tirosh (Chair), *The role of inconsistent ideas in learning mathematics.* Symposium conducted at the annual meeting of American Educational Research Association, New Orleans, LA.

Bell-Gredler, M. E. (1986). *Learning and instruction: Theory into practice.* New York: Macmillan.

Bendick, J. (1962). *Archimedes and the door of science.* New York: Franklin Watts.

Beneke, W. N., & Harris, M. B. (1972). Teaching self-control of study behavior. *Behaviour Research and Therapy, 10*, 35–41.

Berkowitz, L., & LePage, A. (1967). Weapons as aggression-eliciting stimuli. *Journal of Personality and Social Psychology, 7*, 202–207.

Berlyne, D. E. (1960). *Conflict, arousal, and curiosity.* New York: McGraw-Hill.

Bersh, P. J. (1951). The influence of two variables upon the establishment of a secondary reinforcer for operant responses. *Journal of Experimental Psychology, 41*, 62–73.

Bilodeau, I. M., & Schlosberg, H. (1951). Similarity in stimulating conditions as a variable in retroactive inhibition. *Journal of Experimental Psychology, 41*, 199–204.

Birch, H. G., & Rabinowitz, H. S. (1951). The negative effect of previous experience on productive thinking. *Journal of Experimental Psychology, 41*, 121–125.

Birnbaum, J. C. (1982). The reading and composing behaviors of selected fourth- and seventh-grade students. *Research in the Teaching of English, 16*, 241–260.

Bjork, R. A. (1972). Theoretical implications of directed forgetting. In A. W. Melton & E. Martin (Eds.), *Coding processes in human memory.* Washington, DC: Winston.

Bloom, B. S., Englehart, M. B., Furst, E. J., Hill, W. H., & Krathwohl, D. R. (1956). *Taxonomy of educational objectives. The classification of educational goals. Handbook I: Cognitive domain.* New York: Longman Green.

Bobango, J. C. (1988, April). The effect of phase-based instruction on high school geometry students' van Hiele levels and achievement. Paper presented at the American Educational Research Association, New Orleans, LA.

Bobrow, S., & Bower, G. H. (1969). Comprehension and recall of sentences. *Journal of Experimental Psychology, 80,* 455–461.

Boe, E. E., & Church, R. M. (1967). Permanent effects of punishment during extinction. *Journal of Comparative and Physiological Psychology, 63,* 486–492.

Bolles, R. C. (1975). *Theory of motivation* (2nd ed.). New York: Harper & Row.

Bolstad, O., & Johnson, S. (1972). Self-regulation in the modification of disruptive classroom behavior. *Journal of Applied Behavior Analysis, 5,* 443–454.

Born, D. G., & Davis, M. L. (1974). Amount and distribution of study in a personalized instruction course and in a lecture course. *Journal of Applied Behavior Analysis, 7,* 365–375.

Bourne, L. E., Jr. (1967). Learning and utilization of conceptual rules. In B. Kleinmuntz (Ed.), *Concepts and the structure of memory.* New York: Wiley.

Bourne, L. E., Jr. (1982). Typicality effects in logically defined concepts. *Memory and Cognition, 10,* 3–9.

Bourne, L. E., Jr., Dominowski, R. L., Loftus, E. F., & Healy, A. F. (1986). *Cognitive processes* (2nd ed.). Englewood Cliffs, NJ: Prentice-Hall.

Bourne, L. E., Jr., Ekstrand, D. R., & Dominowski, R. L. (1971). *The psychology of thinking.* Englewood Cliffs, NJ: Prentice-Hall.

Bousfield, W. A. (1953). The occurrence of clustering in the recall of randomly arranged associates. *Journal of General Psychology, 49,* 229–240.

Bower, G. H. (1972). Mental imagery and associative learning. In L. W. Gregg (Ed.), *Cognition in learning and memory.* New York: Wiley.

Bower, G. H., Black, J. B., & Turner, T. J. (1979). Scripts in memory for text. *Cognitive Psychology, 11,* 177–220.

Bower, G. H., & Clark, , M. C. (1969). Narrative stories as mediators for serial learning. *Psychonomic Science, 14,* 181–182.

Bower, G. H., Clark, M. C., Lesgold, A. M., & Winzenz, D. (1969). Hierarchical retrieval schemes in recall of categorized word lists. *Journal of Verbal Learning and Verbal Behavior, 8,* 323–343.

Bower, G. H., & Hilgard, E. R. (1981). *Theories of learning* (5th ed.). Englewood Cliffs, NJ: Prentice-Hall.

Bower, G. H., & Holyoak, K. J. (1973). Encoding and recognition memory for naturalistic sounds. *Journal of Experimental Psychology, 101,* 360–366.

Bower, G. H., Karlin, M. B., & Dueck, A. (1975). Comprehension and memory for pictures. *Memory and Cognition, 3,* 216–220.

Bower, G. H., & Springston, F. (1970). Pauses as recoding points in letter series. *Journal of Experimental Psychology, 83,* 421–430.

Bragstad, B. J., & Stumpf, S. M. (1982). *A guidebook for teaching study skills and motivation.* Boston: Allyn and Bacon.

Bramel, D., Taub, B., & Blum, B. (1968). An observer's reaction to the suffering of his enemy. *Journal of Personality and Social Psychology, 8,* 384–392.

Bransford, J. D., & Franks, J. J. (1971). The abstraction of linguistic ideas. *Cognitive Psychology, 2,* 331–350.

Bransford, J. D., & Johnson, M. K. (1972). Contextual prerequisites for understanding: Some investigations of comprehension and recall. *Journal of Verbal Learning and Verbal Behavior, 11,* 717–726.

Braukmann, C. J., Kirigin, K. A., & Wolf, M. M. (1981). Behavioral treatment of juvenile delinquency. In S. W. Bijou & R. Ruiz (Eds.), *Behavior modification: Contributions to education.* Hillsdale, NJ: Erlbaum.

Breitmeyer, B. B., & Ganz, L. (1976). Implications of sustained and transient channels for theories of visual pattern masking, saccadic suppression, and information processing. *Psychological Review, 83,* 1–36.

Brewer, W. F., & Treyens, J. C. (1981). Role of schemata in memory for places. *Cognitive Psychology, 13,* 207–230.

Briggs, L. J., & Reed, H. B. (1943). The curve of retention for substance material. *Journal of Experimental Psychology, 32,* 513–517.

Broadbent, D. E. (1958). *Perception and communication.* London: Pergamon Press.

Broden, M., Hall, R. V., & Mitts, B. (1971). The effect of self-recording on the classroom behavior of two eighth grade students. *Journal of Applied Behavior Analysis, 4,* 191–199.

Bronfenbrenner, U. (1970). *Two worlds of childhood: U.S. and U.S.S.R.* New York: Russell Sage Foundation.

Brooke, R. R., & Ruthren, A. J. (1984). The effects of contingency contracting on student performance in a PSI class. *Teaching of Psychology, 11,* 87–89.

Brooks, L. R. (1978). Nonanalytic concept formation and memory for instances. In E. Rosch & B. B. Lloyd (Eds.), *Cognition and categorization.* Hillsdale, NJ: Erlbaum.

Brooks, L. W., & Dansereau, D. F. (1987). Transfer of information: An instructional perspective. In S. M. Cormier & J. D. Hagman (Eds.), *Transfer of learning: Contemporary research and applications.* San Diego: Academic Press.

Brown, A. L. (1978). Knowing when, where, and how to remember: A problem of metacognition. In R. Glaser (Ed.), *Advances in instructional psychology,* Hillsdale, NJ: Erlbaum.

Brown, A. L., Campione, J., & Day, J. (1981). Learning to learn: On training students to learn from texts. *Educational Researcher, 10* (2), 14–21.

Brown, J. (1968). Reciprocal facilitation and impairment of free recall. *Psychonomic Science, 10,* 41–42.

Brown, R., & Herrnstein, R. J. (1975). *Psychology.* Boston: Little, Brown.

Brown, R., & McNeill, D. (1966). The "tip of the tongue" phenomenon. *Journal of Verbal Learning and Verbal Behavior, 5,* 325–337.

Bruner, J. S. (1957). On going beyond the information given. In *Contemporary approaches to cognition.* Cambridge, MA: Harvard University Press.

Bruner, J. S. (1961a). The act of discovery. *Harvard Educational Review, 31,* 21–32.

Bruner, J. S. (1961b). *The process of education.* Cambridge, MA: Harvard University Press.

Bruner, J. S. (1966). *Toward a theory of instruction.* New York: Norton.

Bruner, J. S., Goodnow, J., & Austin, G. (1956). *A study of thinking.* New York: Wiley.

Bryan, J. H. (1975). Children's cooperation and helping behaviors. In E. M. Hetherington (Ed.), *Review of child development research* (Vol. 5). Chicago: University of Chicago Press.

Buckhout, R. (1974). Eyewitness testimony. *Scientific American, 231* (6), 23–31.

Buckland, P. R. (1968). The ordering of frames in a linear program. *Programmed Learning and Educational Technology, 5,* 197–205.

Bufford, R. K. (1976). Evaluation of a reinforcement procedure for accelerating work rate in a self-paced course. *Journal of Applied Behavior Analysis, 9,* 208.

Bugelski, B. R. (1962). Presentation time, total time, and mediation in paired-associate learning. *Journal of Experimental Psychology, 63,* 409–412.

Bugelski, B. R., & Alampay, D. A. (1961). The role of frequency in developing perceptual sets. *Canadian Journal of Psychology, 15,* 205–211.

Bugelski, B. R., Kidd, E., & Segmen, J. (1968). Image as a mediator in one-trial paired-associate learning. *Journal of Experimental Psychology, 76,* 69–73.

Bushell, D., Wrobel, P. A., & Michaelis, M. L. (1968). Applying "group" contingencies to the classroom study behavior of preschool children. *Journal of Applied Behavior Analysis, 1,* 55–61.

Calfee, R. (1981). Cognitive psychology and educational practice. In D. C. Berliner (Ed.), *Review of Research in Education* (Vol. 9). Washington, DC: American Educational Research Association.

Carmichael, L., Hogan, H. P., & Walters, A. A. (1932). An experimental study of the effect of language on the reproduction of visually perceived form. *Journal of Experimental Psychology, 15,* 73–86.

Catania, A. C. (1985). The two psychologies of learning: Blind alleys and nonsense syllables. In S. Koch & D. E. Leary (Eds.), *A century of psychology as science.* New York: McGraw-Hill.

Catania, A. C., & Reynolds, G. S. (1968). A quantitative analysis of the responding maintained by interval schedules of reinforcement. *Journal of the Experimental Analysis of Behavior, 11,* 327–383.

Cavanaugh, J. C., & Perlmutter, M. (1982). Metamemory: A critical examination. *Child Development, 53,* 11–28.

Cermak, L. S., & Craik, F. I. M. (Eds.). (1979) *Levels of processing in human memory.* Hillsdale, NJ: Erlbaum.

Champagne, A. B., Klopfer, L. E., & Gunstone, R. F. (1982). Cognitive research and the design of science instruction. *Educational Psychologist, 17,* 31–53.

Chase, W. G., & Chi, M. T. H. (1980). Cognitive skill: Implications for spatial skill in large-scale environments. In J. Harvey (Ed.), *Cognition, social behavior, and the environment.* Potomac, MD: Erlbaum.

Chase, W. G., & Simon, H. A. (1973). Perception in chess. *Cognitive Psychology, 4*, 55–81.

Cheng, P. W. (1985). Restructuring versus automaticity: Alternative accounts of skill acquisition. *Psychological Review, 92*, 414–423.

Cheng, P. W., Holyoak, K. J., Nisbett, R. E., & Oliver, L. M. (1986). Pragmatic versus syntactic approaches to training deductive reasoning. *Cognitive Psychology, 18*, 293–328.

Cherry, E. C. (1953). Some experiments on the recognition of speech, with one and with two ears. *Journal of the Acoustical Society of America, 25*, 975–979.

Cheyne, J. A., & Walters, R. H. (1970). Punishment and prohibition: Some origins of self-control. In T. M. Newcomb (Ed.), *New directions in psychology*. New York: Holt, Rinehart & Winston.

Chi, M., Feltovich, P., & Glaser, R. (1981). Categorization and representation of physics problems by experts and novices. *Cognitive Science, 5*, 121–152.

Chiesi, H. L., Spilich, G. J., & Voss, J. F. (1979). Acquisition of domain-related information in relation to high and low domain knowledge. *Journal of Verbal Learning and Verbal Behavior, 18*, 257–273.

Chomsky, N. (1957). *Syntactic structures*. The Hague: Mouton.

Christen, F., & Bjork, R. A. (1976). On updating the loci in the method of loci. Paper presented at the annual meeting of the Psychonomic Society, St. Louis, MO.

Clark, D. C. (1971). Teaching concepts in the classroom: A set of teaching prescriptions derived from experimental research. *Journal of Educational Psychology, 62*, 253–278.

Coates, B., & Hartup, W. W. (1969). Age and verbalization in observational learning. *Developmental Psychology, 1*, 556–562.

Cochran, K. F. (1988, April). Cognitive structure representation in physics. Paper presented at the annual meeting of American Educational Research Association New Orleans, LA.

Cofer, C. (1971). Properties of verbal materials and verbal learning. In J. Kling & L. Riggs (Eds.), *Woodworth and Schlosberg's experimental psychology*. New York: Holt, Rinehart & Winston.

Collier, G., Hirsh, E., & Hamlin, P. H. (1972). The ecological determinants of reinforcement in the rat. *Physiology and Behavior, 9*, 705–716.

Collins, A. M., & Loftus, E. F. (1975). A spreading-activation theory of semantic processing. *Psychological Review, 82*, 407–428.

Collins, A. M., & Quillian, M. R. (1969). Retrieval time from semantic memory. *Journal of Verbal Learning and Verbal Behavior, 8*, 240–247.

Collins, A. M., & Quillian, M. R. (1972). How to make a language user. In E. Tulving & W. Donaldson (Eds.), *Organization of memory*. New York: Academic Press.

Coltheart, M., Lea, C. D., & Thompson, K. (1974). In defense of iconic memory. *Quarterly Journal of Experimental Psychology, 26*, 633–641.

Conrad, R. (1962). An association between memory errors and errors due to acoustic masking of speech. *Nature, 193*, 1314–1315.

Conrad, R. (1964). Acoustic confusions in immediate memory. *British Journal of Psychology, 55*, 75–84.

Conrad, R. (1971). The chronology of the development of covert speech in children. *Developmental Psychology, 5,* 398–405.

Conrad, R. (1972). Short-term memory in the deaf: A test for speech coding. *British Journal of Psychology, 63,* 173–180.

Conrad, R., & Hull, A. J. (1964). Information, acoustic confusion, and memory span. *British Journal of Psychology, 55,* 429–432.

Cook, L. K. (1983). Instructional effects of text structure-based reading strategies on the comprehension of scientific prose. (Doctoral dissertation, University of California, Santa Barbara.) *Dissertation Abstracts International, 44,* 2411A.

Cooper, L. A., & Shepard, R. N. (1973). The time required to prepare for a rotated stimulus. *Memory and Cognition, 1,* 246–250.

Cormier, S. M. (1987). The structural processes underlying transfer of training. In S. M. Cormier & J. D. Hagman (Eds.), *Transfer of learning: Contemporary research and applications.* San Diego: Academic Press.

Cormier, S. M., & Hagman, J. D. (1987). Introduction. In S. M. Cormier & J. D. Hagman (Eds.), *Transfer of learning: Contemporary research and applications.* San Diego: Academic Press.

Corte, H. E., Wolf, M. E., & Locke, B. J. (1971). A comparison of procedures for eliminating self-injurious behavior of retarded adolescents. *Journal of Applied Behavior Analysis, 4,* 201–214.

Craik, F. I. M., & Lockhart, R. S. (1972). Levels of processing: A framework for memory research. *Journal of Verbal Learning and Verbal Behavior, 11,* 671–684.

Craik, F. I. M., & Tulving, E. (1975). Depth of processing and the retention of words in episodic memory. *Journal of Experimental Psychology: General, 104,* 268–294.

Craik, F. I. M., & Watkins, M. J. (1973). The role of rehearsal in short-term memory. *Journal of Verbal Learning and Verbal Behavior, 12,* 598–607.

Crespi, L. P. (1942). Quantitative variation of incentive and performance in the white rat. *American Journal of Psychology, 55,* 467–517.

Crowder, N. A., & Martin, G. (1961). *Trigonometry.* Garden City, NY: Doubleday.

Crowley, T. J. (1984). Contingency contracting treatment of drug-abusing physicians, nurses, and dentists. *National Institute on Drug Abuse: Research Monograph Series, 46,* 68–83.

Cuvo, A. J. (1975). Developmental differences in rehearsal and free recall. *Journal of Experimental Child Psychology, 19,* 65–78.

Dallett, K. M. (1964). Implicit mediators in paired-associate learning. *Journal of Verbal Learning and Verbal Behavior, 3,* 209–214.

D'Amato, M. R. (1955). Secondary reinforcement and magnitude of primary reinforcement. *Journal of Comparative and Physiological Psychology, 48,* 378–380.

D'Amato, M. R. (1970). *Experimental psychology: Methodology, psychophysics, and learning.* New York: McGraw-Hill.

Daneman, M., & Carpenter, P. A. (1980). Individual differences in working memory and reading. *Journal of Verbal Learning and Verbal Behavior, 19,* 450–466.

Dansereau, D. F., Collins, K. W., McDonald, B. A., Holley, C. D., Garland, J. C., Diekhoff, G., & Evans, S. H. (1979). Development and evaluation of a learning strategy training program. *Journal of Educational Psychology, 71,* 64–73.

Darley, J. M., & Gross, P. H. (1983). A hypothesis-confirming bias in labeling effects. *Journal of Personality and Social Psychology, 44,* 20–33.

Darwin, C. J., Turvey, M. T., & Crowder, R. G. (1972). An auditory analogue of the Sperling partial report procedure: Evidence for brief auditory storage. *Cognitive Psychology, 3,* 255–267.

Davis, G. A. (1966). Current status of research and theory in human problem solving. *Psychological Bulletin, 66,* 36–54.

deCharms, R. (1968). *Personal causation.* New York: Academic Press.

Deci, E. L. (1971). Effects of externally mediated rewards on intrinsic motivation. *Journal of Personality and Social Psychology, 18,* 105–115.

Deci, E. L., & Porac, J. (1978). Cognitive evaluation theory and the study of human motivation. In M. R. Lepper & D. Greene (Eds.), *The hidden costs of reward.* Hillsdale, NJ: Erlbaum.

deGroot, A. D. (1965). *Thought and choice in chess.* The Hague: Mouton.

Dempster, F. N., & Rohwer, W. D. (1974). Component analysis of the elaborative encoding effect in paired-associate learning. *Journal of Experimental Psychology, 103,* 400–408.

Denny, M. R., & Weisman, R. G. (1964). Avoidance behavior as a function of the length of nonshock confinement. *Journal of Comparative and Physiological Psychology, 58,* 252–257.

Deregowski, J. B. (1972). Pictorial perception and culture. *Scientific American, 227* (5), 82–88.

DeVries, R. (1969). Constancy of generic identity in the years three to six. *Monographs of the Society for Research in Child Development, 34* (Whole No. 127).

Dinsmoor, J. A. (1954). Punishment: I. The avoidance hypothesis. *Psychological Review, 61,* 34–46.

Dinsmoor, J. A. (1955). Punishment: II. An interpretation of empirical findings. *Psychological Review, 62,* 96–105.

DiVesta, F. J., & Ingersoll, G. M. (1969). Influence of pronounceability, articulation, and test mode on paired-associate learning by the study-recall procedure. *Journal of Experimental Psychology, 79,* 104–108.

Doctorow, M., Wittrock, M. C., & Marks, C. (1978). Generative processes in reading comprehension. *Journal of Educational Psychology, 70,* 109–118.

Dodd, D. H., & White, R. M. (1980). *Cognition: Mental structures and processes.* Boston: Allyn and Bacon.

Dominowski, R. L., & Jenrick, R. (1972). Effects of hints and interpolated activity on solution of an insight problem. *Psychonomic Science, 26,* 335–338.

Dooling, D. J., & Christiaansen, R. E. (1977). Episodic and semantic aspects of memory for prose. *Journal of Experimental Psychology: Human Learning and Memory, 3,* 428–436.

Dowaliby, F. J., & Schumer, H. (1973). Teacher-centered vs. student-centered mode of college classroom instruction is related to manifest anxiety. *Journal of Educational Psychology, 64*, 125–132.

Downs, R. M., & Stea, D. (1977). *Maps in minds*. New York: Harper & Row.

Doyle, W. (1983). Academic work. *Review of Educational Research, 53*, 159–199.

Drabman, R. S. (1976). Behavior modification in the classroom. In W. E. Craighead & M. J. Mahoney (Eds.), *Behavior modification principles, issues, and applications*. Boston: Houghton Mifflin.

Drabman, R. S., & Spitalnik, R. (1973). Social isolation as a punishment procedure: A controlled study. *Journal of Experimental Child Psychology, 16*, 236–249.

Dressel, P. L. (1977). The nature and role of objectives in instruction. *Educational Technology, 17*(5), 7–15.

DuBois, N. F. (1987, April). Training students to become autonomous learners. Paper presented at American Educational Research Association, Washington, DC.

DuBois, N. F., Kiewra, K. A., & Fraley, J. (1988, April). Differential effects of a learning strategy course. Paper presented at American Educational Research Association, New Orleans, LA.

Duell, O. K. (1986). Metacognitive skills. In G. D. Phye & T. Andre (Eds.), *Cognitive classroom learning: Understanding, thinking, and problem solving*. Orlando, FL: Academic Press.

DuNann, D. G., & Weber, S. J. (1976). Short- and long-term effects of contingency managed instruction on low, medium, and high GPA students. *Journal of Applied Behavior Analysis, 9*, 375–376.

Duncker, K. (1945). On problem solving. *Psychological Monographs, 58* (Whole No. 270).

Dunn, C. S. (1983). The influence of instructional methods on concept learning. *Science Education, 67*, 647–656.

Dyer, H. S. (1967). The discovery and development of educational goals. *Proceedings of the 1966 Invitational Conference on Testing Problems*. Princeton, NJ: Educational Testing Service.

Eaton, J. F., Anderson, C. W., & Smith, E. L. (1984). Students' misconceptions interfere with science learning: Case studies of fifth-grade students. *Elementary School Journal, 84*, 365–379.

Ebbinghaus, H. (1913). *Memory: A contribution to experimental psychology* (H. A. Ruger & C. E. Bussenius, trans.). New York: Teachers College Press. (Original work published 1885.)

Ebert, J. D., Loewy, A. G., Miller, R. S., & Schneiderman, H. A. (1973). *Biology*. New York: Holt, Rinehart & Winston.

Elliott, R., & Vasta, R. (1970). The modeling of sharing: Effects associated with vicarious reinforcement, symbolization, age, and generalization. *Journal of Experimental Child Psychology, 10*, 8–15.

Ellis, H. C. (1978). *Fundamentals of human learning, memory, and cognition* (2nd ed.). Dubuque, IA: William C. Brown.

Ellis, H. C., & Hunt, R. R. (1983). *Fundamentals of human memory and cognition* (3rd ed.). Dubuque, IA: William C. Brown.

English, H. B., Welborn, E. L., & Killian, C. D. (1934). Studies in substance memorization. *Journal of General Psychology, 11,* 233–260.

Epstein, H. (1978). Growth spurts during brain development: Implications for educational policy and practice. In J. Chall & A. Mirsky (Eds.), *Education and the brain: The 77th yearbook of the National Society for the Study of Education, Part II.* Chicago: University of Chicago Press.

Estes, W. K. (1969a). New perspectives on some old issues in association theory. In N. J. Mackintosh & W. K. Honig (Eds.), *Fundamental issues in associative learning.* Halifax, Canada: Dalhousie University Press.

Estes, W. K. (1969b). Outline of a theory of punishment. In B. A. Campbell & R. M. Church (Eds.), *Punishment and aversive behavior.* New York: Appleton-Century-Crofts.

Evans, G. W., & Oswalt, G. L. (1968). Acceleration of academic progress through the manipulation of peer influence. *Behaviour Research and Therapy, 6,* 189–195.

Fagen, J. W., & Rovee, C. K. (1976). Effects of qualitative shifts in a visual reinforcer in the instrumental response of infants. *Journal of Experimental Child Psychology, 21,* 349–360.

Fantino, E. (1973). Aversive control. In J. A. Nevin & G. S. Reynolds (Eds.), *The study of behavior.* Glenview, IL: Scott, Foresman.

Farnham-Diggory, S. (1972). The development of equivalence systems. In S. Farnham-Diggory (Ed.), *Information processing in children.* New York: Academic Press.

Faust, G. W., & Anderson, R. C. (1967). Effects of incidental material in a programmed Russian vocabulary lesson. *Journal of Educational Psychology, 58,* 3–10.

Feldhusen, J. F. (1963). Taps for teaching machines. *Phi Delta Kappan, 44,* 265–267.

Ferster, C. B., & Skinner, B. F. (1957). *Schedules of reinforcement.* Englewood Cliffs, NJ: Prentice-Hall.

Fisk, A. D. (1986). Frequency encoding is not inevitable and is not automatic: A reply to Hasher & Zacks. *American Psychologist, 41,* 215–216.

Fitzsimmons, R. J., & Loomer, B. M. (1977). *Spelling research and practice.* Des Moines, IA: Iowa State Department of Public Instruction.

Flaherty, C. F. (1985). *Animal learning and cognition.* New York: Knopf.

Flavell, J. H. (1963). *The developmental psychology of Jean Piaget.* New York: Van Nostrand Reinhold.

Flavell, J. H. (1976). Metacognitive aspects of problem solving. In L. B. Resnick (Ed.), *The nature of intelligence.* Hillsdale, NJ: Erlbaum.

Flavell, J.H. (1985) *Cognitive development* (2nd ed.). Englewood Cliffs, NJ: Prentice-Hall.

Flavell, J. H., Friedrichs, A. G., & Hoyt, J. D. (1970). Developmental changes in memorization processes. *Cognitive Psychology, 1,* 324–340.

Flavell, J. H., & Wellman, H. M. (1977). Metamemory. In R. V. Kail, Jr., & J. W. Hagen (Eds.), *Perspectives on the development of memory and cognition.* Hillsdale, NJ: Erlbaum.

Fleishman, E. A. (1987). Foreword. In S. M. Cormier & J. D. Hagman (Eds.), *Transfer of learning: Contemporary research and applications.* San Diego: Academic Press.

Fong, G. T., Krantz, D. H., & Nisbett, R. E. (1986). The effects of statistical training on thinking about everyday problems. *Cognitive Psychology, 18,* 253–292.

Foxx, R. M., & Shapiro, S. T. (1978). The timeout ribbon: A nonexclusionary timeout procedure. *Journal of Applied Behavior Analysis, 11,* 125–136.

Franks, J. J., & Bransford, J. D. (1971). Abstraction of visual patterns. *Journal of Experimental Psychology, 90,* 65–74.

Frase, L. T. (1975). Prose processing. In G. H. Bower (Ed.), *The psychology of learning and motivation* (Vol. 9). New York: Academic Press.

Frederiksen, N. (1984). Implications of cognitive theory for instruction in problem-solving. *Review of Educational Research, 54,* 363–407.

Freiburgs, V., & Tulving, E. (1961). The effect of practice on utilization of information from positive and negative instances in concept identification. *Canadian Journal of Psychology, 15,* 101–106.

Freud, S. (1922). *Beyond the pleasure principle.* London: International Psychoanalytic Press.

Friedrich, L. K., & Stein, A. H. (1973). Aggressive and pro-social television programs and the natural behavior of preschool children. *Society for Research in Child Development Monographs, 38* (Whole No. 151).

Frith, U. (1978). From print to meaning and from print to sound, or how to read without knowing how to spell. *Visible Language, 12,* 43–54.

Frith, U. (1980). Unexpected spelling problems. In U. Frith (Ed.), *Cognitive processes in spelling.* London: Academic Press.

Furst, E. J. (1981). Bloom's taxonomy of educational objectives for the cognitive domain: Philosophical and educational issues. *Review of Educational Research, 51,* 441–453.

Gage, N. L., & Berliner, D. C. (1984). *Educational psychology* (3rd ed.) Boston: Houghton Mifflin.

Gagné, E. D. (1985). *The cognitive psychology of school learning.* Boston: Little, Brown.

Gagné, R. M. (1982). Developments in learning psychology: Implications for instructional design; and effects of computer technology on instructional design and development. *Educational Technology, 22* (6), 11–15.

Gagné, R. M. (1983). Some issues in the psychology of mathematics instruction. *Journal of Research in Mathematics Education, 14* (1), 7–18.

Gagné, R. M. (1985). *The conditions of learning and theory of instruction* (4th ed.). New York: Holt, Rinehart & Winston.

Gagné, R. M., Briggs, L. J., & Wager, W. W. (1988). *Principles of instructional design* (3rd ed.). New York: Holt, Rinehart & Winston.

Gagné, R. M., & Brown, L. T. (1961). Some factors in the programming of conceptual learning. *Journal of Experimental Psychology, 62*, 313–321.

Gagné, R. M., & Driscoll, M. P. (1988). *Essentials of learning for instruction* (2nd ed.). Englewood Cliffs, NJ: Prentice-Hall.

Gagné, R. M., & Smith, E. C. (1962). A study of the effects of verbalization on problem solving. *Journal of Experimental Psychology, 63*, 12–18.

Garb, J. L., & Stunkard, A. J. (1974). Taste aversions in man. *American Journal of Psychiatry, 131*, 1204–1207.

Gardner, M. (1978). *Aha! Insight.* New York: Scientific American.

Gasper, K. L. (1980). The student perspective. *Teaching Political Science, 7*, 470–471.

Gerst, M. S. (1971). Symbolic coding processes in observational learning. *Journal of Personality & Social Psychology, 19*, 7–17.

Gibson, E., & Rader, N. (1979). Attention: The perceiver as performer. In G. A. Hale & M. Lewis (Eds.), *Attention and cognitive development.* New York: Plenum Press.

Gick, M. L., & Holyoak, K. J. (1980). Analogical problem solving. *Cognitive Psychology, 12*, 306–355.

Gick, M. L., & Holyoak, K. J. (1983). Schema induction and analogical transfer. *Cognitive Psychology, 15*, 1–38.

Gick, M. L., & Holyoak, K. J. (1987). The cognitive basis of knowledge transfer. In S. M. Cormier & J. D. Hagman (Eds.), *Transfer of learning: Contemporary research and applications.* San Diego: Academic Press.

Gillingham, M. G., Garner, R., & Wright, J. (1988, April). Adults confuse importance and interestingness in expository text. Paper presented at the American Educational Research Association, New Orleans, LA.

Glanzer, M., & Cunitz, A. R. (1966). Two storage mechanisms in free recall. *Journal of Verbal Learning and Verbal Behavior, 5*, 351–360.

Glaser, R. (1979). Trends and research questions in psychological research on learning and schooling. *Educational Researcher, 8*, 6–13.

Glass, A. L., & Holyoak, K. J. (1975). Alternative conceptions of semantic memory. *Cognition, 3*, 313–339.

Glass, A. L., Holyoak, K. J., & O'Dell, C. (1974). Production frequency and the verification of quantified statements. *Journal of Verbal Learning and Verbal Behavior, 13*, 237–254.

Glass, A. L., Holyoak, K. J., & Santa, J. L. (1979). *Cognition.* Reading, MA: Addison-Wesley.

Gleitman, H. (1985). Some trends in the study of cognition. In S. Koch & D. E. Leary (Eds.), *A century of psychology as science.* New York: McGraw-Hill.

Glenberg, A. (1976). Monotonic and nonmonotonic lag effects in paired-associated and recognition memory paradigms. *Journal of Verbal Learning and Verbal Behavior, 15*, 1–16.

Glover, J., & Gary, A. L. (1976). Procedures to increase some aspects of creativity. *Journal of Applied Behavior Analysis, 9*, 79–84.

Glucksberg, S. (1962). The influence of strength of drive on functional fixedness and perceptual recognition. *Journal of Experimental Psychology, 63*, 36–41.

Glucksberg, S., & Weisberg, R. W. (1966). Verbal behavior and problem solving: Some effects of labeling in a functional fixedness problem. *Journal of Experimental Psychology, 71*, 659–664.

Glueck, S., & Glueck, E. (1950). *Unraveling juvenile delinquency.* Cambridge, MA: Harvard University Press.

Glynn, S. M., & DiVesta, F. J. (1977). Outline and hierarchical organization as aids for study and retrieval. *Journal of Educational Psychology, 69*, 89–95.

Godden, D. R., & Baddeley, A. D. (1975). Context-dependent memory in two natural environments: On land and underwater. *British Journal of Psychology, 66*, 325–332.

Good, T. L. (1987). Two decades of research on teacher expectations: Findings and future directions. *Journal of Teacher Education, 38* (4), 32–47.

Good, T. L., & Brophy, J. E. (1984). *Looking in classrooms.* New York: Harper & Row.

Good, T. L., & Brophy, J. E. (1986). *Educational psychology: A realistic approach.* New York: Longman.

Gorman, A. M. (1961). Recognition memory for nouns as a function of abstractness and frequency. *Journal of Experimental Psychology, 61*, 23–29.

Grabe, M. (1986). Attentional processes in education. In G. D. Phye & T. Andre (Eds.), *Cognitive classroom learning: Understanding, thinking, and problem solving.* Orlando, FL: Academic Press.

Gray, J. A., & Wedderburn, A. A. I. (1960). Grouping strategies with simultaneous stimuli. *Quarterly Journal of Experimental Psychology, 12*, 180–184.

Gray, W. D., & Orasanu, J. M. (1987). Transfer of cognitive skills. In S. M. Cormier & J. D. Hagman (Eds.), *Transfer of learning: Contemporary research and applications.* San Diego: Academic Press.

Greeno, J. G. (1973). The structure of memory and the process of solving problems. In R. L. Solso (Ed.), *Contemporary issues in cognitive psychology: The Loyola Symposium.* Washington, DC: Winston.

Greenspoon, J., & Ranyard, R. (1957). Stimulus conditions and retroactive inhibition. *Journal of Experimental Psychology, 53*, 55–59.

Greer, R. D. (1983). Contingencies of the science and technology of teaching and pre-behavioristic research practices in education. *Educational Researcher, 12*(1), 3–9.

Greiner, J. M., & Karoly, P. (1976). Effects of self-control training on study activity and academic performance: An analysis of self-monitoring, self-reward, and systematic planning components. *Journal of Counseling Psychology, 23*, 495–502.

Grimes, J. W., & Allinsmith, W. (1961). Compulsivity, anxiety and school achievement. *Merrill-Palmer Quarterly, 7*, 247–271.

Groninger, L. D. (1971). Mnemonic imagery and forgetting. *Psychonomic Science, 23*, 161–163.

Gross, T. F., & Mastenbrook, M. (1980). Examination of the effects of state anxiety on problem-solving efficiency under high and low memory conditions. *Journal of Educational Psychology, 72,* 605–609.

Guthrie, E. R. (1935). *The psychology of learning.* New York: Harper & Row.

Guthrie, E. R. (1942). Conditioning: A theory of learning in terms of stimulus, response, and association. In *The psychology of learning,* 41st Yearbook of the National Society for the Study of Education, Part II. Chicago: University of Chicago Press.

Hale, G. A. (1983). Students' predictions of prose forgetting and the effects of study strategies. *Journal of Educational Psychology, 75,* 708–715.

Hall, J. F. (1966). *The psychology of learning.* Philadelphia: Lippincott.

Hall, J. F. (1971). *Verbal learning and retention.* Philadelphia: Lippincott.

Hall, R. V., Axelrod, S., Foundopoulos, M., Shellman, J., Campbell, R. A., & Cranston, S. S. (1971). The effective use of punishment to modify behavior in the classroom. *Educational Technology, 11* (4), 24–26. Reprinted in K. D. O'Leary & S. O'Leary (Eds.) (1972), *Classroom management: The successful use of behavior modification.* New York: Pergamon Press.

Hallahan, D. P., Marshall, K. J., & Lloyd, J. W. (1981). Self-recording during group instruction: Effects of attention to task. *Learning Disabilities Quarterly, 4,* 407–413.

Hansen, J., & Pearson, P. D. (1983). An instructional study: Improving the inferential comprehension of good and poor fourth-grade readers. *Journal of Educational Psychology, 75,* 821–829.

Harari, H., & McDavid, J. W. (1973). Name stereotypes and teachers' expectations. *Journal of Educational Psychology, 65,* 222–225.

Haring, T. G., Roger, B., Lee, M., Breen, C., & Gaylord-Ross, R. (1986). Teaching social language to moderately handicapped students. *Journal of Applied Behavior Analysis, 19,* 159–171.

Harlow, H. F. (1949). The formation of learning sets. *Psychological Review, 56,* 51–65.

Harlow, H. F. (1950). Analysis of discrimination learning by monkeys. *Journal of Experimental Psychology, 40,* 26–39.

Harlow, H. F. (1959). Learning set and error factor theory. In S. Koch (Ed.), *Psychology: A study of science.* New York: McGraw-Hill.

Harlow, H. F., & Zimmerman, R. R. (1959). Affectional responses in the infant monkey. *Science, 130,* 421–432.

Harris, K. R. (1986). Self-monitoring of attentional behavior versus self-monitoring of productivity: Effects of on-task behavior and academic response rate among learning disabled children. *Journal of Applied Behavior Analysis, 19,* 417–423.

Harris, M. (1985). Visualization and spelling competence. *Journal of Developmental Education, 9* (2), 2–5; 31.

Harris, R. J. (1977). Comprehension of pragmatic implications in advertising. *Journal of Applied Psychology, 62,* 603–608.

Harris, V. W., & Sherman, J. A. (1973). Use and analysis of the "Good Behavior Game" to reduce disruptive classroom behavior. *Journal of Applied Behavior Analysis, 6,* 405–417.

Harter, S. (1983). Developmental perspectives on the self-system. In E. M. Hetherington (Ed.), *Handbook of child psychology. Vol. 4: Socialization, personality, and social development.* New York: Wiley.

Hasher, L., & Zacks, R. T. (1984). Automatic processing of fundamental information. *American Psychologist, 39,* 1372–1388.

Hastings, W. M. (1977). In praise of regurgitation. *Intellect, 105,* 349–350.

Hayes, K. J., & Hayes, C. (1952). Imitation in a home-raised chimpanzee. *Journal of Comparative and Physiological Psychology, 45,* 450–459.

Hayes, S. C., Rosenfarb, I., Wulfert, E., Munt, E. D., Korn, Z., & Zettle, R. D. (1985). Self-reinforcement effects: An artifact of social standard setting? *Journal of Applied Behavior Analysis, 18,* 201–214.

Hayes-Roth, B., & Thorndyke, P. W. (1979). Integration of knowledge from text. *Journal of Verbal Learning and Verbal Behavior, 18,* 91–108.

Haygood, R. C., & Bourne, L. E., Jr. (1965). Attribute- and rule-learning aspects of conceptual behavior. *Psychological Review, 72,* 175–195.

Henle, M. (1985). Rediscovering gestalt psychology. In S. Koch & D. E. Leary (Eds.), *A century of psychology as science.* New York: McGraw-Hill.

Herbert, J. J., & Harsh, C. M. (1944). Observational learning by cats. *Journal of Comparative Psychology, 37,* 81–95.

Hergenhahn, B.R. (1988) *An introduction to theories of learning* (3rd ed.). Englewood Cliffs, NJ: Prentice Hall.

Herrnstein, R. J. (1969). Method and theory in the study of avoidance. *Psychological Review, 76,* 49–69.

Herrnstein, R. J. (1977). The evolution of behaviorism. *American Psychologist, 32,* 593–603.

Herrnstein, R. J., Nickerson, R. S., de Sánchez, M., & Swets, J. A. (1986). Teaching thinking skills. *American Psychologist, 41,* 1279–1289.

Hess, R. D., & McDevitt, T. M. (1984). Some cognitive consequences of maternal intervention techniques: A longitudinal study. *Child Development, 55,* 2017–2030.

Higbee, K. L. (1976). Can young children use mnemonics? *Psychological Reports, 38,* 18.

Hildreth, G. (1955). *Teaching spelling.* New York: Holt.

Hillerich, R. L. (1976). *Spelling: An element in written expression.* Columbus, OH: Merrill Publishing Co.

Hintzman, D. L. (1978). *The psychology of learning and memory.* San Francisco: Freeman.

Hiroto, D. S. (1974). Locus of control and learned helplessness. *Journal of Experimental Psychology, 102,* 187–193.

Hiroto, D. S., & Seligman, M. E. P. (1975). Generality of learned helplessness in man. *Journal of Personality and Social Psychology, 31,* 311–327.

Hobbs, T. R., & Holt, M. M. (1976). The effects of token reinforcement on the behavior of delinquents in cottage settings. *Journal of Applied Behavior Analysis, 9,* 189–198.

Hockman, C. H., & Lipsitt, L. P. (1961). Delay-of-reward gradients in discrimination learning with children for two levels of difficulty. *Journal of Comparative and Physiological Psychology, 54,* 24–27.

Hokanson, J. E., & Burgess, M. (1962). The effects of three types of aggression on vascular processes. *Journal of Abnormal and Social Psychology, 64,* 446–449.

Holley, C. D., & Dansereau, D. F. (1984). The development of spatial learning strategies. In C. D. Holley & D. F. Dansereau (Eds.), *Spatial learning strategies.* Orlando, FL: Academic Press.

Holley, C. D., Dansereau, D. F., McDonald, B. A., Garland, J. C., & Collins, K. W. (1979). Evaluation of a hierarchical mapping technique as an aid to prose processing. *Contemporary Educational Psychology, 4,* 227–237.

Holz, W. C., & Azrin, N. H. (1962). Recovery during punishment by intense noise. *Psychological Reports, 11,* 655–657.

Homme, L. E., Csanyi, A. P., Gonzales, M. A., & Rechs, J. R. (1970). *How to use contingency contracting in the classroom.* Champaign, IL: Research Press.

Homme, L. W., deBaca, P. C., Devine, J. V., Steinhorst, R., & Rickert, E. J. (1963). Use of the Premack principle in controlling the behavior of nursery school children. *Journal of the Experimental Analysis of Behavior, 6,* 544.

Hopkins, R. H., & Atkinson, R. C. (1968). Priming and the retrieval of names from long-term memory. *Psychonomic Science, 11,* 219–220.

Horn, E. (1919). Principles of methods in teaching spelling as derived from scientific investigation. *Eighteenth Yearbook of the National Society for the Study of Education, Part II.* Bloomington, IN: Public School Publishing.

Hovland, C. I., & Weiss, W. (1953). Transmission of information concerning concepts through positive and negative instances. *Journal of Experimental Psychology, 43,* 175–182.

Howard, D. V. (1983). *Cognitive psychology: Memory, language, and thought.* New York: Macmillan.

Howe, M. J. A. (1970). Using students' notes to examine the role of the individual learner in acquiring meaningful subject matter. *Journal of Educational Research, 64,* 61–63.

Howe, M. J. A. (1980). *The psychology of human learning.* New York: Harper & Row.

Hudspeth, W. J. (1985). Developmental neuropsychology: Functional implications of quantitative EEG maturation. [Abstract] *Journal of Clinical and Experimental Neuropsychology, 7,* 606.

Hull, C. L. (1920). Quantitative aspects of the evolution of concepts: An experimental study. *Psychological Monographs, 28,* (Whole No. 123).

Hull, C. L. (1934). The concept of the habit-family hierarchy and maze learning. *Psychological Review, 41,* 33–54.

Hull, C. L. (1937). Mind, mechanism, and adaptive behavior. *Psychological Review, 44,* 1–32.

Hull, C. L. (1938). The goal-gradient hypothesis applied to some "field-force" problems in the behavior of young children. *Psychological Review, 45,* 271–299.

Hull, C. L. (1943). *Principles of behavior: An introduction to behavior theory.* New York: Appleton-Century-Crofts.

Hull, C. L. (1951). *Essentials of behavior.* New Haven, CT: Yale University Press.

Hull, C. L. (1952). *A behavior system: An introduction to behavior theory concerning the individual organism.* New Haven, CT: Yale University Press.

Humphreys, L. G. (1939). Acquisition and extinction of verbal expectations in a situation analogous to conditioning. *Journal of Experimental Psychology, 25,* 294–301.

Hundert, J. (1976). The effectiveness of reinforcement, response cost, and mixed programs on classroom behaviors. *Journal of Applied Behavior Analysis, 9,* 107.

Hunt, E. B. (1962). *Concept learning: An information processing problem.* New York: Wiley.

Hyde, T. S., & Jenkins, J. J. (1969). Differential effects of incidental tasks on the organization of recall of a list of highly associated words. *Journal of Experimental Psychology, 82,* 472–481.

Inhelder, B., & Piaget, J. (1958). *The growth of logical thinking from childhood to adolescence.* (A. Parsons & S. Milgram, Trans.) New York: Basic Books.

Iwata, B. A. (1987). Negative reinforcement in applied behavior analysis: An emerging technology. *Journal of Applied Behavior Analysis, 20,* 361–378.

Iwata, B. A., & Bailey, J. S. (1974). Reward versus cost token systems: An analysis of the effects on students and teacher. *Journal of Applied Behavior Analysis, 7,* 567–576.

James, W. (1890). *Principles of psychology.* New York: Holt.

Jenkins, J. J., & Russell, W. A. (1952). Associative clustering during recall. *Journal of Abnormal and Social Psychology, 47,* 818–821.

Johnson, M. K., Bransford, J. D., & Solomon, S. K. (1973). Memory for tacit implications of sentences. *Journal of Experimental Psychology, 98,* 203–205.

Johnson, R. E. (1975). Meaning in complex learning. *Review of Educational Research, 45,* 425–459.

Johnson, T. D., Langford, K. G., & Quorn, K. C. (1981). Characteristics of an effective spelling program. *Language Arts, 58,* 581–588.

Johnson-Laird, P. N., & Wason, P. C. (1977). Introduction to conceptual thinking. In P. N. Johnson-Laird & P. C. Wason (Eds.), *Thinking: Readings in cognitive science.* Cambridge, England: Cambridge University Press.

Jones, B. F., & Hall, J. W. (1982). School applications of the mnemonic keyword method as a study strategy by eighth graders. *Journal of Educational Psychology, 74,* 230–237.

Jones, H. E., & English, H. B. (1926). Notional vs. rote memory. *American Journal of Psychology, 37,* 602–603.

Jones, M. C. (1924). The elimination of children's fears. *Journal of Experimental Psychology, 7,* 382–390.

Judd, C. H. (1932). Autobiography. In C. Murchison (Ed.), *History of psychology in autobiography* (Vol. 2). Worcester MA: Clark University Press.

Kahneman, D. (1973). *Attention and effort.* Englewood Cliffs, NJ: Prentice-Hall.

Kahneman, D., & Tversky, A. (1972). Subjective probability: A judgment of representativeness. *Cognitive Psychology, 3,* 430–454.

Kahneman, D., & Tversky, A. (1973). On the psychology of prediction. *Psychological Review, 80,* 237–251.

Kamin, L. J. (1956). The effects of termination of the CS and avoidance of the US on avoidance learning. *Journal of Comparative and Physiological Psychology, 49,* 420–424.

Kamin, L. J., Brimer, C. J., & Black, A. H. (1963). Conditioned suppression as a monitor of fear of the CS in the course of avoidance training. *Journal of Comparative and Physiological Psychology, 56,* 497–501.

Kaufman, A., Baron, A., & Kopp, R. E. (1966). Some effects of instructions on human operant behavior. *Psychonomic Monograph Supplements, 1,* 243–250.

Kazdin, A. E. (1972). Response cost: The removal of conditional reinforcers for therapeutic change. *Behavior Therapy, 3,* 533–546.

Keele, S. W., & Chase, W. G. (1967). Short-term visual storage. *Perception and Psychophysics, 2,* 383–385.

Keller, F. S. (1968). Goodbye teacher. *Journal of Applied Behavior Analysis, 1,* 79–89.

Keller, F. S. (1974). An international venture in behavior modification. In F. S. Keller & E. Ribes-Inesta (Eds.), *Behavior modification: Applications to education.* New York: Academic Press.

Kendler, H. H. (1985). Behaviorism and psychology: An uneasy alliance. In S. Koch & D. E. Leary (Eds.), *A century of psychology as science.* New York: McGraw-Hill.

Kendler, H. H., & Kendler, T. S. (1961). Effect of verbalization on reversal shifts in children. *Science, 134,* 1619–1620.

Kendler, H. H., & Kendler, T. S. (1962). Vertical and horizontal processes in problem solving. *Psychological Review, 69,* 1–16.

Kendler, T. S. (1961). Concept formation. *Annual Review of Psychology, 13,* 447–472.

Kendler, T. S., & Kendler, H. H. (1959). Reversal and nonreversal shifts in kindergarten children. *Journal of Experimental Psychology, 58,* 56–60.

Keppel, G., & Underwood, B. J. (1962). Proactive inhibition in short-term retention of single items. *Journal of Verbal Learning and Verbal Behavior, 1,* 153–161.

Kiewra, K. A. (1985). Investigating notetaking and review: A depth of processing alternative. *Educational Psychologist, 20,* 23–32.

Kiewra, K. A., DuBois, N. F., Christian, D., McShane, A., Meyerhoffer, M., & Roskelly, D. (1988, April). Theoretical and practical aspects of taking, reviewing and borrowing conventional, skeletal or matrix lecture notes. Paper presented at American Educational Research Association, New Orleans, LA.

Kintsch, W., Mandel, T. S., & Kozminsky, E. (1977). Summarizing scrambled stories. *Memory and Cognition, 5,* 547–552.

Klatzky, R. L. (1975). *Human memory.* San Francisco: Freeman.

Klein, S. B. (1987). *Learning: Principles and Applications.* New York: McGraw-Hill.

Kletzien, S. B. (1988, April). Achieving and non-achieving high school readers' use of comprehension strategies for reading expository text. Paper presented at the American Educational Research Association, New Orleans, LA.

Knight, S. L. (1988, April). Examining the relationship between teacher behaviors and students' cognitive reading strategies. Paper presented at the American Educational Research Association, New Orleans, LA.

Koffka, K. (1935). *Principles of Gestalt psychology.* New York: Harcourt, Brace.

Kohler, I. (1962) Experiments with goggles. *Scientific American, 206* (5), 62–72.

Köhler, W. (1925). *The mentality of apes.* London: Routledge & Kegan Paul.

Köhler, W. (1929). *Gestalt psychology.* New York: Liveright.

Köhler, W. (1938). *The place of value in a world of facts.* New York: Liveright.

Köhler, W. (1940). *Dynamics in psychology.* New York: Liveright.

Köhler, W. (1947). *Gestalt psychology: An introduction to new concepts in modern psychology.* New York: Liveright.

Köhler, W. (1959). Gestalt psychology today. *American Psychologist, 14,* 727–734.

Köhler, W. (1969). *The task of Gestalt psychology.* Princeton, NJ: Princeton University Press.

Kosslyn, S. M., & Pomerantz, J. R. (1977). Imagery, propositions, and the form of internal representations. *Cognitive Psychology, 9,* 52–76.

Kreutzer, M. A., Leonard, C., & Flavell, J. H. (1975). Prospective remembering in children. *Monographs of the Society for Research in Child Development, 40* (Whole No. 159).

Krueger, W. C. F. (1929). The effect of overlearning on retention. *Journal of Experimental Psychology, 12,* 71–78.

Krumboltz, J. D., & Krumboltz, H. B. (1972). *Changing children's behavior.* Englewood Cliffs, NJ: Prentice-Hall.

Kulhavy, R. W., Peterson, S., & Schwartz, N. H. (1986). Working memory: The encoding process. In G. D. Phye & T. Andre (Eds.), *Cognitive classroom learning: Understanding, thinking, and problem solving.* Orlando, FL: Academic Press.

Kulhavy, R. W., Schwartz, N. H., & Shaha, S. H. (1983). Spatial representation of maps. *American Journal of Psychology, 96,* 337–351.

Kulik, J. A., & Kulik, C. C. (1988). Timing of feedback and verbal learning. *Review of Educational Research, 58,* 79–97.

Kulik, J. A., Kulik, C. C., & Cohen, P. A. (1979). A meta-analysis of outcome studies of Keller's Personalized System of Instruction. *American Psychologist, 34,* 307–318.

Kulik, J. A., Kulik, C. C., & Cohen, P. A. (1980). Effectiveness of computer-based college teaching: A meta-analysis of findings. *Review of Educational Research, 50,* 525–544.

LaBerge, D., & Samuels, S. J. (1974). Toward a theory of automatic information processing in reading. *Cognitive Psychology, 6,* 293–323.

Landauer, T. K. (1962). Rate of implicit speech. *Perceptual and Motor Skills, 15,* 646.

Lange, P. C. (1972). What's the score on programmed instruction? *Today's Education, 61,* 59.

Larkin, J. H. (1980). Teaching problem solving in physics: The psychological lab and the practical classroom. In D. T. Tuma & F. Reif (Eds.), *Problem solving and education: Issues in teaching and research.* Hillsdale, NJ: Erlbaum.

Leff, R. (1969). Effects of punishment intensity and consistency on the internalization of behavioral suppression in children. *Developmental Psychology, 1,* 345–356.

Leherissey, B. L., O'Neil, H. F., & Hansen, D. N. (1971). Effects of memory support on state anxiety and performance in computer-assisted learning. *Journal of Educational Psychology, 62,* 413–420.

Lepper, M. R., & Greene, D. (Eds.) (1978). *The hidden costs of reward.* Hillsdale, NJ: Erlbaum.

Lepper, M. R., Greene, D., & Nisbett, R. E. (1973). Understanding children's intrinsic interest with extrinsic rewards: A test of the "overjustification" hypothesis. *Journal of Personality and Social Psychology, 28,* 129–137.

Lett, B. T. (1973). Delayed reward learning: Disproof of the traditional theory. *Learning and Motivation, 4,* 237–246.

Lett, B. T. (1975). Long delay learning in the T-maze. *Learning and Motivation, 6,* 80–90.

Levin, G. R. (1983). *Child psychology.* Monterey, CA: Brooks/Cole.

Levin, J. R. (1981). The mnemonic '80s: Keywords in the classroom. *Educational Psychologist, 16,* 65–82.

Levin, J. R., McCormick, C. B., Miller, G. E., Berry, J. K., & Pressley, M. (1982). Mnemonic versus nonmnemonic vocabulary learning strategies for children. *American Educational Research Journal, 19,* 121–136.

Levine, M. A. (1966). Hypothesis behavior by humans during discrimination learning. *Journal of Experimental Psychology, 71,* 331–338.

Lewis, D. J., & Maher, B. A. (1965). Neural consolidation and electroconvulsive shock. *Psychological Review, 72,* 225–239.

Linden, M., & Wittrock, M. C. (1981). The teaching of reading comprehension according to the model of generative learning. *Reading Research Quarterly, 17,* 44–57.

Lindsay, P. H., & Norman, D. A. (1977). *Human information processing.* New York: Academic Press.

Lipsitt, L. P., & Kaye, H. (1964). Conditioned sucking in the human newborn. *Psychonomic Science, 1,* 29–30.

Lipsitt, L. P., & Kaye, H. (1965). Change in neonatal response to optimizing and non-optimizing sucking stimulation. *Psychonomic Science, 2,* 221–222.

Loftus, E. F., & Loftus, G. R. (1980). On the permanence of stored information in the human brain. *American Psychologist, 35,* 409–420.

Loftus, E. F., & Palmer, J. C. (1974). Reconstruction of automobile destruction: An example of the interaction between language and memory. *Journal of Verbal Learning and Verbal Behavior, 13,* 585–589.

Loftus, G. R., & Loftus, E. F. (1976). *Human memory: The processing of information.* New York: Wiley.

Lovitt, T. C., & Curtiss, K. A. (1969). Academic response rate as a function of teacher- and self-imposed contingencies. *Journal of Applied Behavior Analysis, 2,* 49–53.

Lovitt, T. C., Guppy, T. E., & Blattner, J. E. (1969). The use of free-time contingency with fourth graders to increase spelling accuracy. *Behaviour Research and Therapy, 7,* 151–156.

Luchins, A. S. (1942). Mechanization in problem solving: The effect of Einstellung. *Psychological Monographs, 54* (Whole No. 248).

Luchins, A. S., & Luchins, E. (1950). New experimental attempts at preventing mechanization in problem solving. *Journal of General Psychology, 42,* 279–297.

Mace, F. C., Page, T. J., Ivancic, M. T., & O'Brien, S. (1986). Effectiveness of brief time-out with and without contingent delay: A comparative analysis. *Journal of Applied Behavior Analysis, 19,* 79–86.

Macfarlane, A. (1978). What a baby knows. *Human Nature, 1,* 74–81.

MacPherson, E. M., Candee, B. L., & Hohman, R. J. (1974). A comparison of three methods for eliminating disruptive lunchroom behavior. *Journal of Applied Behavior Analysis, 7,* 287–297.

Madsen, C. H., Becker, W. C., & Thomas, D. R. (1968). Rules, praise, and ignoring: Elements of elementary classroom control. *Journal of Applied Behavior Analysis, 1,* 139–150.

Mager, R. F. (1962). *Preparing instructional objectives.* Belmont, CA: Fearon.

Mager, R. F. (1972). *Goal analysis.* Belmont, CA: Fearon.

Mahoney, M. J., & Thoresen, C. E. (1974). *Self-control: Power to the person.* Monterey, CA: Brooks/Cole.

Maier, N. R. F. (1945). Reasoning in humans III: The mechanisms of equivalent stimuli and of reasoning. *Journal of Experimental Psychology, 35,* 349–360.

Maier, N. R. F., & Janzen, J. C. (1968). Functional values as aids and distractors in problem solving. *Psychological Reports, 22,* 1021–1034.

Maier, S. F., & Seligman, M. E. P. (1976). Learned helplessness: Theory and evidence. *Journal of Experimental Psychology: General, 105,* 3–46.

Mandler, G., & Pearlstone, Z. (1966). Free and constrained concept learning and subsequent recall. *Journal of Verbal Learning and Verbal Behavior, 5,* 126–131.

Mandler, J. M., & Johnson, N. S. (1976). Some of the thousand words a picture is worth. *Journal of Experimental Psychology: Human Learning and Memory, 2,* 529–540.

Mandler, J. M., & Parker, R. E. (1976). Memory for descriptive and spatial information in complex pictures. *Journal of Experimental Psychology: Human Learning and Memory, 2,* 38–48.

Mandler, J. M., & Ritchey, G. H. (1977). Long-term memory for pictures. *Journal of Experimental Psychology: Human Learning and Memory, 3,* 386–396.

Masur, E. F., McIntyre, C. W., & Flavell, J. H. (1973). Developmental changes in apportionment of study time among items in a multitrial free recall task. *Journal of Experimental Child Psychology, 15,* 237–246.

Mathews, J. R., Friman, P. C., Barone, V. J., Ross, L. V., & Christophersen, E. R. (1987). Decreasing dangerous infant behaviors through parent instruction. *Journal of Applied Behavior Analysis, 20,* 165–169.

Matlin, M. W. (1983). *Cognition.* New York: Holt, Rinehart & Winston.

Maurer, A. (1974). Corporal punishment. *American Psychologist, 29,* 614–626.

Mayer, G. R., & Butterworth, T. N. (1979). A preventive approach to school violence and vandalism: An experimental study. *Personnel Guidance Journal, 57,* 436–441.

Mayer, R. E. (1974). Acquisition processes and resilience under varying testing conditions for structurally different problem solving procedures. *Journal of Educational Psychology, 66,* 644–656.

Mayer, R. E. (1975). Information processing variables in learning to solve problems. *Review of Educational Research, 45,* 525–541.

Mayer, R. E. (1977). *Thinking and problem solving: An introduction to human cognition and learning.* Glenview, IL: Scott, Foresman.

Mayer, R. E. (1979a). Can advance organizers influence meaningful learning? *Review of Educational Research, 49,* 371–383.

Mayer, R. E. (1979b). Twenty years of research on advance organizers: Assimilation theory is still the best predictor of results. *Instructional Science, 8,* 133–167.

Mayer, R. E. (1982). Memory for algebra story problems. *Journal of Educational Psychology, 74,* 199–216.

Mayer, R. E. (1983a). Can you repeat that? Qualitative effects of repetition and advance organizers on learning from science prose. *Journal of Educational Psychology, 75,* 40–49.

Mayer, R. E. (1983b). *Thinking, problem solving, and cognition.* New York: Freeman.

Mayer, R. E. (1984). Aids to text comprehension. *Educational Psychologist, 19,* 30–42.

Mayer, R. E. (1987). *Educational psychology: A cognitive approach.* Boston: Little, Brown.

Mayer, R. E., & Greeno, J. G. (1972). Structural differences between learning outcomes produced by different instructional methods. *Journal of Educational Psychology, 63,* 165–173.

Mayzner, M. S., & Tresselt, M. E. (1958). Anagram solution times: A function of letter-order and word frequency. *Journal of Experimental Psychology, 56,* 350–376.

Mayzner, M. S., & Tresselt, M. E. (1966). Anagram solution times: A function of multiple-solution anagrams. *Journal of Experimental Psychology, 71,* 66–73.

McAllister, W. R., & McAllister, D. E. (1965). Variables influencing the conditioning and the measurement of acquired fear. In W. F. Prokasy (Ed.), *Classical conditioning.* New York: Appleton-Century-Crofts.

McAshan, H. H. (1979). *Competency-based education and behavioral objectives.* Englewood Cliffs, NJ: Educational Technology.

McCallin, R. C. (1988). *Knowledge application orientation, cognitive structure, and achievement.* Unpublished doctoral dissertation, University of Northern Colorado, Greeley, CO.

McCloskey, M. E., & Glucksberg, S. (1978). Natural categories: Well-defined or fuzzy sets? *Memory and Cognition, 6,* 462–472.

McCord, W., McCord, J., & Zola, I. K. (1959). *Origins of crime: A new evaluation of the Cambridge-Somerville Youth Study.* New York: Columbia University Press.

McCrary, J. W., & Hunter, W. S. (1953). Serial position curves in verbal learning. *Science, 117,* 131–134.

McGeoch, J. A. (1942). *The psychology of human learning.* New York: McKay.

McHale, M. A., Brooks, Z., & Wolach, A. H. (1982). Incentive shifts with different massed and spaced trial cues. *Psychological Record, 32,* 85–92.

McKenzie, H. S., Clark, M., Wolf, M. M., Kothera, R., & Benson, C. (1968). Behavior modification of children with learning disabilities using grades as tokens and allowances as back up reinforcers. *Exceptional Children, 34,* 745–752.

McLaughlin, T. F., & Malaby, J. (1972). Intrinsic reinforcers in a classroom token economy. *Journal of Applied Behavior Analysis, 5,* 263–270.

Meehl, P. E. (1950). On the circularity of the law of effect. *Psychological Bulletin, 47,* 52–75.

Melton, A. W. (1963). Implications of short-term memory for a general theory of memory. *Journal of Verbal Learning and Verbal Behavior, 2,* 1–21.

Melton, A. W., & Irwin, J. M. (1940). The influence of degree of interpolated learning on retroactive inhibition and the overt transfer of specific responses. *American Journal of Psychology, 53,* 173–203.

Melton, R. F. (1978). Resolution of conflicting claims concerning the effect of behavioral objectives on student learning. *Review of Educational Research, 48,* 291–302.

Merrill, M. D., & Tennyson, R. D. (1977). *Concept teaching: An instructional design guide.* Englewood Cliffs, NJ: Educational Technology.

Merrill, M. D., & Tennyson, R. D. (1978). Concept classification and classification errors as a function of relationships between examples and non-examples. *Improving Human Performance, 7,* 351–364.

Meyer, B. J. F., Brandt, D. H., & Bluth, G. J. (1980). Use of top-level structure in text: Key for reading comprehension of ninth-grade students. *Reading Research Quarterly, 16,* 72–103.

Michael, J. L. (1974). The essential components of effective instruction and why most college teaching is not. In F. S. Keller & E. Ribes-Inesta (Eds.), *Behavior modification: Applications to education.* New York: Academic Press.

Miller, G. A. (1956). The magical number seven, plus or minus two: Some limits on our capacity for processing information. *Psychological Review, 63,* 81–97.

Miller, G. A., Galanter, E., & Pribram, K. H. (1960). *Plans and the structure of behavior.* New York: Holt, Rinehart & Winston.

Miller, N. E. (1948). Studies of fear as an acquirable drive: I. Fear as motivation and fear-reduction as reinforcement in the learning of new responses. *Journal of Experimental Psychology, 38,* 89–101.

Miller, N. E., & Dollard, J. C. (1941). *Social learning and imitation.* New Haven, CT: Yale University Press.

Mischel, W., & Grusec, J. E. (1966). Determinants of the rehearsal and transmission of neutral and aversive behaviors. *Journal of Personality and Social Psychology, 3,* 197–205.

Moletzsky, B. (1974). Behavior recording as treatment: A brief note. *Behavior Therapy, 5,* 107–111.

Mooney, C. M. (1957). Age in the development of closure ability in children. *Canadian Journal of Psychology, 11,* 219–226.

Moray, N., Bates, A., & Barnett, R. (1965). Experiments on the four-eared man. *Journal of the Acoustical Society of America, 38,* 196–201.

Morris, C. D., Bransford, J. D., & Franks, J. J. (1977). Levels of processing versus transfer appropriate processing. *Journal of Verbal Learning and Verbal Behavior, 16,* 519–533.

Morris, P. (1977). Practical strategies for human learning and remembering. In M. J. A. Howe (Ed.), *Adult learning: Psychological research and applications.* London: Wiley.

Morris, R. J. (1985). *Behavior modification with exceptional children: Principles and practices.* Glenview, IL: Scott, Foresman.

Mowrer, O. H. (1938). Preparatory set (expectancy): A determinant in motivation and learning. *Psychological Review, 45,* 62–91.

Mowrer, O. H. (1939). A stimulus-response analysis and its role as a reinforcing agent. *Psychological Review, 46,* 553–565.

Mowrer, O. H. (1956). Two-factor learning theory reconsidered, with special reference to secondary reinforcement and the concept of habit. *Psychological Review, 63,* 114–128.

Mowrer, O. H. (1960). *Learning theory and behavior.* New York: Wiley.

Mowrer, O. H., & Lamoreaux, R. R. (1942). Avoidance conditioning and signal duration: A study of secondary motivation and reward. *Psychological Monographs, 54* (Whole No. 247).

Neisser, U. (1967). *Cognitive psychology.* New York: Appleton-Century-Crofts.

Neisser, U. (1981). John Dean's memory: A case study. *Cognition, 9,* 1–22.

Neisser, U., & Weene, P. (1962). Hierarchies in concept formation. *Journal of Experimental Psychology, 64,* 644–645.

Nelson, T. O. (1971). Savings and forgetting from long-term memory. *Journal of Verbal Learning and Verbal Behavior, 10,* 568–576.

Nelson, T. O. (1977). Repetition and depth of processing. *Journal of Verbal Learning and Verbal Behavior, 16,* 151–171.

Nelson, T. O. (1978). Detecting small amounts of information in memory: Savings for nonrecognized items. *Journal of Experimental Psychology: Human Learning and Memory, 4,* 453–468.

Nelson, T. O., & Rothbart, R. (1972). Acoustic savings for items forgotten from long-term memory. *Journal of Experimental Psychology, 93,* 357–360.

Neumann, P. G. (1974). An attribute frequency model for the abstraction of prototypes. *Memory and Cognition, 2,* 241–248.

Neumann, P. G. (1977). Visual prototype formation with discontinuous representation of dimensions of variability. *Memory and Cognition, 5,* 187–197.

Newell, A., Shaw, J. C., & Simon, H. A. (1958). Elements of a theory of human problem solving. *Psychological Review, 65,* 151–166.

Newell, A., & Simon, H. (1972). *Human problem solving.* Englewood Cliffs, NJ: Prentice-Hall.

Nisbett, R. E., & Bellows, N. (1977). Verbal reports about causal influences on social judgments: Private access versus public theories. *Journal of Personality and Social Psychology, 35,* 613–624.

Nisbett, R. E., & Wilson, T. D. (1977). Telling more than we can know: Verbal reports on mental processes. *Psychological Review, 84,* 231–259.

Norman, D. A. (1969). *Memory and attention: An introduction to human information processing.* New York: Wiley.

Norman, D. A. (1976). *Memory and attention: An introduction to human information processing* (2nd ed.). New York: Wiley.

Norman, D. A. (1980). Cognitive engineering and education. In D. T. Tuma & F. Reif (Eds.), *Problem solving and education: Issues in teaching and research.* Hillsdale, NJ: Erlbaum.

Norman, D. A., & Bobrow, D. G. (1975). On data-limited and resource-limited processes. *Cognitive Psychology, 7,* 44–64.

Norman, D. A., & Rumelhart, D. E. (1975). *Explorations in cognition.* San Francisco: Freeman.

Olds, J., & Milner, P. (1954). Positive reinforcement produced by electrical stimulation of septal area and other regions of rat brain. *Journal of Comparative and Physiological Psychology, 47,* 419–427.

O'Leary, K. D., & Becker, W. C. (1967). Behavior modification of an adjustment class: A token reinforcement program. *Exceptional Children, 33,* 637–642.

O'Leary, K. D., Kaufman, K. F., Kass, R. E., & Drabman, R. S. (1970). The effects of loud and soft reprimands on the behavior of disruptive students. *Exceptional Children, 37,* 145–155.

O'Leary, K. D., & O'Leary, S. G. (Eds.) (1972). *Classroom management: The successful use of behavior modification.* New York: Pergamon Press.

Ormrod, J. E. (1979). Cognitive processes in the solution of three-term series problems. *American Journal of Psychology, 92,* 235–255.

Ormrod, J. E. (1985). Proofreading *The Cat in the Hat*: Evidence for different reading styles of good and poor spellers. *Psychological Reports, 57,* 863–867.

Ormrod, J. E. (1986a). Differences between good and poor spellers in reading style and short-term memory. *Visible Language, 20,* 437–447.

Ormrod, J. E. (1986b). Learning to spell: Three studies at the university level. *Research in the Teaching of English, 20,* 160–173.

Ormrod, J. E. (1986c). Learning to spell while reading: A follow-up study. *Perceptual and Motor Skills, 63,* 652–654.

Ormrod, J. E., & Jenkins, L. (1988, April). Study strategies for learning spelling: What works and what does not. Paper presented at the annual meeting of the American Educational Research Association, New Orleans, LA.

Ormrod, J. E., Ormrod, R. K., Wagner, E. D., & McCallin, R. C. (1988). Reconceptualizing map learning. *American Journal of Psychology, 101,* 425–433.

Ormrod, J. E., & Wagner, E. D. (1987, October). Spelling conscience in undergraduate students: Ratings of spelling accuracy and dictionary use. Paper presented at Northern Rocky Mountain Educational Research Association, Park City, UT.

Ornstein, R. E. (1972). *The psychology of consciousness*. San Francisco: Freeman.

Osborn, A. F. (1963). *Applied imagination* (3rd ed.). New York: Scribner.

Osborne, J. G. (1969). Free-time as a reinforcer in the management of classroom behavior. *Journal of Applied Behavior Analysis, 2*, 113–118.

Osgood, C. E. (1949). The similarity paradox in human learning: A resolution. *Psychological Review, 56*, 132–143.

Owen, S., Blount, H., & Moscow, H. (1978). *Educational psychology: An introduction*. Boston: Little, Brown.

Owens, J., Bower, G. H., & Black, J. B. (1979). The "soap opera" effect in story recall. *Memory and Cognition, 7*, 185–191.

Packard, R. G. (1970). The control of "classroom attention": A group contingency for complex behavior. *Journal of Applied Behavior Analysis, 3*, 13–28.

Paivio, A. (1963). Learning of adjective-noun paired associates as a function of adjective-noun word order and noun abstractness. *Canadian Journal of Psychology, 17*, 370–379.

Paivio, A. (1971). *Imagery and verbal processes*. New York: Holt, Rinehart & Winston.

Palermo, D. S. (1973). More about less: A study of language comprehension. *Journal of Verbal Learning and Verbal Behavior, 12*, 211–221.

Palincsar, A. S., & Brown, A. L. (1984). Reciprocal teaching of comprehension-fostering and comprehension-monitoring activities. *Cognition and Instruction, 1*, 117–175.

Paris, S. G., Cross, D. R., & Lipson, M. Y. (1984). Informed strategies for learning: A program to improve children's reading awareness and comprehension. *Journal of Educational Psychology, 76*, 1239–1252.

Paris, S. G., Newman, R., S. & McVey, K. A. (1982). Learning the functional significance of mnemonic actions: A microgenetic study of strategy acquisition. *Journal of Experimental Child Psychology, 34*, 490–509.

Park, O. (1984). Example comparison strategy versus attribute identification strategy in concept learning. *American Educational Research Journal, 21*, 145–162.

Parke, R. D., & Deur, J. L. (1972). Schedule of punishment and inhibition of aggression in children. *Developmental Psychology, 7*, 266–269.

Parke, R. D., & Walters, R. H. (1967). Some factors determining the efficacy of punishment for inducing response inhibition. *Monograph for the Society for Research in Child Development, 32* (Whole No. 109).

Parrish, J. M., Cataldo, M. F., Kolko, D. J., Neef, N. A., & Egel, A. L. (1986). Experimental analysis of response covariations among compliant and inappropriate behaviors. *Journal of Applied Behavior Analysis, 19*, 241–254.

Pavlov, I. P. (1927). *Conditioned reflexes*. (G. V. Anrep, Trans.). London: Oxford University Press.

Penfield, W. (1958). Some mechanisms of consciousness discovered during electrical stimulation of the brain. *Proceedings of the National Academy of Sciences, 44,* 51–66.

Penfield, W. (1959). Consciousness, memory, and man's conditioned reflexes. In K. Pribram (Ed.), *On the biology of learning.* New York: Harcourt Brace & World.

Penfield, W., & Roberts, L. (1959). *Speech and brain-mechanisms.* Princeton, NJ: Princeton University Press.

Pepper, J. (1981). Following students' suggestions for rewriting a computer programming textbook. *American Educational Research Journal, 18,* 259–270.

Perfetti, C. A., & Hogaboam, T. (1975). The relationship between single word coding and reading comprehension skill. *Journal of Educational Psychology, 67,* 461–469.

Perfetti, C. A., & Lesgold, A. M. (1979). Coding and comprehension in skilled reading and implications for reading instruction. In L. B. Resnick & P. Weaver (Eds.), *Theory and practice of early reading* (Vol. 1). Hillsdale, NJ: Erlbaum.

Perin, C. T. (1943). A quantitative investigation of the delay-of-reinforcement gradient. *Journal of Experimental Psychology, 32,* 37–51.

Perry, D. G., & Perry, L. C. (1983). Social learning, causal attribution, and moral internalization. In J. Bisanz, G. L. Bisanz, & R. Kail (Eds.), *Learning in children: Progress in cognitive development research.* New York: Springer-Verlag.

Peterson, L. R., & Peterson, M. J. (1959). Short-term retention of individual items. *Journal of Experimental Psychology, 58,* 193–198.

Peterson, L. R., & Peterson, M. J. (1962). Minimal paired-associate learning. *Journal of Experimental Psychology, 63,* 521–527.

Peterson, P. L. (1988). Teachers' and students' cognitional knowledge for classroom teaching and learning. *Educational Researcher, 17* (5), 5–14.

Pezdek, K. (1977). Cross-modality semantic integration of sentence and picture memory. *Journal of Experimental Psychology: Human Learning and Memory, 3,* 515–524.

Pfiffner, L. J., & O'Leary, S. G. (1987). The efficacy of all-positive management as a function of the prior use of negative consequences. *Journal of Applied Behavior Analysis, 20,* 265–271.

Pfiffner, L. J., Rosen, L. A., & O'Leary, S. G. (1985). The efficacy of an all-positive approach to classroom management. *Journal of Applied Behavior Analysis, 18,* 257–261.

Phillips, E. L., Phillips, E. A., Fixsen, D. L. & Wolf, M. M. (1971). Achievement place: Modification of the behaviors of predelinquent boys within a token economy. *Journal of Applied Behavior Analysis, 4,* 45–59.

Piaget, J. (1928). *Judgment and reasoning in the child.* (M. Warden, Trans.). New York: Harcourt, Brace.

Piaget, J. (1952). *The origins of intelligence in children.* (M. Cook, Trans.). New York: Norton.

Piaget, J. (1959). *The language and thought of the child* (3rd ed.). (M. Gabain, Trans.). New York: Humanities Press.

Piaget, J. (1970). Piaget's theory. In P. H. Mussen (Ed.), *Carmichael's manual of psychology*. New York: Wiley.

Piaget, J. (1971). *Psychology and epistemology: Towards a theory of knowledge.* (A. Rosin, Trans.). New York: Viking.

Piaget, J. (1972). *The principles of genetic epistemology.* (W. Mays, Trans.). New York: Basic Books.

Piaget, J. (1980). *Adaptation and intelligence: Organic selection and phenocopy* (S. Eames, Trans.). Chicago: University of Chicago Press.

Piaget, J., & Inhelder, B. (1969). *The psychology of the child.* (H. Weaver, Trans.). New York: Basic Books.

Pianko, S. (1979). A description of the composing processes of college freshmen writers. *Research in the Teaching of English, 13,* 5–22.

Piersel, W. C. (1987). Basic skills education. In C. A. Maher & S. G. Forman (Eds.), *A behavioral approach to education of children and youth.* Hillsdale, NJ: Erlbaum.

Pigott, H. E., Fantuzzo, J. W., & Clement, P. W. (1986). The effects of reciprocal peer tutoring and group contingencies on the academic performance of elementary school children. *Journal of Applied Behavior Analysis, 19,* 93–98.

Piliavin, I. M., Piliavin, J. A., & Rodin, J. (1975). Costs, diffusion, and the stigmatized victim. *Journal of Personality and Social Psychology, 32,* 429–438.

Piliavin, J. A., Dovidio, J. F., Gaertner, S. L., & Clark, R. D., III (1981). Responsive bystanders: The process of intervention. In J. Grzelak & V. Derlega (Eds.), *Living with other people: Theory and research on cooperation and helping.* New York: Academic Press.

Piontkowski, D., & Calfee, R. (1979). Attention in the classroom. In G. A. Hale & M. Lewis (Eds.), *Attention and cognitive development.* New York: Plenum Press.

Plummer, S., Baer, D. M., and LeBlanc, J. M. (1977). Functional considerations in the use of procedural time out and an effective alternative. *Journal of Applied Behavior Analysis, 10,* 689–706.

Polya, G. (1957). *How to solve it.* Garden City, NY: Doubleday.

Popham, W. J. (1988). *Educational evaluation* (2nd ed.). Englewood Cliffs, NJ: Prentice-Hall.

Posner, G. J. (1978, April). Cognitive science: Implications for curricular research and development. Paper presented at the annual meeting of the American Educational Research Association, Toronto.

Posner, G. J., & Rudnitsky, A. N. (1986). *Course design: A guide to curriculum development for teachers* (3rd ed.). New York: Longman.

Posner, M. I., Goldsmith, R., & Welton, K. E., Jr. (1967). Perceived distance and the classification of distorted patterns. *Journal of Experimental Psychology, 73,* 28–38.

Posner, M. I., & Keele, S. W. (1968). On the genesis of abstract ideas. *Journal of Experimental Psychology, 77,* 353–363.

Posner, M. I., & Keele, S. W. (1970). Retention of abstract ideas. *Journal of Experimental Psychology, 83,* 304–308.

Postman, L. (1964). Short-term memory and incidental learning. In A. W. Melton (Ed.), *Categories of human learning.* New York: Academic Press.

Postman, L., & Phillips, L. (1965). Short-term temporal changes in free recall. *Quarterly Journal of Experimental Psychology, 17,* 132–138.

Postman, L., & Underwood, B. J. (1973). Critical issues in interference theory. *Memory and Cognition, 1,* 19–40.

Premack, D. (1959). Toward empirical behavior laws: I. Positive reinforcement. *Psychological Review, 66,* 219–233.

Premack, D. (1963). Rate differential reinforcement in monkey manipulation. *Journal of Experimental Analysis of Behavior, 6,* 81–89.

Prentice, N. M. (1972). The influence of live and symbolic modeling on prompting moral judgments of adolescent delinquents. *Journal of Abnormal Psychology, 80,* 157–161.

Pressey, S. L. (1926). A simple apparatus which gives tests and scores—and teaches. *School and Society, 23,* 373–376.

Pressey, S. L. (1927). A machine for automatic teaching of drill material. *School and Society, 24,* 549–552.

Pressley, M., Levin, J. R., & McCormick, C. B. (1980). Young children's learning of foreign language vocabulary: A sentence variation of the keyword method. *Contemporary Educational Psychology, 5,* 22–29.

Pressley, M., Snyder, B. L., & Cariglia-Bull, T. (1987). How can good strategy use be taught to children? Evaluation of six alternative approaches. In S. M. Cormier & J. D. Hagman (Eds.), *Transfer of learning: Contemporary research and applications.* San Diego: Academic Press.

Pylyshyn, Z. W. (1973). What the mind's eye tells the mind's brain: A critique of mental imagery. *Psychological Bulletin, 80,* 1–24.

Rachlin, H., & Herrnstein, R. J. (1969). Hedonism revisited: On the negative law of effect. In B. A. Campbell & R. M. Church (Eds.), *Punishment and aversive behavior.* New York: Appleton-Century-Crofts.

Radebaugh, M. R. (1985). Children's perceptions of their spelling strategies. *The Reading Teacher, 38,* 532–536.

Radke-Yarrow, M., Zahn-Waxler, C., & Chapman, M. (1983). Children's prosocial dispositions and behavior. In E. M. Hetherington (Ed.), *Handbook of child psychology. Vol. 4: Socialization, personality, and social development.* New York: Wiley.

Rapport, M. D., Hurphy, M. A., & Bailey, J. S. (1982). Ritalin vs. response cost in the control of hyperactive children: A within-subject comparison. *Journal of Applied Behavior Analysis, 15,* 205–216.

Rapport, M. D., & Bostow, D. E. (1976). The effects of access to special activities on performance in four categories of academic tasks with third-grade students. *Journal of Applied Behavior Analysis, 9,* 372.

Raugh, M. R., & Atkinson, R. C. (1975). A mnemonic method for learning a second language vocabulary. *Journal of Educational Psychology, 67,* 1–16.

Reber, A. S., & Allen, R. (1978). Analogical and abstraction strategies in synthetic grammar learning: A functionalist interpretation. *Cognition, 6,* 189–221.

Reber, A. S., Kassin, S. M., Lewis, S., & Cantor, B. (1980). On the relationship between implicit and explicit modes in the learning of a complex rule structure. *Journal of Experimental Psychology: Human Learning and Memory, 6,* 492–502.

Redd, W. H., Morris, E. K., & Martin, J. A. (1975). Effects of positive and negative adult-child interactions on children's social preference. *Journal of Experimental Child Psychology, 19,* 153–164.

Reder, L. M. (1982). Plausibility judgment versus fact retrieval: Alternative strategies for sentence verification. *Psychological Review, 89,* 250–280.

Reder, L. M., & Ross, B. H. (1983). Integrated knowledge in different tasks: Positive and negative fan effects. *Journal of Experimental Psychology: Human Learning and Memory, 8,* 55–72.

Reed, S. K., Ernst, G. W., & Banerji, R. (1974). The role of analogy in transfer between similar problem states. *Cognitive Psychology, 6,* 436–450.

Reese, H. W., & Lipsitt, L. P. (1970). *Experimental child psychology.* New York: Academic Press.

Reese, H. W., & Parnes, S. J. (1970). Programming creative behavior. *Child Development, 41,* 413–423.

Reif, F., & Heller, J. I. (1982). Knowledge structure and problem solving in physics. *Educational Psychologist, 17,* 102–127.

Reiser, R. A., & Sullivan, H. J. (1977). Effects of self-pacing and instructor-pacing in a PSI course. *Journal of Educational Research, 71,* 8–12.

Reitman, J. S. (1974). Without surreptitious rehearsal, information in short-term memory decays. *Journal of Verbal Learning and Verbal Behavior, 13,* 365–377.

Reitman, W. R. (1964). Heuristic decision procedures, open constraints, and the structure of ill-defined problems. In M. W. Shelley & G. L. Bryan (Eds.), *Human judgments and optimality.* New York: Wiley.

Reitman, W. R. (1965). *Cognition and thought: An information processing approach.* New York: Wiley.

Repp, A. C., & Deitz, S. M. (1974). Reducing aggressive and self-injurious behavior of institutionalized retarded children through reinforcement of other behaviors. *Journal of Applied Behavior Analysis, 7,* 313–325.

Resnick, L. B. (1976). Task analysis in instructional design: Some cases from mathematics. In D. Klahr (Ed.), *Cognition and instruction.* Hillsdale, NJ: Erlbaum.

Resnick, L. B., & Glaser, R. (1976). Problem solving and intelligence. In L. B. Resnick (Ed.), *The nature of intelligence.* Hillsdale, NJ: Erlbaum.

Restle, F., & Davis, J. H. (1962). Success and speed of problem solving by individuals and groups. *Psychological Review, 69,* 520–536.

Reynolds, G. S. (1975). *A primer of operant conditioning* (rev. ed.). Glenview, IL: Scott, Foresman.

Rimm, D. C., & Masters, J. C. (1974). *Behavior therapy: Techniques and empirical findings.* New York: Academic Press.

Rips, L. J., Shoben, E. J., & Smith, E. E. (1973). Semantic distance and the verification of semantic relations. *Journal of Verbal Learning and Verbal Behavior, 12,* 1–20.

Ritter, K., Kaprove, B. H., Fitch, J. P., & Flavell, J. H. (1973). The development of retrieval strategies in young children. *Cognitive Psychology, 5,* 310–321.

Roberts, K. T., & Ehri, L. C. (1983). Effects of two types of letter rehearsal on word memory in skilled and less skilled beginning readers. *Contemporary Educational Psychology, 8,* 375–390.

Robinson, F. P. (1961). *Effective study.* New York: Harper & Row.

Robinson, N. M., & Robinson, H. B. (1961). A method for the study of instrumental avoidance conditioning with children. *Journal of Comparative and Physiological Psychology, 54,* 20–23.

Roediger, H. L. (1980). Memory metaphors in cognitive psychology. *Memory and Cognition, 8,* 231–246.

Roediger, H. L., & Crowder, R. G. (1976). A serial position effect in recall of United States presidents. *Bulletin of the Psychonomic Society, 8,* 275–278.

Rogers, T. B., Kuiper, N. A., & Kirker, W. S. (1977). Self-reference and the encoding of personal information. *Journal of Personality and Social Psychology, 35,* 677–688.

Rolider, A., & Van Houten, R. (1985). Movement suppression time-out for undesirable behavior in psychotic and severely developmentally delayed children. *Journal of Applied Behavior Analysis, 18,* 275–288.

Rosch, E. H. (1973a). Natural categories. *Cognitive Psychology, 4,* 328–350.

Rosch, E. H. (1973b). On the internal structure of perceptual and semantic categories. In T. E. Moore (Ed.), *Cognitive development and the acquisition of language.* New York: Academic Press.

Rosch, E. H. (1975). Cognitive representations of semantic categories. *Journal of Experimental Psychology: General, 104,* 192–253.

Rosch, E. H. (1977a). Classification of real-world objects: Origins and representations in cognition. In P. N. Johnson-Laird & P. C. Wason (Eds.), *Thinking: Readings in cognitive science.* Cambridge, England: Cambridge University Press.

Rosch, E. H. (1977b). Human categorization. In N. Warren (Ed.), *Advances in cross-cultural psychology* (Vol. 1). London: Academic Press.

Rosch, E. H. (1978). Principles of categorization. In E. Rosch & B. Lloyd (Eds.), *Cognition and categorization.* Hillsdale, NJ: Erlbaum.

Rosch, E. H., & Mervis, C. B. (1975). Family resemblances: Studies in the internal structure of categories. *Cognitive Psychology, 7,* 573–605.

Rosch, E. H., Mervis, C. B., Gray, W. D., Johnson, D. M., & Boyes-Braem, P. (1976). Basic objects in natural categories. *Cognitive Psychology, 8,* 382–439.

Rosch, E. H., Simpson, C., & Miller, R. S. (1976). Structural bases of typicality effects. *Journal of Experimental Psychology: Human Perception and Performance, 2,* 491–502.

Rosenthal, R., & Jacobson, L. (1968). *Pygmalion in the classroom: Teacher expectation and pupils' intellectual development.* New York: Holt, Rinehart & Winston.

Rosenthal, T. L., Alford, G. S., & Rasp, L. M. (1972). Concept attainment, generalization, and retention through observation and verbal coding. *Journal of Experimental Child Psychology, 13,* 183–194.

Rosenthal, T. L., & Bandura, A. (1978). Psychological modeling: Theory and practice. In S. L. Garfield & A. E. Begia (Eds.), *Handbook of psychotherapy and behavior change: An empirical analysis* (2nd ed.). New York: Wiley.

Rosenthal, T. L., & Zimmerman, B.J. (1978). *Social learning and cognition.* New York: Academic Press.

Roughead, W. G., & Scandura, J. M. (1968). What is learned in mathematical discovery. *Journal of Educational Psychology, 59,* 283–289.

Royer, J., M., & Cable, G. W. (1976). Illustrations, analogies, and facilitation of transfer in prose learning. *Journal of Educational Psychology, 68,* 205–209.

Rubin, D. C. (1977). Very long-term memory for prose and verse. *Journal of Verbal Learning and Verbal Behavior, 16,* 611–621.

Rueger, D. B., & Liberman, R. P. (1984). Behavioral family therapy for delinquent substance-abusing adolescents. *Journal of Drug Abuse, 14,* 403–418.

Rumelhart, D. E., Lindsay, P. H., & Norman, D. A. (1972). A process model for long-term memory. In E. Tulving & W. Donaldson (Eds.), *Organization of memory.* New York: Academic Press.

Rumelhart, D. E., & Ortony, A. (1977). The representation of knowledge in memory. In R. C. Anderson, R. J. Spiro, & W. E. Montague (Eds.), *Schooling and the acquisition of knowledge.* Hillsdale, NJ: Erlbaum.

Rundus, D. (1971). Analysis of rehearsal processes in free recall. *Journal of Experimental Psychology, 89,* 63–77.

Rundus, D., & Atkinson, R. C. (1971). Rehearsal processes in free recall: A procedure for direct observation. *Journal of Verbal Learning and Verbal Behavior, 9,* 99–105.

Rushton, J. P. (1975). Generosity in children: Immediate and long-term effects of modeling, preaching, and moral judgment. *Journal of Personality and Social Psychology, 31,* 459–466.

Rushton, J. P. (1982). Social learning theory and the development of prosocial behavior. In N. Eisenberg (Ed.), *The development of prosocial behavior.* New York: Academic Press.

Sachs, J. S. (1967). Recognition memory for syntactic and semantic aspects of connected discourse. *Perception and Psychophysics, 2,* 437–442.

Safren, M. A. (1962). Associations, sets, and the solution of word problems. *Journal of Experimental Psychology, 64,* 40–45.

Saltz, E. (1971). *The cognitive bases of human learning.* Homewood, IL: Dorsey.

Samuel, A. L. (1963). Some studies in machine learning using the game of checkers. In E. A. Feigenbaum & J. Feldman (Eds.), *Computers and thought.* New York: McGraw-Hill.

Samuels, S. J. (1967). Attentional processes in reading: The effect of pictures in the acquisition of reading responses. *Journal of Educational Psychology, 58,* 337–342.

Samuels, S. J., & Turnure, J. E. (1974). Attention and reading achievement in first-grade boys and girls. *Journal of Educational Psychology, 66,* 29–32.

Sasso, G. M., & Rude, H. A. (1987). Unprogrammed effects of training high-status peers to interact with severely handicapped children. *Journal of Applied Behavior Analysis, 20,* 35–44.

Sax, G. (1980). *Principles of educational and psychological measurement and evaluation* (2nd ed.). Belmont, CA: Wadsworth.

Saxe, G. B. (1988). Candy selling and math learning. *Educational Researcher, 17* (6), 14–21.

Scandura, J. M. (1974). Role of higher order rules in problem solving. *Journal of Experimental Psychology, 102*, 984–991.

Schank, R. C. (1975). *Conceptual information processing.* New York: Elsevier.

Schank, R. C., & Abelson, R. P. (1977). *Scripts, plans, goals, and understanding: An inquiry into human knowledge structures.* Hillsdale, NJ: Erlbaum.

Schepis, M. M., Reid, D. H., & Fitzgerald, J. R. (1987). Group instruction with profoundly retarded persons: Acquisition, generalization, and maintenance of a remunerative work skill. *Journal of Applied Behavior Analysis, 20*, 97–105.

Schliefer, M., & Douglas, V. I. (1973). Effects of training on the moral judgment of young children. *Journal of Personality and Social Psychology, 28*, 62–67.

Schmidt, R. A., & Young, D. E. (1987). Transfer of movement control in motor skill learning. In S. M. Cormier & J. D. Hagman (Eds.), *Transfer of learning: Contemporary research and applications.* San Diego: Academic Press.

Schneider, W., & Shiffrin, R. M. (1977). Controlled and automatic human information processing: I. Detection, search, and attention. *Psychological Review, 84*, 1–66.

Schoenfeld, A. H. (1979). Explicit heuristic training as a variable in problem solving performance. *Journal for Research in Mathematics Education, 10*, 173–187.

Schoenfeld, A. H., & Herrmann, D. J. (1982). Problem perception and knowledge structure in expert and novice mathematical problem solvers. *Journal of Experimental Psychology: Learning, Memory, and Cognition, 8*, 484–494.

Schramm, W. (1964). *The research on programed instruction: An annotated bibliography.* Washington, DC: U.S. Government Printing Office.

Schunk, D. C. (1981). Modeling and attributional effects on children's achievement: A self-efficacy analysis. *Journal of Educational Psychology, 73*, 93–105.

Schwartz, S. H. (1971). Modes of representation and problem solving: Well evolved is half solved. *Journal of Experimental Psychology, 91*, 347–350.

Schwebel, A. I., & Cherlin, D. L. (1972). Physical and social distancing in teacher-pupil relationships. *Journal of Educational Psychology, 63*, 543–550.

Scoville, W. B., & Milner, B. (1957). Loss of recent memory after bilateral hippocampal lesions. *Journal of Neurology, Neurosurgery, and Psychiatry, 20*, 11–19.

Sears, R. R., Maccoby, E. E., & Levin, H. (1957). *Patterns of child rearing.* Evanston, IL: Row Peterson.

Seddon, G. M. (1978). The properties of Bloom's taxonomy of educational objectives for the cognitive domain. *Review of Educational Research, 48*, 303–323.

Selfridge, O. G. (1955), Pattern recognition and modern computers, *Proceedings of the Western Joint Computer Conference,* New York: Institute of Electrical and Electronics Engineers.

Seligman, M. E. P. (1975). *Helplessness.* San Francisco: Freeman.

Seligman, M. E. P., & Campbell, B. A. (1965). Effects of intensity and duration of punishment on extinction of an avoidance response. *Journal of Comparative and Physiological Psychology, 59*, 295–297.

Seligman, M. E. P., & Johnston, J. C. (1973). A cognitive theory of avoidance learning. In F. J. McGuigan & D. B. Lumsden (Eds.), *Contemporary approaches to conditioning and learning.* Washington, DC: Winston.

Seligman, M. E. P., & Maier, S. F. (1967). Failure to escape traumatic shock. *Journal of Experimental Psychology, 74,* 1–9.

Shafto, F., & Sulzbacher, S. (1977). Comparing treatment tactics with a hyperactive preschool child: Stimulant medication and programmed teacher intervention. *Journal of Applied Behavior Analysis, 10,* 13–20.

Shepard, R. N. (1967). Recognition memory for words, sentences, and pictures. *Journal of Verbal Learning and Verbal Behavior, 6,* 156–163.

Shepard, R. N., & Metzler, J. (1971). Mental rotation of three-dimensional objects. *Science, 171,* 701–703.

Shiffrin, R. M., & Cook, J. R. (1978). Short-term forgetting of item and order information. *Journal of Verbal Learning and Verbal Behavior, 17,* 189–218.

Shiffrin, R. M., & Schneider, W. (1977). Controlled and automatic human information processing: II. Perceptual learning, automatic attending, and a general theory. *Psychological Review, 84,* 127–190.

Shimmerlick, S. M., & Nolan, J. D. (1976). Reorganization and the recall of prose. *Journal of Educational Psychology, 68,* 779–786.

Shimoff, E., Catania, A. C., & Matthews, B. A. (1981). Uninstructed human responding: Sensitivity of low-rate performance to schedule contingencies. *Journal of the Experimental Analysis of Behavior, 36,* 207–220.

Shulman, H. G. (1971). Similarity effects in short-term memory. *Psychological Bulletin, 75,* 399–415.

Shulman, H. G. (1972). Semantic confusion errors in short-term memory. *Journal of Verbal Learning and Verbal Behavior, 11,* 221–227.

Siegel, S., & Andrews, J. M. (1962). Magnitude of reinforcement and choice behavior in children. *Journal of Experimental Psychology, 63,* 337–341.

Siegler, R. S. (1986). *Children's thinking.* Englewood Cliffs, NJ: Prentice-Hall.

Simon, H. A. (1973). The structure of ill-structured problems. *Artificial Intelligence, 4,* 181–201.

Simon, H. A. (1974). How big is a chunk? *Science, 183,* 482–488.

Simon, H. A. (1978). Information-processing theory of human problem solving. In W. K. Estes (Ed.), *Handbook of learning and cognitive processes. Vol. 5. Human information processing.* Hillsdale, NJ: Erlbaum.

Simon, H. A. (1980). Problem solving and education. In D. T. Tuma & F. Reif (Eds.), *Problem-solving and education: Issues in teaching and research.* Hillsdale, NJ: Erlbaum.

Simon, H. A., & Hayes, J. R. (1976). Understanding complex task instructions. In D. Klahr (Ed.), *Cognition and instruction.* Hillsdale, NJ: Erlbaum.

Skinner, B. F. (1938). *The behavior of organisms: An experimental analysis.* Englewood Cliffs, NJ: Prentice-Hall.

Skinner, B. F. (1948a). Superstition in the pigeon. *Journal of Experimental Psychology, 38,* 168–172.

Skinner, B. F. (1948b). *Walden Two.* New York: Macmillan.

Skinner, B. F. (1953). *Science and human behavior.* New York: Macmillan.

Skinner, B. F. (1954). The science of learning and the art of teaching. *Harvard Educational Review, 24,* 86–97.

Skinner, B. F. (1957). *Verbal behavior.* New York: Appleton-Century-Crofts.

Skinner, B. F. (1958). Reinforcement today. *American Psychologist, 13,* 94–99.

Skinner, B. F. (1963). Behaviorism at fifty. *Science, 140* (3570), 951–958.

Skinner, B. F. (1966a). An operant analysis of problem solving. In B. Kleinmuntz (Ed.), *Problem solving: Research, method and theory.* New York: Wiley.

Skinner, B. F. (1966b). What is the experimental analysis of behavior? *Journal of the Experimental Analysis of Behavior, 9,* 213–218.

Skinner, B. F. (1967). B. F. Skinner . . . An autobiography. In E. G. Boring & G. Lindzey (Eds.), *A history of psychology in autobiography* (Vol. 5). New York: Irvington.

Skinner, B. F. (1968). *The technology of teaching.* New York: Appleton-Century-Crofts.

Skinner, B. F. (1971). *Beyond freedom and dignity.* New York: Knopf.

Skinner, B. F. (1973). The free and happy student. *Phi Delta Kappan, 55,* 13–16.

Skinner, B. F., & Epstein, R. (1982). *Skinner for the classroom.* Champaign, IL: Research Press.

Smith, F. (1988). *Understanding reading* (4th ed.). Hillsdale, NJ: Erlbaum.

Smith, S. M., Glenberg, A., & Bjork, R. A. (1978). Environmental context and human memory. *Memory and Cognition, 6,* 342–353.

Smoke, K. L. (1932). An objective study of concept formation. *Psychological Monographs, 42* (Whole No. 191).

Snowman, J. (1986). Learning tactics and strategies. In G. D. Phye & T. Andre (Eds.), *Cognitive classroom learning: Understanding, thinking, and problem solving.* Orlando, FL: Academic Press.

Snyder, M., & Swann, W. B. (1978). Behavioral confirmation in social interaction: From social perception to social reality. *Journal of Experimental Social Psychology, 14,* 148–162.

Sokal, R. R. (1977). Classification: Purposes, principles, progress, prospects. In P. N. Johnson-Laird & P. C. Wason (Eds.), *Thinking: Readings in cognitive science.* Cambridge, England: Cambridge University Press.

Solnick, J. V., Rincover, A., & Peterson, C. R. (1977). Some determinants of the reinforcing and punishing effects of timeout. *Journal of Applied Behavior Analysis, 10,* 415–424.

Solomon, R. L., & Wynne, L. C. (1954). Traumatic avoidance learning: Acquisition in normal dogs. *Psychological Monographs, 67* (Whole No. 354).

Sperling, G. (1960). The information available in brief visual presentations. *Psychological Monographs, 74* (Whole No. 498).

Sperling, G. (1967). Successive approximations to a model for short-term memory. *Acta Psychologia, 27,* 285–292.

Spielberger, C. D., & DeNike, L. D. (1966). Descriptive behaviorism versus cognitive theory in verbal operant conditioning. *Psychological Review, 73,* 306–326.

Spilich, G. J., Vesonder, G. T., Chiesi, H. L., & Voss, J. F. (1979). Text processing of domain-related information for individuals with high and low domain knowledge. *Journal of Verbal Learning and Verbal Behavior, 18,* 275–290.

Spiro, R. J. (1980a). Accommodative reconstruction in prose recall. *Journal of Verbal Learning and Verbal Behavior, 19,* 84–95.

Spiro, R. J. (1980b). Constructive processes in prose comprehension and recall. In R. J. Spiro, B. C. Bruce, & W. F. Brewer (Eds.), *Theoretical issues in reading comprehension.* Hillsdale, NJ: Erlbaum.

Standing, L. (1973). Learning 10,000 pictures. *Quarterly Journal of Experimental Psychology, 25,* 207–222.

Standing, L., Conezio, J., & Haber, R. N. (1970). Perception and memory for pictures: Single-trial learning of 2560 visual stimuli. *Psychonomic Science, 19,* 73–74.

Stazyk, E. H., Ashcraft, M. H., & Hamann, M. S. (1982). A network approach to mental multiplication. *Journal of Experimental Psychology: Learning, Memory, and Cognition, 8,* 320–335.

Steele, B. G., & Pollack, C. B. (1968). A psychiatric study of parents who abuse infants and small children. In R. E. Helfer & C. H. Kempe (Eds.), *The battered child.* Chicago: University of Chicago Press.

Stein, B. S. (1978). Depth of processing reexamined: The effects of the precision of encoding and test appropriateness. *Journal of Verbal Learning and Verbal Behavior, 17,* 165–174.

Stein, B. S., & Bransford, J. D. (1979). Constraints on effective elaboration: Effects of precision and subject generation. *Journal of Verbal Learning and Verbal Behavior, 18,* 769–777.

Stein, B. S., Bransford, J.,D., Franks, J. J., Owings, R. A., Vye, N. J., & McGraw, W. (1982). Differences in the precision of self-generated elaborations. *Journal of Experimental Psychology: General, 111,* 399–405.

Steinmetz, S. K. (1977). *The cycle of violence.* New York: Praeger.

Stephens, C. E., Pear, J. J., Wray, L. D., & Jackson, G. C. (1975). Some effects of reinforcement schedules in teaching picture names to retarded children. *Journal of Applied Behavior Analysis, 8,* 435–447.

Sternberg, S. (1966). High-speed scanning in human memory. *Science, 153,* 652–654.

Steuer, F. B., Applefield, J. M., & Smith, R. (1971). Televised aggression and the interpersonal aggression of preschool children. *Journal of Experimental Child Psychology, 11,* 442–447.

Stevenson, H. C., & Fantuzzo, J. W. (1986). The generality and social validity of a competency-based self-control training intervention for underachieving students. *Journal of Applied Behavior Analysis, 19,* 269–276.

Stinessen, L. (1975). Conditions which influence acquisition and application of verbal representations in problem solving. *Psychological Reports, 36,* 35–42.

Strage, A., Christopoulos, J., Rohwer, W. D., Thomas, J. W., Delucchi, J. J., & Curley, R. G. (1988, April). Grade-level differences in study activities as a function of perceived and observed course characteristics. Paper presented at the American Educational Research Association, New Orleans, LA.

Strauss, M. A., Gelles, R. J., & Steinmetz, S. K. (1980). *Behind closed doors: Violence in the American family.* Garden City, NY: Doubleday.

Sulin, R. A., & Dooling, D. J. (1974). Intrusions of a thematic idea in retention of prose. *Journal of Experimental Psychology, 103,* 255–262.

Sulzer-Azaroff, B. (1981). Issues and trends in behavior modification in the class-room. In S. W. Bijou & R. Ruiz (Eds.), *Behavior modification: Contributions to education.* Hillsdale, NJ: Erlbaum.

Sund, R. B. (1976). *Piaget for educators.* Columbus, OH: Merrill Publishing Co.

Sussman, D. M. (1981). PSI: Variations on a theme. In S. W. Bijou & R. Ruiz (Eds.), *Behavior modification: Contributions to education.* Hillsdale, NJ: Erlbaum.

Swanson, H. L. (1987). Information processing theory and learning disabilities: An overview. *Journal of Learning Disabilities, 20,* 3–7.

Sweller, J., & Levine, M. (1982). Effects of goal specificity on means-end analysis and learning. *Journal of Experimental Psychology: Learning, Memory, and Cognition, 8,* 463–474.

Swenson, L. C. (1980). *Theories of learning: Traditional perspectives/contemporary developments.* Belmont, CA: Wadsworth.

Tanner, B. A., & Zeiler, M. (1975). Punishment of self-injurious behavior using aromatic ammonia as the aversive stimulus. *Journal of Applied Behavior Analysis, 8,* 53–57.

Taylor, B. M. (1982). Text structure and children's comprehension and memory for expository material. *Journal of Educational Psychology, 74,* 323–340.

Taylor, M. J., & Kratochwill, T. R. (1978). Modification of preschool children's bath-room behaviors by contingent teacher attention. *Journal of School Psychology, 16,* 64–71.

Tennyson, C. L., Tennyson, R. D., & Rothen, W. (1980). Content structure and instructional control strategies as design variables in concept acquisition. *Journal of Educational Psychology, 72,* 499–505.

Tennyson, R. D., & Cocchiarella, M. J. (1986). An empirically based instructional design theory for teaching concepts. *Review of Educational Research, 56,* 40–71.

Tennyson, R. D., & Park, O. (1980). The teaching of concepts: A review of instructional design literature. *Review of Educational Research, 50,* 55–70.

Tennyson, R. D., & Tennyson, C. L. (1975). Rule acquisition design strategy variables: Degree of instance divergence, sequence, and instance analysis. *Journal of Educational Psychology, 67,* 852–859.

Tennyson, R. D., Youngers, J., & Suebsonthi, P. (1983). Concept learning by children using instructional presentation forms for prototype formation and classification-skill development. *Journal of Educational Psychology, 75,* 280–291.

Terrell, G., & Ware, R. (1961). Role of delay of reward in speed of size and form discrimination learning in childhood. *Child Development, 32,* 409–415.

Thomas, E. L., & Robinson, H. A. (1972). *Improving reading in every class: A sourcebook for teachers.* Boston: Allyn and Bacon.

Thompson, R., & McConnell, J. (1955). Classical conditioning in the planarian, *Dugesia dorotocephala. Journal of Comparative and Physiological Psychology, 48,* 65–68.

Thorndike, E. L. (1898). Animal intelligence: An experimental study of the associative processes in animals. *Psychological Review Monograph Supplement, 2* (8).

Thorndike, E. L. (1903). *Educational psychology.* New York: Lemcke & Buechner.

Thorndike, E. L. (1911). *Animal intelligence.* New York: Macmillan.

Thorndike, E. L. (1913). *Educational psychology: The psychology of learning* (Vol. 2). New York: Teachers College Press.

Thorndike, E. L. (1924). Mental discipline in high school studies. *Journal of Educational Psychology, 15,* 1–22; 83–98.

Thorndike, E. L. (1932a). *The fundamentals of learning.* New York: Teachers College Press.

Thorndike, E. L. (1932b). Reward and punishment in animal learning. *Comparative Psychology Monograph, 8* (39).

Thorndike, E. L. (1935). *The psychology of wants, interests, and attitudes.* New York: Appleton-Century-Crofts.

Thorndike, E. L., & Woodworth, R. S. (1901). The influence of improvement in one mental function upon the efficiency of other functions. *Psychological Review, 8,* 247–261, 384–395, 553–564.

Thyne, J. M. (1963). *The psychology of learning and techniques of teaching.* London: University of London Press.

Timberlake, W., & Allison, J. (1974). Response deprivation: An empirical approach to instrumental performance. *Psychological Review, 81,* 146–164.

Tirosh, D., & Graeber, A. O. (1988, April). Inconsistencies in preservice elementary teachers' beliefs about multiplication and division. In D. Tirosh (Chair), *The role of inconsistent ideas in learning mathematics.* Symposium conducted at the annual meeting of American Educational Research Association, New Orleans, LA.

Tolman, E. C. (1932). *Purposive behavior in animals and men.* New York: Century.

Tolman, E. C. (1938). The determiners of behavior at a choice point. *Psychological Review, 45,* 1–41.

Tolman, E. C. (1942). *Drives toward war.* New York: Appleton-Century.

Tolman, E. C. (1959). Principles of purposive behavior. In S. Koch (Ed.), *Psychology: A study of a science* (Vol. 2). New York: McGraw-Hill.

Tolman, E. C., & Honzik, C. H. (1930). Introduction and removal of reward, and maze performance in rats. *University of California Publications in Psychology, 4,* 257–275.

Tolman, E. C., Ritchie, B. F., & Kalish, D. (1946). Studies in spatial learning. I. Orientation and the short-cut. *Journal of Experimental Psychology, 36,* 13–24.

Trachtenberg, D. (1974). Student tasks in text material. What cognitive skills do they tap? *Peabody Journal of Education, 52,* 54–57.

Travers, R. M. W. (1982). *Essentials of learning* (5th ed.). New York: Macmillan.

Treisman, A. M. (1964). Verbal cues, language and meaning in selective attention. *American Journal of Psychology, 77,* 215–216.

Trenholme, I. A., & Baron, A. (1975). Intermediate and delayed punishment of human behavior by loss of reinforcement. *Learning and Motivation, 6,* 62–79.

Trowbridge, M. H., & Cason, H. (1932). An experimental study of Thorndike's theory of learning. *Journal of General Psychology, 7,* 245–252.

Tryon, G. S. (1980). The measurement and treatment of test anxiety. *Review of Educational Research, 50,* 343–372.

Tulving, E. (1962). Subjective organization in free recall of "unrelated" words. *Psychological Review, 69,* 344–354.

Tulving, E. (1968). Theoretical issues in free recall. In T. R. Dixon & D. L. Horton (Eds.), *Verbal behavior and general behavior theory.* Englewood Cliffs, NJ: Prentice-Hall, 1968.

Tulving, E. (1975). Ecphoric processes in recall and recognition. In J. Brown (Ed.), *Recall and recognition.* London: Wiley.

Tulving, E., & Psotka, J. (1971). Retroactive inhibition in free recall: Inaccessibility of information available in the memory store. *Journal of Experimental Psychology, 87,* 1–8.

Tulving, E., & Thomson, D. M. (1971). Retrieval processes in recognition memory: Effects of associative context. *Journal of Experimental Psychology, 87,* 116–124.

Tulving, E., & Thomson, D. M. (1973). Encoding specificity and retrieval processes in episodic memory. *Psychological Review, 80,* 352–373.

Turnbull, C. M. (1961). *The forest people.* New York: Simon & Schuster.

Turnure, J., Buium, N., & Thurlow, M. (1976). The effectiveness of interrogatives for promoting verbal elaboration productivity in young children. *Child Development, 47,* 851–855.

Turvey, M .T., & Kravetz, S. (1970). Retrieval from iconic memory with shape as the selection criterion. *Perception and Psychophysics, 8,* 171–172.

Tversky, B. (1981). Distortions in memory for maps. *Cognitive Psychology, 13,* 407–433.

Uhl, C. N. (1973). Eliminating behavior with omission and extinction after varying amounts of training. *Animal Learning and Behavior, 1,* 237–240.

Uhl, C. N., & Garcia, E. E. (1969). Comparison of omission with extinction in response elimination in rats. *Journal of Comparative and Physiological Psychology, 69,* 554–562.

Ullmann, L. P., & Krasner, L. A. (1969). *A psychological approach to abnormal behavior.* Englewood Cliffs, NJ: Prentice-Hall.

Underwood, B. J. (1948). "Spontaneous recovery" of verbal associations. *Journal of Experimental Psychology, 38,* 429–439.

Underwood, B. J. (1954). Studies of distributed practice: XII. Retention following varying degrees of original learning. *Journal of Experimental Psychology, 47,* 294–300.

Underwood, B. J. (1957). Interference and forgetting. *Psychological Review, 64,* 49–60.

Underwood, B. J. (1961). Ten years of massed practice on distributed practice. *Psychological Review, 68,* 229–247.

Underwood, B. J. (1983). *Attributes of memory.* Glenview, IL: Scott, Foresman.

Underwood, B. J., & Erlebacher, A. H. (1965). Studies of coding in verbal behavior. *Psychological Monographs, 79.*

Underwood, B. J., Kapelak, S., & Malmi, R. (1976). The spacing effect: Additions to the theoretical and empirical puzzles. *Memory and Cognition, 4,* 391–400.

Underwood, B. J., & Schulz, R. W. (1960). *Meaningfulness and verbal learning.* Philadelphia: Lippincott.

Van Rossum, E. J., & Schenk, S. M. (1984). The relationship between learning conception, study strategy and learning outcome. *British Journal of Educational Psychology, 54,* 73–83.

Voss, J. A., Greene, T. R., Post, T. A., & Penner, B. D. (1983). Problem-solving skill in the social sciences. In G. H. Bower (Ed.), *The psychology of learning and motivation* (Vol. 17). New York: Academic Press.

Vurpillot, E., & Ball, W. A. (1979). The concept of identity and children's selective attention. In G. A. Hale & M. Lewis (Eds.), *Attention and cognitive development.* New York: Plenum Press.

Waddill, P. J., McDaniel, M. A., & Einstein, G. O. (in press). Illustrations as adjuncts to prose: A text-appropriate processing approach. *Journal of Educational Psychology.*

Wadsworth, B. J. (1984). *Piaget's theory of cognitive and affective development* (3rd ed.). New York: Longman.

Wagner, E. D. (1988, April). Improving visual literacy: Strategies for using symbolic shorthand. Paper presented at National Society for Performance and Instruction, Washington, DC.

Wagner, E. D. (1989, February). Graphic facilitation effects: Instructional strategies to improve intentional learning outcomes. Paper presented at Association for Educational Communications and Technology, Dallas, TX.

Walker, B. S. (1974). Vividness of imagery and spelling errors. *Perceptual and Motor Skills, 39,* 823–825.

Walker, J. E., & Shea, T. M. (1984). *Behavior management: A practice approach for educators* (3rd ed.). St. Louis, MO: Times Mirror/Mosby.

Wallas, G. (1926). *The art of thought.* New York: Harcourt Brace Jovanovich.

Walters, G. C., & Grusec, J. E. (1977). *Punishment.* San Francisco: Freeman.

Walters, R. H. (1964). Delay of reinforcement gradients in children's learning. *Psychonomic Science, 1,* 307–308.

Walters, R. H., & Parke, R. D. (1964). Influence of response consequences to a social model on resistance to deviation. *Journal of Experimental Child Psychology, 1,* 269–280.

Walters, R. H., Parke, R. D., & Cane, V. A. (1965). Timing of punishment and the observation of consequences to others as determinants of response inhibition. *Journal of Experimental Child Psychology, 2,* 10–30.

Walters, R. H., & Thomas, E. L. (1963). Enhancement of punitiveness by visual and audiovisual displays. *Canadian Journal of Psychology, 17,* 244–255.

Walters, R. H., Thomas, E. L., & Acker, W. (1962). Enhancement of punitive behavior by audio-visual displays. *Science, 136,* 872–873.

Ward, M. H., & Baker, B. L. (1968). Reinforcement therapy in the classroom. *Journal of Applied Behavior Analysis, 1,* 323–328.

Watkins, M. J., & Watkins, O. C. (1974). Processing of recency items for free-recall. *Journal of Experimental Psychology, 102,* 488–493.

Watson, J. B. (1913). Psychology as the behaviorist views it. *Psychological Review, 20,* 158–177.

Watson, J. B. (1914). *Behavior: An introduction to comparative psychology.* New York: Holt, Rinehart & Winston.

Watson, J. B. (1916). The place of a conditioned reflex in psychology. *Psychological Review, 23,* 89–116.

Watson, J. B. (1919). *Psychology from the standpoint of a behaviorism.* Philadelphia: Lippincott.

Watson, J. B. (1925). *Behaviorism.* New York: Norton.

Watson, J. B., & Rayner, R. (1920). Conditioned emotional reactions. *Journal of Experimental Psychology, 3,* 1–14.

Watts, G. H., & Anderson, R. C. (1971). Effects of three types of inserted questions on learning from prose. *Journal of Educational Psychology, 62,* 387–394.

Weinstein, C. F., & Mayer, R. F. (1986). The teaching of learning strategies. In M. C. Wittrock (Ed.), *Handbook of research on teaching* (3rd ed.). New York: Macmillan.

Weisberg, R., DiCamillo, M., & Phillips, D. (1979). Transferring old associations to new situations: A nonautomatic process. *Journal of Verbal Learning and Verbal Behavior, 17,* 219–228.

Welch, G. J. (1985). Contingency contracting with a delinquent and his family. *Journal of Behavior Therapy and Experimental Psychiatry, 16,* 253–259.

Welford, A. T. (1977). Serial reaction-times, continuity of task, single-channel effects and age. In S. Dornic (Ed.), *Attention and performance VI.* Hillsdale, NJ: Erlbaum.

Wells, G. L., & Loftus, E. F. (Eds.) (1984). *Eyewitness testimony.* Cambridge, England: Cambridge University Press.

Welsh, R. S. (1976). Severe parental punishment and delinquency: A developmental theory. *Journal of Clinical Child Psychology, 5,* 17–23.

Wertheimer, M. (1912). Experimentelle Studien über das Sehen von Bewegung. *Zeitschrift für Psychologie, 61,* 161–265.

Wertheimer, M. (1945). *Productive thinking.* New York: Harper.

Wertheimer, M. (1959). *Productive thinking* (enl. ed., edited by Michael Wertheimer). New York: Harper.

Whitlock, C. (1966). Note on reading acquisition: An extension of laboratory principles. *Journal of Experimental Child Psychology, 3,* 83–85.

Wickelgren, W. A. (1973). The long and the short of memory. *Psychological Bulletin, 80,* 425–438.

Wickelgren, W. A. (1974). *How to solve problems: Elements of a theory of problems and problem solving.* San Francisco: Freeman.

Wielkiewicz, R. M. (1986). *Behavior management in the schools: Principles and procedures.* New York: Pergamon Press.

Wilkins, A. T. (1971). Conjoint frequency, category size, and categorization time. *Journal of Verbal Learning and Verbal Behavior, 10*, 382–385.

Williams, D. C. (1959). The elimination of tantrum behavior by extinction procedures. *Journal of Abnormal and Social Psychology, 59*, 269.

Wilson, P. S. (1988, April). The relationship of students' definitions and example choices in geometry. In D. Tirosh (Chair), *The role of inconsistent ideas in learning mathematics*. Symposium conducted at the annual meeting of the American Educational Research Association, New Orleans, LA.

Wingfield, A., & Byrnes, D. L. (1981). *The psychology of human memory*. New York: Academic Press.

Winograd, P. (1988, April). Respondent's comments. In R. Peterson (Chair), *What do we know about learning from textbooks? Part I*. Symposium conducted at the American Educational Research Association New Orleans, LA.

Winston, P. (1973). Learning to identify toy block structures. In R. L. Solso (Ed.), *Contemporary issues in cognitive psychology: The Loyola Symposium*. Washington, DC: Winston.

Wolf, M. M., Braukmann, C. J., & Ramp, K. A. (1987). Serious delinquent behavior as part of a significantly handicapping condition: Cures and supportive environments. *Journal of Applied Behavior Analysis, 20*, 347–359.

Wolf, T. M., & Cheyne, J. A. (1972). Persistence of effects of live behavioral, televised behavioral, and live verbal models on resistance to temptation. *Child Development, 43*, 1429–1436.

Wolpe, J. (1958). *Psychotherapy by reciprocal inhibition*. Stanford, CA: Stanford University Press.

Wolpe, J. (1969). *The practice of behavior therapy*. Oxford: Pergamon Press.

Wulbert, M., & Dries, R. (1977). The relative efficacy of methylphenidate (Ritalin) and behavior-modification techniques in the treatment of a hyperactive child. *Journal of Applied Behavior Analysis, 10*, 21–31.

Yarmey, A. D. (1973). I recognize your face but I can't remember your name: Further evidence on the tip-of-the-tongue phenomenon. *Memory and Cognition, 1*, 287–290.

Zacks, R. T., Hasher, L., & Hock, H. S. (1986). Inevitability and automaticity: A response to Fisk. *American Psychologist, 41*, 216–218.

Zahorik, J. A. (1976) The virtue of vagueness in instructional objectives. *Elementary School Journal, 76*, 411–419.

Zazdeh, L. A., Fu, K. S., Tanak, K., & Shimura, M. (Eds.) (1975). *Fuzzy sets and their applications to cognitive and decision processes*. New York: Academic Press.

Zechmeister, E. B., & Nyberg, S. E. (1982). *Human memory: An introduction to research and theory*. Monterey, CA: Brooks/Cole.

Zeiler, M. D. (1971). Eliminating behavior with reinforcement. *Journal of the Experimental Analysis of Behavior, 16*, 401–405.

Zeller, A. F. (1950). An experimental analogue of repression. II. The effect of individual failure and success on memory measured by relearning. *Journal of Experimental Psychology, 40*, 411–422.

Zelniker, T., & Jeffrey, W. E. (1979). Attention and cognitive style in children. In G. A. Hale & M. Lewis (Eds.), *Attention and cognitive development.* New York: Plenum Press.

Zirin, G. (1974). How to make a boring thing more boring. *Child Development, 45,* 232–236.

Zuriff, G. E. (1985). *Behaviorism: A conceptual reconstruction.* New York: Columbia University Press.

AUTHOR INDEX

SUBJECT INDEX